First World War
and Army of Occupation
War Diary
France, Belgium and Germany

37 DIVISION
Divisional Troops
Royal Army Medical Corps
49 Field Ambulance
14 June 1915 - 25 April 1919

WO95/2525/2

The Naval & Military Press Ltd
www.nmarchive.com
Published in association with The National Archives

Published by

The Naval & Military Press Ltd

Unit 10 Ridgewood Industrial Park,

Uckfield, East Sussex,

TN22 5QE England

Tel: +44 (0) 1825 749494

www.naval-military-press.com

www.nmarchive.com

This diary has been reprinted in facsimile from the original. Any imperfections are inevitably reproduced and the quality may fall short of modern type and cartographic standards.

© **Crown Copyright**
Images reproduced by permission of The National Archives, London, England, 2015.

Contents

Document type	Place/Title	Date From	Date To
Heading	WO95/2525/2 49 Field Ambulance RAMC 37 Div Jun 1915-Apr 1919		
Heading	37th Division Medical 49th Field Ambulance 1915 Jun-1919 Apr		
Heading	37th Division 49th Field Ambulance Vol I. 14th June 1915 July 1915		
War Diary	Limerick	14/06/1915	21/06/1915
War Diary	Tidworth Park	22/06/1915	30/07/1915
War Diary	Southampton	30/07/1915	30/07/1915
War Diary	Havre	31/07/1915	31/07/1915
Heading	37th Division 49th Field Ambulance Vol: II August 15		
War Diary	St Omer	01/08/1915	01/08/1915
War Diary	Moringhem	02/08/1915	04/08/1915
War Diary	Campagne	05/08/1915	05/08/1915
War Diary	Paul Balloy Farm	06/08/1915	27/08/1915
War Diary	Mondicourt	28/08/1915	28/08/1915
War Diary	Caumesnil	31/08/1915	31/08/1915
Heading	37th Division 49th Field Ambulance Vol 3 Sept 15		
War Diary	Caumesnil	01/09/1915	02/09/1915
War Diary	Humbercamp	12/09/1915	27/09/1915
Heading	37th Division 49th Field Ambulance Vol 4 Oct 15		
War Diary	Humbercamp	01/10/1915	29/10/1915
Heading	37th Division 49th F.A. Vol: 5 Nov 15		
War Diary	Humbercamp	01/11/1915	03/11/1915
War Diary	Pas	05/11/1915	27/11/1915
Heading	37th Division 49th F.A. Vol. 6 Decr 15		
War Diary	Pas	04/12/1915	30/12/1915
Heading	37th Div 49th F.A Vol: 7 Jan 1916		
War Diary	Pas	04/01/1916	28/01/1916
Heading	49th Field Ambulance Feb 1916		
Miscellaneous	49th F.A. Vol: 8		
War Diary	Pas	02/02/1916	29/02/1916
Heading	37th Div 49 F. Amb Vol 9&10. March 1916 April 1916		
War Diary	Bailleulmont	05/03/1916	19/03/1916
War Diary	Mondicourt	21/03/1916	30/04/1916
Heading	37th Div B 49 F. Amb May 1916		
War Diary	Mondicourt	01/05/1916	01/05/1916
War Diary	St. Amand	02/05/1916	05/05/1916
War Diary	Larbret	06/05/1916	31/05/1916
Heading	C18.49 F.A June 1916		
War Diary	Larbret	01/06/1916	30/06/1916
Heading	37th Division 49th Field Ambulance July 1916		
War Diary	Larbret	01/07/1916	03/07/1916
War Diary	Warlincourt	04/07/1916	12/07/1916
War Diary	Mondicourt	13/07/1916	13/07/1916
War Diary	Houvin-Houvigneul	14/07/1916	14/07/1916
War Diary	Chelers	15/07/1916	15/07/1916
War Diary	Divion	16/07/1916	26/07/1916
War Diary	Les 4 Vents	27/07/1916	31/07/1916

Heading	War Diary Of 49th Field Ambulance From 1st August To 31st August 1916 Vol 14		
War Diary	Les 4 Vents	01/08/1916	13/08/1916
War Diary	Divion	14/08/1916	31/08/1916
Heading	37th Div War Diary Of 49th Field Ambulance From 1st To 30th September 1916 Vol: XIV		
War Diary	Divion	01/09/1916	17/09/1916
War Diary	Coupigny (Hersin)	18/09/1916	20/09/1916
War Diary	Coupigny	21/09/1916	30/09/1916
Heading	37th Div. War Diary Of 49th Field Ambulance From 1st Oct 1916 To 31st Oct 1916 Vol XV		
War Diary	Coupigny (Hersin)	01/10/1916	15/10/1916
War Diary	Fresnicourt	16/10/1916	17/10/1916
War Diary	Chelers	18/10/1916	19/10/1916
War Diary	Liencourt	20/10/1916	20/10/1916
War Diary	Orville	21/10/1916	21/10/1916
War Diary	Arqueves	22/10/1916	23/10/1916
War Diary	Near Varennes Sheet 57.D.O.36.c.93	24/10/1916	29/10/1916
War Diary	Beauval	30/10/1916	31/10/1916
Heading	37th Div War Diary Of 49th Field Ambulance R.A.M.C. For November 1916 Volume XVI		
War Diary	Beauval	01/11/1916	11/11/1916
War Diary	Acheux Wood	12/11/1916	14/11/1916
War Diary	Q 31 G Sheet 57D Near Englebelmer	15/11/1916	20/11/1916
War Diary	Q 31 G Near Engle Belmar	21/11/1916	24/11/1916
War Diary	Q.31 G.7.7 Sheet 57.D Near Engle Belmer	25/11/1916	25/11/1916
War Diary	Raincheval	26/11/1916	30/11/1916
Heading	37th Div War Diary Of 49th Field Ambulance R.A.M.C. From 1st December 1916 To 31st December 1916 Vol 17		
War Diary	Beavquesne	01/12/1916	13/12/1916
War Diary	Barly Near Doullens	14/12/1916	14/12/1916
War Diary	Hautecote	15/12/1916	15/12/1916
War Diary	Bryas	16/12/1916	16/12/1916
War Diary	Raimbert	17/12/1916	17/12/1916
War Diary	Labiette Farm Near Busnes	18/12/1916	21/12/1916
War Diary	Mesplaux Combined Bethune Sheet X14.a.9.6	22/12/1916	27/12/1916
War Diary	Mesplaux	28/12/1916	31/12/1916
Heading	49th Field Ambulance R.A.M.C. War Diary For January 1917 Vol X		
War Diary	Mesplaux Near Locon	01/01/1917	07/01/1917
War Diary	Mesplaux	08/01/1917	31/01/1917
Heading	War Diary Of 49th Field Ambulance From 1st February To 28th February 1917 (Volume 19)		
War Diary	Mesplaux	01/02/1917	01/02/1917
War Diary	Annezin	02/02/1917	11/02/1917
War Diary	Noeux-Les-Mines	12/02/1917	28/02/1917
Heading	War Diary Of 49th Field Ambulance From 1st March 1917 To 31st March 1917 (Volume 20)		
War Diary	Noeux-Les-Mines	01/03/1917	02/03/1917
War Diary	Cantrainne Near Lillers	03/03/1917	03/03/1917
War Diary	Cantrainne	04/03/1917	04/03/1917
War Diary	Ligny-Les-Aire	05/03/1917	08/03/1917
War Diary	Britel-Grossart	09/03/1917	09/03/1917
War Diary	Foufflin-Ricametz	10/03/1917	19/03/1917
War Diary	Foufflin	20/03/1917	25/03/1917

War Diary	Foufflin-Ricametz	26/03/1917	31/03/1917
Heading	37th Div War Diary Of 49th Field Ambulance From 1st April 1917 To 30th April 1917 (Volume 21)		
Miscellaneous	Summary Of Medical War Diaries Of 49th F.A. 37th Div		
Miscellaneous	49th F.A. 37th Div. 6th Corps. 3rd Army Officer Commanding-Lt.Col. W.F. Roe. 18th Corps From April 13th		
War Diary	Foufflin-Ricametz	01/04/1917	04/04/1917
War Diary	Izel-Les-Hameau	05/04/1917	05/04/1917
War Diary	Izel	06/04/1917	06/04/1917
War Diary	Duisan (27.a.6.0 51.C)	07/04/1917	08/04/1917
War Diary	Duisan (L.7.a.6.0)	09/04/1917	13/04/1917
War Diary	Lignereuil	14/04/1917	18/04/1917
War Diary	Gouves	19/04/1917	19/04/1917
War Diary	Oil Factory St. Nicholas	20/04/1917	22/04/1917
War Diary	St. Nicholas Oil Factory	23/04/1917	26/04/1917
War Diary	St. Nicholas	27/04/1917	29/04/1917
War Diary	Liencourt	30/04/1917	30/04/1917
War Diary		22/04/1917	25/04/1917
Heading	War Diary Of 49th Field Ambulance From 1st May To 31st May 1917 (Volume 22)		
Miscellaneous	Summary Of Medical War Diaries Of 49th F.A. 37th Div		
Miscellaneous	49th F.A. 37th Div. 18th Corps. 3rd Army Officer Commanding-Lt. Col. W.F. Roe. 6th Corps From 19th May		
War Diary	Liencourt	01/05/1917	17/05/1917
War Diary	Simencourt	18/05/1917	18/05/1917
War Diary	Arras	19/05/1917	31/05/1917
Heading	War Diary Of 49th Field Ambulance From 1st June 1917 To 30th June 1917 (Volume 23)		
War Diary	Manin	01/06/1917	04/06/1917
War Diary	Croix	05/06/1917	05/06/1917
War Diary	Anvin	06/06/1917	06/06/1917
War Diary	Lisbourg	07/06/1917	21/06/1917
War Diary	Febvin-Palfart	22/06/1917	22/06/1917
War Diary	Thiennes	23/06/1917	23/06/1917
War Diary	Lagstre	24/06/1917	24/06/1917
War Diary	Fermoy Farm Near Locre	25/06/1917	28/06/1917
War Diary	Locre	29/06/1917	30/06/1917
Heading	War Diary Of 49th Field Ambulance From 1st July 1917 To 31st July 1917 (Volume 24)		
War Diary	Locre	01/07/1917	01/07/1917
War Diary	Lindenhoek	02/07/1917	31/07/1917
Miscellaneous			
Heading	War Diary Of 49th Field Ambulance From 1st August To 31st August 1917 (Vol:25)		
War Diary	Lindenhoek	01/08/1917	07/08/1917
War Diary	Locre Hospice	08/08/1917	08/08/1917
War Diary	Locre	09/08/1917	31/08/1917
Heading	War Diary Of 49th Field Ambulance From 1st Sept 1917 To 30th Sept 1917 (Volume 26)		
War Diary	Locre	01/09/1917	12/09/1917
War Diary	Mont Kokereele Farm (R.17.b. 5.2 Sheet 27 S.E)	12/09/1917	20/09/1917
War Diary	Mt. Kokereele Farm	21/09/1917	22/09/1917

War Diary	Mont. Kokoreele	23/09/1917	27/09/1917
War Diary	Voormezeele	27/09/1917	30/09/1917
Heading	War Diary Of 49th Field Ambulance From 1st October 1917 To 31st October 1917 (Vol:27)		
War Diary	Voormezeele	01/10/1917	16/10/1917
War Diary	Kokoreele R.17.b.52 (Sheet 27)	16/10/1917	16/10/1917
War Diary	Kokoreele	17/10/1917	31/10/1917
Heading	War Diary Of 49th Field Ambulance From 1st November 1917 To 30th November 1917 (Vol: 28)		
Miscellaneous			
War Diary	Kokoreele	08/11/1917	09/11/1917
War Diary	Hospice Locre	10/11/1917	11/11/1917
War Diary	Mont Kokoreele R.17.b.5.2. (Sheet 27)	01/11/1917	07/11/1917
War Diary	Hospice Locre	12/11/1917	15/11/1917
War Diary	Kemmel	15/11/1917	30/11/1917
Miscellaneous			
Heading	War Diary Of 49th Field Ambulance From 1st December 1917 To 31st December 1917 (Volume 29)		
War Diary	Kemmel	02/12/1917	31/12/1917
Heading	War Diary Of 49th Field Ambulance From 1st Jan. 1918 To 31st Jan 1918 (Volume 30)		
War Diary	Kemmel	01/01/1918	09/01/1918
War Diary	Ebblinghem	10/01/1918	31/01/1918
Heading	War Diary Of 49th Field Ambulance From 1st February To 28th February 1918 (Volume 31)		
War Diary	Ebblinghem	01/02/1918	13/02/1918
War Diary	Reninghelst	14/02/1918	17/02/1918
War Diary	Menin Road I.9.c.6.6	17/02/1918	19/02/1918
War Diary	Menin Rd I.9.c.6.6 Sheet 28	20/02/1918	22/02/1918
War Diary	Menin Rd I.9.c.6.6 (MDS)	23/02/1918	27/02/1918
War Diary	Menin Rd	28/02/1918	28/02/1918
Heading	War Diary Of 49th Field Ambulance From 1st March 1918 To 31st March 1918 Vol 33		
War Diary	Menin Road I.9.c.6.6 Sheet 28	01/03/1918	06/03/1918
War Diary	Menin Road I.9.c.6.6 Sheet 28 (M.D.S)	07/03/1918	08/03/1918
War Diary	Menin Rd I.9.c.6.6 Centre M.D.S	08/03/1918	11/03/1918
War Diary	Menin Rd M.D.S I.9.c.6.6. (Sheet 28)	12/03/1918	18/03/1918
War Diary	Menin Rd I.9.c.6.6. Sheet 28 M.D.S	19/03/1918	23/03/1918
War Diary	Menin Rd (MDS) I.9.c.6.6 Sheet 28	24/03/1918	25/03/1918
War Diary	Menin Rd I.9.c.6.6 Sheet 25	26/03/1918	27/03/1918
War Diary	Godewaersvelde	27/03/1918	28/03/1918
War Diary	Beauquemaison	29/03/1918	29/03/1918
War Diary	Grincourt Les Pas	30/03/1918	31/03/1918
Heading	War Diary Of 49th Field Ambulance From 1st April To 30th April 1918 Vol 34		
War Diary	Grincourt Lez Pas	01/04/1918	01/04/1918
War Diary	La Cauchie	02/04/1918	03/04/1918
War Diary	Souastre	04/04/1918	09/04/1918
War Diary	Souastre (M.D.S)	10/04/1918	13/04/1918
War Diary	Souastre	14/04/1918	16/04/1918
War Diary	Authie	17/04/1918	23/04/1918
War Diary	Bienvillers E.2.d.5.8. (Sheet 57.D)	24/04/1918	25/04/1918
War Diary	Henu	25/04/1918	30/04/1918
Heading	War Diary Of 49th Field Ambulance From 1st May To 31st May 1918 Volume 34		
War Diary	Henu	01/05/1918	12/05/1918

War Diary	Sheet 57D	12/05/1918	12/05/1918
War Diary	Henu	13/05/1918	18/05/1918
War Diary	Authie St. Leger	18/05/1918	24/05/1918
War Diary	St Leger Les Authie	25/05/1918	30/05/1918
War Diary	Authie St Leger	31/05/1918	31/05/1918
Heading	War Diary Of 49th Field Ambulance From 1st June 1918 To 30th June 1918 Volume 35		
War Diary	Authie St Leger	01/06/1918	05/06/1918
War Diary	Dreuil Les Amiens	06/06/1918	09/06/1918
War Diary	Plachybuyon	10/06/1918	17/06/1918
War Diary	Plachy	18/06/1918	22/06/1918
War Diary	Thievres	23/06/1918	24/06/1918
War Diary	Souastre	25/06/1918	30/06/1918
Heading	War Diary Of 49th. Field Ambulance From 1st July To 31st. July 1918		
Miscellaneous	Appendix IV And V Are Field With Place Under Main Dressing Stations		
Miscellaneous			
War Diary	Souastre	01/07/1918	31/07/1918
Miscellaneous			
Miscellaneous	Objective. 4th Objective		
Miscellaneous	Reports On The Use Of Bicarbonate Of Soda To Counteract The Effects Of Mustard Gas	04/07/1918	04/07/1918
Miscellaneous	A.D.M.S 37th Divn App II	07/07/1918	07/07/1918
Miscellaneous	Q 37th Divn App III	08/07/1918	08/07/1918
Miscellaneous	A.D.M.S. 37th Division. App VI	22/07/1918	22/07/1918
Heading	War Diary Of 49th Field Ambulance From 1st To 31st August 1918 Vol 38		
Miscellaneous	No. 49 F.A. Aug 1918		
War Diary	Souastre	01/08/1918	25/08/1918
War Diary	Near Logeast Wood F.30.a.5.0 (Sheet 57D)	26/08/1918	28/08/1918
War Diary	F.30.a.5.0 (Sh.57D)	28/08/1918	29/08/1918
War Diary	F.30.a.5.0 (Sheet 57D) (Logeast Wood)	29/08/1918	30/08/1918
War Diary	F.30.a.5.0 (Sheet 57D)	30/08/1918	31/08/1918
Miscellaneous	A.D.M.S 37th Divn App I	01/08/1918	01/08/1918
Miscellaneous	A.D.M.S. 37 Division App T-A	05/08/1918	05/08/1918
Heading	War Diary Of 49th Field Ambulance From 1st September To 30th September 1918 Vol 39		
War Diary	F.30.a.5.0 Sheet 57D (Logeast Wood)	01/09/1918	03/09/1918
War Diary	Favreuil H.16.c.2.7 (Sheet 57c)	03/09/1918	03/09/1918
War Diary	Favreuil	03/09/1918	04/09/1918
War Diary	H.17.c.1.7 (Sh 57c)	04/09/1918	10/09/1918
War Diary	Lebucquiere (I.30.a.6.6) Sh. 57c	11/09/1918	11/09/1918
War Diary	Lebucquiere	11/09/1918	21/09/1918
War Diary	La Barque	21/09/1918	22/09/1918
War Diary	Logeast Wood F.30.c.9.9 (Sh 57D)	23/09/1918	23/09/1918
War Diary	Logeast Wood	23/09/1918	30/09/1918
Diagram etc			
Miscellaneous	Report On Recent Operation Appx II	24/09/1918	24/09/1918
Diagram etc			
Miscellaneous			
Heading	War Diary Of 49th Field Ambulance From 1st October 1918 To 31st October 1918 Vol 40		
War Diary	Achiet Le Grand (G.9.b-57c)	01/10/1918	02/10/1918
War Diary	I.31.d (Near Bancourt)	02/10/1918	06/10/1918
War Diary	I.31.b (Sh 57c)	07/10/1918	07/10/1918

War Diary	Metz En Couture	08/10/1918	14/10/1918
War Diary	Haucourt	15/10/1918	15/10/1918
War Diary	Caudry	16/10/1918	21/10/1918
War Diary	Viesly	22/10/1918	22/10/1918
War Diary	Briastre	23/10/1918	23/10/1918
War Diary	Beaurain	24/10/1918	24/10/1918
War Diary	Salesches	25/10/1918	31/10/1918
Heading	War Diary From 1st November To 30th November 1918 49th Field Ambulance Vol 40		
Miscellaneous	Hospital Return For The Week Ended		
Miscellaneous	Hospital And Place		
Miscellaneous			
War Diary	Salesches	01/11/1918	10/11/1918
War Diary	Caudry	11/11/1918	30/11/1918
Heading	War Diary Of 49th Field Ambulance From 1st December To 31st December 1918 Vol 42		
War Diary	Caudry	01/12/1918	01/12/1918
War Diary	Haussy	02/12/1918	02/12/1918
War Diary	Villers Pol	03/12/1918	14/12/1918
War Diary	St Waast	14/12/1918	14/12/1918
War Diary	Sous-Le-Bois	15/12/1918	15/12/1918
War Diary	Rouveroy	17/12/1918	17/12/1918
War Diary	Binche	18/12/1918	18/12/1918
War Diary	Courcelles	19/12/1918	19/12/1918
War Diary	Liberchies	20/12/1918	26/12/1918
Heading	War Diary Of 49th Field Ambulance From 1st Jan 1919 To 31 Jan 1919 Vol 43		
War Diary	Liberchies Belgium	01/01/1919	11/01/1919
War Diary	Liberchies	12/01/1919	29/01/1919
Miscellaneous			
Heading	War Diary Of 49th Field Ambulance From 1st February To 28th February 1919 Vol 44		
War Diary			
War Diary	Liberchies (Belgium)	01/02/1919	25/02/1919
War Diary	Liberchies	26/02/1919	28/02/1919
War Diary			
Heading	War Diary Of 49th Field Ambulance From 1st March To 31st March 1919 Vol 45		
Miscellaneous			
War Diary	Liberchies (Belgium)	01/03/1919	11/03/1919
War Diary	Lodelinsart (Charleroi)	13/03/1919	22/03/1919
War Diary	Lodelinsart	24/03/1919	31/03/1919
Miscellaneous			
Heading	War Diary Of 49th Field Ambulance From 1st April To 25 April 1919 Vol 46		
War Diary			
War Diary	Lodelinsart Belgium	01/04/1919	17/04/1919
War Diary	Antwerp	18/04/1919	20/04/1919
War Diary	Tilbury	21/04/1919	22/04/1919
War Diary	Catterick Yorks	23/04/1919	25/04/1919
War Diary			

WO95/2525-2

49 Field Ambulance RAMC

37 Div

Jun 1915 – Apr 1919

37TH DIVISION
MEDICAL

49TH FIELD AMBULANCE
~~AUG 1915 – DEC 1918~~
1915 JUN – 1919 APL.

121/6242   3yr Burton

49th Field Ambulance

Vol I.

DIARY or INTELLIGENCE SUMMARY

(Erase heading not required.)

Army Form C. 2118

49th Field Amb[ulance]

Place	Date	Hour	Summary of Events and Information	Remarks and references to Appendices
Limerick	14/7/15	3 PM	Took over command of 49th Field ambulance from Training Centre Limerick	17A
"	21/7/15	1.45 PM	49th F.A. entrained at Limerick for Ireland via Roscrea	17A
Tidworth Park	22/7/15	8. a.m	Arrived at Tidworth. Marched to Tidworth Park Camp.	18A
			LIEUTENANT FOLEY J.E. reported his departure to Training Centre Crookham in accordance with War Office Instructions	17A
Tidworth Park	3/7/15		LIEUTENANTS R. McGILVRAY; N.B GRAHAM; A.J. TRINCA; R.W. RYAN; F.W.A PONSFORD arrived from Training Centre Crookham & joined 49th F.A. to complete establishment	18A
Tidworth Park	26/7/15		Sergeant Major CONWAY transferred to Training Centre Farnham in accordance with instrs from R/A in C Records.	18A
Tidworth Park	29/7/15	9 am	Transferred 15' pairs details to 1st Cavly R Warwickshire Regt.	10A
"	30/7/15	3.45 pm	1st of Train left Tidworth station arriving Southampton 5.30am. 5 officers; 118 other ranks; 28 animals, 7 four wheeled, 2 two wheeled vehicles	
			2nd " " " 7 am " " 5 officers 102 other ranks; 2/6 animals; 7 four wheeled & two wheeled vehicles	
		5.20 am		
Southampton		5 PM	4 Officers & 5 other ranks, 56 horses, 14 four wheeled & two wheeled vehicles embarked on HMT "City of Dunkirk" for passage to HAVRE	
		7.30 PM	6 officers & 135 other ranks embarked on HMT "EMPRESS QUEEN" for passage to HAVRE	19A
Havre	31/7/15	7 am	6 officers & 135 other ranks disembarked at HAVRE	8A
		10	85 " 56 horses. 14 four wheeled & two wheeled vehicles & 1 bicycle disembarked at HAVRE	
		2/10	Field Ambulance entrained for area of concentration	8A

121/6787

37th H Strauss

49th Field Ambulance
Vol: II
August. 15

Aug /15

Army Form C. 2118

WAR DIARY
or
INTELLIGENCE SUMMARY
(Erase heading not required.)

Instructions regarding War Diaries and Intelligence Summaries are contained in F.S. Regs., Part II. and the Staff Manual respectively. Title Pages will be prepared in manuscript.

Place	Date	Hour	Summary of Events and Information	Remarks and references to Appendices
St Omer	1/8/15	14.30	49th Field ambulance detrained & marched to billets in MORINGHEM & BARBINGHEM.	DA
MORINGHEM	2/8/15		Ambulance remained in billets, no orders to open up being received.	DA
"	3/8/15		"	DA
"	4/8/15		Ambulance remained in billets	DA
CAMPAGNE	5/8/15	9.30	Ambulance marched to CAMPAGNE & bivouacked in field west of road between it & Somme N of V of ST SYLVESTRE billets	DA
PAUL BALLOY FARM	6/8/15	?	Ambulance marched to FARM PAUL BALLOY 600 yds N of Sergeants & Corporals, 14 Drivers of 7 motor Ambulance waggons & 6 motor bicycles joined	DA
"	7/8/15		Ambulance remained in billets	DA
"	8/8/15		B Section opened for reception of cases	DA
"	9/8/15		All sections opened for duty	DA
"	10/8/15		Ordinary hospital work carried out, Lt Graham transferred to his Stationary Hospital ARCQUES	DA
			Lieut Ronald from 8th Div where 8 men of Somme Capt VEY, Lt RYAN, TRINCA, & PONSFORD, 4 NCO's & 20 men sent to 12th Division for instruction	DA
"	14/8/15		1st Party returned from Instructional course with 12th D	DA
"	16/8/15		2nd Party, Capt Ellague, Lt Selway Lts O M Peter, 4 NCO's & 20 men sent to 12th Division for instruction	DA
"	19/8/15		2nd Party returned	DA
"	20/8/15		3rd Party, Major AHERN, Lt McCAUL, 5 NCO's & 20 men sent to 12th Division for Instruction	DA
"	24/8/15		3rd Party returned	DA
MONDICOURT	27/8/15		Ambulance marched to CASSELL Station & entrained & proceeded to MONDICOURT & billeted	DA
CAUMESNIL	28/8/15		Ambulance marched to billets at CAUMESNIL	DA
	31/8/15	8.	Ambulance settle at CAUMESNIL	DA

Ahern Major RAMC
O.C. 49th Field Ambulance

121/121

37th Division

49th Field Ambulance
Vol 3
Sept. 15.

Sept 15

Army Form C. 2118.

WAR DIARY
or
INTELLIGENCE SUMMARY.
(Erase heading not required.)

Instructions regarding War Diaries and Intelligence Summaries are contained in F. S. Regs., Part II. and the Staff Manual respectively. Title pages will be prepared in manuscript.

Place	Date	Hour	Summary of Events and Information	Remarks and references to Appendices
SAUMESNIL	19/5		B Section marched to HUMBERCAMPS & opened a dressing station at Mme VEUVE RICHE DHEUTTE	A/6
	20/5		Remainder of ambulance marched to HUMBERCAMPS; Advanced dressing station	A/6
HUMBERCAMP	21/5		Opened at BIENVILLERS AU BOIS & BERLES AU BOIS	A/6
			No 36447 A/Sgt Russ F.H recommended for promotion to the rank of Sergeant being recommended to acting rank from that date.	B/6
	24/5		Pris 3674 A/C Parker F transferred to 15th Field Amb Regt & undergone inoculation	C/6
	25/5		Receive information from O/C Records Name & performance of No 34417 A/Sgt Russ F.H as acting Sergeant Major	A/6
	26/5		No 42/02 6472 D YOUNG.T A.S.C transferred duly to 404 Reserve Mechanical Station	A/6
	27/5		No M/7/055085 Pt Douglas E J ASC MT transferred over to No 1 0.0.S	B/6

Donovan Mayor RAMC
O.C. 49^B Field Ambulance

121/7595

37th Division

49th Field Ambulance
Vol 4
Oct 15

Oct 1915

Army Form C. 2118.

WAR DIARY
or
INTELLIGENCE SUMMARY.
(Erase heading not required.)

Place	Date	Hour	Summary of Events and Information	Remarks and references to Appendices
HUMBERCAMP	1/10/15		No T4/078676 Pte Gough C. joined for duty from 37 Div Train	Bq
	4/10/15		No T4/057367 Pte PARKES W. transferred sick to No 4 C.C.S	Bq
	5/10/15		No 39961 T/c MORGAN A E RAMC transferred out to No 19 C.C.S	Bq
	10/10/15		No 36881 Cpl Grant D. transferred to Office of DMS 3rd Army	Bq
	11/10/15		No 39142 P/c Morley S.K. transferred to No 19 C.C. Station (sick)	Bq
	11/10/15		No T3/026775 Dvr Dean A. joined for duty from 3rd Div Train ASC	Bq
	26/10/15		No 38239 Pte Gale W. appointed acting Corporal	Bq
	27/10/15		No T3/022071 Dvr Fay H. joined for duty from 37 Div Train ASC	Bq
	28/10/15		No T3/025678 Dvr King S. ASC transferred to 37 Div Train	Bq
	29/10/15		No 42669 Pte Phillips Reuben transferred sick to No 19 C.C. Station	Bq

Seluin Major Rainer
O C 45th Field Ambulance
31/10/15

37th Kurrum

49 F.Z.a.
Vol: 5

D/
7624

Nov 15

Nov 15

Army Form C. 2118.

WAR DIARY
or
INTELLIGENCE SUMMARY.
(Erase heading not required.)

Instructions regarding War Diaries and Intelligence Summaries are contained in F.S. Regs., Part II. and the Staff Manual respectively. Title pages will be prepared in manuscript.

Place	Date	Hour	Summary of Events and Information	Remarks and references to Appendices
HUMBERCAMP	1/1/15		Ambulance performing Army duties	
	2/1/15		Capt VEY & GILLESPIE with a detachment of NCOs men took on charge of the 37th Divisional Rest Station at MONDICOURT	See
	3/1/15		Lieut McGILLVRAY with a detachment of NCOs & men took on charge of 37th Divisional Baths at PAS	See
PAS	5/1/15		Remainder of 4.4.2 Field Ambulance moved to PAS as Ambulance lying & Field Ambulance	See
	6/1/15		W/3631 Pte Wells R.R. reported acting corporal as from 3/1/15	See
			W/38661 Pte GRIFFIN B.L. transferred back to No 4 C.C. Station	See
	9/1/15		W/DM/s/112356 Pte RICH F.W. joined from F.A.W. Unit	See
	15/1/15		W/M4/04987a Pte JOHNSON M.S. transferred back to No 19 C.C. Station	See
	27/1/15		W/36384 Sgt JONES W. transferred back to No 4 C.C. Station	See

Lieut Major R.A.M.C.
OC 4.9.2 Field Ambulance

37th Kwreun

49th F.a.
Vol. 6

D/7795

Neeg. 15.

Dec. 1915

Army Form C. 2118.

R.A.M.C.
49 F. Amb.

WAR DIARY
or
INTELLIGENCE SUMMARY.
(Erase heading not required.)

Place	Date	Hour	Summary of Events and Information	Remarks and references to Appendices
P.A.S	4/15		CAPTAIN GOSSIP R.A.M.C. S.R. reported his arrival & was taken in strength	Scheme keys of same
	7/12/15		CAPTAIN VEY reported his departure for vacancy 6/12/15 Pte R F.A	10 a
	10/12/15		Sergt. J. Ambulance	Do
	12/12/15		LIEUTENANT TAYLOR R.A.M.C. reported his arrival for duty	Do
	13/12/15		LIEUTENANT McCAUL reported his departure for duty with 6th Lancers Regt	Do
	21/12/15		No 36361 S/Cpl Willis R.R transferred sick to No 19 C.C.S	
	24/12/15		No 34915 Pte Buckley F. transferred to base Amb. W.O 14 releases 114 a 301	Do
	30/12/15		Capt T.P. EDWARDS R.A.M.C. Y attached for temporary duty	Do W.E.
			Captain J.B. Low R.A.M.C. S.C. reported his arrival for duty	

Deven Major Rowe
O C 49 99 Field Ambulance

37

49th F.A.
Vol: 7

37th Div
F119811

Jan 1916

WAR DIARY or INTELLIGENCE SUMMARY

Army Form C. 2118

Place	Date	Hour	Summary of Events and Information	Remarks and references to Appendices
PAS.	4/7/16		M/2/115079 Pte Boyle G. joined for duty & was taken on the strength of the Ambulance	See
	6/7/16		No 69710 Pte JONES J.G; No 69687 Pte LOWE J; No 69364 Pte KAYE W; No 69290 Pte LITTLE W.J; No 69230 Pte HOSKING P; No 69891 Pte MIDGLEY E; No 68905 Pte JONES D; No 68906 Pte JOHN D H; No 48625 Pte JONES H&D reported their arrival & were taken on the strength of the Ambulance	See
	10/7/16		No 33441 2/Cpl R. MACKINSON struck off duty & taken on strength & posted to Private duty in excess of War establishment	See
	10/7/16		No 38637 A/Sgt J. C. EVANS reverted to Corporal	See
	11/7/16		No M/055043 ASC Corpl GARNER A. also MT permanently attached to this Unit as acting Sergt. Vice EVANS reverted	See
	12/7/16		No 34945 A/Cpl Corporal R. J. COOPER promoted to be acting Sergt.	See
			Guthrie D & g VII Corps no 129/16 of 12/7/16	
	17/7/16		No 42878 Pte HEDLEY D & No 1993 Pte HUTCHISON J. transferred to Base Commandant HAVRE for Inoculation list. Authority A.D.M.S. No H/2043 of 14/7/16. Corporal J C EVANS transferred to 32nd Field Ambulance.	See
	17/7/16		No 38637 Corporal J C EVANS transferred to 30 Field Ambulance Authority a Dub 379 Dnd no M 887 of 16/7/16	See
	18/7/16		No 36348 Corporal F E SELLARS reported his arrival from 50th Field Ambulance re Corporal EVANS	See
	21/7/16		Lieutenant J McGILVRAY having reported his departure to report himself at the base of France, on termination of his contract is struck off the strength of this Unit	See
	28/7/16		Major D AHERN is appointed temporary Divisional Censor while in charge of a Field Ambulance (July 12th) Authority issued from the London Gazette supplement Jan 6 published in the times dated 27/1/16	See

Saunders Capt R.A.M.C.
O.C 49th Field Ambulance

31/7/16

Feb 1916

49th Field Ambulance

49th F.a.
Vol: 8

Army Form C. 2118.

WAR DIARY
or
INTELLIGENCE SUMMARY.
(Erase heading not required.)

Instructions regarding War Diaries and Intelligence Summaries are contained in F.S. Regs., Part II. and the Staff Manual respectively. Title pages will be prepared in manuscript.

Place	Date	Hour	Summary of Events and Information	Remarks and references to Appendices
P.A.S	2/7/16		Handed over adv H.Q. of Divisional Rest Station to representative of 111th Field Ambulance	Divisional Order
	3/7/16		40575 Pte Burton O.S. RAMC transferred sick to 5/Highland C.C.S	do
	4/7/16		81188 Pte RARITY T. & 81234 Pte RAE S.W. proceed from No 55 General Base Depot	do
	12/7/16		Advanced Dressing Station opened at BAILEULVAL	do
	19/7/16		Ambulance moved to BAVINCOURT	do
	21/7/16		2Lt BROWN. J. PERRIN. joined 49th Ambulance from No 4 General Hosp.	Officer attd Fce.
	21/7/16		No T/2/015645 Actg Cpl FRY. R.A.S.C. H.T. returned to duty with No 3 Coy 37th Div Train	Officer attd Fce.
	29/7/16		Dressing Station opened at BAILLEULMONT — Remainder of ambulance moved from BAVINCOURT (where site of Rest Station was handed over to Lt Col GULLAN C/113 W Lancs Fams. 55"" Div) + placed in reserve at HENU	Officer attd Fce.
	29/7/16		Capt EDWARDS. T.P. (T.F.) (temporarily attached to 49 D Famb.) left to be attached as M.O. 37th Div Supp. Col A S C	Officer attd Fce.

31st Dec.

49 F Amb
Vol 9 & 10

March 1910
April 1910

COMMITTEE FOR THE
MEDICAL HISTORY OF THE WAR
Date 9 - JUN 1916

Army Form C. 2118.

49 FIELD AMBULANCE
WAR DIARY
or
INTELLIGENCE SUMMARY.
(Erase heading not required.)

Instructions regarding War Diaries and Intelligence Summaries are contained in F. S. Regs., Part II. and the Staff Manual respectively. Title pages will be prepared in manuscript.

Place	Date	Hour	Summary of Events and Information	Remarks and references to Appendices
BAILLEOLMONT	5/7/16		T/3 025794 Pte (Acting Corporal) WEBSTER A G ASC joined from no 9 Corps Amb. B.T.A. Supernumerary train	Within establishment
	7/7/16		Temporary Lieutenant RUSSELL GEORGE HERBERT, HEYWOOD RAMC reported his arrival for duty from No 6 General Hospital, ROUEN	3a
	8/7/16		No 36384 Corporal T. E. SELLARS RAMC evacuated sick to No 19 C.C.S.	13a
	8/7/16		No 42879 Pte E. HERON transferred to England for admission to Cadet School authority W.O. no ln/56 SD3 at/- 25/6 & 37 I Corr No 107/p0/A at/- 2/7/	
	9/7/16		Portion of Ambulance in reserve at HEMU moved into billets at LA HERLIÈRE	14a
	10/7/16		No 72531 Pte ⟨…⟩ FLEMING A W appointed ⟨paid⟩ Lance Corporal from his Supernumerary Rover	15a
	11/7/16		No 36765 Pte BRISTOW J appointed unpaid Lance Corporal; authority DDM 5th Corps no 109/15 6/10/16	3a, 33a, 2a
	11/7/16		No 3924 Pte SAVAGE R admitted No 50 Stationary	
	12/7/16		French Clearing Station opened at LA HERLIÈRE	
	14/7/16		No 37141 QG DEAN T H evacuated sick to no 19 CCS	0a
	14/7/16		No 33790 Pte EVEREST A S evacuated sick to No 19 C.C.S	9a
	19/7/16		Advanced Dressing Station at BAILLEUVAL a Dressing Station BAILLEUMONT closed up to no 10 Field Ambulance	3a
	18/7/16		Advanced party under Captain POUSFORD ⟨…⟩ one from half field ambulance to ADS & HERLIÈRE	3a
MONDICOURT	19/7/16		French dressing station at LA HERLIÈRE handed over to ADS A standing Remainder of Ambulance personnel except R. Worth & MONDICOURT	23a
	19/7/16		No mp/05+548 Pte FAUX R QMG MT ⟨…⟩ Field Ambulance ⟨…⟩ 19a, 3a

Army Form C. 2118.

49th FIELD AMBULANCE
WAR DIARY
or
INTELLIGENCE SUMMARY.
(Erase heading not required.)

Instructions regarding War Diaries and Intelligence Summaries are contained in F. S. Regs., Part II. and the Staff Manual respectively. Title pages will be prepared in manuscript.

Place	Date	Hour	Summary of Events and Information	Remarks and references to Appendices
MONDICOURT	3/4/16	2.5pm	No 36827 Pte TENTY.W RAMC & No 63547 Pte FOX.E RAMC joined from Nos 4 General Base ROUEN	Baru Dpt Roun
			No M/4/115079 Pte BOYLE G evacuated sick to No 1 C.C.S	SC

William Brice Rain
OC 49th Field Ambulance
April 1st 1916

49th FIELD AMBULANCE WAR DIARY

INTELLIGENCE SUMMARY

Army Form C. 2118.

4970mt
Vol 16

Instructions regarding War Diaries and Intelligence Summaries are contained in F. S. Regs., Part II and the Staff Manual respectively. Title pages will be prepared in manuscript.

(Erase heading not required.)

Place	Date	Hour	Summary of Events and Information	Remarks and references to Appendices
MONDICOURT	2/4/16		No 37451 Pte FIELD. S. transferred nich to 41 C.C.S. No M/7/156683 Pte SOUTHGATE H.H. ASC MT reported his arrival for duty from No 1 depot ROUEN & was taken on the strength	Seen to G.R. Roup
	3/4/16		Awarded A.T. TRIM A repatriated to departure for No 43 C.C.S. Lieutenant R.W. RYAN reported his departure for No 14 Z. Division. 1 Lieutenant F.W.A. PONGFORD reported his departure for 37 Z Division. Authority M/n:18 ADMS 37th Division dated 1.4.16	Do
	3/4/16		Lieutenant J. J. O'NEILL reported his arrival for duty from No 43 C.C.S.	Do
	4/4/16		Lieutenant E. HESTERLOW reported his arrival from No 15th Field Ambulance	Do
	5/4/16		Lieutenant H.R. SOUPER reported his arrival from 1 R.I. Division	Do
	5/4/16		No 69710 Pte JONES J. transferred nich to No 4 I.C.C.S.	Do
	7/4/16		No 34945 Corporal (acting Sergeant) R. J. COOPER transferred sick to No 19 C.C.S.	Do
	7/4/16		Lieutenant Colonel D. AHERN handed over command of 49th Field Ambulance to Captain J. GOSSIP authority A. form 37th Division No M 1182 of 7/4/16	Do
			Captain J. GOSSIP handed over command of 49th Field Ambulance to Lieutenant Colonel D. P. WATSON, authority A. Division No. M1142 of 7/4/16 pending arrival of Lieutenant Colonel W. F. ROE. D.S.D. R.A.M.C. who had been ordered to take over command. pencil graph expl. issued.	Morley/Appliances
	8/4/16		Lieutenant Colonel W. F. ROE. D.S.O. R.A.M.C (T.F.) took over command, transferred command of No 11 Field Ambulance	

H Morris Ray
F. C. W. F. Roe Lt Col (T.F.)

WAR DIARY or INTELLIGENCE SUMMARY

Army Form C. 2118.

Place	Date	Hour	Summary of Events and Information	Remarks and references to Appendices
MONDICOURT	1916 April 9		Reported in person to A.D.M.S. 37th Div. & D.D.M.S. (I.P.) Rawe returned from temporary duty with 11 Warwicks. Fine weather. Orders rcg.	ADMS
"	10		Conference of O.C.s Field Ambulances & Second=in=command with A.D.M.S. Harness the question of training, &c. Prisoners went to Lt. Rowan.	ADMS
"	11		Very wet day. A.D.M.S. visited F.A. Amb. 2 pm. Lt. Rowan reported fit during duty with #6 F. Amb.	WM
"	12		Route march by column. Section to LUCHEUX. Very wet. Parade State. 9 Offrs. 20 N.C.Os. 112 men. 26 horses. 12 Ambs. 14 vehicles. Capt. Lew appointed Town Major of MONDICOURT vice Capt. Gillespie. A/Lt. Supern. R.A.M.C. Gazetted Capt. 7.4.16. dateposition 25.3.16. Lt. O'Neill took over medical charge of 9 LEICESTERS temporarily for Capt. Poyser who proceeded on leave to ENGLAND.	WM
	13		Very showery with thin intervals. Clear.	WM
	14		Showery in the morning, fine afternoon. Clear.	WM

WAR DIARY
INTELLIGENCE SUMMARY

Army Form C. 2118.

Place	Date	Hour	Summary of Events and Information	Remarks and references to Appendices
MONDICOURT	15/5/16		St Simon RAMC took over duty of unit by Br Batt. Heavy rain & hail in morning. Fine afternoon. A emergency section of the F.Amb. Ancher to GRENAS and established an advanced dressing station for practice under command of Capt Gillespie. Hostile Aeroplanes dropped bombs in vicinity of MONDICOURT about 10 pm. No damage.	WM
	16/5/16		Fine day. Church parade 11am. Pay parade 2pm. Board for examination of enquests for commissions 2.30 pm. Pres. Lt Col Vulson RAMC. Visited F.Amb. 3 & 5 pm.	WM
	17/5/16		Wet day.	WM
	18/5/16		26 Anti-Typhoid inoculations (TAB 1). Very wet.	WM
	19/5/16		Raining all day.	WM
	20/5/16		Attended to give evidence at a Court Martial on Pte Chile A.S.C. at WARLINCOURT. Pte Green Ambulance was trial by Brig Genl Vaughan. DA & MG VII Corps. 29 Inoculations (TAB 1). Very wet.	WM

WAR DIARY 49 Field Amb
or
INTELLIGENCE SUMMARY.
(Erase heading not required.)

Army Form C. 2118.

Place: MONDICOURT

Date	Hour	Summary of Events and Information	Remarks and references to Appendices
21/4/16		Attended Court Martial at WARLINCOURT on Pte WELLS, & gave further evidence	
22/4/16		CAPT LOW. RAMC. looped over duties as TOWN-MAJOR of MONDICOURT to Capt. DARWELL. 37 Div G.C. Coy. Four reinforcements arrived. Fine morning, rain wet afternoon & night.	
		Dr O'NEILL returned from duty with 9. LEICESTERS.	
		Very wet.	
		26. inoculation T.A.B. I was also inoculated T.A.B.	
23/4/16		A.D.M.S. visited F.Amb. Fine sunny day. Church Parade 3 p.m.	4/A
24/4/16		Lt O'Neill departed for duty with Si Div. Fine sunny day. Administration Conference at DOULLENS 6 p.m. attended by Quatermaster Transport Officer and R.M. Sergeant. D.D.M.S. VII Corps visited and inspected F.Amb.	
		27. inoculation T.A.B.	

WAR DIARY or INTELLIGENCE SUMMARY

Army Form C. 2118.

No. 49 Field Ambulance

Place	Date	Hour	Summary of Events and Information	Remarks and references to Appendices
MONDICOURT	25/4/16		Weather fine & warm	RAMC
	26/4/16		Conference of O.C. Ambulances at A.D.M.S. Temp. medical charge of VII Corps Troops POMMERA. 2/6 T.F.R. [illegible] G.Whiteley detailed for [illegible]	WDR
	27/4/16		Weather fine & warm	WDR
	28/4/16		Weather fine & warm. O.C. 37 Div. Drain in/lecture Transport. 21. T.F.B. [illegible]	WDR
	29/4/16		Weather fine & warm. Raffle [illegible] Rejoined me on duty for Capt Row RAMC detailed for temporary duty with 2/5 Div. VII Corps Troops, POMMERA. Capt Gillespie proceeded on leave. Capt Gossip evacuated sick to 9.C.C.S. Capt Souper with Lt Russell	COR
	30/4/16		Sgt Reynolds + 2 others & 2 M.D.S. Ambulance sent to No 12 Field Ambulance to take over armoured tramway station at BIENVILLERS.	MM

[Signature] R.A.M.C.

May 1914

3-1 M Bde

NB HQ 4. Amb.

COMMITTEE FOR THE
MEDICAL HISTORY O[F] T[HE] WA[R]
Date 26 JUN 1915

Vol 1

WAR DIARY
or
INTELLIGENCE SUMMARY.
(Erase heading not required.)

Army Form C. 2118.

49th Field Ambulance
R.A.M.C.

Place	Date	Hour	Summary of Events and Information	Remarks and references to Appendices
MONDICOURT	1/5/16		Fine weather. Visited ST. AMAND and inspected the billets & Hospital billets occupied by 12 Field Ambulance.	WD
ST. AMAND	2/5/16		Marched from MONDICOURT to ST. AMAND via PASSCHENUV, arrived 3 Officers, 1 W.O., 12 Sgts, 115 O.R., 35 horses, 18 wagons. Marching out state: 3 Officers, 1 W.O., 14 vehicles. Weather fine on the whole.	WD
"	3/5/16		A.D.M.S. 46 Division called & when one to look after sick of this division during the move. Weather fine. A/A.D.M.S. 37 Div called.	
"	4/5/16	2.30 a.m.	Heavy bombardment of our trench in MONCHY-HANNESCAMP salient. We treated 45 Casualties. 3 died at Field Ambulance. D.D.M.S. VII CORPS called to see me. A.D.M.S. 37 Div called to see me. Received 6 sick cases from 37 D. in during move. → 1 Officer & F.O.R. arrived to take over our premises at ST. AMAND for 2/2 LONDON Field Ambulance. 3 Officers +	WD
	5/5/16			

Army Form C. 2118.

WAR DIARY 49 Field Ambulance
INTELLIGENCE SUMMARY.
(Erase heading not required.)

Place	Date	Hour	Summary of Events and Information	Remarks and references to Appendices
ST.AMAND	5/5/16		3 Officers with a section of 3rd North Midland Field Ambulance arrived with instructions from ADMS 46 Div. to take over from us.	WBC
LARBRET	6/5/16		I left my premises at ST AMAND having handed over to the Officer i/c of party from 2/1 LONDON F. Amb. The arrival of the 3rd N.MIDLAND park was during a snowstorm. Marched to LARBRET via HUMBERCAMP & LA HERLIERE, arriving 11.40 a.m. Took over Huts bearing Railway, East of the village. Visited by 9/ADMS 37 Div. — DADMS 37 Div. — AA+QMG 37 Div. — DADMS VII Corps. Weather fine.	MN
"	7.55/5/16		Capt Low, returned from temp duty with VIII Corps troops. Visited by D.D.M.S. VII Corps. & A.D.M.S. 37 Div. Weather Warm & calm.	WBC

Army Form C. 2118.

WAR DIARY 49th Field Ambulance
or R.A.M.C.
INTELLIGENCE SUMMARY.

(Erase heading not required.)

Instructions regarding War Diaries and Intelligence Summaries are contained in F.S. Regs. Part II. and the Staff Manual respectively. Title pages will be prepared in manuscript.

Place	Date	Hour	Summary of Events and Information	Remarks and references to Appendices
LARBRET	8/5/16		Lt BROWNE proceeded to 10.R.N.LANCS. for temp. duty. I visited A.D.S. at BIENVILLERS & found everything satisfactory. 6 T.A.B. inoculation. Weather wet.	WM
"	9/5/16		Capt. EDWARDS. RAMC T.F.) reported for duty from 37 Div. Supply Column. Capt D.S. ROUGH. RAMC (T.C.) reported for duty from No 2 General Hosp. G.O.C. 37 Division inspected the Field Ambulance Hospital. 6 T.A.B. inoculation. Weather wet.	WM
"	10/5/16		Fine day. Capt EDWARDS went to A.D.S. BIENVILLERS for 14 days duty. 6 T.A.B. inoculation.	WM
"	11/5/16		D.D.M.S. VII Corps called. I visited A.D.S. BIENVILLERS and HANNESCAMP. Fine day. 5 T.A.B. inoculation.	WM
"	12/5/16		A.D.M.S. called at 7 a.m. I rode to BAVINCOURT to see A.D.M.S. 3 T.A.B. Capt. GILLESPIE. RAMC (SR) returned from leave for duty. Weather moderate.	WM
"	13/5/16		Went to BAVINCOURT to see A.D.M.S. + C.R.E. with reference to material for constructing dugouts. 5 T.A.B. inoculation. Very wet.	WM

Army Form C. 2118.

WAR DIARY
or
INTELLIGENCE SUMMARY. 49 Field Ambulance

(Erase heading not required.)

Place	Date	Hour	Summary of Events and Information	Remarks and references to Appendices
LARBRET	14/8/16		Wet morning. Overcast in Afternoon. Pay parade 2 pm. A.D.M.S. Inspected Ambulance & officers. Capt. Gillespie & Capt Brough relieved Lt Russell & Capt Edwards at A.D.S. B1.	WM
	15/8/16		Weather light rain. Capt Edwards R.A.M.C. rel. on return to duty.	WM
	16/8/16		6 T.A.R. in circulation.	
			Fine day. Visited A.D.S. at BENVILLERS. Capt Gillespie	WM
	17/8/16		Lt Brown R.A.M.C. rejoined from temp duty with 10 L.N. Lancs. Fine weather.	WM
	18/8/16		A.D.M.S. visited Ambulance 7 a.m. Capt Brough went to 1 Leicester for R.A.M.C. temporary duty. 2 T.A.B. in circulation.	WM
	19/8/16		Fine day, very warm. D.D.M.S. VII Corps visited Ambulance midday. Attended Medical Board at A.D.M.S. Office 2.30. During my absence D.M.S. 3rd Army inspected Ambulance. 2 T.A.B. in circulation.	WM

WAR DIARY / INTELLIGENCE SUMMARY

Army Form C. 2118.

49 Field Ambulance R.A.M.C.

Place	Date	Hour	Summary of Events and Information	Remarks and references to Appendices
LARBRET.	20/8/16		43 Shrapnel Shells issued to Stretcher Bearers. Fine day, very warm. D.D.G.M.S. called & inspected Ambulance. Was out riding at the time so did not see him.	WMC
"	21/8/16		Fine day. Church Parade 11.45 am. Conference of O.C's & 2nd in Commands at A.D.M.S.	WMC
"	22/8/16		Fine day. A.D.M.S. called at 7 a.m. Went with A.D.M.S. to BIENVILLERS & Capt. Orr Paine. Reports of men sent to reinforce hurt at A.D.S. Left Reynolds & men sent to reinforce hurt at A.D.S. Went on leave to Scotland.	WMC
"	23/8/16		Fine day. Went to A.D.S. BIENVILLERS.	WMC
"	24/8/16		Fine morning; Wet afternoon evening. A.D.M.S. Colonel Visitor. Advance Depot of Med Stores at DOULLENS. 3 N.CO's & 20 men sent to BIENVILLERS to work on new DUGOUTS.	WMC

Army Form C. 2118.

WAR DIARY
or
INTELLIGENCE SUMMARY.
(Erase heading not required.) 49 Field Ambulance

Instructions regarding War Diaries and Intelligence Summaries are contained in F.S. Regs., Part II. and the Staff Manual respectively. Title pages will be prepared in manuscript.

Place	Date	Hour	Summary of Events and Information	Remarks and references to Appendices
LABRETS			Wet morning. Fine afternoon. CAPT NICHOLLS 17th LANCERS worked here to give instruction to A.S.C. attached, in horse management for pr 4 days. Went to A.D.S. & then to A.D.M.S.	WBR
"	26/5/16		Fine day. Went to A.D.S. & went round with D.D.M.S. VIIth CORPS. CAPT. EDWARDS returned from leave.	WBR
"	27/5/16		Fine day. CAPT. BROUGH RAMC returned from duty at A.D.S. from duty with 17th Lancers. Lt RUSSELL returned to H.Q. Visited HQ from A.D.S. by D.D.G.M.S. 6.30 pm	WBR
"	28/5/16		Fine day. CAPT EDWARDS RAMC went for temporary duty to 126 Bgde. RFA. Pay invoice & inspection of ambulances. Went to A.D.S. Lt TAYLOR RAMC relieved CAPT GILLESPIE for duty at A.D.S. CAPT GILLESPIE returned tonight at 11-Rs	WBR
"	29/5/16		CAPT. SOUPER RAMC had a leave to Scotland. Weather fine. I go on leave to England at 1.30 p.m.	

W. Armes Major
RAMC

Army Form C. 2118.

WAR DIARY
or
INTELLIGENCE SUMMARY. 49 Field Ambulance R.A.M.C
(Erase heading not required.)

Place	Date	Hour	Summary of Events and Information	Remarks and references to Appendices
TARBRET	29/5/16		Lt. Col. W.F. ROE. D.S.O. R.A.M.C.(T.F.) proceeded England on leave. Weather fine. Visited A.D.S. in afternoon.	7.85.
	30/5/16		LIEUT RUSSELL R.A.M.C. to Divisional GAS School for instruction, four days. A.D.M.S. called at 10 a.m. Lecture by Lt. Col. D.P. WATSON R.A.M.C. on "Treatment of Gassed Cases" in afternoon.	78h. 78g.
	31/5/16		Wet & cold in morning, fine afternoon. Fine day.	

J.R. Gillespie Capt R.A.M.C.
ft O.C. 49th R.A.M.C

June 1916.

CB.49.F.A.

COMMITTEE FOR THE
MEDICAL HISTORY OF THE WAR
Date 5 AUG. 1916

Army Form C.2118.

Please
Vol 12

WAR DIARY 40th Field Ambce
or
INTELLIGENCE SUMMARY.
(Erase heading not required.)

Instructions regarding War Diaries and Intelligence Summaries are contained in F. S. Regs., Part II. and the Staff Manual respectively. Title pages will be prepared in manuscript.

Place	Date	Hour	Summary of Events and Information	Remarks and references to Appendices
LARBRET	1/6/16		Fine day To A.D.M.S. in afternoon	783.
	2/6/16		Fine day. Captain LOW returns from leave. A.D.M.S. called in morning & afternoon.	783.
	3/6/16		Hailstorm in morning fine later. Lieut RUSSELL returned from GAS course at WARLUZEL. Visited A.D.S. in morning. To A.D.M.S. in evening.	783.
	4/6/16		Fine day. D.G.M.S. and D.M.S. 3rd Army visited the Ambulance in afternoon.	783.
	5/6/16		Lieut BROWN returned from 10th Loyal N.L. Lancs. and Lieut RUSSELL to 6th Bedfords 783. D.D.M.S. VII Corps called at 3.30 pm. A.D.M.S. called at 6.30 pm Visited A.D.S. Weather wet & windy.	783.
	6/6/16		Lieut PETCH proceeded on leave. Captain EDWARDS returned from 12th Bde. R.F.A. Captain H.W. EVANS 48 Field Amb reported for temporary duty. Weather wet & windy	783.
	7/6/16			783.

Watermarks - fine afternoon A.D.S.
D.S. Gillespie Capt RAMC A.D.S.

Army Form C. 2118.

WAR DIARY
or
INTELLIGENCE SUMMARY.

(Erase heading not required.)

40th Field Ambulance R.A.M.C.

Instructions regarding War Diaries and Intelligence Summaries are contained in F. S. Regs., Part II. and the Staff Manual respectively. Title pages will be prepared in manuscript.

Place	Date	Hour	Summary of Events and Information	Remarks and references to Appendices
LARBRET	8/6		Returned from leave & resumed command. A.D.M.S. called. 10 km. Capt Evans R.A.M.C. returned tourer with 4 O.R. and Wet weather.	WM
	9/6	7 a.m.	A.D.M.S. called. Capt Souper R.A.M.C returned from leave. Visits A.D.S. Weather overcast + showery his afternoon	WM
	10/6	6.30 a.m.	A.D.M.S. called at 11 a.m. RAILHEAD at LARBRET was shelled from 5.10 a.m. till 9 a.m. 12 shells burst. A few burst with. D.D.M.S. called at 2 or 3 knocked spans of field Aunt. 2 bomiers + one damage to Railway. Unfortunately wet thunder + hailstorms.	WM
	11/6		Capt GILLESPIE appointed Town Major of LARBRET + LAHERLIERE. Conference of O.C. Divisional A.D.M.S. this. Payheure. Wednesday + fine afternoon.	WM
	12/6		To A.D.S. with Capt Souper. Weather overcast.	WM
	13/6		To A.D.M.S. Weather wet all day.	WM

2353 Wt. W2544/1454 700,000 5/15 D. D. & L. A.D.S.S./Forms/C. 2118.

Army Form C. 2118.

WAR DIARY
or
INTELLIGENCE SUMMARY.
(Erase heading not required.)

HQ Field Ambulance, RAMC

Place	Date	Hour	Summary of Events and Information	Remarks and references to Appendices
LARBRET	14/6/16		D.M.S. 3rd Army inspected Field Ambulance & A.D.S. Cyfed Wates for duty. 6/23 Bde. R.F.A. French troops advanced our lines at 11 pm to midnight. Weather overcast.	WM
	15/6/16		To A.D.S. To A.D.M.S. Weather cloudy.	WM
	16/6/16		To A.D.S. Lt. BROWN returned to unit with 3 Amb. from 10 Sqd N. Lanc. Weather fine & warm.	WM
	17/6/16		To A.D.M.S. Lt. PETCH returned from leave. [illegible]	WM
	18/6/16		To A.D.M.S. "am" and "special work" for Division at night. 3 N.Co's & 31 Other did "special work" for Division at night. Left 2 N.Co's & 31 Other. Weather fine & warm.	WM
	19/6/16		Visited A.D.S. weather overcast.	WM
	20/6/16		Fine day. Visited A.D.S. To A.D.M.S. 5:30 pm	WM
	21/6/16		Visited A.D.S. BIENVILLERS + HANNESCAMP with Capt Treleaven & D.A.D.M.S. 27 Div Weather fine	WM

Army Form C. 2118.

WAR DIARY
or
INTELLIGENCE SUMMARY. 49 Field Ambulance
(Erase heading not required.)

Instructions regarding War Diaries and Intelligence Summaries are contained in F.S. Regs., Part II. and the Staff Manual respectively. Title pages will be prepared in manuscript.

Place	Date	Hour	Summary of Events and Information	Remarks and references to Appendices
LABORET	22/6		Very Warm. Called to see ADMS.	WM
	23/6		Received Operation Orders from ADMS verbally at conference 5.30. Visited No 20 C.C.S. Violent thunder storm at 4 pm. Capt GILLESPIE attached for duties of TOWN MAJOR to Major MCKENNA 9 N. STAFFS. Very heavy rain during the night.	WM
	24/6		CAPT GILLESPIE went to A.D.S. on duty. Capt. EDWARDS returned for duty from 123 Bgde R.F.A. Rev. H. STURT. C.F. (C.E.) attached temporarily for duty at F.A.M.B. Fine day. Heavy bombardment by our guns on right of our front.	WM
	25/6		Continue Bombardment by our guns. BIENVILLERS Shelled. 7 or 8 casualties. Fine day. Bombs dropped by German Aircraft near Ambulance at 10 am.	WM
	26/6		Continue Bombardment by our guns. Wet weather.	

Army Form C. 2118.

WAR DIARY
or
INTELLIGENCE SUMMARY.

49th Field Ambulance
RAMC

(Erase heading not required.)

Instructions regarding War Diaries and Intelligence Summaries are contained in F. S. Regs., Part II. and the Staff Manual respectively. Title pages will be prepared in manuscript.

Place	Date	Hour	Summary of Events and Information	Remarks and references to Appendices
LARBERT	27/6/16		Ambulance cleared of all cases unfit to rejoin their units. Cpl EDWARDS R.A.M.C. I.V. Co. & Three sent for temporary duty with 20 C.C.S. Capt Person reported for duty. Lieut RAMAGE #### returned from Temporary duty with 6th Bedfords. 18 cases of pen poisoning received by lorry of Cylinders in our hands by former place available and evacuated to 20 C.C.S. Wet wild rain in torrents.	Cpl EDWARDS WM
	28/6/16		Wet morning, fair later. Gas attack 7.30 to 3.45 p.m. 33rd Reserve.	WM
	29/6/16		Overcast, fine later. Raid on German trenches our Monday by 37 Div. Gas bombs released 11 a.m.	WM
	30/6/16		Very windy overcast in morning, fine later. D.M.S. 2nd Army called with Col. Alexi Thompson R.A.M.C. 12 noon. D.D.M.S. VII Corps called 12.30 pm	

H. Inman Lieut Col
O.C. 49 Field Amb.

39th Division

49th Field Ambulance

July 1916

COMMITTEE FOR THE
MEDICAL HISTORY OF THE WAR
Date 5-SEP. '15

WAR DIARY
INTELLIGENCE SUMMARY.

Army Form C. 2118.

49 Field Ambulance R.A.M.C.

July 1913 Vol.

Place	Date	Hour	Summary of Events and Information	Remarks and references to Appendices
LARBRET	1/7/16		Capt. PEARSON. R.A.M.C. proceeded to 20 C.C.S. for temporary duty. 2nd Lieutenant Capt. EDWARDS who has been for duty to 27 RESERVE PARK. Heavy bombardment on our right commenced 6.30 a.m. Infantry assault & diversions on our Right (46th & 56th Divs) at 7.30. Gas & smoke demonstration by our Division in front of HANNESCAMP. Shell explosion in BIENVILLERS.	WM
"	2/7/16		184 Field Co. R.E. We have friendly at 6 a.m. 16 wounded admitted here, about 15 or 20 killed. D.D.M.S. 3rd Army called.	WM
		7 a.m.	German Shelling L.A. COUCHIE ROAD & STONE DUMP about a mile from here. 3 Shells burst in LARBRET at 4.30 p.m. One horse wounded. 2 Shells burst at Army Pillar + Dump.	WM
"	3/7/16		10/H 1 N.C.O. & 10 men of 2 N. Midland Field Amb. reported at A.D.S. L to make arrangement for taking over from us. Lieut. Colonel .... arr clos by duty Ambulance. Major Turner R.A.M.C. O.C. 2nd N. Midland Field Amb. called here on the ambulance	WM

WAR DIARY 49 Field Ambulance R.A.M.C.

Army Form C. 2118.

INTELLIGENCE SUMMARY
(Erase heading not required.)

Place	Date	Hour	Summary of Events and Information	Remarks and references to Appendices
	3/7/16		To make arrangements to take over from us. Lt Taylor & Lt Schooley & he have returned to H.Q. from BIENVILLERS.	WR
WARLINCOURT	4/7/16		Field Ambulance arrived from our Rest at 10 a.m. and arrived at huts at WARLINCOURT. 37 Division became D.H.Q. Reserve. Capt. GILLESPIE & 35 O.R. returned from BIENVILLERS to H.Q. The rest (30) from L.F. their and who had been at HANNESCAMP returned to this unit at GAUDIEMPRÉ. Fine morning, heavy thunderstorm & rain in afternoon.	WR
	5/7/16		Overcast in morning. Fine afternoon. D.D.M.S. VII Corps called 10.30 a.m. A.D.M.S. called 11.45 a.m. Capt. PEARSON & 9. O.R. returned to H.Q. from 20 C.C.S.	WR
	6/7/16		Commenced a course of Physical Drill. Showery day.	WR
	7/7/16		Fine day. Very quiet day.	WR

Army Form C. 2118.

WAR DIARY
49 Field Ambulance
or
INTELLIGENCE SUMMARY.
R.A.M.C.

(Erase heading not required.)

Instructions regarding War Diaries and Intelligence Summaries are contained in F.S. Regs., Part II. and the Staff Manual respectively. Title pages will be prepared in manuscript.

Place	Date	Hour	Summary of Events and Information	Remarks and references to Appendices
WARLINCOURT	8/6		Fine day day. Payparade at 2 p.m.	MM
	9/6		Church Parade 11.30 a.m. Visited A.D.M.S. afternoon. Fine & warm.	MM
	10/6		Warm & Sunny. Tent Nearly can be Worked to be pitched with tomorrow. Heating.	MM
	11/6		Capt Sullehi with to Mondicourt on Tam Music. Went with A.D.M.S. to look for a suitable place for tactic taken up the Ambulance. Services on a farm at MONDICOURT. Fine day.	MM
	12/6		Went to horse show & selected fillets for Ambulance. Cloudy, some rain in Evg.	MM
MONDICOURT	13/6		Field Ambulance left Huts at WARLINCOURT 10 a.m. Arr' tents were pitched. Rather windy. at MONDICOURT. 10.40 a.m. Showers in morning, fine afterwards.	MM
HOUVIN-HOUVIGNEUL	14/6/13		F. Amb. marched to HOUVIN-HOUVIGNEUL, arrived at 7-40, + handed to fillets, &c. to 102 B godo. Capt. Came under orders of 102 B godo.	MM

Army Form C. 2118.

WAR DIARY 49th Field Ambulance
or R.A.M.C.
INTELLIGENCE SUMMARY.

(Erase heading not required.)

Instructions regarding War Diaries and Intelligence Summaries are contained in F. S. Regs., Part II. and the Staff Manual respectively. Title pages will be prepared in manuscript.

Place	Date	Hour	Summary of Events and Information	Remarks and references to Appendices
CHELERS	15/7/16		74th Ambulance from CHELERS HOUVIN – HOUVIGNEUL – arrived at CHELERS at 10 a.m. + marched to billets. Received orders to take over 102 Regm. First day. Showers evening.	WM
DIVISION	16/7/16		74th Ambulance with 102 Regt from CHELERS (91seu) to DIVISION (1-15 in). Billeted at L'ECOLE MATERNELLE. 13 Lieut's hospital staff. CHELERS WM line of march. Came under IVth CORPS, 1st ARMY. First hospital. Showery afternoon + Evg.	WM
"	17/7/16		A.D.M.S. called here 11 a.m. Showery.	WM
"	18/7/16		D.D.M.S. IVth CORPS called. LT.S.CHILD.R.A.M.C.(T.F.) reported arrival from No.3 General Hospital, & was attached to F.Amb. to pm 15. Overcast.	WM
"	19/7/16		A.D.M.S. called. First weather.	WM

WAR DIARY
or
INTELLIGENCE SUMMARY

Army Form C. 2118.

HQ & Field Ambulance RAMC

Place	Date	Hour	Summary of Events and Information	Remarks and references to Appendices
DIVION	20/7/16		Fine day. Authelu & Brille.	WD
"	21/7/16		Friday. Pay Parade. Route march.	WD WD
"	22/7/16		Saturday. IV Corps Inspector Hospital. Fine day.	
"	23/7/16		Sunday. Church Parade 11.30. Fine day.	
"	24/7/16		Capt GILLESPIE proceeded 3 days leave to proceed to BOULOGNE. Received orders to visit & initiate arrangements to visit 1/5 LONDON Fd. Amb. to take over from them at LES 4 VENTS. 36B.W.9.d. LONDON. Went with Capt SOUPER RAMC & Sarn Ifr. 1/5 F.A.M.B. & visited their A.D.S. at CABARET ROUGE. Arn. Collecting Station at CARENCY and VILLERS AUX BOIS. Fine day.	WD

WAR DIARY *or* **INTELLIGENCE SUMMARY**

49 Field Ambulance
RAMC

Army Form C. 2118.

Place	Date	Hour	Summary of Events and Information	Remarks and references to Appendices
DIVION	25/7/18		Sent party of 1 Officer + NCos under Capt Low RAMC to reconnoitre position occupied by 1/5 London Fd Amb. Three Ministerials received from IV. Corps School. Got some blankets & clothing disinfected. Fine day.	WM
"	26/7/18		Capt B. Dehan ant 13 hammock from A&SaFm. Sent B. Dehan with Capt Low to take over from 1/5 London Fd Amb. Sent 2 Horse Amb, Wgns to follow 102 Bde on the march. 600 disinfements issued to People yesterday. Sent Three disinfectors to 4/5 Fd Amb, more to take over from A.D.M.S. 37. Div.	WM
LES 4 VENTS	27/7/18		Remainder of Ambulance moved to LES 4 VENTS & took over position vacated by 1/5 London F. Amb. Capt. GILLESPIE arrived from A.D.M.S. Office at 4.20. Fine day but cloudy. Short shower.	WM
"	28/7/18		D.D.M.S. inspected Ambulance at 10.20 a.m. I went there A&Sns at Sent Corp. to LARBERT for Shrapnel wound. Fine day. Warm. we left there on 4.7.18	WM

WAR DIARY 49th Field Ambulance

Army Form C. 2118.

INTELLIGENCE SUMMARY.

(Erase heading not required.)

Place	Date	Hour	Summary of Events and Information	Remarks and references to Appendices
Les VENTS	29/7/16		A.D.M.S. called 9.30 a.m. 39 Cases of Sickness to hospital. Mostly from Fine & Sunny later.	WM
"	30/7/16		Conference on @ For Ambulances at A.D.M.S. Office 2. p.m. Visited 1st Field Amb. at GRAND SERVINS. Fine Warm day.	WM
"	31/7/16		First Anniversary of the leaving ⊕ for France of 49. Field Ambulance. Very Hot day. Ex. C.H.L.D. Reported Fresh for duty to O.C. 50 Fd Amb. Water HEPITAL CORNER. Collected stations & VILLERS aux BOIS W.T.M. Ford Car to be sent from V. aux B. Saw M.O. if carriages of collected bath act of am daily	WM

B M
No 45. Fd Amb

87/Ind.
49 F Amb
Vol 14

Aug 1916.

Confidential

War Diary

of

49th Field Ambulance

from 1st August to 31st August 1916

Army Form C. 2118.

WAR DIARY 49 Field Ambulance
INTELLIGENCE SUMMARY.
(Erase heading not required.)

Instructions regarding War Diaries and Intelligence Summaries are contained in F. S. Regs., Part II. and the Staff Manual respectively. Title pages will be prepared in manuscript.

Place	Date	Hour	Summary of Events and Information	Remarks and references to Appendices
LES 4 VENTS	1/8/16		ADMS called 9.30 am. I visited A.D.S. & remained there and spent an afternoon	WBL
	2/8/16		42 cases of Scabies transferred to 41st Field Amb. Weather h.b.	WBL
	3/8/16		S.Aug II Corps called today now in reserve. 11.45 am. Weather hot.	WBR
			Weather cooler.	
	4/8/16		Weather windy & cool. I visited 37 Std. Rest Station, Coucourt. Aplets	WBL
			from G.H.Q. inspected our Motor Ambulances.	
	5/8/16		ADMS 9th Division visited our For. Amb. Capt. Mimms from No 26	WBL
			General Hospital arrived & dispensed on 2 days & assist there with	
			Cancers, Truks & Solcent Solation.	
	6/8/16		Fine day. Review of personnel at Hop line Corner & 1/5th St Omer, 1 Sid Inspy	WBL
			2 Drivers. 1 Cyclist & 1 Orderly Cpn at Orderly Range to 2 Officers 1 Sgt.	
			1 Cpl & 22 men. Adva use there of acid post. 1 Cpl & 9 men.	

Army Form C. 2118.

WAR DIARY
49th Field Ambulance
INTELLIGENCE SUMMARY.
(Erase heading not required.)

Place	Date	Hour	Summary of Events and Information	Remarks and references to Appendices
LES 4 VENTS	7/7/16		Capt Gillespie proceeded for temp. duty with 2/2/6 N. Fusiliers vice Lt Keith R.A.M.C. wounded. Divisional Band played here from 5 to 7 p.m. Hot weather.	WJR
	8/7/16		A.D.M.S. called 9.30 a.m. Weather hot.	WJR
	9/7/16		A.D.M.S. called 10 a.m. Weather hot.	WJR
	10/7/16		Lt.Col Glover R.A.M.C. O.C. 27 Fd Amb. got in touch with me + relieved the Fd Amb Hq + advanced dressing station, preliminary to taking over from me in a few days. O.C. 27 Fd Amb + A.D.M.S. 32 Div. in specting my transport. Went with Divn. to view the 27th Fd Amb. at DIVION. Capt Harrison R.A.M.C. joined from ETAPLES to obtain transport cases to take treatment by Carell's tubes + Dakin's Solution. Weather too hot.	WJR
	11/7/16		Capt Hancock R.A.M.C. #11 O.R. of 27 Fd Amb. proceeded to A.D.S. to replace Capt Low + 11 O.R. of this Ambulance. 10% heat stroke.	WJR

Army Form C. 2118.

WAR DIARY 49 Field Ambce

INTELLIGENCE SUMMARY.

(Erase heading not required.)

Instructions regarding War Diaries and Intelligence Summaries are contained in F. S. Regs., Part II. and the Staff Manual respectively. Title pages will be prepared in manuscript.

Place	Date	Hour	Summary of Events and Information	Remarks and references to Appendices
LES 4 VENTS	12/6/16		HdQrs IV CORPS called + ordered concert the Ambulance. Misty morning hot later.	WMT
"	13/6		A.Brid called 12.30 pm. A.D.S. at CABARET ROUGE & HOSPITAL CORNER handed over to 27 Fd Amb. Capt PEARSON & party returned to H.Q.s. Fine day	WMT
DIVION.	14/6		49 Fd Ambulance marched from LES 4 VENTS at 10 am, having handed over to 27 Fd. Ambulance, via ESTRÉE COUCHIE - GAUCHIN-LE-GAL REBREUVE - HOUDIN - to DIVION. Opened up at School taken over from 98 Fd Amb. Dull morning, cool. Heavy rain commenced at 1 p.m. & again we arrived here. Took over 9 Scabies cases from 98 Fd Amb.	WMT
"	15/6		Showery weather.	WMT
"	16/6		Fine day.	WMT
"	17/6		SgaDm S 37 Div Orders. Fine day	WMT

Army Form C. 2118.

WAR DIARY 49 Field Ambulance
INTELLIGENCE SUMMARY. TPMC

(Erase heading not required.)

Instructions regarding War Diaries and Intelligence Summaries are contained in F. S. Regs., Part II. and the Staff Manual respectively. Title pages will be prepared in manuscript.

Place	Date	Hour	Summary of Events and Information	Remarks and references to Appendices
DIVISION	18/7/16		D.D.M.S. IV CORPS Called 12.20 p.m. Sent Ford car to Duffey Coben to be fitted with armour plates. Pay horse stables. 2 N.C.O's & 6 men sent to 37 Divisional Remounts for temporary duty. Gunnery.	WD
"	19/7/16		Capt Pearson went to Kleinmary duck with 26 N.F. trenches. A & B nil cases. 11.30 Gym.	WD
			Capt Ritchie Foster 40 cases. Wednesday. Capt Moss Sanitary Officer in 37 Div cases.	WD
"	20/7/16		D.D.M.S. IV CORPS called 11 am. Fine day.	WD
"	21/7/16		Capt Pearson returned from temp duty with 26 N.F. Walker. Overcast & cool.	WD
"	22/7/16		T.A.B. 2nd to 37 Div. Called 10.45 am. 102 & 103 Brigade's left 37 Div & 111 & 112 Brigade's arrived. Weather Fine & Cool day.	WD

2353 Wt. W2544/1454 700,000 5/15 D. D. & L. A.D.S.S./Forms/C. 2118.

Army Form C. 2118.

WAR DIARY 49 Field Ambulance RAMC

INTELLIGENCE SUMMARY.

(Erase heading not required.)

Instructions regarding War Diaries and Intelligence Summaries are contained in F.S. Regs., Part II. and the Staff Manual respectively. Title pages will be prepared in manuscript.

Place	Date	Hour	Summary of Events and Information	Remarks and references to Appendices
DIVISION.	23/8/16		Capt Penson went for temp duty to 13 K.R.R. Weather cloudy.	WAR
"	24/8/16		Lieut Russell went for temp duty to 13 R.F. A.D.M.S. called in afternoon. Route march 2 - 4 p.m.	WAR
"	25/8/16		Showery.	WAR
"	26/8/16		A.D.M.S. called 3 p.m. Route march 2 - 4 p.m. Heavy showers. Lieut Brown R.A.M.C. 49 Fd Amb. admitted sick.	WAR
"	27/8/16		Showery.	40M
"	28/8/16		A.D.M.S. called 10 a.m. D.D.M.S. IV Corps called 12 noon. Ambulance Showery.	WM
"	29/8/16		13th K.R.R.C. & 13 R.F. left the bivouan Encampment, fed horses & gave 2 Scant them. Heavy rain.	WM
"	30/8/16		Very hot & low key day.	40M
"	31/8/16		Fine day.	40M

W. Penson
O.C. 49 Fd Amb.
1.9.16

140/1734

31.10.

Confidential

War Diary
— of —
49th Field Ambulance

from 1st to 30th September 1916

Vol: XIV

COMMITTEE FOR THE
MEDICAL HISTORY OF THE WAR
Date 30 OCT. 1916

M

Army Form C. 2118.

WAR DIARY 49 Field Ambulance
or
INTELLIGENCE SUMMARY.
RAMC

(Erase heading not required.)

Place	Date	Hour	Summary of Events and Information	Remarks and references to Appendices
DIVION	1/9/16		ADMS called 11 am. Capt J.C.L. Vey. R.A.M.C. temporarily attached from 125th Bde. R.F.A. Pay Parade 5 pm. Sent in recommendations for advancement to WR Rets of Cpls. Pay of Pte. Hosp: Cairns, Fletcher, Parsons, Hodgkinson, Butler, Brown & Baxter. Weather fine.	WR
"	2/9/16		A.D.M.S. called 11 am. Capt Vey proceeded to 2/E. LANCS. for duty. Sent in recommendations for S/Sgt Burden to be Q.M.S. and Sgt Reynolds to be S/Sgt. Weather fine.	WR
"	3/9/16		Capt B Church Parade 2.30. Weather fine.	WR
"	4/9/16		Capt Dr McCLELLAN. 10 York + Lancs, a patient in hospital, placed under arrest by his own C.O. for "rendering himself unfit for duty by means of alcohol". Officers from 10 Y + L's took summary of evidence in the known. Weather wet & windy.	WR
"	5/9/16		A.D.M.S. called + in Spectre F.A. + Horse Lines. One evac to hosp, rest efficient.	WR
"	6/9/16		D.D.M.S. IV CORPS called 11.30. Weather fine	WR

Army Form C. 2118.

WAR DIARY

49th Field Ambulance
R.A.M.C.

INTELLIGENCE SUMMARY.

(Erase heading not required.)

Instructions regarding War Diaries and Intelligence Summaries are contained in F. S. Regs., Part II. and the Staff Manual respectively. Title pages will be prepared in manuscript.

Place	Date	Hour	Summary of Events and Information	Remarks and references to Appendices
DIVION	7/7/16		Capt. GILLESPIE R.A.M.C. rejoined for duty from 26th N.F. New Dummery. Spiridee is taken by Aug. 10 Y & Les in the line of Capt. McCleelan. Fine Weather.	WR
"	8/9/16		G.O.C. 37 Division Called & W. Spain + Self rejoined the F.A. at home lines. Weather fine.	WR
"	9/9/16		Capt. PEARSON permanently attached to 13. K.R.R. for duty, + Shirth of this F.A. Personnel received new to 5 receiving officers. One cart.	WR
"	10/9/16		Weather fine.	WR
"	11/9/16		Fine Weather.	WR
"	12/9/16		A.D.M.S. Called. Fine weather. Lt. J.P. Brown sent to Y Some Cots for temporary duty.	WR
"	13/9/16		Capt. Gillespie R.A.M.C. admitted to hospital A.sh. Weather fine.	WR
"	14/9/16		A.D.M.S Called 11.15 a.m. Weather fine. Maillie + Vivier & Grand.	WR

Army Form C. 2118.

WAR DIARY
or
INTELLIGENCE SUMMARY.
(Erase heading not required.)

149th Field Ambulance

Place	Date	Hour	Summary of Events and Information	Remarks and references to Appendices
DIVION	15/9/16		Capt. McClellan, Lt. Y + L. Anidrages this unit were arrest. Pay/Nurse Senior Inspection + Inspection of Khaki helmets. Copy/Letter. Route Marches prohibited July. Weather fine	WR
	16/9/16		Lt Taylor admitted to Ophthalmic Hosp. Weather fine	WR
	17/9/16		Church Parade 9.30 am. I visited 1st (R.N.D.) Field Amb. + arranged with O.C. to take over his transport. (COURIGNY). Received orders from A.D.M.S. to have to COURIGNY and take over from 1st (R.N.D.) Field Amb. Tomorrow. Fine weather.	WR
COURIGNY (HERSIN)	18/9/16		Jnr Ambulance moved to COURIGNY arriving at 12.30 pm and took over from 1st (R.N.D.) Field Amb. Heavy Showers.	WR
	19/9/16		Lt. Q.T. Symons RAMC temporarily attached. Heavy rain.	WR
	20/9/16		A.D.M.S. called 10.30 am. A.D.M.S. called 4.15 pm called at 8 pm. Weather wet.	WR

Army Form C. 2118.

WAR DIARY
INTELLIGENCE SUMMARY. 49% Field Amber.
(Erase heading not required.)

Place	Date	Hour	Summary of Events and Information	Remarks and references to Appendices
COUPIGNY	21/9/16		L/Cpl T. Symons R.A.M.C. sent by L/F.F Ambt. for duty. Capt Gillespie R.A.M.C. sent to 48 Fd Ambt. for temporary duty. Weather uncertain	
"	22/9		Staff officer Lt. & Qm. Peter administer Protective Ain. (IVth Corps) Weather overcast with fine intervals	
"	23/9		A.D.M.S. arrived 11 am A.D.M.S. arrived 2.30 pm Weather overcast	
"	24/9		Conference of F.A. Commanders Mine at A.D.M.S 2.30. Church Parade 11 am Fine weather. 9 messages sent with Instructions. A.D.M.S. at A+K NOULETTE from 48 Fd Amb. M.A.D.M.S Itching ones on 26/9/16.	MR
"	25/9		Sent 2 Sept 19 Sgt Symons to 48 Field Ambulance for duty as A.D.S. 1 Visited A.D.S with Capt Bough. R.M.C. and inspected MR him Mining Station & advanced Air Post. Lt Russell returned to duty from 13 R.F. GAS ALARM. 10.30 pm which however out to be a false one.	

2353 Wt. W2544/1454 700,000 5/15 D. D. & L. A.D.S.S./Forms/C. 2118.

Army Form C. 2118.

WAR DIARY
or
INTELLIGENCE SUMMARY. 49th Field Ambce

(Erase heading not required.)

Place	Date	Hour	Summary of Events and Information	Remarks and references to Appendices
COUPIGNY	26/9/16		Capt. Brough R.A.M.C. + 20 O.R. proceeded for duty at A.D.S. at Couplency. I took over the A.D.S. but all cars are to return through 48th Fd Amb. at Fosse 10. Capt Gillespie returned for duty from 48th Fd Amb & took over charge of A.D.S. at Couplency Aix-Noulette. A Fatigue Pm R.A.M.C. Antilegres from Aubigne. Weather fine.	WDR
	27/9/16		A.D.M.S. called. 37 Div Band players in Aub. 5 – 6.30 P.m.	WDR
	28/9/16		Weather rainy. I visited the A.D.S.s of 47th for look out at BULLY-GRENAY.	WDR
	29/9/16		D.D.M.S. called at 12 noon. Pay Parade. Inspection of funeral ladders. D.A.R.M.C. + G.S.O.I. 37 Div + Inspection of No. 3 a Amb. 4 p.m. Funerary	WDR
	30/9/16		I visited A.D.S. ——— Aix-Noulette & Aux Aubigne & all the evacuating points. Capt McClellan 10 + 2 cars reported to Asst of 4 th who asked Collect 10 am. "Dismissed H. M. Service. He was evacuated to 22 C.C.S. Fine day manufactured Sanitaire. J.U.C.N. H. Jameson For Committee, Lt Col, Commanding 5 Fd Ambulance.	WDR

2353/Wt. W5544/1454 700,000 5/15 D. D. & L. A.D.S.S./Forms/C. 2118.

140/815

Oct. 1916. 31st Dec.

Confidential

War Diary
of
149th Field Ambulance

from 1st Oct. 1916 to 31st Oct. 1916

COMMITTEE FOR THE
MEDICAL HISTORY OF THE WAR
Date — 9 DEC. 1916

Vol. XV

M

WAR DIARY
INTELLIGENCE SUMMARY. 49th "Field Ambulance"

(Erase heading not required.)

Army Form C. 2118.

Instructions regarding War Diaries and Intelligence Summaries are contained in F. S. Regs., Part II. and the Staff Manual respectively. Title pages will be prepared in manuscript.

Place	Date	Hour	Summary of Events and Information	Remarks and references to Appendices
COUPIGNY (HERSIN)	1/10/16		Capt G.H.F. Pritchard finished his duty at 2.30 pm. Lt Taylor 10th arr. temporary duty as M.O. 15th Heavy Artillery Group. Fine day. Visited both M. Ambulances at Fossé 9.	WR
"	2/10/16		Capt Soper RAMC proceeded 140 Field Ambulance for temporary duty. Lt Russel to 1st Somersets for temporary duty in relief of Lt J.P. Brown. Wet morning.	WR
"	3/10/16		Capt Gillespie handed over charge of A.D.S. at Aix-Noulette to Capt. Brumf & proceeded for duty to 17th Corps. Lt J.P. Brown proceeded for duty to 63 (RN) Division. Capt Soper returned from duty 140 Fd Amb. A.D.M.S. Corps. Wethering. Fine afternoon.	WR
"	4/10/16		A.D.M.S. called. 37 Sic Brund Blargies ar 1st Amb. 3-5 pm. Wet day.	WR
"	5/10/16 6/10/16		H.D.M.S. (Col. Duckering) called. Wet day. Capt Soper & Lt Qu Pitol visited A.D.S. Weather New Cart.	WR WR

WAR DIARY / INTELLIGENCE SUMMARY

Army Form C. 2118.

49th Field Ambulance

Place	Date	Hour	Summary of Events and Information	Remarks and references to Appendices
COUPIGNY (HERSIN)	7/10/16		Capt Rm Raine attended a demonstration of smell Box Respirator at 37 Div G.A.S. School. G.O.C. 37 Div in District Field Ambulance. Weather Showery.	WR
"	8/10/16		Medical Board consisting of myself as President and Capts. Dow & Soper as members assembled & examined report upon fitness of 2/Lt T.H. THORNE for a permanent commission. Weather Showery. This Ambulance in turn First Aid is Completion between the 3 Fd Ambulances for the best A.S. Wagon & Pair Horses. Seen by 37 Div Team.	MAL
"	9/10/16		I visited the A.D.S. in the afternoon. A.D.M.S. called. I went later A.D.M.S. at 7 p.m. Weather overcast.	WR
"	10/10/16		A Medical Board consisting of Myself, Capt Cooke & Capt Dow members to examine & report upon fitness of 2/Lt Raven still on permanent Commission. Capt Cooke proceeded to A.D.S. to visit Capt Bump. returned to H.Q. from A.D.S. I visited the Municeboat ABLAIN-St-NAZAIRE to bitumen. Weather fine.	WR

ABLAIN-St-NAZAIRE to bitumen.

WAR DIARY 4/9th Field Ambulance

INTELLIGENCE SUMMARY

Army Form C. 2118.

(Erase heading not required.)

Place	Date	Hour	Summary of Events and Information	Remarks and references to Appendices
COUPIGNY (HERSIN)	11/6/16		A.D.M.S. called and left some ambulance to F.A. Mercer reported for temporary duty from 50th Field Ambulance & proceeded to A.D.S. Wet weather.	WR
"	12/6/16		Very light work.	WR
"	13/6/16		Capt. attended at A.D.M.S. 12 men treceived instructions re impending move of Division. I called on 6.B Brigade at Aux NOULETTE. Sgt Major Rue attended dressing station & Small Boy Ruprieto and Dr Gr School. Pay Parade & inspected in section. Amos inspection Aux Nulette re. Fine but humid weather.	WR
"	14/6/16		A.D.M.S. called this morning. Lt. F.D. Mercer returned to 50th Fd Amb. and for duty.	WR
"	15/6/16		Two M.O.s from 6th Canadian Fd. Amb. arrived to take arrangements for the taking over from position at 5pm. The 6th Canadian Fd Amb took over A.D.S. at Aux Noulette. Lt. G.S. Burges returned for duty from 4 Fd Amb. Fair weather.	WR

Army Form C. 2118.

49th Field Ambulance

WAR DIARY
INTELLIGENCE SUMMARY.
(Erase heading not required.)

Place	Date	Hour	Summary of Events and Information	Remarks and references to Appendices
FRESNICOURT	16/10/16		71 Ambulance relieved by 6th Canadian Field Ambulance (Major Murphy) C.A.M.C, and marched to FRESNICOURT and came under orders of 63rd Inf. Brigade. Fine day. Met A.D.M.S. 37 Div. Who mentioned Lt Taylor reporting on being relieved from temporary duty with 15th Group Heavy Artillery.	WK
"	17/10/16		I went to HERMIN & prepared me a Medical Officer a Member, with Capt Low & Sapper as members, to investigate the mental condition of Pte Wood MK & Sapper as members. Weather fine. 1st Middlesex Regt.	WK
CHELERS	18/10/16		71 Amb. marched from Fresnicourt to CHELERS, arriving 1pm. Wet morning, fine but over cast later. I went to THURSDAY to make arrangements with O.C. 42 C.C.S. to receive cases from this Amb.	WK
"	19/10/16		Remained at CHELERS. Very wet day.	WK
LIENCOURT	20/10/16		Marched to LIENCOURT with 63rd Brigade. Called tree A.D.M.S. at LE CAUROY. Fine weather had very cold.	WK

Army Form C. 2118.

WAR DIARY
of 49th Field Ambulance
INTELLIGENCE SUMMARY
(Erase heading not required.)

Instructions regarding War Diaries and Intelligence Summaries are contained in F.S. Regs., Part II. and the Staff Manual respectively. Title pages will be prepared in manuscript.

Place	Date	Hour	Summary of Events and Information	Remarks and references to Appendices
ORVILLE	21/10/16		Marched to ORVILLE with 63rd Brigade. Weather fine but cold. Went into Billets.	WMcR
ARQUEVES	22/10/16		Marched to ARQUEVES with 63rd Brigade. Visited No 3 C.C.S. and marked for evacuation of cases through Nos 3 & 44 C.C.S. at PUCHVILLERS. Very cold & frosty.	WMcR
"	23/10		Remained in billets at ARQUEVES. 15 O.R. sent for stamping duty to Special Hospital WARLOY have now orders from A.D.M.S. 37.Div. Very wet day.	WMcR
VARENNES 24/10/16 Sheet 57.D. O.36.c.93.			I proceeded to reconnoitre a position at O.36.c.9.3. near VARENNES & arranged to move my Fd Amb. there & take over from 3rd (R.N.D.) Fd Amb. The Ambulance moved down less the 3 Bearer Subdivisions. March order of A.D.M.S. 37 Div. 2/L 3 Bearer Subdivisions teams, Wagon Orderlies with Capt. Brough & Lt. Burger proceeded to VARENNES & reported to O.C. Watson R Amc Convoy. Convoy consisted of Bearer Subdvns. Capt. Soper reported for the tram such & to O.C. 1st (RND) Field Amb. Divisional Main Dressing Station at HEDAUVILLE.	WMcR

Army Form C. 2118.

WAR DIARY 49th Field Ambulance

INTELLIGENCE SUMMARY.

(Erase heading not required.)

Place	Date	Hour	Summary of Events and Information	Remarks and references to Appendices
VARENNES O.36.c.93 Sheet 57.D.	25/10/16		Lt J.A.S. Piggott R.A.M.C. reported for duty. Very hot weather.	W/R
	26/10/16		Capt Brown & Lt R Burgess with Bearer Division returned to this unit after temporary occupation & return & Lt Col Evans in addition to command than at A.H.M. Amb. Very cold work.	W/R
	27/10/16		An Officer & S.O.O.T.R. of the Devons Division join our work. Conference of C.O. at A.D.M.S. at MARIEUX 2.30 pm. Very cold work.	W/R
	28/10/16		An Officer & S.O.O.T.R. on road work. I met Lt Kethyn & rode to the Casualty Dressing Station of 37th & 63rd Divisions between ENGLEBELMER & MARTINSART. Sheet 57.D. Q.31.8. & inspected the arrangements for the evacuation of slightly wounded cases. A.D.M.S. called at 12 am & Lee Par to Capt Long a long absence. I visited Advanced troops in the day. Very windy & rain in afternoon.	W/R

WAR DIARY

49th Field Ambulance

INTELLIGENCE SUMMARY

Army Form C. 2118.

(Erase heading not required.)

Instructions regarding War Diaries and Intelligence Summaries are contained in F.S. Regs., Part II. and the Staff Manual respectively. Title pages will be prepared in manuscript.

Place	Date	Hour	Summary of Events and Information	Remarks and references to Appendices
Near VARENNES O.36.c.9.3 (Sheet 51D)	29/10/16		Very wet & stormy. An Officer & 3rd O.R. & 10 O.R.'s of No. 2 Section employed on road work.	
BEAUVAL	30/10/16		Received orders to proceed to Beauval. Tent Subdivision (Capt Day & Relieft) sent transport Divisional Dressing Station (Bruce & 17th) Relieft at 8.45 a.m. Received orders from A.D.M.S. to hand in to O.C. Field Ambulance an Motor Ambulance our transport, our party arrived Cap't Inglis from Ambulance as with 87th Brigade. Head party on horses. Rect Division; and Officers & horses the Ambulance. All three pictures moving hay horses Rect Division 37th Division. Rect A.M.H. from 37th Division. the Ambulance moved to BEAUVAL arriving 9 marquee tattoos. Very heavy rain all day but time to rear returned to Villers-Bocage. Arrived at 11 pm. Men and equipment had their tea at 5 pm. Men and clothes through the state of the roads were the chief damage done. Fine weather. Am. Shires ten they off.	
"	31/10/16		Arrived Cellent 10.30 am Fine weather. After cleanup up.	

W.m = Ames
Lt. Col.
Au og.49. Fld. Amb.

31st Div

140/66/
1917

Confidential

War Diary
— of —
HQ 142nd Field Ambulance, R.A.M.C.
for November 1916

Volume XVI

COMMITTEE FOR THE
MEDICAL HISTORY OF THE WAR
Date -3 JAN. 1917

Army Form C. 2118.

WAR DIARY 49th Field Ambulance

INTELLIGENCE SUMMARY.

(Erase heading not required.)

Instructions regarding War Diaries and Intelligence Summaries are contained in F.S. Regs., Part II. and the Staff Manual respectively. Title pages will be prepared in manuscript.

Place	Date	Hour	Summary of Events and Information	Remarks and references to Appendices
BEAUVAL	1/11/16		Capt R.C. Pope Raws (T.C.) joined for duty from 47th Fld Amb. 3.30pm. Called in afternoon. Weather fine.	WR
"	2/11/16		Very showery weather. Leavers of 9th personnel down with P.U.O. 602.	WR 602
"	3/11/16		Capt Sorper H.R. Rams. evacuated sick to 29 C.C.S. Weather showery.	602
"	4/11/16		A/Col. Victor. Loudy 47th F.A. Amb. called to inoculate to Pont-Remy & Abbeville. Ray B7. Frank & Colcutt. Overseas. with fine intervals. Heavy rain in the night. The Inf. Ambulance is still lacked up nearly the whole time, but we have tapped the Pricky of the 63rd Pyre Amp. On Oct 27.1916 17-Lt M. Reynolds F. has (No 32372) been answered the Military Ambulance. We are now 20 O.R. Short in our personnel.	WR
"	5/11/16		Church Parade 11am. Very high wind. Still standing out & known.	WR 602
"	6/11/16		Wet with fine intervals. Beaver Surain being expected every day for the lorry Convoy. Loaded sketches across Camp Top.	602

2333 Wt. W2544/1454 700,000 5/15 D. D. & L. A.D.S.S./Forms/C. 2118.

WAR DIARY

49th Field Ambulance

INTELLIGENCE SUMMARY

Army Form C. 2118.

(Erase heading not required.)

Place	Date	Hour	Summary of Events and Information	Remarks and references to Appendices
BEAUVAL	7/6		Very hot sultry weather. Pay Parade.	WD
"	8/6		Fair weather	WD
"	9/6		Fine day weather.	
"	10/6		Fine fine weather. 2 bombs dropped from enemy aeroplane in the Vicinity of BEAUVAL at 7.45 p.m. No damage done.	WD
"	11/6		Fine weather. Conference at 10 a.m. at 5 pm re operations on 13.XI.16. (with 63rd Brigade)	WD
ACHEUX WOOD	12/6		1st Ambulance in a check from BEAUVAL to ACHEUX WOOD. (HQ) O/C. 37 Division in Tentacle Column on the march. Weather in and out & misty. Bearer Subdivisions & one Tent Subdivision been in reserve to move as instructions.	WD
"	13/6		Z. Day. (5.45 a.m.) Intense bombardment by our artillery commenced at 5.45 a.m. Lt. Burgess R.A.M.C. & 31.OR. proceeded at 5.20 a.m. to report to O/C. 63rd Division Collecting Station at @ 31.5.77. Sheet 57.D. @ Zero hour Subdivision Standing to ready to move to nearest to both 63rd Regt from 6. a.m. Weather cloudy & damp.	

2353 Wt. W2544/1454 700,000 5/15 D.D. & L. A.D.S.S./Forms/C. 2118.

WAR DIARY
or
INTELLIGENCE SUMMARY.

Army Form C. 2118.

4 9th Field Ambulance

(Erase heading not required.)

Place	Date	Hour	Summary of Events and Information	Remarks and references to Appendices
ACHEUX WOOD	14/6/16		Fine day. Sent 6 horse Ambulance cars to report for temporary duty.	
			A.D.M.S. 2nd Division at BERTRANCOURT, under instructions of D.D.M.S. VIII Corps. Sent 2 horsed Ambulance Wagons to relieve Wagons temporary duty with 63rd Div Collecting Station, to relieve Augustans. Capt Brough R.A.M.C. & Sgt Pink with 2 horse Ambulance proceeded to Q.25.d Sheet 57D for duty with 63rd Brigade.	LMR
Q.31.C. Sheet 57D near ENGLEBELMER	15/6/16		Moved remainder of Ambulance to Q.31.C. (63rd Div Collecting Station) + took over from 2nd (RND) Field Ambulance. Caps Lent & Piggott with a tent Sub Division from near the A.D.S. at MESNIL. Very near K.A. & heavy. Enemy commenced bombardment Bay tram distillery has been firing on since 13th inst.	
ditto	16/6/16		Very calm - busy in morning - Enemy later. 1 visited A.D.S. at MESNIL.	MR
ditto	17/6/16		19 reinforcement (Ptes) Infantry. No of wounded from hour 1st from 17th 19. Sick 13. (37 Siw)	MR

WAR DIARY
INTELLIGENCE SUMMARY. 4th Field Ambulance

Army Form C. 2118.

Place	Date	Hour	Summary of Events and Information	Remarks and references to Appendices
Q.31.b Sht 57.D near ENGLEBELMER	18/1/16		Heavy frost last night & this morning. Colonel Rhyzam R.S. Rail Etc. my Colonel Subt. to hand. D.D.M.S. vice Capt. Callen 11 am. 3rd (Cnd) for Ambulance. Effort of the line. I received 6 mules Ambulance Conform 30 R.A.M.C. hd. artyres. Who knew are chap check Sept 1, 19. 32 O.T.S. elsewhere. Wounded & Sickfor being getting up trench today with - 35 T.O. 3 Seven a trouver tonight. A.D.M.S. called.	MR
ditto	19/1/16		Colder, wet own cart. A.D.M.S. called 11 am. Capt. Mullins R.A.M.C reported for temporary duty. Sick to 12 rom 53. Wounded 12 - 120. Corp of trench fever.	1912
ditto	20/1/16		Fine weather, but cold. Wind from 1/6 to 2 am 20. Attached 85 Sick 162. A.D.M.S. 11th Division called with Sr Brig 37 Brig & O.C. 3rd Field Amb. to look over our arm station. A.D.S. 150th - View Fishing over. Fighting a over our arm station. A.D.S. 150th - View Fishing over. Fighting a 2 officers sent from 33 rd Field Ambulance arrived & preceded to A.D.S. MESNIL Family.	WAR

WAR DIARY or INTELLIGENCE SUMMARY

Army Form C. 2118.

HQ Field Ambce

Place	Date	Hour	Summary of Events and Information	Remarks and references to Appendices
D31.b. near ENGLEBELMER	21/4/16		Cold weather, heavy mist all day. Capt Brough, Lt Rogers, & 4 Orderlies with 3 bearer subdivisions returned to camp. All very tired but in good spirits. Ambulance brought heavy duty ration parties. 2 killed, 12 wounded. Captain, Lt Piggott & B. Sec Tent subdivision returned to camp having handed over A.D.S. at MESNIL # 33rd Field Ambulance & 37 Div Collr. Capt AT Marshall RAMC returned to this HQ for duty. Noon 20 to noon 21. Wounded 19. Irish std.	WR
ditto	22/4/16		Fine day. Not so cold. Capt Brough with A + C Sections keen Volunteers proceeded to repair 37 Divisional Beams at HEMEL. Noon 21th to Noon 22th. Wounded 1. Died 85.	WR
ditto	23/4/16		Misty morning — Guns our Survey Lect, his entre: Nov 22 - Nov 23 wounded 4. Irish 20. Arms S. Collen	WM
ditto	24/4/16		A.A.D.M.S. Called. C. Section Bearer Sub-Division under Cpt Caray returned to camp. Weath Cold & overcast. Noon 23 to noon 24. 6th Div. 0. Wounded	WR

WAR DIARY

49th Field Ambulance

INTELLIGENCE SUMMARY

Army Form C. 2118.

Place	Date	Hour	Summary of Events and Information	Remarks and references to Appendices
Q.31.c.77 Sheet 57D Nr ENGLEBELMER	25/6		Very heavy rain all day.	
ditto RENCHEVAL	26/6		A Sect. Bearer Sub. Division returned to Camp under Capt Gough. The Field Ambulance marched from Q.31.6.77 (Sheet 57 D.) to RAINCHEVAL. to relieve orders of G.O.C. 63rd Brigade. Arrived under heavy rain. went into billets after our arrival. Found main body the hard attend. at RAINCHEVAL. Slept after our arrival. Ran in the Eng & morning. Very tired. Our Marine Chapel.	WOR
ditto	27/6		Capt Payer proceeded to take over Medical Charge of 37 Divisional Train in the town of R.A.M.C. Weather fair but cold.	
ditto	28/6		Capt Powe of attached flesh after the sick in the interim of No 2 Cos, 37 Divisional Train. Pay Parade 5 p.m. Frost morning. Weather overcast & damp.	WOL
ditto	29/6		R.A.M.C. called at 9 a.m. + took a lock round the Ambulance billets. Fine Weather, frost + cold.	Ditts WOR

Army Form C. 2118.

WAR DIARY
or
INTELLIGENCE SUMMARY.

49 Field Ambce

(Erase heading not required.)

Place	Date	Hour	Summary of Events and Information	Remarks and references to Appendices
RAINCHEVAL	30/11		I went to BEAUQUESNE with A.D.M.S. + Staff Captain 13nd Dyn. to find a position for the Field Ambulance; interviewing the TOWN MAJOR + arranging billets. Weather colder + overcast.	

W. Morris Copple
Comdg. 49th Field Ambulance
30. XI. 16

Confidential

War Diary
of
49th Field Ambulance, R.A.M.C.

From 1st December 1916 to 31st December 1916

Vol: 17.

COMMITTEE FOR THE
MEDICAL HISTORY OF THE WAR
Date 31 JAN. 1917

WAR DIARY
or
INTELLIGENCE SUMMARY.

(Erase heading not required.)

Army Form C. 2118.

HQ 149th Field Ambulance

Place	Date	Hour	Summary of Events and Information	Remarks and references to Appendices
BEAUVESNE	1916 1/12		149 Field Ambulance moved from RAINCHEVAL to BEAUVESNE and opened up at RUE de FOSSES. A Bond ceded to temporarily Lt W.C. MENCE RAMC reported for duty. Weather overcast	MR
"	2/XII/16		Lt Right went to 7th Somersets for temporary duty. Lt Burgess with a composite bearer Sub division went to VARENNES for temporary duty. Pitching lists for No. 47 C.C.S. I.N. Co & Garrison to C.R.E. for temporary duty. Weather fine	49A
	3/XII/16		Capt. Burgh went to temporary duty at 8th Canadian. Weather overcast	49A
	4/XII/16		Weather fine but cooler	49A
	5/XII/16		Weather wet & cooler	49A
	6/XII/16		A.D.M.S. called about 2-30pm. Weather overcast	49A
	7/XII/16		A.D.M.S. called about 10-30 am. Had a long interview. Went to camp of 149 Winter training, field ambulance	49A

Army Form C. 2118.

WAR DIARY 49th Field Ambulance
or
INTELLIGENCE SUMMARY.
(Erase heading not required.)

Instructions regarding War Diaries and Intelligence Summaries are contained in F. S. Regs., Part II. and the Staff Manual respectively. Title pages will be prepared in manuscript.

Place	Date	Hour	Summary of Events and Information	Remarks and references to Appendices
BEAUQUESNE	8/12/16		Medical board myself President. Capt Taylor Rouse Member. Holden 10 a.m. at my office. Ireland 3/ Received Boot Oven, Weather wet & cold	LPR
	9/12/16		Wet weather + cold	LPR
	10/12/16		Wet weather + cold	LPR
	11/12/16		A.D.M.S. called at 11 a.m. I lectured representative M.O.s on sanitation. Wet afternoon. Fine morning + frost. Wet afternoon.	LPR
	12/12/16		Capt Brough returned to duty from 7th Lincolns. Lt Burgess returned from VARENNES with 33 O.R. 15 O.R. returned from Aug at Phoenix Hospital WARLOY. Conference CO's at A.D.M.S office 2.30. Received instructions for march on 14th with Pay Parade 5.30 p.m. Cold weather - snow	LPR
	13/12/16		10 O.R. returned from duty (fatigues) with C.R.E. Weather colder. Snow - Fog.	LPR

Army Form C. 2118.

WAR DIARY
or
INTELLIGENCE SUMMARY.

(Erase heading not required.)

49th Field Ambulance

Instructions regarding War Diaries and Intelligence Summaries are contained in F.S. Regs., Part II. and the Staff Manual respectively. Title pages will be prepared in manuscript.

Place	Date	Hour	Summary of Events and Information	Remarks and references to Appendices
BARLY near DOULLENS	14/12/16		Marched from BEAUQUESNE to BARLY & went into billets for the night. We are in charge with 63rd Brigade & conveying their made to hand by means of Horse Ambulances. Motor Ambulances to a hutted hospital has been allotted to Brigade. Coer + one cpt. Some rain. Capt Tay tn left for England for 14 days Special leave in termination of his Contract. We picked up 6 Stragglers on the march.	MO
HAUTE-COTE	15/12/16		Marched from BARLY to HAUTE-COTE. Billets in farm mills + byres. Picked up 74 Stragglers. Snowy.	MO
BRYAS	16/12/16		Marched from HAUTE COTE to BRYAS & billeted for the night. Very cold turncoat. Some rain. Picked up 130 Stragglers.	MO
RAMBERT	17/12/16		Marched from BRYAS to RAMBERT. Fine day. Inspected by G.O.C. 37. Div whilst passing through PERNES. 80 Stragglers picked up.	MO

Army Form C. 2118.

WAR DIARY
or
INTELLIGENCE SUMMARY.

2/2 2nd Field Ambulance

(Erase heading not required.)

Place	Date	Hour	Summary of Events and Information	Remarks and references to Appendices
LABIETTE FARM Near BUSNES	18.12.16		Marched from RAMBERT to LABIETTE FARM. 4.2 Stragglers kept up. Fine but very cold.	WD
"	19.12.16		Conference of C.Os at A.D.M.S. 10 a.m. Received instructions to take over the Collection of Sick of Rubis fm 13th Fd Amb. I went to LOCON, MESPLAUX and LE TOURET and made arrangements with O.C. 13th Fd Amb for taking over 22nd. Fine but cold.	WD
"	20.12.16		Sent Capt Brough with M.O.R. for duty at A.D.S. of 13th Fd Amb at LE TOURET. Fine but cold.	WD
"	21.12.16		Capt Low & Tent Subdivision proceeded to 13th Fd Ambulance MESPLAUX for duty & to take over the hospice formerly in Bethune. Capt Low & charge of Bethune 13th to be sent to LE TOURET & take over A.D.S at LE TOURET. Capt Brough took over A.D.S at LE TOURET. Lieut Hope from 13th Fd Amb to A.R. Lieut Hope Completed hospital party. Wet & colder.	WD

WAR DIARY or INTELLIGENCE SUMMARY.

Army Form C. 2118.

40th Field Ambulance

(Erase heading not required.)

Place	Date	Hour	Summary of Events and Information	Remarks and references to Appendices
MESPLAUX Content BETHUNE Road X.14.a.9.6	22/12/16		The remainder of the 3rd Division moved to MESPLAUX FARM & C/M on the transfer from 13th Div Ambulance. Showery weather	WSL
				WSL
ditto	23/12/16		A.D.M.S. called 9.30 a.m. Lt Piggott went to A.D.S. on duty. Windy.	WSL
"	24/12/16		I went to A.D.S. in afternoon. Pay Parade 2.30 pm. Capt Rm forwarder Hughes left on 14 days leave on expiration of his contract 17/12. Weather fine, holiday	WSL
	25/12/16		I went to A.D.S. in afternoon. Weather colder	WSL
"	26/12/16		D.A.D.M.S. called in afternoon. Weather overcast	WSL
"	27/12/16		Gen. Thick fog at night	WSL

Army Form C. 2118.

WAR DIARY
49th Field Ambulance
INTELLIGENCE SUMMARY.
(Erase heading not required.)

Place	Date	Hour	Summary of Events and Information	Remarks and references to Appendices
MEAULTE	27/12/16		I went round the Coys Lines & visited the Regimental Aid Post. Am seen both to stand & C.O. Sanitary Section. A.D.M.S. called & there I went round the Ambulance & premises in afternoon. Heavy mist.	WDR
"	29/12/16		Over twenty two men on leave	WDR
"			Capt Tay ?? returned from leave	
"	30/12/16		I visited & inspected the premises of the 24th Balloon Section. Fine day, rather milder but windy.	WDR
"	31/12/16		Mild weather. Church Parade 11 a.m.	WDR

31.XII.16

W Morris
Lt Col
Commanding 49th Field Ambulance

49th Field Ambulance. R.A.M.C.

War Diary

January 1917.

Confidential

37

Vol. 19

Vol: XVIII

COMMITTEE FOR THE
MEDICAL HISTORY OF THE WAR
Date 13 MAR. 1917

Army Form C. 2118.

WAR DIARY
or
INTELLIGENCE SUMMARY.

49th Field Ambce

(Erase heading not required.)

Instructions regarding War Diaries and Intelligence Summaries are contained in F. S. Regs., Part II. and the Staff Manual respectively. Title pages will be prepared in manuscript.

Place	Date	Hour	Summary of Events and Information	Remarks and references to Appendices
MESPLAUX NEAR LOCON	1917 Jan 1		A.D.M.S called 11 a.m. Went to A.D.S. 3 p.m. Weather fair	W/R
"	2		I walked to LA COUTURE & LA TOURET & investigated Tramway Line. Left R.A.P. La Couture. Found it was impracticable for use with our A.D.S. Fine weather	W/R
"	3		A.D.M.S. called 11 a.m. I visited Mr Bajolet bros at Pain. Weather overcast & showery.	W/R
"	4		Weather showery	W/R
"	5		Visited BETHUNE. Weather fine	W/R
"	6		Small Boys Inspection Hall 11 a.m. Head on inspection 2 p.m. Showery weather.	W/R
"	7		Church Parade 11 a.m. Pay Parade at 2 p.m. I visited M.O.T. Weather windy	W/R

WAR DIARY 49th Field Ambulance
INTELLIGENCE SUMMARY.

Army Form C. 2118.

Place	Date	Hour	Summary of Events and Information	Remarks and references to Appendices
NEF PLAUX	8.17		Distribution of medical returns to 37 Division to G.O.C. XIth Corps at MERVILLE. 1/Cpl CARDI, A.C. Private NORRIS.A. and PARSONS.H. received the Military Medal ribbons. Capt Low returned from leave. Fine morning, hot at night.	W/M
"	9th		A.D.M.S. proceeded to ENGLAND to leave. Arch Watson 4th Hussars Acting A.D.M.S. Showery weather.	W/M ##
"	10th		S.A.D.M.S. called between 3.30 pm Weather Colder Capt to Inspection H Q 4/2 M.A.H./1273 M/2 Munros from 111 Wrestling Som Coy in my absence at Corp	W/M
"	11th		a/A.D.M.S. called. I went to A.D.S. + in any absence at Corps XIth Corps visited the Ambulance. Lt T. JAUNTON R.A.M.C. (T.C.) Reported for duty from England Cold weather, sleet.	W/M
"	12th		Very cold weather.	W/M

Army Form C. 2118.

WAR DIARY
or
INTELLIGENCE SUMMARY.

49th Field Ambulance

(Erase heading not required.)

Place	Date	Hour	Summary of Events and Information	Remarks and references to Appendices
WESTOUTRE	13th		Pt. TAUNTON proceeded to 37 D.A.C. for temporary duty. Pte McKinnon R.A.M.C. proceeded on 10 days leave to England. Weather cold.	MM
	14th		Capt. J.R.W. proceeded to 37 Div. for School for course of instruction. C.O. 37 Div. with A/ADMS & DDMS inspected the Fd Ambulance in afternoon. Very cold & frosty.	MM
	15th		Lt. W.C. Meune proceeded to 124 Brigade R.F.A. for temporary duty. Capt Berry proceeded on 10 days leave to England. Capt Taylor returned. Capt Brough at A.D.S.J. No.2 E.Z./011,554. Dr T. WESTOBY reported being's bently B & cleared him Bühlthum reported at from X.20.b.63. Returned ambulance struck about a mile per hour Cold & frosty.	MM
	16th		I attended opening meeting of Notaire Museum at D.H.Q. 2 pm. Capt Renwick reported for temporary duty with Fd Ambulance. Cold & frosty.	MM

Army Form C. 2118.

WAR DIARY
or
INTELLIGENCE SUMMARY. 49th Field Ambulance

(Erase heading not required.)

Instructions regarding War Diaries and Intelligence Summaries are contained in F. S. Regs., Part II. and the Staff Manual respectively. Title pages will be prepared in manuscript.

Place	Date	Hour	Summary of Events and Information	Remarks and references to Appendices
WESTHOEK	17		Heavy fall of Rain. No 61051 Pnte S.L Prince transferred to 76 Field Amb. I visited A.D.S. L.of.Com. Sgt Pearson proceeded on leave to 10 temp to England	WR
"	18		Capt Hare returned leave from Bir Gas School. Temp Lieut Hare gazetted Captain in Gazette 21/1/1918. Snow - very cold	WR
"	19		Medical Board convened here to examine myself & candidate for Commission in R.F.C. myself prominent. Capt Hay & S/Sgt Renwich to proceed. Capt Renwich returned to 4th Fd Amb for duty	WR
"	20		Very Cold.	WR
"	21		Sgt Byram proceeded to Bir C.R.T. School from Course of Instruction. I visited A.D.S in afternoon. Pay Parade 12 noon	WR
"	22		Very cold. S Hoar frost.	WR

Army Form C. 2118.

WAR DIARY
or
INTELLIGENCE SUMMARY. 49th Field Ambulance

(Erase heading not required.)

Place	Date	Hour	Summary of Events and Information	Remarks and references to Appendices
MESOPOT.	23/17		At Bughra + 20 O.R. attended lecture in the Censorship held at 112 Brigade H.Qrs. 9 a.m. Venyales, transport.	4 PM
	24/17		Arrived, called 3-45 a.m. Steeplechasing race.	10c
	25/17		Attended a conference called by D.D.M.S. II Corps held at H.Qs of 37th S.M. + 5th Divisions and O.C. H. 9 Field Ambulance. Instrs. made between F.A.'s and R.E. Corps delivered to anyone persons which was principally in carrying the means for training in their duties the new Medical Officers posted to Fd Ambulances. Still keeping him. I fell into a huge dyke + injured flexor fibres of my right thigh adductors.	4Dc
	26/17		I am informed that Indian Board (myself, Capt. Law + Lt. Brydges) has been ordered to assembled in my room to examine 10 Lieuts re applications for permanent Commission in Indian Army. Very heavy trade.	W3K

Army Form C. 2118.

WAR DIARY
or
INTELLIGENCE SUMMARY. 49th Field Ambulance
(Erase heading not required.)

Place	Date	Hour	Summary of Events and Information	Remarks and references to Appendices
MESPLAUX.	27/7		Gun still on finishers. Lt Pigot attended detmch lectures XI Corps at 4TK Field Ambulance. ZELOBES. Rev. Chillew. C.F. C/E addressed W/R a parade on the subject of the Nation's Mission. Still very hard frost. 11 German Lives burnt at A.D.S. in RUE DE BOIS, one nearby the Billet occupied by the R.A.M.C. personnel. Capt Brough returned from leave.	W/R
	28/7		Capt. M. Pigot attended another lecture as yesterday. Ham got frost bite as yesterday. 5 N.C.O. and 3 men from H.Q. company in N.N. LANCS on adjmt. We have sent home 4 and 2 passed forward through our Ambulance. 11 wounded & 2 ...	W/L
	29/7		Confined to Billet. Capt Mervin detailed to visit Mil. Brigade School, GONNEHEM. LA COUTURE, Clearly for medical standing duty. Still freezing hard.	W/R
	30/7		Cold still very ... from snow. 1 N.C.O. & 3 men attended distribution by G.O.C. 1st Army SOMERVILLE. Capt Brough, Mehan & Pigott at A.D.S. Staff Capts H.Q. 1st, 15th, 49th Ambulance or a visit. 3 men frost & snow. Received orders to hand over to 15th F. Ambulance on a raise. Still unable to get out.	W/L
	31/7		Carry by 49th Fd. Ambulance M. Gran in ... Lt Col.

Confidential

War Diary
of
49th Field Ambulance

from 1st February to 28th February 1917

(Volume 19)

Vol 20

COMMITTEE FOR THE
MEDICAL HISTORY OF THE WAR
Date 4th APR. 1917

M

Army Form C. 2118.

WAR DIARY
or
INTELLIGENCE SUMMARY.

49th Field Ambulance

(Erase heading not required.)

Place	Date	Hour	Summary of Events and Information	Remarks and references to Appendices
MESPLAUX	1/2/17		Lt. Col. H. F. ROE, D.S.O., R.A.M.C., proceeded to England on leave. A.D.M.S. 37th Div. called at 11.45 am. Weather cloudy.	
ANNEZIN	2/2/17		Field Ambulance moved to ANNEZIN, being relieved at MESPLAUX by the 15th Field Ambulance (1 Section). Cold & frosty weather.	
	3/2/17		Went to see A.D.M.S. in morning. A.D.M.S. called in afternoon. Weather still very cold.	
	4/2/17		Pay parade 2 p.m. Frosty weather.	
	5/2/17		Route march in morning. D.D.M.S. XI Corps called in the afternoon. Snow fell during the night. Still very cold.	
	6/2/17		D.A.D.M.S. called in afternoon re field Ambulance & transport marches.	
	7/2/17		G.O.C. 37th Division inspected field Ambulance & transport. A.D.M.S. present. Cold but sunny weather.	
	8/2/17		A.D.M.S. & A.D.V.S. (now afterwards to visit the 1st Corps Rest. Station (74th field Ambulance) at LABEUVRIÈRE will inspect Quartermaster & Sergt-major. Had a Route march with transport in the afternoon. Attended a conference & O.Cs Field Ambulances at A.D.M.S. Office at 6 pm. Weather cold but sunny.	
	9/2/17		Weather still cold.	

Army Form C. 2118.

WAR DIARY of 49th Field Ambulance
INTELLIGENCE SUMMARY.
(Erase heading not required.)

Place	Date	Hour	Summary of Events and Information	Remarks and references to Appendices
ANNEZIN	10/2/17		Visited 17th Field Ambulance (1 section) at NOEUX-les-MINES with Q.M. & Supt-Major. Weather fresh.	
	11/2/17		Visited 63rd Brigade. Arranged for ambulance wagons & stores to proceed in the much bigger amount. Capt. D.S. BROUGH & 20 O.R. proceeded to 48th Field Ambulance for duty at their A.D.S. Weather fine, but cold.	
NOEUX-les-MINES	12/2/17		Field Ambulance moved to Staff School, Rue Sadi, NOEUX-les-MINES, a bit over 1km. the 17th Field Ambulance. Thaw began.	
	13/2/17		Major-General KELLY (from Hinflame) & Brigadier-General English visited the Ambulance in the morning. Shaw continued.	
	14/2/17		A.D.M.S. 37th Div. inspected the ambulance in the morning. Visited 37th D.A.C. (Hotchkiss) & 28th Mobile Veterinary Sect. (Drowsing) & their sect. Many found his condition in the afternoon.	
	15/2/17		Visited to 48th Field Ambulance for Lectures dept. Lt. A.P. PISSET to 48th D.M. A.D.S. Visited the 4th A.D.S. at PHILOSOPHE in the afternoon. Weather cold but fine.	

Army Form C. 2118.

WAR DIARY 49th Field Ambulance
INTELLIGENCE SUMMARY.

(Erase heading not required.)

Place	Date	Hour	Summary of Events and Information	Remarks and references to Appendices
NOEUX-LES-MINES	16/2/17		A/DADMS 37th Divn. called this morning. Weather overcast.	
	17/2/17		Weather cloudy.	
	18/2/17		ADMS called in morning. Church parade 10 a.m. Weather overcast.	
	19/2/17		DDMS I.Corps inspected the Field Ambulance at 2 p.m. With the ADMS. Lt P.H. ASHMORE reported for duty in place of Lt T.J. TAUNTON (37th D.A.C.) Weather dull.	
	20/2/17		Pay Parade 2 p.m. Visited ADS at PHILOSOPHE. Coyle. W.C. MENCE to ADS in relief of Capt. D.S. BROUGH. ADMS called in evening. Wet day.	
	21/2/17		Conference of O/Cs Field Ambulances at ADMS Office at 9.30 a.m. Capt. BROUGH returned to Hd.Qrs from ADS. Weather overcast. Lt BURGES to 48th Field Ambulance for temporary duty. ADMS examination by Capt. ROBERTS	
	22/2/17		Called at 12 noon. Post-mortem examination on body of patient who died of cerebro- (21st Mobile Laboratory) or body of patient who died of cerebro-spinal meningitis. Weather dull.	
	23/2/17		Weather overcast.	
	24/2/17		A.D.M.S. called in afternoon. Weather this dull.	

J.W. Cow
A.D.M.S.

WAR DIARY
INTELLIGENCE SUMMARY

Army Form C. 2118.

4.O.% Field Ambce

Place	Date	Hour	Summary of Events and Information	Remarks and references to Appendices
NOEUX-LES-MINES	25/2/17		I arrived at NOEUX-LES-MINES & took over command of 4/4 Field Ambulance on any return for leave 16 days. & thence 7 days. Conference of O.C.'s Fd Ambulances at 8 p.m. Church Parade 10 a.m. & fine weather. 6 p.m.	WR
	26/2/17		Coy H.Q. Engineers on the ice without leave of 35771 Pte Cox F. H. R.A.M.C. Pro. Capt A. McName members Cy Bing of the Indian A.M.C. I called to see A.D.M.S. W. Burgess evacuated to 4/4Th Field Amb to 33 C.C.S. Fine frosty weather.	WR
	27/2/17		Weather to be A.D.M.S. 7 p.m. O.C. 174Th Fd Amb. called to arrange to take over from the Ambulance on 3rd Prox. Fine weather.	WR
	28/2/17		A.D.M.S. visit Fd Amb & eat amount lent. Dr. J. Violet 63rd Gene Karage about paying move with th Major... & A Hot. Conference of O.C. Fd Ambs full day Genl M.Gavin Ray A.D.S.S. Auch.	WR

25.D.17

37

140/2042

Vol 21

37 F Amb

Confidential

War Diary
of
49th Field Ambulance

From 1st March 1917 to 31st March 1917

(Volume 20)

COMMITTEE FOR THE
MEDICAL HISTORY OF THE WAR
Date 11 MAY. 1917

March 1917

51

M

WAR DIARY of 2/4th West Riding Field Ambulance

INTELLIGENCE SUMMARY

Place	Date	Hour	Summary of Events and Information	Remarks and references to Appendices
NOEUX-LES-MINES	1/3/17		Went to RUITIEUX AREA to arrange for billetting. Weather fine but keen.	WM
"	2/3/17		Went to MAZINGARBE + arranged with 63rd Brigade about billetting on 4.3.17. Capt Menow + 20 O.R. returned from temporary duty with 4/5th D.L.I. Capt Menow + 20 O.R. 7th Ambulance at A.D.S. at PHILOSOPHE. Lt Piggot returned from temporary duty with 4/5th from temporary duty from MAZINGARBE to Field Ambulance. 7th Rhodes moved from MAZINGARBE to BETHUNE. 2 men frozen up on route by own ambulance car. Weather damp + cold.	WM
CONTRAINES	3/3/17		Handed over at NOEUX-LES-MINES to 7th Fd Ambulance. moved to billets at CONTRAINES. My car followed on the march. 7th incoles, 63rd M.G.C. + 63rd T.M.B. and picked up the stragglers. 7th Incoles 3. Weather fine + cold. Ambulance Lillers to West Riding C.C.S LILLERS	WM
near LILLERS				

WAR DIARY 49th Field Ambulance

INTELLIGENCE SUMMARY.

Army Form C. 2118.

(Erase heading not required.)

Place	Date	Hour	Summary of Events and Information	Remarks and references to Appendices
AU CANTRAINNE	4/3/17		7th Ambulance remained here. My Ambulance Cars proceeded to Brigade on the march and picked up the following numbers. 1st Middlesex – 3. 8th Somersets – 3. 4th Middlesex – 3. 10th Yorks – 4th. Pay Parade 5 pm. Weather fine but Green.	W.P.L.
LIGNY-LES- AIRE.	5/3/17		7th Ambulance marched to LIGNY-LES-AIRE. 17th and 1st Billets. Ambulance cars followed march of 35th Brigade + picked up the following. 7th Somersets – 10. 10th Yorks Lancs – 7. 4th Middlesex – 1. Snow fell this morning. Very Cold.	W.P.L.
"	6/3/17		7th Ambulance remained here. A.B.M.S. called this morning. C.O's infection approved. Rain fell morning. 2pm Ambulance cars proceeded & picked up as follows:- 10th Yorks/Lancs – 1. 4th Middlesex – 1. 1st Middlesex – 1.	W.P.L.
"	7/3/17		7th Ambulance remained here. Capt Mance R.A.M.C. sent sick to Week Regg C.C.S. Very cold frosty.	W.P.L.

Army Form C. 2118.

WAR DIARY
INTELLIGENCE SUMMARY

HQ 4th Field Ambulance

Place	Date	Hour	Summary of Events and Information	Remarks and references to Appendices
LIGNY-LEZ-AIRE	8/3/17		Sunny. Cold rising. Frozen in tent. Morning. Orderly Piquet & Sanitary adrem on Fire Orders. Inspection of march light in billets 8.30 P.M. Cold	
BRITEL-BROSSART	9/3/17		Fd. Ambulance moved from LIGNY-LES-AIRE to BRITEL, Brois.	
FOUFLINN-RICAMETZ	10/3/17		Fd Ambulance moved from BRITEL to RICAMETZ & opened up to receive WOR sick from units in 62nd Regtl. Area. A.D.M.S. called today. A fine day.	
"	11/3/17		I went to IZEL-LES-HAMEAU & arranged for take over Section School from 45th Fd Ambulance. Private Craig H. brought back to Fd Ambulance YE-F sick WOR. Place is an Infant Room passing in direction of APM 37 Div.	
"	12/3/17		Cool weather.	
"	13/3/17		Captain Lt. Pigott & B. Lect Tent Subdivision & proceeded to HOUVIN- HOUVIGNEUL & opened up a Brig. Dressing Station. Private A. Craig MM Started with Fd without leave. Placed in custody of escort. returned to unit	

WAR DIARY
INTELLIGENCE SUMMARY.

Army Form C. 2118.

49th Field Ambulance

Place	Date	Hour	Summary of Events and Information	Remarks and references to Appendices
FOUFFLIN RICAMETZ	14/3/17		Capt Brough - Lt Johnson & Park of C. Section proceeded to Izel over the Jenkins S/Sgt from 45th Field Ambulance. Lt + Qm Petel proceeded to Ireland on 10 days special leave. Visited HOUVIN and IZEL. Col. Henry Reid in the afternoon.	HQR
"	15/3/17		Attended Conference at St Paul M. Eph. Visited IZEL. Capt Olley M.C. R.A.M.C. Reported for Temporary duty from 50th Fd Amb on [illegible]	HQR
"	16/3/17		Attended Conference at [illegible] 5.30pm Fd [illegible]	HQR
"	17/3/17		Visited HOUVIN. Capt Way released by Cpt Keogh from 50th Fd Amb and transferred to [illegible] temporarily returned to [illegible]	HQR
"	18/3/17		Pay Parade 3 pm. Visited IZEL. Called on Colonel 4.30 pm 9 reinforcements arrived from the Base.	HQR
"	19/3/17		Went IZEL in morning. Capt Murphy 10 days sick leave in consequence of [illegible] illness. Visited CADIAL, Saffeyste R.A.M.C Returned to duty from 10 Corps Rest Station. Weather Overcast	HQR

Army Form C. 2118.

WAR DIARY
or
INTELLIGENCE SUMMARY.

(Erase heading not required.)

494th Field Ambulance

Instructions regarding War Diaries and Intelligence Summaries are contained in F. S. Regs., Part II. and the Staff Manual respectively. Title pages will be prepared in manuscript.

Place	Date	Hour	Summary of Events and Information	Remarks and references to Appendices
FOUFFLIN	20.3.17		H.Q.M.S. called 12.30 & told me that he might have leave shortly. Went to see & attended a Confce. of Capt. R.M.O. Kelly & G.O.C. 87 Bde. at Houvin. 2 p.m. Snow fell heavily.	
"	21/3/17		Went to ARRAS with D. C. of Nichols, Range. & Capt. Prehn. Return. Staging & recommend. a Dis Station & visited valley Rly. Coy. Very Cold. Snow fell to-day.	
"	22/3/17			
"	23/3/17		Very Cold. Went & arrans transport matters & ordnance pack mules. & 13.M.B.R. with A. D. M. S. R.A.M.C.	
"	24/3/17		Frosty. A.D.M.S. called in afternoon & went with him to T.F.S.M.S. & visit 477 Field Ambulance.	
"	25/3/17		Capt Leith R.A.M.C. to report for duty to 1/2 E.L. Lt Burgess R.A.M.C. came but he not reported. Confce. as at Avenug. 5-30 p.m.	

Army Form C. 2118.

WAR DIARY
INTELLIGENCE SUMMARY. 49th Field Ambulance
(Erase heading not required.)

Place	Date	Hour	Summary of Events and Information	Remarks and references to Appendices
FOUFFLIN-RICAMETZ	26/3/17		Attended Demonstration by Consulting Surgeon 3rd Army at 10.0 v/m	
"	27/3/17		HOUVIN[REVEL] — No 33032 Pte Parnaby W.J. Lints. Labour Battn. admitted with acute Rheumatism. Large Photo store.	
		2.15 pm	Patrol of No 20 Mobile Laboratory formed Enquiry in [illegible]	
			[illegible] of No 33032 Pte Parnaby which Lieut Butt [illegible] attached gave Indication [illegible] his Kit & [illegible] white lice taken from form of [illegible] & winter clothing. In afternoon + HOUVIN Barr.	
"	28/3/17		Poor Weather. Capt Brough returned from leave	MR
"	29/3/17	2 pm	Called in ADMS 2 pm. Afterwards visited 50th Field Ambulance.	
"	30/3/17		Conference at HQrs 1st Corps of ADsMS. OsC [illegible]. DsDMS. 3rd Army present.	MR
"	31/3/17		Relief of Much [illegible] by Argd. H am. Conference OsC 71st Ind. + RMOs as [illegible] MR. [illegible] Tried by FGCM. Reacquit guilty. Conning + 5 [illegible].	

Confidential

War Diary
of
149th Field Ambulance

From 1st April 1917 to 30th April 1917

(Volume 21)

COMMITTEE FOR THE
MEDICAL HISTORY OF THE WAR
Date 6 JUN. 1917

B.E.F.

Summary of Medical War Diaries of 49th F.A. 37th Div.

    6th Corps   3rd ARMY.

    18th Corps from April 13th.

    17th Corps from April 19th.

    18th Corps from April 30th.

    6th Corps from 19th May.

O.C. Lieut. Col. W.F. Roe.

Operations on Western Front - 1917- April - May.

Summarised under the following headings :-

Phase "B" - Battle of Arras - April - May 1917.

1st Period - Attack on Vimy Ridge - April.

2nd Period - Capture of Siegfried Line - May.

B.E.F.

49th F.A. 37th Div. 6th Corps. 3rd ARMY.   WESTERN FRONT.
                                            April 1917.
Officer Commanding - Lt.Col. W.F. ROE.

18th Corps from April 13th.

PHASE "B" - Battle of Arras - April - May 1917.
        1st Period - Attack on Vimy Ridge - April.

Headquarters at Fofflin-Ricametz.

April 5th.	Moves. To Izel-Les-Hameau.
7th.	To Duisans. L7.a.6.0. (Sheet 51c).
8th.	Moves. Detachment.) "A" Br. S.D. and "B" T.S.D. moved Medical Arr.) forward under Officer Commanding 48th F.A. Officer Commanding 49th Field Ambulance took over command of remainder of 48th and 49th Field Ambulances (R.A.M.C. Reserve.)
9th.	Moves Detachment. 1 and B & C Br. S.D's moved forward with 63rd Infantry Brigade.
10th.	Moves Transport. 2 Horse Ambulances from 48th Field Ambulance and 1 from 49th Field Ambulance sent for duty between Tilloy and Arras.
11th.	Moves Detachment. 2 and 1 Reserve T.S.D. of 48th Field Ambulance and 2 of 49th Field Ambulance to Arras under Officer Commanding 48th Field Ambulance.
	Medical Arrangements. 2 A.D.S.'s formed by Div. R.A.M.C. 1 at Feuchy and 1 at Tilloy.
	Moves Transport. 3 Horse Ambulances sent to A.D.S. Tilloy.
	Casualties R.A.M.C. 0 & 2 killed, 0 & 3 wounded.
12th.	Casualties R.A.M.C. 0 & 10 wounded.
	0 & 1 died of wounds.
13th.	Moves. Detachment & Transport. Personnel and Transport of 48th and 49th Field Ambulances under Officer Commanding 48th Field Ambulance returned to Duisans.
	Transfer. To 18th Corps.

B.E.F.

49th F.A. 37th Div. 18th Corps. 3rd ARMY.   WESTERN FRONT.
Officer Commanding - Lt.Col. W.F. ROE.   April 1917.

17th Corps from 19th April.

PHASE "B" - Battle of Arras - April - May 1917.
    1st Period - Attack on Vimy Ridge - April.

H.Q. at Lignereul.
April 13th.	Transfer. To 18th Corps.
14th.	Moves. To Lignereuil.
19th.	Transfer. To 17th Corps.

B.E.F.

<u>49th F.A. 37th Div. 17th Corps. 3rd ARMY. WESTERN FRONT.</u>
April 1917.
<u>Officer Commanding - Lt.Col. W.F. ROE.</u>

<u>PHASE "B" - Battle of Arras - April - May 1917.</u>
<u>-1st Period - Attack on Vimy Ridge - April.</u>
<u>H.Q. Arras.</u>

April 19th. <u>Transfer.</u> To 17th Corps.

19-20th. <u>Moves.</u>) To Arras. Took over Oil
<u>Medical Arrangements.</u>) Factory from 11th F.A.

"B" T.S.D. took over Div. Col. S. under 17th Corps orders.

22nd. <u>Moves Detachment.</u> "C" Br. S.D. to 50th F.A. for duty as Stretcher Bearers. "A" and "B" Br. S.D's to 63rd Brigade.

<u>Medical Arrangements.</u>) Reserve R.A.M.C. Depot at Oil
<u>Transport.</u>) Factory under Officer Commanding 49th Field Ambulance with Massed Ambulance Wagons and Cars of 37th Div. Field Ambulances and 10 Motor Ambulances of 24th M.A.C.

23rd. <u>Medical Arrangements.</u> 2 and "A" T.S.D. with "A" T.S.D. of 50th Field Ambulance established A.D.S. on St. Laurent - Blangy - Gavrelle Road.

<u>Casualties R.A.M.C.</u> Lt. Burgess wounded died 24th.

24th. <u>Medical Arrangements.</u>) 37th Div. Band sent to A.D.S.
<u>Assistance.</u>) to act as Stretcher Bearers.

28th. <u>Operations.</u> 37th Division attacked 4.30 a.m.

<u>Medical Arrangements.</u>) 8 ambulance wagons sent out
<u>Evacuation.</u>) to carry walking wounded to D.C.S.

<u>Operations Enemy.</u> Several shells fell in vicinity of Oil Factory.

<u>Moves Detachment.</u> "A" and "B" Br. S.D. returned to Headquarters from the front line.

"C" Br. S.D. returned to Headquarters
29th. from the front line.

B.E.F.

49th F.A. 37th Division. 17th Corps. 3rd ARMY. WESTERN FRONT. April 1917.

Officer Commanding = Lt. Col. W.F. ROE.

18th Corps from 30th April.

PHASE "B" - Battle of Arras - April - May 1917.
-1st Period - Attack on Vimy Ridge - April.

April 30th. Medical Arrangements. A.D.S. and D. Col. S. handed over to S.A.F.A.

Moves. To Liencourt.

Casualties R.A.M.C. Between 22nd and 25th.
- 0 & 3 killed.
- 0 & 13 wounded.

Casualties A.S.C. M.T. attd. 0 and 1 wounded.

Transfer. 37th Division transferred to 18th Corps.

B.E.F.

49th F.A. 37th Div. 6th Corps. 3rd ARMY. WESTERN FRONT.
April 1917.
Officer Commanding - Lt.Col. W.F. ROE.
18th Corps from April 13th.

PHASE "B" - Battle of Arras - April - May 1917.

    1st Period - Attack on Vimy Ridge - April.

Headquarters at Fofflin-Ricametz.

April 5th.   Moves. To Izel-Les-Hameau.

7th.   To Duisans. L7.a.6.0. (Sheet 51c).

8th.   Moves. Detachment.) "A" Br. S.D. and "B" T.S.D. moved
Medical Arr.   )
forward under Officer Commanding 48th F.A. Officer
Commanding 49th Field Ambulance took over command of
remainder of 48th and 49th Field Ambulances (R.A.M.C.
Reserve.)

9th.   Moves Detachment. 1 and B & C Br. S.D's moved forward
with 63rd Infantry Brigade.

10th.   Moves Transport. 2 Horse Ambulances from 48th Field
Ambulance and 1 from 49th Field Ambulance sent for
duty between Tilloy and Arras.

11th.   Moves Detachment. 2 and 1 Reserve T.S.D. of 48th Field
Ambulance and 2 of 49th Field Ambulance to Arras under
Officer Commanding 48th Field Ambulance.
Medical Arrangements. 2 A.D.S.'s formed by Div. R.A.M.C.
1 at Feuchy and 1 at Tilloy.
Moves Transport. 3 Horse Ambulances sent to A.D.S. Tilloy.
Casualties R.A.M.C. O & 2 killed O & 3 wounded.

12th.   Casualties R.A.M.C. O & 10 wounded.
                 O & 1 died of wounds.

13th.   Moves. Detachment Personnel and Transport of 48th and
& Transport.
49th Field Ambulances under Officer Commanding 48th Field
Ambulances returned to Duisans.
Transfer. To 18th Corps.

B.E.F.

49th F.A. 37th Div. 18th Corps. 3rd ARMY. WESTERN FRONT.
Officer Commanding - Lt.Col. W.F. ROE.   April 1917.

17th Corps from 19th April.

PHASE "B" - Battle of Arras - April - May 1917.
    1st Period - Attack on Vimy Ridge - April.

           H.Q. at Lignereul.

April 13th.   Transfer. To 18th Corps.
    14th.   Moves. To Lignereuil.
    19th.   Transfer. To 17th Corps.

B.E.F.

49th F.A.   37th Div. 17th Corps. 3rd ARMY. WESTERN FRONT.
                                                April 1917.
Officer Commanding - Lt.Col. W.F. ROE.

H.Q. Arras.

PHASE "B" - Battle of Arras - April - May 1917.
    -1st Period - Attack on Vimy Ridge - April.

April 19th. Transfer. To 17th Corps.

19-20th. Moves.   ) To Arras. Took over Oil
          Medical Arrangements.   )
          Factory from 11th F.A.

                            "B" T.S.D. took over Div. Col. S.
          under 17th Corps orders.

22nd.   Moves Detachment. "C" Br. S.D. to 50th F.A. for duty
         as Stretcher Bearers. "A" and "B" Br. S.D's to 63rd
         Brigade.

         Medical Arrangements.) Reserve R.A.M.C. Depot at Oil
         Transport.   )
         Factory under Officer Commanding 49th Field Ambulance
         with Massed Ambulance Wagons and Cars of 37th Div.
         Field Ambulances and 10 Motor Ambulances of 24th M.A.C.

23rd.   Medical Arrangements. 2 and "A" T.S.D. with "A" T.S.D.
         of 50th Field Ambulance established A.D.S. on St.
         Laurent - Blangy - Gavrelle Road.

         Casualties R.A.M.C. Lt. Burgess wounded died 24th.

24th.   Medical Arrangements.   ) 37th Div. Band sent to A.D.S.
         Assistance.   )
         to act as Stretcher Bearers.

28th.   Operations. 37th Division attacked 4.30 a.m.

         Medical Arrangements.   ) 8 ambulance wagons sent out
         Evacuation.   )
         to carry walking wounded to D.C.S.

         Operations Enemy. Several shells fell in vicinity of Oil
         Factory.

         Moves Detachment. "A" and "B" Br. S.D. returned to
         Headquarters from the front line.

                            "C" Br. S.D. returned to Headquarters
29th.   from the front line.

B.E.F.

49th F.A. 37th Division. 17th Corps. 3rd ARMY.   WESTERN FRONT.
                                                  April 1917.
Officer Commanding = Lt. Col. W.F. ROE.

18th Corps from 30th April.

PHASE "B" - Battle of Arras - April - May 1917.
   -1st Period - Attack on Vimy Ridge - April.

April 30th. Medical Arrangements. A.D.S. and D. Col. S. handed over to

S.A.F.A.

Moves. To Liencourt.

Casualties R.A.M.C. Between 22nd and 25th.

   O & 3 killed.

   O & 13 wounded.

Casualties A.S.C. M.T. attd. O and 1 wounded.

Transfer. 37th Division transferred to 18th Corps.

WAR DIARY
or
INTELLIGENCE SUMMARY.

49th Field Ambulance

Army Form C. 2118.

(Erase heading not required.)

Place	Date	Hour	Summary of Events and Information	Remarks and references to Appendices
FOUFFLIN-RICAMETZ	1/4/17		Wet weather.	AQ/1
"	2/4/17		Attended Administrative Conference 3785 at HOUVIN. Heavy Snow.	AQ/2
"	3/4/17		A.D.M.S. called 11 a.m. I promulgated the sentence of F.G.C.M. on #3 Private CRAIG R.A.M.C. 10 months imprisonment with H.L. which 6 months was remitted by G.O.C. 83rd Inf. Bgde. as it G.O.C. meant that Pvte Craig should and be imprisoned till further orders. I released him from custody. Snow falling.	AQ/3
"	4/4/17		Fair weather.	AQ/4
IZEL-LES-HAMEAU	5/4/17		The H.Qs. of the Field Ambulance moved to IZEL + 1st Bearer Sec. Tent Subdivision moved from HOUVIN to IZEL + all went into billets. The Advance + 1 Car were to proceed to 37 C.C.S. for duty only. I entrained 250900 9/16 D.D.&L. Ltd. Forms/C2118/13. At Frevent-market DIVISION. Very cold.	AQ/5

Army Form C. 2118.

WAR DIARY
or
INTELLIGENCE SUMMARY.

(Erase heading not required.) 4 9th Field Ambulance

Instructions regarding War Diaries and Intelligence Summaries are contained in F. S. Regs., Part II. and the Staff Manual respectively. Title pages will be prepared in manuscript.

Place	Date	Hour	Summary of Events and Information	Remarks and references to Appendices
IZEL	6/5/17		Fine sunny day. Field Ambulance remained in billets at IZEL-LES-HAMEAU. Shoes formed & former dumbest cleaned up. Went to ARRAS. B.23.a.S.1 (5.18)	WOR
DUISAN (L.7.a.6.0) S.I.C.	7/5/17		Fine weather, hot cold wind. The Field Ambulance moved to camp in huts on AGNEZ-DUISAN Road. Rd S.I.C. L.7.a.6.0. I have former ... dump of public structures	WOR
"	8/5/17		Fine & sunny. Capt Marsham R.A.M.C reported for temp. duty. Capt Way R.A.M.C reported from 15th ... Amb. for temp. duty. Capt. ... Rev.n G. Forman 48th ... amb for temp duty. B. Tent Subdiv. under Capt M Law and Capt Way & Lt Pupper moved off at 2 p.m. under orders of the M.P. Watson R.A.M.C to accompany the 11th Bgde. ... A.R.C.A.S. transit ... to...	

Army Form C. 2118.

WAR DIARY
or
INTELLIGENCE SUMMARY. 4/1st Field Ambulance

(Erase heading not required.)

Place	Date	Hour	Summary of Events and Information	Remarks and references to Appendices
DUISANS (L.7.a.6.0)	9/4/17	"Z" 5.30 am	Capt Brough with B & C Bearers Subsections moved off at 6.30 am with 62nd Brigade. Heavy Rain & Snow. Wind and snowing. Iain breaks later. heavy snow at night. Three Ambulance Wagons [10/4th & 2 of 49th (2nd) Field Ambulances?]	WR
"	10/4/17		Reem Snow, Very Cold, Strong winds. 2 Cld Wagons for 4 F.A. & Capt Very M.C.	WR Capt Very M.C.
"	11/4/17		1 for 49th Fd Amb. Left for duty between Tilloy & Arras. RAMC reported for duty. Capt Very M.C. proceeded to ARRAS to Relief stations. 37th Division for duty on A.D.S. Two A.D.S. have been formed by Division R.A.M.C. 1 at HEUCHY & 1 at TILLOY yesterday. Capts Marshall + Godfrey R.A.M.C. with 1 Reserve Tent Subdivision of 4/1st & 2 of 4/9th Field Ambulances proceeded to what to duty to Lt Col. Hahn R.A.M.C. at Advanced Dressing Stns. ARRAS. Cold windy day. Rain. Heavy snow afternoon and night. 3 Ambulance Wagons returning from duty at Wagonlieu & New Bank (adj. to TILLOY).	WR

Army Form C. 2118.

WAR DIARY
or
INTELLIGENCE SUMMARY.

(Erase heading not required.) 69th Field Ambulance

Place	Date	Hour	Summary of Events and Information	Remarks and references to Appendices
DUISAN L.7.a.63	12/4/17		Note to Col. Falkus. Windy morning. Closing with Pamphlets and Rifles. Following casualties reported:- 36631 Pte J Smyth wounded, 35176 Pte J Brick wounded, 69330 Pte E Hopkins wounded	51 CCS (Both to R.I.M.R.) 51 CCS
			7.0 P.M. 8 men lent as hush arrived both 1st & 69 Fd R's returned. Enemy, no wounded	M.E.
"	13/4/17		This bright morning Inniskilling Ceb. Personnel + Transport of 4th F.A. & 9th Fgh Auth returned. Ceb to our command reported later. The following Casualties also occurred during the Battle of ARRAS:- Killed No 36833 Pte Rillington J (11/17) 36743 Ycpl Bamford JH. (11/17). 2nd Johnson 39712 Pte Howard AG (12/17) Wounded No 42602 Pte Kenny J - 31560 Pte Green R.E. 38495 Pte Swan R (Cpl 11/7) 36876. Pte Foreman R.M. 33802 Pte Swan E. 21902 Pte Hutchinson W.9 1815.87 Pte O'Neill P.J. 36787 Pte Brown M.A. 86020 Pte 10116 24257 Pte Parker R all 12/17	

Army Form C. 2118.

WAR DIARY
or
INTELLIGENCE SUMMARY.

49th Field Ambulance

(Erase heading not required.)

Place	Date	Hour	Summary of Events and Information	Remarks and references to Appendices
DIEVAL	14/4/17		The Field Ambulance moved into Billets at LIGNEREUIL & relieved up present trick of 87th Field Brigade - Friday.	WAR
LIGNEREUIL	15/4/17		Remained in billets, men rested. Adm's Conference of O.O.C. 5.30 pm	WAR
"	16/4/17		Medical Board assembled to examine 2/Lt S. Silkstone, 4th Middlesex for fitness for permanent commission in the Regular Army. Capt W.J. Rae, Res. Retire. President. Capt M.L.W. & D. Lyppet members. C.O. paraded 2 pm. 1 promptly acknowledged letter received from A.D.M.S 33 Div. expressing appreciation of the work done by the Divisional R.A.M.C. during the Battle of ARRAS.	WAR
"	17/4/17		13 Reinforcements reported for duty from the Base. Pay Parade 5 pm. Wet weather.	WAR

Army Form C. 2118.

WAR DIARY
40th Field Ambulance
INTELLIGENCE SUMMARY.

(Erase heading not required.)

Instructions regarding War Diaries and Intelligence Summaries are contained in F. S. Regs., Part II. and the Staff Manual respectively. Title pages will be prepared in manuscript.

Place	Date	Hour	Summary of Events and Information	Remarks and references to Appendices
Sept 1917 LIGNEREUIL	18/9/17		Capt McClumpha R.A.M.C. (S.R.) reported for duty. Wet weather.	WJL
GOUVES	19/9/17		2A Ambulance moved from LIGNEREUIL to GOUVES with 63rd Brigade. Halting point his billets for the night.	WJL
DIL FACTORY ST NICHOLAS	20/9/17		2A Ambulance moved to OIL FACTORY ST NICHOLAS. HQ R.A.M.S. Took over from 11th Field Ambulance of 63rd M.R.L.D.R. Took over B. Tents Divisional Rest Station. Divisional Walking Wagon were Rest Station.	WJL
"	21/9/17		D.D.M.S. XVIIth Corps called. ADMS called.	WJL
"	22/9/17		ADMS XVIIth Capt called. ADMS called. Capt Brough with C. Beam Major. reported for oc. 50th Fd Amb. for duty in reserve. Sketch Renew. Lt Broyle with A. & B. Beam Subdivisions reported for duty with 63rd Brigade. WJL I took over Command of Reserve R.A.M.C. Units at Oil Factory. 50th Field Ambulance arrived at OIL FACTORY and commenced working. Nicht R.A.M.C. 10 Motor Ambulances on relation to relief from M.A.C. of the Messrs Ambulances & Australians.	WJL

Army Form C. 2118.

WAR DIARY
or
INTELLIGENCE SUMMARY.
(Erase heading not required.) 49th Field Ambulance

Place	Date	Hour	Summary of Events and Information	Remarks and references to Appendices
ST NICHOLAS OIL FACTORY	23/4/17	Zero 4.35 a.m.	LT BURGES R.A.M.C. transferred to join Unit to relieve Capt Taylor sent to relieve him 2.20 a.m. Capt McKenzie & Capt Elliott with A Tent Subdivision of 49th & 50th Fd Ambulances moved up & opened an advanced Dressing Station in the ST LAURENT — BLANGY — GAVRELLE ROAD abt 7—3.0 p.m. 4.30 pm — got the following from Bm HQrs 4/9th Regt of 9th Nth Staffs asking in clipping & making skeleton.	WOR
		abt 2.45 pm	I sent 37 stretcher Bearers up to A.D.S. lines & stretcher Bearers stuck closer. I visited ADS at 5.30pm and ADMS	WOR
"	25/4/17		D.C. & 5th Fd Amblce reported Vted Lt Burges who died afterwards at Canadian C.C.S on 24/4.17. I visited ADMS in afternoon.	WOR
"	26th		ADMS called re-stretcher bearers arrangements to support Lt Burgess. During our Advances tri HQ I visited ADS & ADMS Lt Ewing R.A.M.C reported for duty from 6th H.A.G. R.G.A. annexed posted to duty at Divisional Collecting Station.	WOR

Army Form C. 2118.

WAR DIARY
or
INTELLIGENCE SUMMARY.
(Erase heading not required.)

49th Field Ambulance

Instructions regarding War Diaries and Intelligence Summaries are contained in F. S. Regs., Part II. and the Staff Manual respectively. Title pages will be prepared in manuscript.

Place	Date	Hour	Summary of Events and Information	Remarks and references to Appendices
ST NICHOLAS	27/5		Opened Camp kitchen at Div. Adv. H.Qrs. Adms 9th Division called with Chief A.D.M.S. called. A.D.M.S. 37 Div. called. I took Capt Lowthorp & Lt R.Sgt. to visit the A.D.S. & afterwards to visit adjmts, and the kitchen A.D.S. run by Lt Col A. Nicholls 50th Field Ambulance.	WJR
	28/7		Attach by 37 Div. A.D.S. report 5 Regn. Ambulances improper sword to carry wounded — prefer transport by M.A.C. — to 4th Army H.Q. 3.30 p.m. I went to see the Lieut-Col & 4th Feb 2 obs (illegible) & & B Bearer [illegible] returned to O.C. Factory Adrms. 8pm.	W
	29/7		Prov Note: called 9.30 am. I called at T. C. D. C. [illegible] 19th Div [illegible] A.B.C Bearer [illegible] [illegible] M.O. I.s. Sent with Tel Call [illegible] [illegible] [illegible] bearer divs & Rear [illegible] [illegible] [illegible] [illegible] [illegible] [illegible] changed their steeds to the horsey, much stricken [illegible] B.T. & head.	W
LIPINCOURT	30/5		[largely illegible entry]	W

(P.T.O)

Army Form C. 2118.

WAR DIARY
of 49th Field Ambulance
INTELLIGENCE SUMMARY.
(Erase heading not required.)

Place	Date	Hour	Summary of Events and Information	Remarks and references to Appendices
	22/4/17		Casualties among personnel between 22/4/17 & 25/4/17	
			Lieut J.C.S. BURGES, R.A.M.C. wounded — Died of wounds at No 1 Canadian Casualty Clearing Station 24/4/17	
	23/4/17		Killed: No 40820 Pte J.E. MORRISON & No 76477 Pte E. CHAPMAN	
			Wounded: No 36335 Pte L.J. MAYO; No 36201 L/Cpl J. AINSWORTH; No 36689 A/L/Cpl R. KINNON & No 36658 Pte J.H. PEDEN; No 39280 Pte W. BARRY; No 48236 Pte D. McJOHN; No 69790 Pte W.J. LYTTLE; No 22434 Pte C. BUTTERWORTH; No 69527 Pte J. LOWE; No 35999 Pte J. CURRY (to duty); No 32409 Pte J. NAYLOR; No 5820 Pte J. FALLOW; No 34 Pte S. PRATT	
	24/4/17		Killed: No 90634 Pte J. BUTLER	
	25/4/17		Wounded: No M/2/054790 Sgt. J.J. CHELLEW (A.S.C. M.T. attached)	
	30/4/17			

M. Munro
Lieut Colonel
Commanding 49th Field Ambulance

Confidential

War Diary
of
49th Field Ambulance
from 1st May to 31st May 1917

(Volume 22)

Medical

B.E.F.

Summary of Medical War Diaries of 49th F.A. 37th Div.

   6th Corps 3rd ARMY.
   18th Corps from April 13th.
   17th Corps from April 19th.
   18th Corps from April 30th.
   6th Corps from 19th May.

O.C. = Lt. Col. W.F. ROE.

Operations on Western Front - 1917- April - May.

Summarised under the following headings :-

Phase "B" - Battle of Arras - April - May 1917.
1st Period - Attack on Vimy Ridge - April.
2nd Period - Capture of Siegfried Line - May.

B.E.F.

49th F.A. 37th Div. 18th Corps. 3rd ARMY. WESTERN FRONT.
May 1917.

Officer Commanding - Lt. Col. W.F. ROE.

6th Corps from 19th May.

PHASE "B" - Battle of Arras - April - May 1917.
 -2nd Period - Capture of Siegfried Line - May.

H.Q. at Liencourt.

May 2nd.	Moves. Detachment.O and 44 to 19th C.C.S.
3rd-11th.	Operations R.A.M.C. Routine.
11th.	Decoration. Sgt Dyson R. awarded M.M.
18-19th.	Moves.) To Hôpital St. Jean Arras and took Medical Arrangements.) over Divl. M.D.S. from 2/2nd London Field Ambulance.
	Transfer. 37th Division transferred to 6th Corps.

B.E.F.

49th F.A. 37th Div. 6th Corps. 3rd ARMY.   WESTERN FRONT.
May 1917.
Officer Commanding - Lt.Col. W.F. ROE.

PHASE "B" - Battle of Arras - April - May 1917.
2nd Period - Capture of Siegfried Line - May.

H.Q. Hôpital St. Jean ARRAS.

May 19th. **Transfer.** 37th Division transferred to 6th Corps.

20th. **Operations Enemy.** Arras, occasionally shelled by long distance guns.

29th. **Moves. Detachment.** 1 and Br. S.D. to 87th F.A. to assist bearers clearing 29th Div. front. Returned 31st.

30th. **Decorations.** Sgt Cardy awarded bar to M.M.

        L/Cpl Lintott.)
        L/Cpl Midgeley)   awarded M.M.
        Sgt Chellew (A.S.C.M.T. attd.)

All for gallantry in action 23rd - 30th April.

31st. **Casualties R.A.M.C.** 0 and 2 wounded in small operation on 29th Div. Front.

B.E.F.

49th F.A. 37th Div. 18th Corps. 3rd ARMY. WESTERN FRONT.
May 1917.
Officer Commanding - Lt. Col. W.F. ROE.

6th Corps from 19th May.

PHASE "B" - Battle of Arras - April - May 1917.
-2nd Period - Capture of Siegfried Line - May.

H.Q. at Liencourt.

May 2nd.   Moves. Detachment.O and 44 to 19th C.C.S.

3rd-11th.   Operations R.A.M.C. Routine.

11th.   Decoration. Sgt Dyson R. awarded M.M.

18-19th.   Moves.   ) To Hopital St. Jean Arras and took
            Medical Arrangements.)
            over Divl. M.D.S. from 2/2nd London Field Ambulance.

            Transfer. 37th Division transferred to 6th Corps.

B.E.F.

49th F.A. 37th Div. 6th Corps. 3rd ARMY.   WESTERN FRONT.
                                           May 1917.
Officer Commanding - Lt.Col. W.F. ROE.

PHASE "B" - Battle of Arras - April - May 1917.

2nd Period - Capture of Siegfried Line - May.

H.Q. Hopital St. Jean Arras.

May 19th.   Transfer. 37th Division transferred to 6th Corps.

20th.   Operations Enemy. Arras occasionally shelled by long distance guns.

29th.   Moves. Detachment. 1 and Br. S.D. to 87th F.A. to assist bearers clearing 29th Div. front. Returned 31st.

30th.   Decorations. Sgt Cardy awarded bar to M.M.

        L/Cpl Lintott.   )
        L/Cpl Midgeley   )   awarded M.M.
        Sgt Cheller (A.S.C.M.T. attd.)

All for gallantry in action 23rd - 30th April.

31st.   Casualties R.A.M.C. O and 2 wounded in small operation on 29th Div. Front.

Army Form C. 2118.

WAR DIARY
or
INTELLIGENCE SUMMARY. 49th Field Ambulance

(Erase heading not required.)

Place	Date	Hour	Summary of Events and Information	Remarks and references to Appendices
LIENCOURT	1/5/17		Spent the day resting & cleaning up. On th. whole all ranks are very fit. A.D.M.S. called. Fine Sunny weather.	
"	2/5/17		We took over Large Field Kits vacated by 28th Fd Ambulance. 3 pm Sept/Cpl Broom & 43 O.R. sent to W Company with 3 G.S. & Motor Amb/L LEZ BOISON. 4 hors. Frictioning day.	None
"	3/5/17		Fine warm day. We commenced Flexle in patients huts to be Registered as Lectures from 4 Pm to 5 Pm Fer Cook, halt hour lecture. Went for the horses in afternoon.	
"	4/5/17		Fine warm day. ADMS called to see Pay Parade 9 am. 12 n.z. Lect. Th. Commun. transferred to S.O.R. Fer Quit. for duty.	None

A5834 Wt.W4973 M687. 750,000 8/16 D.D. & L. Ltd. Forms/C.2118/13.

Army Form C. 2118.

WAR DIARY
or
INTELLIGENCE SUMMARY.
(Erase heading not required.)

Instructions regarding War Diaries and Intelligence Summaries are contained in F. S. Regs., Part II. and the Staff Manual respectively. Title pages will be prepared in manuscript.

Place	Date	Hour	Summary of Events and Information	Remarks and references to Appendices
LIENCOURT	5/5/17		Preliminary Transport Inspection by O.C. 37th Bn. Train. 1st & 4th Coy arrived. Officers & N.Co's attended a lecture in Res. by main 4th & 5th Fd Amb. lecture on AMBULANCES. Commenced re-inoculating with T.A.B. on line system. 1st Regtl Canadian transport to 37th Monarchs.	1431
"	6/5/17		Friday. B.A.M'S allens in afternoon. 1st Brewing and Preliminary duty to 37th but Keever.	472
"	7/5/17		Sun day. Practices formation 17th B.T.I. in afternoon. Church present.	491
"	8/5/17		Wet morning.	
"	9/5/17		Fine day. Fair some vehicles to Divnl. Transport Competition. Rank Nos 1st & 5th Fd Amb... 2nd 4th Fd Amb. 3rd 4th Fd Artillery.	

Army Form C. 2118.

WAR DIARY
or
INTELLIGENCE SUMMARY.
(Erase heading not required.)

Place	Date	Hour	Summary of Events and Information	Remarks and references to Appendices
Nov 1917 LIEN COURT	10/9		R.A.M.S. Lecture to [illegible] the [illegible]. At 5.30 p.m. attended Conference of Field Ambulance Officers & N.C.O.s of Asst Dir. [illegible] [illegible].	M.G.R.
	11/9		Col P.W. Hughes C.M.G. A.D.M.S. [illegible] [illegible] Brown in hospital [illegible] No 34499 Pte R. Dyson [illegible] [illegible] Co. C.P.S. Sent to [illegible] [illegible] (D.R.O. No 2465 4/11/17)	M.G.R.
			A.D.M.S. XVth Corps 37th	
			R.A.M.C. Divisional Military [illegible] [illegible].	M.G.R.
	12/9		Fine weather.	
	13/9		Fine day. Car broke down D.T.O. A.M.S. took men up to H.Q. & to 37 Div.	M.G.R.
	14/9		Fine day.	
	15/9		Dr Endny R.A.M.C. went to 4th Middlesex for [illegible] [illegible] [illegible] [illegible] Capt. [illegible] Attch. G.O.C. D.D. inspected [illegible] [illegible] [illegible] of A.D.S. & 2 [illegible] [illegible] [illegible] Capt. [illegible] [illegible].	M.G.R.

A5834 Wt.W4973/M687 750,000 8/16 B.D.& L.Ltd. Forms/C.2118/13.

Army Form C. 2118.

WAR DIARY
INTELLIGENCE SUMMARY.
(Erase heading not required.) 4 G.H. Field Ambulance

Place	Date	Hour	Summary of Events and Information	Remarks and references to Appendices
LIENCOURT	16/9		Wet afternoon. Pay Parade 5.30pm. Orders	WK
"	17.9		I attended lecture by O.C. 8 VIII Corps + Div. H.Q. subject "Recent Operations". Attended conference at Adv'nd Stn. Unreceive situation on arrival Tomorrow. Showery weather. M.O. at work.	WK
SIMENCOURT	18/9 /17		Ft. Amb. moved to SIMENCOURT with 62nd Bge & reverted to billets for the nights WK Friday. Handed over to 142 nd Ft. Amb.	WK
ARRAS	19.9 /17		Ft. Amb. moved to HOPITAL ST JEAN, ARRAS & took over as divisional Main DRESSING STATION from 2/2nd London Ft. Amb. Fine warm day.	WK
"	20.9 /17		Fine day. ARRAS still shelled occasionally by long distance & high velocity shell.	WK
"	21/9		Fine weather. Don S. called. We may have the hilling cleaner & later. with German prisoner of war.	WK

WAR DIARY
or
INTELLIGENCE SUMMARY.

(Erase heading not required.) L.9th Field Ambulance

Army Form C. 2118.

Place	Date	Hour	Summary of Events and Information	Remarks and references to Appendices
ARRAS	22/5/17		Lt Col. more returns from temporary duty with 37 C.C.S. Heavy rain. Several shells burst in near the hospital in the night.	A.9/36
"	23/5/17		Fine weather. Capt Guy proceeded to join the London Fd Amb. Capt Welsh took over period charge of hospital pro Tem Commandant.	A.9/37
"	24/5/17		Inspection of Fr Ambulance by D.D.M.S. 4th Army. 4th B.g.M.S. returning from leave visited hut s lot 8 General Hospital. Fine weather.	A.9/38
"	25/5/17		Conference of ADsMS + OCs C.T. F.As of 17th Corps. 2.30 pm	A.9/39
"	26/5/17		Draft of 1/field b men admitted to hospital from base.	A.9/40
"	27/5/17		G.O.C. 17th Corps inspected the hospital. About 61 Even Critty to view the hospital previous for establishment.	A.9/41
"	28/5/17			A.9/42

WAR DIARY
INTELLIGENCE SUMMARY

Army Form C. 2118.

Place	Date	Hour	Summary of Events and Information	Remarks and references to Appendices
ARRAS	29/5		O.C. 2/1 (I) Middlesex called for the emergency rations and purchase in June 10th. Capt. Knollwo... begin to... to Infantry units of 97th Div Ambulance, to ensure... having cleaning the 2/97 5th June.	
	30/5		Capt. Lei & McKenna did Div Advance to HQ and came onto the 97th Dir for check. Got cars back up from late 5 New forms Military board... of F/L Miller A.C.C. N.T. B/Y3 late. To Capt. Middleton. Rev. Middleton has... to Ambulance Infirmary in return Arrival April 23 + 30...	
	31/5		Capts have Service & Young with Advanced Parties from O/C. Still Movement for Ambulance relation to... and Temporary D. Advance not to Temporary camp.	

Army Form C. 2118.

WAR DIARY
or
INTELLIGENCE SUMMARY.   48th Bn Australian

(Erase heading not required.)

Place	Date	Hour	Summary of Events and Information	Remarks and references to Appendices
ARRAS	31/5/17		Fine Warm weather. Capt Low & Benson Intelligence returning from Army HQrs with 7th Tel ambulance a brewed passing WOR on the 29 Hanover inst. Two Riflemen & Pvte Jefferies have left slight wounds but returns to duty.	

31/5/17

Vol 24

149230

CONFIDENTIAL

War Diary
— of —
49th Field Ambulance

from 1st June 1917 to 30th June 1917

(Volume 23)

COMMITTEE FOR THE
MEDICAL HISTORY OF THE WAR
Date -7 AUG. 1917

Army Form C. 2118.

WAR DIARY
or
INTELLIGENCE SUMMARY. 49 Field Ambulance

(Erase heading not required.)

Instructions regarding War Diaries and Intelligence Summaries are contained in F. S. Regs., Part II. and the Staff Manual respectively. Title pages will be prepared in manuscript.

Place	Date	Hour	Summary of Events and Information	Remarks and references to Appendices
MANIN	1/6/17		Field Ambulance Lawrier over the Hopital ST JEAN, ARRAS to the O.C. 3rd Stationary Ambulance at 10 am. by Transport undex to MANIN with the transport of the 6 Bare Brigade. Sir mounted personnel proceeded by bus Convoy to MANIN. 6.10 pm. Divisions at MANIN. with 8 am. Ending 12 m.c. parties for permanent billity. Fine weather at Q.H. Ending 12 m.c. parties for permanent billity. Billet 4th Middlesex.	WoR
"	2/17		Remained at MANIN getting cleaner up & settle in. Theatre. Pay Parade 2 pm. a great success.	WoR
"	3/5/17		Remained at MANIN to improve. This N mention. Church Parade. Lt Ashmore reported took trick from 4 Field Ambulance.	WR
"	4/17		Took on temporary duty Lt.Col. S. Sturf during absence on leave of Col Morthelp: HQ at LIGNEREUIL	WR

WAR DIARY
or
INTELLIGENCE SUMMARY

(Erase heading not required.) 49th Field Ambulance

Army Form C. 2118.

Place	Date	Hour	Summary of Events and Information	Remarks and references to Appendices
CROIX	5/5/17		Ambulance horse drawn arrived at CROIX. Took over personnel by two M.T. 63rd Brigade. Division came under administration of 1st Army. Remained at Div. H.Q. LIGNEREUIL. Visited the Ambulance at CROIX in afternoon. Lt Ashmore sent to Tournay this with 5th East Lancs in relief of Capt. VEY M.C. Sick. Frowarden.	War
ANVIN	6/5/17		1st Ambulance marched from CROIX to ANVIN. Bivouac with Divisional Train.	War
LISBOURG	7/5/17		H. Ambulance marched from ANVIN to LISBOURG and Bivouac up at the New War Girls School.	War
"	8/5/17		Moved to BOMY with Div H.Q. AA + Q.M.G. and Staff H.Q. Visited the other Ambulance.	War
"	9/5/17		R.A.M.C. training commenced.	War

WAR DIARY or INTELLIGENCE SUMMARY

Army Form C. 2118.

(Erase heading not required.) 1st Ain Field Ambulance

Place	Date	Hour	Summary of Events and Information	Remarks and references to Appendices
LISBOURG	10/6/17		Church Parade 9 a.m. Sgt Bryson returned to duty from Base.	WR
"	11/6/17		Training continued. Instructed 3 O. Ranks to attend HQrs in morning. Rain.	WR
"	12/6/17		Lt. R.F. KIEFFER U.S. Med. Corps reported for duty from Base. Fine.	WR
"	13/6/17		S.C.O.R. returned re reinforcements from Base. Capt BEOUGH RAMC. Awarded the Military Cross. D.R.O. 2574 of 1/3/17.	WR
"	14/6/17		Training still continues daily. Fine weather.	WR
"	15/6/17		Instructed 4 other Ambulances re horse lines to stands.	WR
"	16/6/17		Army & Corps collar the morning. Dental Officer attended from No 58 C.C.S. Pay Parade 4.30 pm. Wet afternoon.	WR

WAR DIARY
or
INTELLIGENCE SUMMARY.

(Erase heading not required.) 4 9th Field Ambulance

Army Form C. 2118.

Place	Date	Hour	Summary of Events and Information	Remarks and references to Appendices
LISBORG	17/6/17		Lee Cpl SAVAGE discharged to Divisional Laundry. Detachment which went to B. mid Brigade for Divisions. I visited 63rd rd. Brigade — Officers + arranged to hold classes for instructors in Sanitation + visited sites at 4 9th Fd Ambulance LISBORG. Commencing 18th inst. Fine hot day	W.R.
	18/6/17		Heavy thunder storm at 3 pm	W.R.
	19/6/17		Classes for Instruction in Sanitation State + Water duties for the 63rd Brigade commenced here. Capts Rice and Brough R.A.M.C Lecturers in Sanitation QMSI + Collectors Garment committeework by asst. B + C sections over a last Reserve Addition.	W.R.
	20/6/17		Sanitation Class broken up on account of Brigade's move to FRUGES.	W.R.
	21/6/17		Division Presentation of Special Ribbons by 1st Army Commander at FRUGES. The following received: Lieut-Col Archibald attached Capt Brough Lt. M.C. Lt Colonel. Pte Rideoff an nursing orderly. Cpl Fol Sole Whiteley McElhinnon Cpl Ruston an nursing orderly. Cpl Mac Clenahan + 25 O.R. all W.Mc as denies Distinguish Cont. Ram. Slenany	W.R.

WAR DIARY

or

INTELLIGENCE SUMMARY

Army Form C. 2118.

Place	Date	Hour	Summary of Events and Information	Remarks and references to Appendices
FEBVIN-PALFART	22/7/17		7th Ambulance hoped from [illegible] O.C. 65th Brigade. Capt McClurkin sent with Private Backhouse + a Corp to his Ambulance to STEENBECQUE to attain 9th Nth Staffords + 89 Bd R.E. on the march to LOCRE. Capt Bromiley Roome proceeded Hallowes for 14 days leave on completion of his contract. Not written.	WAR
THIENNES	23/7/17		7th Ambulance moved to THIENNES + went into billets. Staff Capts RAMC	WAR
CAESTRE	24/7/17		Moved from THIENNES to CAESTRE. Inspected + marched up. G.O.C. 37 Div. Capt McClurkin + party returned from LOCRE to 9th N. Staff + 89 Bd R.E. Twenty five transferred to 9th Corps from Canc to to 2nd Army.	WAR
FERMOY FARM near LOCRE	25/7/17		March to FERMOY FARM near LOCRE & went into camp. Attend casualty pudd A.D.S. 9/11.25 to bunk at [illegible] KLEIN VIERSTRAAT. Capt R.E. Spengin RAMC reported for duty from 49 General hospital.	WAR

WAR DIARY
or
INTELLIGENCE SUMMARY

Army Form C. 2118.

Place	Date	Hour	Summary of Events and Information	Remarks and references to Appendices
FERMOY FARM NEAR LOCRE	26/6/17		Heavy enemy cal night. I trailer 110 Fd Amb. The HOPPICS LOCRE + shed unserviceable. & between 2am by 2 guns N 29 f. n.t. Cpl Cuddy of main procured jinkeys to 110 Fd Amb. A.D.S. at 10.30 pm hostile aeroplane dropped 4 bombs on the remains of the Camp. Casualties 2 R.A.M.C. + 3 A.S.C. (H.T.) horses 5 vans + 1 mule killed, 4 other animals wounded.	W.R.
"	27/6/17		A.D.M.S 1st Corps and A.D.M.S Green. Capt N.B. Low with 1 Tent Subdivision + 1 Bearer Subdivision proceeded to 110 Fd Trench Mor A.D.S. for duty. Lieut Puppet with 1 Tent Subdivision proceeded to 110 Fd Amb Main Dressing Station at LOCRE for duty.	W.R.
"	28/6/17		Capt A. Chapman with 1 Bearer Subdivision marched to KLEIN VIERSTRAAT and completed relief of 110 Fd Amb A.D.S. + Bearer Post at 6 p.m.	W.R.

WAR DIARY
or
INTELLIGENCE SUMMARY

(Erase heading not required.) 4th Field Ambulance

Army Form C. 2118.

Place	Date	Hour	Summary of Events and Information	Remarks and references to Appendices
LOCRE	29/9/17		Remainder of Field Ambulance moved to LOCRE and took over from 110th Fd Amb. at HOSPICE. 62 patients transferred to 49th Fd Amb b/110 Fd Amb. O.C. 49th Fd Amb took over Corps Collecting Station at BRULOOZE from 50th Fd Amb and now runs it. Returns, rations & IN & R items.	MC
"	30/9/17		O.C. 59th Fd Amb called and arranged [illegible] over Artillery of our front line; and Adj. to view stretcher [?] O.C. 49th Fd Amb visited 2nd NY Corps [illegible] at CELESTINES & arranged [illegible] & found w. Then to see on the 2nd July. He then reconnoitred LINDENHOEK & ROMMEL huts & knew the Ambulance stations there now (April 3) Divis took over Fd Amb by 50th Fd and after hands occupations by Field Amb [illegible]	MC

Confidential

War Diary
of
49th Field Ambulance

From 1st July 1917 to 31st July 1917

[Volume 24]

COMMITTEE FOR THE
MEDICAL HISTORY OF THE WAR
Date 10 SEP. 1917

Medical

WAR DIARY
or
INTELLIGENCE SUMMARY

Army Form C. 2118.

4/7th Field Ambulance

Place	Date	Hour	Summary of Events and Information	Remarks and references to Appendices
LOCRE	1/7/17		Capt McRae coming down from the Bearer Post yesterday evening admitted to Hospital with influenza. Capt Russell & O.R.S. returned to IX Corps Scabies & Anti-Tet. as an advance part. Submission of a Tet. pestilence. Returning lilies have been received by 57th Field Ambulance. 57th Field Ambulance collect transport for sitting at the Hospice Tournant. (RTF Collecting Station at BRULOOZE). Remits over to OC 57 Fld Ambulance.	W.R.
LINDENHOEK	2/7/17		Handed over the Hospice Locre to O.C. 57th Field Ambulance. 12 noon and handed to LINDENHOEK via KEMMEL. Took over an A.D.S. position from Capt (Chief) Rame for O.C. 5th Fd Amb & returned to Beau poste below the Brasserie KEMMEL. hop races out to hand them over and troops in cleaning the lines. We have moved an armoured dugout explosive at KEMMEL & have two Capt McClarkin, Capt Lys & Lt Dunn Petrol with the remainder of Fd. Amb.to H.Q. Capt McClarkin - proceed on 14 days leave to ENGLAND from IX Corps Scabies Hosp from 5/9/17 3rd Amb. Lt Sgt N. Stafford in proceed to CAESTRE + R/I. on IX Corps Scabies Hosp from 5/9/17 3rd Amb. temporary duty.	W.R.

Army Form C. 2118.

WAR DIARY
or
INTELLIGENCE SUMMARY.
(Erase heading not required.)

49th Field Ambulance

Place	Date	Hour	Summary of Events and Information	Remarks and references to Appendices
LINDENHOEK	3/7/17		Several H.E. & Gas shells dropped in the vicinity of HQ. Gas to be [?] morning between 3 & 4 a.m. Pay Parade 7 pm.	WAL
"	4/7/17		Admd Cullen 4.30 am. Went to CHAPITRE & afterwards to N Hoster 18 CORPS SCABIES HOSPITAL. H.M.T. N.R.B & Piche. Than Neighbourhood than Asylum & house through KEMMEL. We are working on improvement of existing dugouts dwellings. Inspected detachment at BRASSERIE. KEMMEL also 63 wt & t Brigde. HQ. We are now collecting sick from 63 wt 112 B Brigades 9 H.N. Staff (Pioneers) ent 152, 153, 157 Fd Cops R.E. and attending better Sick & Wounded.	WAL
"	5/7/16			
"	6/7/17		Ecole hôtel shelling in vicinity of any ante between 9.30 & 10 pm. 1 NCo & 10 Men proceeded to A.D.S. & 50 th Fd Amb. THEREN F.M. in noon Company for relief of Bearers of Scottish Amb. in the line.	WAL

Army Form C. 2118.

WAR DIARY
or
INTELLIGENCE SUMMARY
(Erase heading not required.) 4th K Field Ambulance

Place	Date	Hour	Summary of Events and Information	Remarks and references to Appendices
LINDENHOEK	7/7/17		Lt. A.P. Pugh proceeded to England for 10 days leave. Capt Spengler proceeded to IX Corps Scabies Hosp. in his relief. ADMS called during the morning. Capt Brough returned this pm leave & took up charge of detachment at KEMMEL	WD
"	8/7/17		Heavy thunderstorm & rain in early morning. 1 N.C.O. & 36 men proceeded to KARRAN FARM, A.D.S. of 50th Fd Ambulance at 4.30 am to relieve similar number of bearers of 50th Fd Ambulance and to take orders of O.C. 50th Field Ambulance	WD
"	9/7/17	11am	Previous officers Mounted training – an officer to pass an examination in Scott Fd Ambulance. ADMS called at 10.30 am. I visited the IXth Corps Scabies Hospital this afternoon.	WD
"	10/7/17		Waited in all day expecting visit from ADMS, who did not come	WD

Army Form C. 2118.

WAR DIARY
or
INTELLIGENCE SUMMARY.

(Erase heading not required.)

49. Field Ambulance

Instructions regarding War Diaries and Intelligence Summaries are contained in F. S. Regs., Part II. and the Staff Manual respectively. Title pages will be prepared in manuscript.

Place	Date	Hour	Summary of Events and Information	Remarks and references to Appendices
LINDENHOEK	11/7/17	9.30 am	I visited Bonn posts at WYTCHAETE &c. with Capt Taylor & Capt Wray. M.C. near our camp	WR
		2 pm	4 of our Balloons attacked & brought down by hostile aeroplane. 2nd Casualty Capt Low whereto sick. Capt Brough M.C. proceeded to CAESTRE HOSP. over charge of IX Corps Scabies Hospital.	
	12/7/17		One our aeroplane brought down by German plane near our camp. Pilot slightly wounded. Observer (R. BINKLEY. 28th by British Canadian) at 5.30 am Supplies R.F.C. killed. We brought in the body and conveyed it to BAILLEUL. I visited CAESTRE (Scabies Hospital)	WR
	13/7/17		Capt N.B. Low R.A.M.C. evacuated sick to New Zealand C.C.S. HAZEBROUCK	
	14/7/17		Conference Conditions. Interview, plans for improving sanitary, Visited IX Corps Scabies Hospital & then visited II Corps & left a message with Capt Powell Rame representing the in interviews	WR

Army Form C. 2118.

WAR DIARY
or
INTELLIGENCE SUMMARY
(Erase heading not required.)

AQ Field Ambulance 38

Place	Date	Hour	Summary of Events and Information	Remarks and references to Appendices
LINDEN HOEK			Supply of water for bathing the patients, and any suggestion for improvement. I visited ADS (so called) with Capt Pelerman O.C. 50th Fd Amb (acting) + arranged together If mor. Received a wire from O.C. A.S.C. Depot (A T+S) HAVRE losing Hong Army Aun. Sutherland D.T/4/083185 had his received there whole close arrest, ower enquiring whether he belongs this Unit; the has proceeded leave to U.K. from 25/6/17 to 5/7/17 and had been absent since 5/7/17.	NMC
"	15/7/17		Under orders of A.D.M.S. 29 Div. I handed over A.D.S. at KEMMEL W.B. to O.C. 59th Field Ambulance. Pay Parade.	W.B.
"	16/7/17		Took over A.D.S. at PARRAN FARM from 50th Fd Amb. Capt Taylor & Mr Tearbotsworth proceeded on leave to england. It is a Divisional Collecting Station. Railway line begins not far Operations. Artery shelled during	

Army Form C. 2118.

WAR DIARY
or
INTELLIGENCE SUMMARY.
(Erase heading not required.)

49th Field Ambulance

Place	Date	Hour	Summary of Events and Information	Remarks and references to Appendices
LINDENHOEK	16/2/17	Cont. morning.	I went to IX Corps Scabies Hospital + arranged for a bed in the vicinity. The Newcomer to a Canne part full kept to the bathing of patients. Others billeted at LINDENHOEK near PARRAN FARM during my absence.	WR
"	17/7		Capt Run reported evacuated to base from New Zealand C.C.S.	WR
"	18/7		Sent 23 Reinfts to South Fd Ambulance. Any Bearers in the line. Attended demonstration of the YUKON pack at LINDENHOEK. Capt Taylor R.A.M.C. Fd Ambulance Arks.	WR
"	19/7		Lt Pyper returned from leave. I went to IX Corps Scabies Hospl & also to Mont Kokereele in an ambulance, bringing back D.S. Cuttleworth A.R.C.H.S. brought with him to Fd Ambulance. from H.Q. 2, transport with temp abscess.	WR

Army Form C. 2118.

WAR DIARY
or
INTELLIGENCE SUMMARY.
(Erase heading not required)

4 O/R FIELD AMBULANCE

Place	Date	Hour	Summary of Events and Information	Remarks and references to Appendices
LINDENHOEK	20/3/17		to Sutherland remanded for Admission of Case at A.D.M.S. 2.S.-Reserve. Lieut F Scott for Andrew Fulsier whose amnesia of any kind in the line. Lt A.V. BOYLE R.A.M.C. (T.C.) reported for duty from the Base.	War
"	21/3/17		to Sutherland demanded for evidence of the Balance to writing. I took Evidence & gave it to Sutherland am viewed it & writings.	War
"	22/3/17		I went to the A.D.M.S with reference to the running function. Capt TAYLOR returned for duty from 10th Fd Amb Scottish Corps.	War
"	23/3/17		O/R was called & went with him to A.D. Station at PARRAIN FARM. Capt Taylor was to take charge of Scabies Hospital, CAESTRE. O/R was called from Capt Brough who returned for duty at H.Q. Army FARM. I went to 1st Can Fd Amb Scabies Hospital. Commander called at the Camp at 7 pm.	War

Army Form C. 2118.

WAR DIARY
or
INTELLIGENCE SUMMARY
(Erase heading not required.)

49th FIELD AMBULANCE

Place	Date	Hour	Summary of Events and Information	Remarks and references to Appendices
LINDENHOEK	24/7/17		Inspected transports lines of 6th Bedfords, 11th Warwicks and 63rd M.G. Coy. A.D.M.S. called in evg.	WR
"	25/7		Attended at Scottish Aid & Crowler with O.C. 48th & 59th Fd Ambs re to making transport vehicles with G.H.Q. Divisional Supply in uniform manner. Lived with Capt Brough at WYTSCHAETE to make arrangements for shelter for walking wounded during forthcoming active operations. Detailed ophthalmic to supervise the sanitation of #1 Bulleu section.	WR
"	26/7/17		Received instructions to arrange for hospital attachment of personnel of Divnl R.E. as Capt Knightly has been admitted to hospital with W.R.) Notified Capt Brough for this duty, & arranged for his return from at LINDENHOEK D.S. I have is spoken to (A)SHIRE (Rep. Hospital)	WR

Army Form C. 2118.

WAR DIARY
or
INTELLIGENCE SUMMARY.
(Erase heading not required.)

49th Field Ambulance

Place	Date	Hour	Summary of Events and Information	Remarks and references to Appendices
LINDENHOEK	27/9/17		Lt Kieffer U.S. Med Service attached to 6th Bedfords for duty. O.C. 49th Field Ambulance called to various arrangements for conveyance of walking wounded during forthcoming active operations.	WR
"	28/9/17		Lt Sutherland D. taken by P.G.C.M. for being an absentee without leave.	WR
"	29/9/17		Very severe thunder storm from 10 p.m. to 4 a.m. Capt Brough M.C. proceeded to duty & took charge at IX Corps Scabies Hosp. Capt Shapin returning to H.Q. Ambce.	
"	30/9/17		1 promulgation Sentence of F.G.C.M. on Lt Sutherland, i.e. 60 days field punishment No 2. Capt Shapin proceeded to duty with 9th N. Staffs. Capt Clarke returned to duty with R.R. Stroman and Hazen reported that they had Ptes Abbott, [illegible] 49th Field Amb.	

Army Form C. 2118.

WAR DIARY
or
INTELLIGENCE SUMMARY
(Erase heading not required.)

49th Field Ambulance

Place	Date	Hour	Summary of Events and Information	Remarks and references to Appendices
LINDENHOEK	31/7/17		IX Corps attacked at 3.50 a.m. b 3rd Brigade in the line. I am opening an A.D.S. at PARRAIN FARM (de Pujin + Le Bizet), 46 Bearers have arrived here prior under orders of O.C. 50th Field Ambulance. I am carrying walking wounded from WYTSCHAETE to Walking Wounded Station at KEMMEL (O.C. 50th 2nd amb.). I visited WYTSCHAETE with Major about 6.30 a.m. and arranged to send 8 Fords however Kelly can only get in with his however to motor Ambulance as cars which can not get into town of WYTSCHAETE in recently built rating ground. I sympathized sending wounded out being brought down by Light Railway to Corps Collecting Station. Weather wet & rather colder.	[signature]

31/7

Confidential

War Diary
of
49th Field Ambulance

From 1st August to 31st August 1917

(Vol: 25)

COMMITTEE FOR THE
MEDICAL HISTORY OF THE WAR
Date -1 OCT. 1917

WAR DIARY

Army Form C. 2118.

INTELLIGENCE SUMMARY: 49th Field Ambulance

Place	Date	Hour	Summary of Events and Information	Remarks and references to Appendices
LINDENHOEK	1/8/14		Casualties treated at POTIJZE FARM from 6 am 31/7 to 6 am 1/8 37 Other Ranks. 4 Offs: 51 O.R. Other Division O.R. 3. GERMAN O.R. 1. Much rain. Wounded are brought in very late. 2 of my H.D. horses attached to Field Wagon killed by shell this am WYTSCHAETE. JL horses and Wagons are being used for conveying walking cases from LAMPPOST CORNER for about ½ mile known Ambulances will commute per my around front posts of the road.	MR
"	2/8		Quiet day. Ford Car No. 13 collided with a lorry & was driver-knocked on the DRANOUTRE-LINDENHOEK Rd. Car struck W.S.C. in driving. Car collected by D.S.C. Rd to 6. Wounded. Casualties at POTIJZE FARM HOT 6am Aug 1 37 Bn O.S. O.R. 15. CORPS TROOPS O.R.1 to 6am Aug 2 " "	WR

Army Form C. 2118.

WAR DIARY
or
INTELLIGENCE SUMMARY.
(Erase heading not required.)

49 Field Ambulance

Place	Date	Hour	Summary of Events and Information	Remarks and references to Appendices
LINDENHOEK	3/8/17		Very wet all day. Front Line Cropped. D.D.M.S. IX th Corps called here this morning. Quiet day. Casualties passed through A.D.S. PARRAIN FARM from 6 a.m. Aug 2 to 6 a.m. Aug 3. 37th Div. Offr. 1. O.R. 8. Other Divs. nil.	W.R.
"	4/8/17		Casualties passed through A.D.S. PARRAIN FARM from 6 a.m. Aug 3 to 6 a.m. Aug 4. 37 Divs O.R.6. Weather still wet. Settled rain begins on KENNEL — WYTSCHAETE road, but casualties have not increased. The Relieving unit A.D.M.S. I have withdrawn walking wounded collecting post from D.15.d.5.17. and the horse ambulance wagons, walking wounded are to join the ordinary course of evacuation. 3 Ford Wagons returned to O.C. 47th Field Ambulance.	W.R. W.R.
"	5/8/17		Whole unit of A.Div.S. Hay Bearers in the Line, relieved by Bearers of 50th Field Ambulance, returned to H.Qrs. O.C. & H.Qs. & Bearers of O.C. & H.F.A. (50th Fld Amb) responsible to deal with all cases at M.D.S. & Rid & line on all cars to M.D.S. (50th Fld Amb). O.C. 50th F.A. responsible to clear Tr. Corps Paris Bishop CHESTER from the line to O.A.S. O.C. builds Tr. Corps Paris Bishop CHESTER.	W.R.

Army Form C. 2118.

WAR DIARY
INTELLIGENCE SUMMARY

4/9th Field Ambulance

(Erase heading not required.)

Place	Date	Hour	Summary of Events and Information	Remarks and references to Appendices
LINDENHOEK	6/7/17		Casualties treated at PARRAIN FARM A.D.S. 6 am 5th to 6 am 6th 37 Divn 19. O.R. B[B]rs. Divisional Pay Parade. Men or N.C.O.'s and Privates of Bearer Division under Lt HARDY. to PARRAIN FARM to act in reserve and to improve R.O.C. Post for Ambulance. No deaths. Returning Officer to the Election for the State of ALBERTA, CANADA. I sent the Polls for the State for 14th inst.	W.O.O.
"	7/7/17		Casualties treated at PARRAIN FARM, A.D.S. 6 am 6th to 6 am 7th 37 Divn. O.R. 22. Stretcher O.R.S. Lt WILLCOCK returned to duty from the Base on 5th inst. & went to LOCRE Hospice. Lt. Piggott Orderly Patrol with an 57th Field Ambulance on tomorrow. I sent Lt. Piggott Orderly Patrol with an Advanced Party in Sup to HOSPICE LOCRE. & places & personal information returned to H.Q. Advanced Party from 12th Australian F.A. arrived to take over the Dressing Station at LINDENHOEK.	W.O.O.
LOCRE HOSPICE	8/7/17		Handed over Dressing Station, LINDENHOEK to O.C. 12 Australian Fld Ambulance. Handed over A.D.S. PARRAIN FARM to O.C. A.F.H. Fld Amb. A.F.H. F.A. and marched to LOCRE & took over the Hospital at the Hospice from O.C. 5th Nor Field Ambulance. Took over & transferred 47 patients. Heavy Thunder Storm.	

Army Form C. 2118.

WAR DIARY or INTELLIGENCE SUMMARY

49th Field Ambulance

(Erase heading not required.)

Place	Date	Hour	Summary of Events and Information	Remarks and references to Appendices
LOCRE	9/8/17	7.30 to 9 pm 9/8/17	Casualties passing through this Main Dressing Station 12 own 8/8/17. 1 Off. 49 O.R. (including 11 Gas cases) 49th Fd Ambulance is forming Main Dressing Station for the Division/front.	WD-?
"	10/8/17	7.30 pm 9/8/17 to 7.30 pm 10/8/17	Without collect + intact throughout & none of. 2 new to Fr Cases Services D.S. Casualties admitted from 7.30 pm 9/8/17 to 7.30 pm 10/8/17. 2 Off. 28 O.R. Onl/Sergeant.	WD
"	11/8/17	10/8/17 to 7.30 pm 11/8/17	Capt Tay ln R.A.M.C proceeded on leave to U.K. Casualties from 7.30 pm 10/8/17 to 7.30 pm 11/8/17. Off. nil. O.R. 6. (1 Gas, 5 Acc). Heavy rain & thunder at night.	WD
"	12/8/17	Casualties from 7.30 pm 11/8/17 to 7.30 pm 12/8/17	Off. 1 O.R. 27 General. Off. 1 O.R. 37 Generals. 378 R.A. H.Q. 1 premier at Medical Board to examine T/S/Major H. Adams, 378 R.A. H.Q. for temporary Commission. Capt Foot R.A.M.C. SR. rejoined in duty.	WD
"	13/8/17	Casualties from 7.30 pm 12/8/17 to 7.30 pm 13/8/17	O.R. 295 General. O.1. O.R. 295 General. D. Willcocks proceeded to duty. Brig Gen MacLachlan buried at Hospice. D/ADMS (52?) Centre Wiltshire Mid (MESTRE) at 18 Corps Schools Wiltshire Mid (MESTRE)	WD

WAR DIARY
INTELLIGENCE SUMMARY

49th Field Ambulance

Army Form C. 2118.

Place	Date	Hour	Summary of Events and Information	Remarks and references to Appendices
Locre	14/8/17		Casualties from 7pm 13th to 7pm 14th. O. 1 O.R. 10. 5 sick. O. 1 Col. C.Q. Walton C.M.C. Consulting Surgeon Second Army called and gave a demonstration of the application of Thomas' Splints.	WD
"	15/8/17		Casualties from 7pm 14th to 7pm 15th. Off. 3. O.R. 19. Gunshot W.O. Off. — O.R. 6 sick. O	WD
"	16/8/17		Casualties from 7pm 15th to 7pm 16th. Off. 3. O.R. 19. Gunshot Wd. Off. nil. O.R. 39. (including 5 gunshot wd.)	WD
"	17/8/17		Casualties from 7.30 16th to 7.30 17th. Off. nil. O.R. 39 (including 5 gunshot wd.)	WD
"	18/8/17		A.D.M.S. called 10.30 a.m. Casualties from 7.30pm 17th to 7.30 18th. Off. 2. O.R. 20. (including 2 Off + 4 O.R. gunshot wounds)	WD
"	19/8/17		Pay Parade 2 p.m. Lt. KIEFFER. U.S.M.S. attached for instruction in duties of Lt. attached to 6th Bedfords. Lt. BOYCE sent to 10 Yorks & Lancs. MacConnell wounded. Casualties from 7.30 18th to 7.30 19th. Off. 1. O.R. 13. (includes 1 O.R. gassed (shell). Off. 1 O.R. (minor)	WD

WAR DIARY or INTELLIGENCE SUMMARY

Army Form C. 2118.

49th Field Ambulance

Place	Date	Hour	Summary of Events and Information	Remarks and references to Appendices
LOCRE	20/8/17		Casualties from 7.30pm 19th to 7.30pm 20th = 1 Off. 12 O.R. nil prisoners.	WM
"	21/8/17		Capt. Foott. R.A.M.C. proceeded for temporary duty with 123 Bgde R.F.A. vice Irvine. IX Corps Scabies hospital in afternoon. I.i.S.keaton En/a B 37 D.A.C. away of 4M. No I Car. 37th Div Train. Casualties 7.30pm 20th to 7.30pm 21st Off. nil O.R. 16 (including 1 prisoner (shell).	WM
"	22/8/17		Casualties from 7.30pm 21st to 7.30pm 22/8/17 Off. nil O.R. 4. nil prisoners	WM
"	23/8/17		Capt Taylor R.Am.C returns from leave to U.K. Chaseletion 7.30pm 22nd to 7.30pm 23rd. 14 O.R. nil of same. 40 Cases of Wincham him fever to Corps Dysentery Camp. Total 1 Scabs, Officer of down below transferred to Enic 10.7.17 = 297. Casualties 7.30pm 23rd to 7.30pm 24th = O.R. 1.	WL
"	24		Friends Am. Car. Sect to Corps Dysentery Camp = 36. Returned overnight after Capt W. Clinton Baker to U.K. France, amenity 4/8/17 5/8/17	

WAR DIARY
INTELLIGENCE SUMMARY

49th Field Ambulance

Army Form C. 2118.

Place	Date	Hour	Summary of Events and Information	Remarks and references to Appendices
LOCRE	25/8/17		Lt. Col. W. F. Roe, D.S.O., R.A.M.C. proceeded on leave to England. 9 O.R. took over command of the Field Ambulance. Lieut. A. V. Bagall VR.O.M.C. proceeded from 10th Yorks & Lancs. 1 O.R. to 8th Somersett L.I. 9 O.R. 21 Diarrhoea cases sent to Dysentry Camp. Casualties admitted 2 O.R.	TWell
"	26/8/17		O.C. 37 Divl. Train inspected transport & horse lines - Lt. Wilcocks and 13 O.R. returned from duty at T.X. Cooper Seaton D.S. 10 Diarrhoea cases sent to Dysentry Camp. Casualties admitted 1 O.R.	TWell
"	27/8/17		Medically examined 50 men of the ambulance categorization. Casualties 2 Officers 7 O.R. 22 Diarrhoea cases sent to Dysentry Camp	TWell
"	28/8/17		O.C. 48 Field Ambulance called this morning as to 2 Bearer Sections for working the new line. - Medically examined 43 personnel for categorization. Sgt Carey with 66 hours proceeded to O.C. 48 Field Ambce for duty. Casualties admitted 2 other ranks. 38 Diarrhoea cases sent to Dysentry Camp.	TWell
"	29/8/17		A.D.M.S. 37 Div. called this morning. 35 Diarrhoea cases sent to Dysentry Camp. Casualties admitted. 1 Officer	TWell

Army Form C. 2118.

WAR DIARY
or
INTELLIGENCE SUMMARY.
(Erase heading not required.)

Instructions regarding War Diaries and Intelligence Summaries are contained in F. S. Regs., Part II. and the Staff Manual respectively. Title pages will be prepared in manuscript.

Place	Date	Hour	Summary of Events and Information	Remarks and references to Appendices
ROUEN	30/8/17		F.G.C.M. on Pte Church of this ambulance assembled at 11h. Infantry Brigade Depot.	
			27 Diarrhoea cases sent to Dysentery Camp. Casualties admitted 2 O.R.	1 Tpt
"	31/8/17		21 Diarrhoea cases sent to Dysentery Camp - Casualties admitted 1 Off. 2 O.R.	1 Tpt

J M Matthew
Capt. R.A.M.C.
O.C. 4/9 Fd Amb
C of E

Confidential

War Diary
of
49th Field Ambulance

From 1st Sept: 1917 to 30th Sept: 1917

(Volume 26)

COMMITTEE FOR THE
MEDICAL HISTORY OF THE WAR
Date -5 NOV.1917

Army Form C. 2118.

WAR DIARY
INTELLIGENCE SUMMARY.
(Erase heading not required.)

49th Field Ambulance

Instructions regarding War Diaries and Intelligence Summaries are contained in F. S. Regs., Part II. and the Staff Manual respectively. Title pages will be prepared in manuscript.

Place	Date	Hour	Summary of Events and Information	Remarks and references to Appendices
LOCRE	1/9/17		Promulgated sentence of 90 days F.P. No.2 on Pte. R Church 22 Diarrhoea cases to Dysentery Camp - Gas dumpshot 24 hrs 2 off 4 OR	Three
"	2/9/17		18 Diarrhoea cases to Dysentery Camp. Casualties during past 24 hrs 4 OR Pay Parade in afternoon - Col. Cheek, Medic. Comdg 13th K.R.R.C. (Killed in action) buried in Hospice garden in afternoon. About 11-15 p.m. hostile aircraft dropped 5 bombs near Hospice 2 dropped at M 30 a 2.8. (Sheet 28) demolishing a cottage and burying the occupants who were extricated by our personnel Casualties - killed 1 civilian woman, wounded 5, 1 civilian woman - 2 other civilians buried and treated here.	Three
"	3/9/17		A.D.M.S. 37 Div. called in morning - 6 Diarrhoea cases sent to Dysentery Camp. Casualties during past 24 hours - 24 OR (including 11 OR of 37 D.A.C. wounded by bomb dropped by hostile aircraft early this morning 1 of these men died here.)	Three
"	4/9/17		18 Diarrhoea cases sent to Dysentery Camp. 9 "P.B." men reported for duty from No. 234 Employment Coy, in relief of A.S.C.	

Army Form C. 2118.

WAR DIARY
INTELLIGENCE SUMMARY.
(Erase heading not required.)

49th Field Ambulance

Place	Date	Hour	Summary of Events and Information	Remarks and references to Appendices
LOCRE	4/9/17		batmen & grooms to be returned to H.T. Base Depot in accordance with A.G. No C/408/3	Three
"	5/9/17		11 Stretcher Cases sent to Dysentery Camp. Casualties during past 24 hours 2 Off 8 O.R.	Three
		24 hours – 10 O.R. (includes 2 Second [Schell?]) Lt. Col. Nicholson R.F.A. - Comdg 104 Bde R.F.A. (killed by bomb dropped by hostile aircraft) buried at Kospice this evening	
		Lieut A.G. Welsh Ramb. to 6th Bgd.mby to E Company duty vice Lt. R.T. Keffer (sick)	Three
	6/9/17	9 A.S.C. men sent to H.T. & S.S. Base Depot Havre this morning	
		21 Diarrhoea cases to Dysentery Camp. Handed over command of Field Ambulance to Lt. Col. W.T. Roe DSO who returned from leave this afternoon	

McMurtrie RAMC
Capt.
49 Field Ambulance

WAR DIARY
INTELLIGENCE SUMMARY. 49 Field Ambulance

Army Form C. 2118.

Place	Date	Hour	Summary of Events and Information	Remarks and references to Appendices
LOCRE	7/9/17		Divl Gas Officer gave demonstration in use of new Officer Bryce in the act of taking over Medical Charge of 10th Yorks (Lanc) (temporarily) on his relieved by Capt Tom lin. 5th Somerset. Convalescents from 7 p.m. 6 & 7 p.m. 7th. 1 Off. 10 O.R (includes 1 Off. + 4 O.R (Quart-Sleve). 17 cases of Convalescents to Hazebrouck Camp.	WR
"	8/9/17		10 Cases to Hazebrouck Camp. Convalescents from 7 p.m. 7th to 7 p.m. 8th. 6 O.R. S.B.Ns. 9th Corps Collect 6 prise in bay Wound Collect 12.15 p.m.	WR
"	9/9/17		Absence. 18 Cases to Hazebrouck Camp. Convalescents 7 p.m. 8th to 7 p.m. 9/17. 19 O.R.	WR
"	10/9/17		O.C. 57th Fd Amb Called Hazebrouck for taking over the Hopkin on 12/9/17. I visited KONEREEZE FARM R.17. b.5.2. Sheet 27 S.E. I view & arrange & take over from the O.C. 57th Fd Amb. on 12/9/17. Cases to Hazebrouck Camp 19. Convalescents from 7 p.m. 9/9/17 to 7 p.m. 10/9/17 - 2 Off. 19 O.R. (includes 4 Queen's Slive)	WR

WAR DIARY
INTELLIGENCE SUMMARY

Army Form C. 2118.

49th Fd Ambulance

Place	Date	Hour	Summary of Events and Information	Remarks and references to Appendices
LOCRE	11/9/17		19 Cans to Hazebrook Camp. Casualties from 7am 10/9 to 7 pm 11/9. 23. O.R. (nil gassed). Lt Pigott R.A.M.C. with advance party proceeded to BOESCHEPE FARM. 12 O KOREELE taken over from O.C. 5-Fd Fd Ambulance. A Durie held in abeyance. A Durie held in abeyance. Leave to U.K. in afternoon. I am acting A.D.M.S. during his absence. Officer R.A.M.C. & Advance party from 5-7 Fd Fd Ambce. arrived here 5 pm	W.R.
-	12/9/17		Mobile Loree & 18th Corps Reserve Stores handed over to O.C. 5-7 Fd Ambulance under command of A/Capt MacClurkin. MacClurkin marched off at 12 noon to KOKEREELE. I proceeded to 37 Div H.Qrs. ST JEAN CAPELLE. & A.D.M.S. acting 12 noon. Capt MacClurkin R.A.M.C. taken over temporary command of 49 Fd Ambulance (454).	W.R.

Army Form C. 2118.

WAR DIARY
or
INTELLIGENCE SUMMARY. 49th Field Ambulance.
(Erase heading not required.)

Place	Date	Hour	Summary of Events and Information	Remarks and references to Appendices
MONT KOKEREELE FARM (R.17.C.5.2 Sheet 27 S.E)	12/9/17		Ambulance arrived at Mt Kokereele about 1-30 p.m.	TMR
	13/9/17		Casualties 11 O.R. (includes 8 gassed). Lt. Col. Roe D.S.O. R.A.M.C., acting A.D.M.S. called MR in afternoon.	MR
	14/9/17		Acting A.D.M.S. & D.A.D.M.S. called this afternoon.	TMR
	15/9/17		I handed over command of the Field Ambulance to Capt. A.C. Taylor R.A. M.C.	TMR

T Wotherspoon
Capt R.A.M.C.
a/g F.A

WAR DIARY or INTELLIGENCE SUMMARY.

Army Form C. 2118.

49th Field Ambulance

Place	Date	Hour	Summary of Events and Information	Remarks and references to Appendices
Mt KOKEREELE FARM (R.11. & 5.2) Sheet 29 S.E.	15/9/17		Capt. T. McCLURKIN. R.A.M.C.(S.R.) and Lieut. A.G.E. WILCOCK. R.A.M.C.(S.R.) proceeded to ENGLAND for duty. 9 took over commands of the Field Ambulance from Capt. W. McCLURKIN.	A.F.J.
	16/9/17		Church Parade in morning - Pay Parade at 5 p.m.	A.F.J.
	17/9/17		o/ A.D.M.S. 39th Div. called	A.F.J.
	18/9/17		Lieut. and Qr.M. G.W. PETCH. R.A.M.C. proceeded to IRELAND on 15 days leave.	A.F.J.
	19/9/17		o/ A.D.M.S. called - Our Motor Ambulance followed 63rd/112th Inf. Brigade to KEMMEL area this night - this area full units. 1 Sister (on full C) 1 Brown Sub-division sent to it to ours.	A.F.J.
	20/9/17		o/ A.D.M.S. called in morning - Capt. WISHART. R.A.M.C reported for temp. duty - photos from 48th Field Ambulance and later man attached for duty, all nos. 2. C.C.S.	A.F.J

WAR DIARY
or
INTELLIGENCE SUMMARY.

Army Form C. 2118.

Place	Date	Hour	Summary of Events and Information	Remarks and references to Appendices
MT. KOKEREELE FARM.	21/9/17		Ambulance followed 63rd and 112th Inf. Brigades from KEMMEL over to MONT KOKEREELE and MONT NOIR area — now full out. Lt. Col. W.F. Roe. D.S.O. R.A.M.C. returned from H.Q. F. Taylor Capt. R.A.M.C.	
	22/9/17	11.30 a.m.	Received orders from A.D.M.S. to have 1 Section + 1 Bearer Subdivision ready to move at 2 hours notice. The remainder (minus detachment at CASSEL) to be ready to move at any short notice. Patients likely to be fit for duty in 14 days to be sent immediately to 50th Fd Ambulance at BOESEVE. Those not likely to be fit for duty in 14 days to be sent to C.C.Stn. Ambulance with W[?]R	
		6.30 p.m.	Received orders that 1 Off & 50 bearers to report to O.C. 134th Fd. Amb. BRASSERIE VIERSTRAAT — SCHERPBURG Road by 12 midnight. The team was between and sent. Also 1 Cpl M.A.Cav. Complies with Caps Forest R.A.M.C. returns from Mains Amt-will Cap & Briges R.F.A.	

Army Form C. 2118.

WAR DIARY
or
INTELLIGENCE SUMMARY.   49th Fd Ambulance

(Erase heading not required.)

Instructions regarding War Diaries and Intelligence Summaries are contained in F. S. Regs., Part II. and the Staff Manual respectively. Title pages will be prepared in manuscript.

Place	Date	Hour	Summary of Events and Information	Remarks and references to Appendices
MONT. KOKEREELE	23/9/17		Church Parade 10.20 a.m.	WPR
"	24/9/17		Lt Boyall RAMC returned from duty Infantry Batt with 10 Yorks & Lancs. Capts Buchanan & Proctor M.C. reported for duty from Black Pool. ADMS. event in the morn.	WPR
"	25/9/17		Capt Foott detailed to 13 K.R.R Corps for embarking. Aug 5? H Rogers left to leave to England. Capt A.C. Taylor wounded by shell which is observer of stretcher Bearers & evacuation to No.2 C.C.S. Capt Proctor detailed to replace him in the line, reporting to O.C. 59th Fd Ambulance.	
"	26/9/17		Capt Taylor evacuated to Base.	
"	27/9/17		Received orders to take over collection of line from 134th Fd Ambulance. Proceed to A.D.S. at VOORMEZEELE (Hd.q. of 134 Fd Amb) and arranged takeover up at noon 28/9/17. Capt Buchanan & Lt Pigott with A.D.S.	

Army Form C. 2118.

WAR DIARY

49th Field Ambulance

(Erase heading not required.)

Place	Date	Hour	Summary of Events and Information	Remarks and references to Appendices
MONT-KOKEREELE	27/9/17	6am	Unit proceeded to VOORMEZEELE to form to O.C. 134th Fd. Amb. Ambulance Transport proceeded to KLEIN VIERSTRAAT. Bread Buses proceeded to BRASSERIE, near VIERSTRAATE to take over from	
VOORMEZEELE	"		O/Ms of 134th Fd. Amb. H.Qs. of Fd Amb proceeded to VOORMEZEELE. Capt Scott with 1 Officer + 2 Bearer Subdivisions Reported to O.C. 45th Fd Amb for temporary duty & under his orders proceeded to the line group took over the following positions from Offrs of 134th Fd Ambulance (further particulars Capt Buchanan + 10 Bear Pers 45th Fd Amb were attached to this party); Bearer Posts CANADA STREET I 20.c.4.2. HEDGE STREET. I 30.6.2.5. A.D.S.'s at LARCH WOOD I 29.c.c.7. DOCKS.	SHEET 28. N.W.
VOORMEZEELE	28/9/17		I visited LOCK 8. + LARCH WOOD at 8 a.m. as Shelling during our visit. 10 am took over A.D.S VOORMEZEELE + A.D.S. LOCK.8. I.32. a.F.5.? & the BRASSERIE, VIERSTRAAT from O.C. 134 Fd Ambulance. Returns. S. called & informed A.D.S VOORMEZEELE. Wounded sent in being Evacuated to CORPS MAIN DRESSING STATION. HOSPICE. LOCRE. 57k Field Ambulance. Capt Proctor + the Bearer party reported for duty	

Army Form C. 2118.

WAR DIARY
or
INTELLIGENCE SUMMARY.
(Erase heading not required.)

Place	Date	Hour	Summary of Events and Information	Remarks and references to Appendices
VOORMEZEELE	28/9/17		having been relieved in the line by an Ambulance of the 19th Divn. Whilst in the line the following Casualties occurred amongst the personnel :- Capt Taylor R.A.M.C. wounded. S.O.R. wounded (Shellshock and duty) 12 OR Gassed to hosp. 2 OR sick. 1 OR missing. Capt Proctor to his unit. Proceeded to the A.D.S. Locke to take off Capt Proctor. Lieut Capt Purdie Proceeded to the line in place of Capt Proctor. No temporary Advanced Change B 10 P.F. in place of Kent Hore. U.S.A. M.R. Kidd. Evacuation from the line is by trolley line to Larch Wood from Hedge St. & Canada St. thence by Cavalry Ambulance to VOORMEZEELE via SPOIL BANK. The cars are being subjected to point rests of pleafire both at LARCH WOOD & on the road down. The question of keeping down Cases from LARCH WOOD — to VOORMEZEELE by trench tramway is being Considered. W.J.R.	
	29/9/17		LIEUT. ROTE U.S.A.M.R. & 24 O.R. from 48th Field Ambulance reported for duty & proceeded to LARCH WOOD to relieve O/c Bearers. Adv. Party 14R Divn Cavalers & Ambulance the possibility of the trench	

Army Form C. 2118.

WAR DIARY
or
INTELLIGENCE SUMMARY

(Erase heading not required.)

49th Field Ambulance

Place	Date	Hour	Summary of Events and Information	Remarks and references to Appendices
VOORMEZEELE	29/9/17		Tramways from LARCH WOOD to VOORMEZEELE being withdrawn by 37th r 15th Div to bring down transport & so entirely the motor ambulances which are authorized for any place for an A.D.S. was to what ventured. A.D.M.S 37 Div ordered cellar about	
		3pm	with me to look I + 2 LARCH WOOD. We also went to the A.D.S. at T28.b.2.4 on VERBRANDEN ROAD. Orders were now to take it over from Jon Amb of 23rd Div, but later cancelled the order. Wounded passing through A.D.S. from 10am 28th to 10am 29th. 37 Div. 29 O.R. other troops 1 Officer 52 O.R. Germans 2 O.R.	W.D.U. 37 Div. 28 O.R.
"	30/9/17		Wounded passing through A.D.S. from 10am 29th to 10am 30th other troops 2 Off. 65 O.R.	

W. Francis
Lt.Col.
Commdg 49th F.Amb.

30.9.17

Confidential Vol 283

War Diary
of
49th Field Ambulance

From 1st October 1917 to 31st October 1917

(Vol: 2)

COMMITTEE FOR THE
MEDICAL HISTORY OF THE WAR
Date -8 DEC. 1917

Army Form C. 2118.

WAR DIARY
or
INTELLIGENCE SUMMARY.
(Erase heading not required.)

49th Field Ambulance

Place	Date	Hour	Summary of Events and Information	Remarks and references to Appendices
VOORMEZEELE	1/10/17		37th First Casualties passing through A.D.S. for 24 hrs ending 12 noon Oct.1. Off 2. W. O.R. 14 Sick. 39 Wounded.	W.O.R.
"	2/10/17		376W Casualties through ADS for 24 hrs ending 12 noon Oct 2. Off 3. Wd. O.R. 12 Sick. 63. Wd. ADMS called to consult re plans active operations. Vicinity W.O.R. A.D.S. VOORMEZEELE shelled 3.45pm to 5pm + from 6.40 to 7pm. OffW.3; OR. Q. 21. W.67.	
	3/10/17		37 P.m Casualties 12 to 12 (noon) 2 1/10-3 1/10. In the 4th Division Received orders from ADMS to prepare for active operations. In the 49th Division order to Off Bearer to equip R.A.Po Smith by In Stretchers. Planks. O.C.'s of Field Ambulance called Forward + Dumps. Splints. Known Relinc himself. One is bringing them the Taken cross cooperation between ADMS. to preparing from the Brow. Look 8 by Trolley Line. 22 Rein for cases to arrive to stay in the several S/Bs removal of dug out Viretin by my Own + all Medical hospital from Company and from BRASSERIE. 2. N.C.O.s + 49 Bearer reported afternoon the S.H. Field Ambulance. Heavily No.S. Beaver in tooking R.C.A Club by. ABS and Rit Corps. S/Bs 14 Cars. any Several Lean 3 pm + be discussed arrangements for Evans A.Sup 4th Available bearers fr 4th 44th SDH for Cad.s not Battle. All Available bearers for 4th 44th SDH for Cad.s not	

WAR DIARY
INTELLIGENCE SUMMARY

Army Form C. 2118.

Place	Date	Hour	Summary of Events and Information	Remarks and references to Appendices
VOORMEZEELE	3/10/17		Tonight in the Divis'n in readiness for tomorrow.	
"	4/10/17		Attached to 37 Div Comm'r 57th Amb. 49th Fd Amb. is acting Walking A.D.S. 57th Fd Amb as Corps M.D.S. 48th Fd Amb is Evacuating Walking Cases from Corps Line through Collecting Stn. Cars, thence by Motor Lorry to S-8th Fd Ambulance KEMMEL. Evacuation from the front line very difficult owing to heavy shelling & sniping, the casualties are very many owing to rain last night & today, the ground is very bad for progression. Casualties pouring through A.D.S. 12-12 (noon) 3-4 pm. 5/Av. D/S./IV. Off IV W. 137 div & 37 corps stns & ashes collected using Relay Bearers (S.Av.) 37 div 2 other corps O.R. 105.	
"	14/3/10/30		Lined up to LARCH WOOD A.D.S. & CANADA ST TUNNELS & found that evacuation on proper or well as Avenue d'Ancre permitted. Also visited 63rd Dgn H.Q. et also to Glen ten proof & found that they have obtained some R.E. personnel to Left piece & line. It can only be done evening by 8 bearers. S.O.R. the trip line. 19.O.R. Sewers up & Lines as bearers reported to reinforce n/Ba plans.	
"	5/10/17		1 returned from the lines at 4 a.m. 17 O.R. reported to temporary certify 50th F. Amb. Col. P. 8.15 A. + these 8 sent up the line as bearers. Relief. 6 Bearers Situation Right N. Sat. portion Relief the line firing in Sub. party. 4-5.30	Off 9. OR 109. C.Pri. 1. OR Off. 9. OR 109.

Army Form C. 2118.

WAR DIARY
or
INTELLIGENCE SUMMARY
(Erase heading not required.)

49th Fd Ambulance

Place	Date	Hour	Summary of Events and Information	Remarks and references to Appendices
VOORMEZEELE	6/10		Casualties passing through A.D.S. 12 O.R. 12 Sit-up 6½. O.2. O.R. 65. I sent Lieut Foster Sharp to take charge of forward bearers & reorganize their disposition & arrange a system of reliefs. Lieut Scott U.S.M.R. reported at H.Q. & has returned to 47th Fd Amb & is being relieved in the line by Capt Hockett from 45th Fd Amb. 1 N.C.O. & 24 Bearers of B & SK F.A. & 10 Bearers of 45 F.A. returned to H.Q. for a rest.	Rain
	7/10		Casualties for 12 to 12 6-7 O.R. 2 Off. 27 O.R. 19 Sit-up. Practor Service in our tent. A.D.M.S. called & conferred with me & O.C. 45th Fd Ambulance about arrangements for future operations. 1 N.C.O. 3 Bearers of 45 Fd Amb came down here for rest. Dr Boyall returned from leave.	Heavy Rain M.O.R
	8/10		Casualties for 12-12 7½-6½ 1 Off. 15 Wdd. A.D.M.S. called and instructors are that I am to be responsible for evacuation from LARCH WOOD 15.0.C.R.6. line & losses and that D.C. & I.K. Fd Amb bearers take over evacuation from our WOOD for tomorrow's operations. All available bearers rationed here proceeded to A.D.S. LANCH WOOD for duty—the line. C. Bicycle proceeded A.D.S.	Fine day Cold wind
	6pm		LARCH WOOD for duty & to relieve Pt R of E. I Sh-M over Company	

Army Form C. 2118.

WAR DIARY
or
INTELLIGENCE SUMMARY.   49. Field Ambulance
(Erase heading not required.)

Place	Date	Hour	Summary of Events and Information	Remarks and references to Appendices
VOORMEZEELE	8/10/17		Walking wounded Station at Voormezeele from O.C. 45th Fd Amb. who took over Command of forward Bearers in front of LARCH WOOD from Lieut. Pt Scott. U.S.M.R. reported true to duty.	Wet day.
"	9/10/17		Pt Rotz. U.S.M.R. reported here from LARCH WOOD & 1 Sick came from 45th Fd Amb. for duty. 14 O.R. 45th Fd Amb. came down to the lines for a rest this morning. (Casualties 12-12(noon) 8-9/17. 2 Off. 18 O.R.	Fine day. hot bright breeze
"	10/10/17		(Casualties 12-12(noon) 9-10/17. 2 Off. 20 O.R. Prs Boyer reported not fit for duty having been relieved at LARCH WOOD by an Offr. 9554 Pt Fd Amb.	Prs Boyer reported not fit for West.
"	11/10/17		Casualties 12-12 noon) 10-11/17. 2 Off. 36 O.R. Lt. Scott. U.S.M.R. proceeded to 10 Y & L. in the line to replace (temporarily) Capt. Harlwell however. Capt. Craswell reported for duty (letterway) from 10th Fd Amb. N.O.R.	Fine day.
"	12/10/17		Casualties 12-12(noon) 11-12/17. 1 Off. 32 O.R. 8 Duty cases. Report Current O.C. 133 Fd Amb. Crees to arrange for taking over the line from ours in 14/15 Oct. O.C. 45 Fd Amb. Command of Forward Bearers time at 10 P.m. N.R.	Wet day.

D. D. & L., London, E.C. (A804) Wt.W1777/M211 750,000 5/17 Sch: 53 Forms/C2118/14

Army Form C. 2118.

WAR DIARY
or
~~INTELLIGENCE SUMMARY~~

(Erase heading not required.)

49th Field Ambulance

Place	Date	Hour	Summary of Events and Information	Remarks and references to Appendices
VOORMEZEELE	13/7/17		Casualties 12-13 12/13 2 Off. 6 S.O.R. 2 Officers & 7 O.R. of 132 Fd Amb reported as advance party & proceeded up to MARCH WOOD to commence relief of 37th Divn R.A.M.C. in the line	
		10.35p	Received telephone message from F.D.M.S. postponing relief & moves for 24 hours, to night of 14/9/16.	
VOORMEZEELE	14/7/17		Casualties 13-14 (noon) 13-14 20/26 O Off 38 O.R.	
		1pm to 3pm	About 30 H.V. Shells, including several termed "duds" fired at VOORMEZEELE. One direct hit on A.D.S., but very slight damage. 2 there rentered in the same. (R.S.A.C.) buildings hit on A.D.S. & con trench for check	
		5.30pm	Several shells started to fall with view of A.D.S. & con trench for check Capt Jergman & 6 parts of Bearers from 133 Fd Ambulance reported for duty with O.C. 132 Fd Amb. As the relief is postponed I am keeping them here till tomorrow. 8 O Bearers of 37th Divisions have been relieved Capt Maxwell R.A.M.C. & Capt Pruneto has been ordered by A.D.M.S. to take over Permanent hospital Officer of 10 R.F. Today.	

A. J. 13th R.F.

Army Form C. 2118.

WAR DIARY
or
INTELLIGENCE SUMMARY.
(Erase heading not required.)

49th Field Ambulance

Place	Date	Hour	Summary of Events and Information	Remarks and references to Appendices
VOORMEZEELE	15th 1/9	1pm	Relief of 37 Div R.A.M.C. by 35th Div. in progress. WAC	Train Parry
	16/10/17	11:30pm	Relief Completed of 37 Div R.A.M.C. by 35th Div. O.C. 132 and 7th Ambulance taken over collection from lines, and Adv. Posts & Bearer Posts at VOORMEZEELE, LARCHWOOD & CANADA St TUNNELS. 49th Fd Ambulance proceeded to KOKOREELE R.7.b.5.2 (Personnel by lorry) & took over from O.C. 134 Fd Ambulance. Bearers & Motor Ambulance Cars of 41st & 158th Field Ambulance returned to their units. A.S. & Sgt Collett. WAC	
KOKOREELE R.7.b.5.2 (Sheet 17)				
KOKOREELE	17/10/17		Collecting Sick from 112 & 63. Brigades. Submitted plans for improvements of Ambulance of site to A.D.M.S. 9th Corps. Casualties to personnel of 49th Marines Fd. Amb. between 22 Sept & 16th Oct = Capt Taylor R.A.M.C wounded & Evacd. to Eng. Wounded & evacd. 32 (10 Gunshot Flesh) Wounded & remaining with Ambulance 7 (all 5 wood Flesh) Wounded to duty 6 Missing 1 Pvt Pritt R.A.M.C. Staff Sgt Wormoth reported for duty from the base. WAC	

WAR DIARY or INTELLIGENCE SUMMARY

Army Form C. 2118.

49th Field Ambulance

Place	Date	Hour	Summary of Events and Information	Remarks and references to Appendices
KOKOREELE	18/10/17		Day spent in cleaning up & refitting. S/Sgt Personnel who were working at A.D.S. at LARCH WOOD went into rest employment. Sgt. Symons from Place Coy. Several cases of trench fever admitted from 63rd Brigade. Cont. of enquiries held into inoculation case of Private W. Fitch who has been advising since Sept 22.1917. 9 reinforcements reported from the Base.	Rainy
"	19/10/17		Medical Board held here to examine candidates for Commissions in Indian Army. Dr.Cy.(Clarke R.A.M.C. Comdy 4 F.A. for Aust. President. Inoculation(antityphoid) being proceeded with amongst the personnel.	W.B.C.
"	20/10/17		Capt. Scrimshirk. R.A.M.C. (T.F.) reported for duty from the Base.	W.B.C.
"	21/10/17		Several of the personnel are still suffering from the effects of Shell gas, Symptom of the throat & temporary being the prevailing Symptom. 63rd Brigade moved to M.E.GRIS over & sent transport for him. Felling out.	W.B.C.
"	22/10/17		Personnel engaged in general cleaning up & stretcher drive. All the equipment now through. 112 Brigade & 247 T.M.B. is being pur through. 63rd Brigade now on collecting.	W.B.C.

Army Form C. 2118.

WAR DIARY
or
INTELLIGENCE SUMMARY. 49th Field Ambulance

(Erase heading not required.)

Place	Date	Hour	Summary of Events and Information	Remarks and references to Appendices
KOKOFELE	23/10/17		Further orders of A.D.M.S. 37 Div. Lt Boyle proceeded to take over medical charge of 11th Warwicks vice Capt Alcock to England wounded, and Capt Buchanan proceeded to take temporary medical charge of 9th North Staffs. Vic Capt Sprague on leave to U.K.	W/C
"	24/10/17		Lt Price proceeded for temporary duty to No. 44 C.C.S.	W/C
"	26/10/17		Court of Enquiry re Absence of Private W. FRITH assembled, showing considered the evidence were unable to come to a definite conclusion as to the cause of his absence. No. 36209 a/L/Cpl CLARK E. J. awarded the Military Medal for gallantry in the Field by Corps Commander	W/C
"	27/10/17		Pay Parade 5.30 pm.	W/C
				IX Corps
				S.D. orders to relieve 12.30 pm	W/C
"	29/10/17		6 Sisters called morning.	W/C
	30/10/17		Lt. Tonkin U.S.M.R.C. reported for duty. Am. Born.	W/C
	31/10/17		C/O Director honoured of 1st Cond. in France	W/C

CONFIDENTIAL Vol 29

War Diary
—of—
49th Field Ambulance

From 1st November 1917 to 30th November 1917

(Vol: 28)

COMMITTEE FOR THE
MEDICAL HISTORY OF THE WAR
Date   17 JAN. 1918

49TH
FIELD AMBULANCE.
No................
Date..............

Army Form C. 2118.

WAR DIARY
or
INTELLIGENCE SUMMARY.

(Erase heading not required.)

Instructions regarding War Diaries and Intelligence Summaries are contained in F. S. Regs., Part II. and the Staff Manual respectively. Title pages will be prepared in manuscript.

Place	Date	Hour	Summary of Events and Information	Remarks and references to Appendices

(A8001) Wt. W1771/M2031 730,000 5/17 D. D. & L., London, E.C. **Sch. 52** Forms/C2118/14

Army Form C. 2118.

WAR DIARY
or
INTELLIGENCE SUMMARY

49th Field Ambulance

(Erase heading not required.)

Place	Date	Hour	Summary of Events and Information	Remarks and references to Appendices
KOROMBEKE	8/11/17		Capt Adams R.A.M.C. to temporary duty with 10 York & Lancs. Capt McLean and 1 Lieut Int. Division proceed to report to O.C. 41st Field Ambulance for temporary duty at MEERSBROOK.	WM
"	9/11/17		Pte Tinsley U.S.N.R. & S.T.O.R. proceed to report to O.C. 48th Field Ambulance for temporary duty in the line. Capt Gigot R.A.M.C. & 1 Lieut Int. Division proceeded to HOSPICE, LOCRE, in advance party. Capt Brough M.C. Leaves B on IK Corps Sanitary Inspector as CRESTER to an office of S.S./Lt Field Ambulance & returned with his hut & kits. Capt Brough proceeded to 250 Tunnelling Coy for temporary duty till 24th Nov.	WM
HOSPICE LOCRE	10/11/17	10 a.m.	Remainder of Ft Ambulance arrived at Hospice Locre & took over from O.C. 57th Field Ambulance, took over 43 patients. Lt. Col. H.E. H.Q. in acting as M.D.S. for 376 Div. No leave has been over the line from 19th Division.	
"	11/11/17		The following awards have been made in connection with recent active operations. D.C.M. to 37/25. Cpl of B/H Carry A.C. 3-VII-17. Military Medals to: 92216. Pte Poon A.C.3-X-17. M/2-153490 Pte R. McKELLAN. A.S.C. Att. 2-XI-17. 36309. Pte. J. CLARKE 2-XI-17. 36765. Cpl. S. BRISTOW. 2-XI-17.	WM

D. D. & L., London, E.C.
Wt. W1771/M2031 750,000 5/17 Sch. 52 Forms/C2118/14

Army Form C. 2118.

WAR DIARY
or
INTELLIGENCE SUMMARY.   49th Field Ambulance
(Erase heading not required.)

Instructions regarding War Diaries and Intelligence Summaries are contained in F. S. Regs., Part II. and the Staff Manual respectively. Title pages will be prepared in manuscript.

Place	Date	Hour	Summary of Events and Information	Remarks and references to Appendices
Mont NoirOrigeus	1/4/17		The unit is still at rest.	WR
R.N.L.S.2.. (Sheet 27)	2/4/17		Inspection of transport personnel & by C.O.	WR
	3/4/17		A.D.M.S. 37 Div inspected the personnel (all dismounted), the 3 Ambulance Wagons & the Motor Ambulance Cars at 3 o'clock p.m. Personnel were drawn up in Column of Sections under Command of C.O.	WR
	4/4/17		Capt Buchanan returned to duty from temporary duty with 9th N. Staffs. at Regtl. Inspection Capt. (Oct 7.1917)	WR
	6/4/17		Went to see A.D.M.S. to receive instructions for pushing move to the line.	WR
	7/4/17		Sent Capt. Piggott to see O.C. 4th F.A. 57th F.A. Ambs. & 57th Fd. Amb. to make arrangements about sending a lorries? attachment to 49th & in B Sect. Transport on own in march to 57th main station. (40th Fd. Amb. 104. 45th Fd Amb. 204) Capt Piggott in Grand Transport Show (RAMC (TC) reported for duty from the Base.)	WR

Army Form C. 2118.

WAR DIARY
or
INTELLIGENCE SUMMARY.
(Erase heading not required.)

49th Field Ambulance.

Place	Date	Hour	Summary of Events and Information	Remarks and references to Appendices
HOSPICE, LOCRE	12/4/17		I went with A.D.M.S. to see new M.D.S. position at KEMMEL, with view to taking it over from O.C. 4th Fd. Amb. Nissen huts are being erected by IX Corps R.E. One Section of 14th Aust. Fd Amb. is here, working in with us, with a view to taking over on 13th inst.	
"	13/4/17		I took over premises at KEMMEL from O.C. 48th Fd Amb. and put a holding party there. I commenced carrying R.E. & IX Corps medical stores from here to KEMMEL.	
"	14/4/17		Capt Regent and advanced party proceeded to KEMMEL to prepare the new premises for the reception of patients tomorrow. I am gradually clearing invalid stores from here to KEMMEL & transferring patients to C.C.S. & 48th Fd Amb (McGILLICAN CAMP).	
"	15/4/17		I handed over the Hospice Locre to O.C. 14th Fd Ambulance (ANZAC) and proceeded to KEMMEL. A station hospital is being built and preceded to KEMMEL. 49th Fd Amb is acting	

Army Form C. 2118.

WAR DIARY
or
INTELLIGENCE SUMMARY.
(Erase heading not required.)

Place	Date	Hour	Summary of Events and Information	Remarks and references to Appendices
KEMMEL	15/1/17 contd		As M.D.S. 4th Fd Amb. is acting as A.D.S. Clearing the line. Wounded we being dealt direct at 4th Fd Amb. 40th F.A. passed through any A.D.S. Book. Sick we being admitted to right Fd Amb. We also admit a large number of Corps & Army troops, as we collect in Dvsn amb. A.D.C. 37 Dvn in Reserve the Infantry Battns this afternoon.	
"	16/1/17		Work of construction & fitting Camp Carriere on. 4 Paris returned to duty from 44.C.C.S.	
"	17/1/17		Capt Buchanan & tent Sub division returned from 45th Fd Amb. Am the horse amb trans here.	
"	18/1/17		A.D.M.S. called. Work of construction still proceeding.	
"	19/1/17		Capt Thomas R.A.M.C. whom Kemp from Factory Amb with 10 yh + horses.	

Army Form C. 2118.

WAR DIARY
or
INTELLIGENCE SUMMARY

(Erase heading not required.)

49th Field Ambulance

Instructions regarding War Diaries and Intelligence Summaries are contained in F.S. Regs., Part II. and the Staff Manual respectively. Title pages will be prepared in manuscript.

Place	Date	Hour	Summary of Events and Information	Remarks and references to Appendices
KEMMEL	20/4/17		A.D.M.S. IX Corps called & inspected the Construction work in progress	WR
"	21/4/17		Capt. Buchanan to Corps duty with F.E. Lanes. Vice Capt Ashmore sick.	WR
"	22/4/17		A.D.M.S. called & looked round.	WR
"	23/4/17		Work of Construction Still Continues	
"	26/4/17		Pay Parade. 2.o/c Any horses not from 48th Fd Ambulance for the home prosperous prospect of Creation of horse Standings. A.D.M.S. called.	
"	27/4/17		I have much annoyance with O.C. 4 Fd. Ambulance that he will not now have 20 horses (he charges every 2 days for fatigues. Construction of horse Standing proceeding). Also the Conservator with Indian hospital gardener Capt. B. absent without leave of No. 46177 Pte. P.J. Merrick Nursing Orderly. Capt. Leuvish & members Capt. Ryper & Lt. Price. As Continue present. Capt. Brough received at 2.30 Incoming Coy by Capt Leuvish W. R. 2 Press. Capt. Brough R.A.M.C. proceeded to U.K. on leave.	WR
	28/4/17			

Army Form C. 2118.

WAR DIARY
or
INTELLIGENCE SUMMARY.
(Erase heading not required.)

49th FIELD AMBULANCE

Place	Date	Hour	Summary of Events and Information	Remarks and references to Appendices
NEFMNEL	28th/17		Lt Prio proceeded in relief of Capt Ahern. Capt H. Prio Ahern on relief proceeded to G.H. Staff Supernumerary in relief of Capt Sprague to England on completion of Contract. Medical Board held here 11 a.m. to examine 3 Officers for Permanent Commission. President Lt Col Clark. Names. Members Capt. Sennwick & Capt Prest.	
"	29/17			
"	30/17		Returns called in Council (48th Fd Amb) from the A.D.S. We are now receiving Casualties from the A.D.S. (48th Fd Amb) Work of construction still progressing.	W Simon Major Commanding 49th Fd Amb. 30.XI.17

Army Form C. 2118.

WAR DIARY
or
INTELLIGENCE SUMMARY.

(*Erase heading not required.*)

Instructions regarding War Diaries and Intelligence Summaries are contained in F. S. Regs., Part II. and the Staff Manual respectively. Title pages will be prepared in manuscript.

Place	Date	Hour	Summary of Events and Information	Remarks and references to Appendices

(A8001) Wt. W1771/M2031 750,000 5/17 **Sch. 52** Forms/C2118/14
D. D. & L., London, E.C.

Confidential

War Diary
— of —
49th Field Ambulance

From 1st December 1917 to 31st December 1917.

(Volume 29)

Army Form C. 2118.

WAR DIARY
of 49th Field Ambulance

INTELLIGENCE SUMMARY.
(Erase heading not required.)

Instructions regarding War Diaries and Intelligence Summaries are contained in F. S. Regs., Part II. and the Staff Manual respectively. Title pages will be prepared in manuscript.

Place	Date	Hour	Summary of Events and Information	Remarks and references to Appendices
KEMMEL	2/12/17		Capt Buchanan joined for temporary duty to 5th Sct armd vice D Ashmore invaliding sick. Adms. Called.	MPL
	3/12/17		Lt Price returned for duty from temp duty with 26th Lumbering Coy.	MPL
	5/12/17		15 O.R. proceeded to 50th Fd Ambulance for temporary duty. Adms. Called.	MPL
	6/12/17		Body of Capt HYLTON, A.V.C. brought in, he was killed in trying to board a moving motor lorry (12.30 pm)	MPL
	7/12/17		Medical Board, President Lt Col W.F. Roe. D.S.O. members Capt Opp. considered recently P.B. men in Kemmel Area. Body of Capt Hylton buried Remy of Locre Military.	MPL
			53 C.C.S. for postmortem examination	
			Work on construction of Hospital, billets + horse lines proceeding.	MPL
	8/12/17		Adms called. Hospital visited by members of U.S.A. Food Commission	MPL
	9/12/17		No 308809 Pte MANIK. W. 2 Yorkshire Regt a patient in hospital suffering from Bullet wound of hand placed under arrest under escort to C.C.S. No 53. on suspicion of being self inflicted, a report to his Unit.	MPL

D. D. & L., London, E.C. (A5001) Wt. W1771/M2031 750,000 5/17 Sch. 52 Forms/C2118/14

Army Form C. 2118.

WAR DIARY
or
INTELLIGENCE SUMMARY.
(Erase heading not required.)

49 Field Ambulance

Place	Date	Hour	Summary of Events and Information	Remarks and references to Appendices
KEMMEL	10/12/17		Lt Price Beaune proceeded to England on leave. Instructions of D.G. A.M.S. G.H.Q. 2nd Echelon. Proceeded further from duty with 13 R.F. vice Capt Quin sick. 1877 Pte WILDEN J. 13 GLOSTERS, not returned last change sheet in respect of ...., admitted to Hospital on Nov 29th 1917, to A.P.M. 37 Div.	W.R.
	11/12/17		Huts & Standing & hospitat previously prepared, construction.	W.R.
	12/12/17		A.T.M.S. arrived	W.R.
	13/12/17		Capt Brough M.C. returned to duty from leave.	W.R.
	14/12/17		A.D.M.S. IX Corps visited & inspected the Ambulance & previous plans running in camp & construction.	W.R.
	15/12/17		Lt J.M. SCANLON, M.R.C. U.S.A. reported for duty from the Base.	W.R.

WAR DIARY

INTELLIGENCE SUMMARY. 49th Field Ambulance

Army Form C. 2118.

Place	Date	Hour	Summary of Events and Information	Remarks and references to Appendices
KEMMEL	16/12/17		I acted as Auth'n men Whites in Commonwealth Mentrulein Military Reperdamen 15.7. & took vote from patient in hospital.	WOL
"	17/12/17		Snowfell during night. Lt Scenter MORC U.S.A. Lieut of II Corps Rest Station. (N.C.C.S.) Suffering from Scabies.	WOL
"	18/12/17		Very heavy frost.	WOL
"	19/12/17		Activity visits Fd. Amb. Capts P.A. CREUK and J.R. MENZIES, R.A.M.C. reported for duty from Base. Heavy frost continues	WOL
"	20/12/17		Heavy frost continues. I have evac. temporarily command of Fd Amb as to Capt Scentrick R.A.M.C. also inspected accompt & proceeded to by 50, 37 Div. to take on duty as A.D.M.S. during absence on leave of Col Morphew. D.S.O. A.M.S.	WOL

W Alex M. Nairne W.O.C.
Comde 49th Fd Amb

Army Form C. 2118.

WAR DIARY
or
INTELLIGENCE SUMMARY.
(Erase heading not required.)

49th Field Ambulance

Place	Date	Hour	Summary of Events and Information	Remarks and references to Appendices
KEMMEL	21/12/17		Visited D.C. No 2 Car Train & arranged for today's evacuation	W.S.
	22/12/17		A/ADMS and D.A.D.M.S. called in the afternoon.	W.S.
	23/12/17		Transport routed him at Poolage, & took over home storage at Kennel	W.S.
			Capt Nyght proceeded to England on leave	
			G.O.C. 37th Division & A/A.D.M.S. inspected Field Ambulance & Horse	W.S.
			Lines thoroughly. Pay Parade in afternoon	
	24/12/17		Visited Four Cabins	W.S.
	25/12/17		Hard Frost 8 mm	W.S.
	26/12/17		Court of Estents to Personnel in evening	W.S.
	27/12/17		Hut Constructor Officer, R.E, called respecting Hospital.	W.S.
			A/A.D.M.S. called in evening	
	28/12/17		Inspected Transport Personnel	W.S.
	29/12/17		Lieut. I.M. Render returned from leave from 11 Car.	W.S.

Army Form C. 2118.

WAR DIARY
or
INTELLIGENCE SUMMARY.

(Erase heading not required.)

Place	Date	Hour	Summary of Events and Information	Remarks and references to Appendices
Kemmel	30/12/17		Capt Event Proceeded to IX Corps Gas School, Brethen, for 5 days course	W-
			Lieut. W.H. Loulan MORC, USA, posted to formwart Medical charge, 13" R. Two.	W-
	31/12/17		Visited 63 M.S.C., Essex Camp, & inspection sanitary condition thereof.	W-

Wakenrick
Capt. RAMC.
Comdg 49° Field Ambulance

Confidential

War Diary
of
49th Field Ambulance

From 1st Jan. 1918 to 31st Jan 1918.

[Volume 30]

COMMITTEE FOR ...
MEDICAL HISTORY OF THE WAR
Date —4 MAR. 1918

Army Form C. 2118.

WAR DIARY
or
INTELLIGENCE SUMMARY. 49 Field Ambulance
(Erase heading not required.)

Instructions regarding War Diaries and Intelligence Summaries are contained in F. S. Regs., Part II. and the Staff Manual respectively. Title pages will be prepared in manuscript.

Place	Date	Hour	Summary of Events and Information	Remarks and references to Appendices
KEMMEL	1/8		New feet dresses to no returned from line duty. A.D.M.S. O S.D.M.S. called.	E.S.
	2/8		Confirmation of the medical examination of latrine etc of 342 Road Construction Coy (R.E.)	E.S.
	3/8		Capt. J.R. Menzies R.A.M.C. (T.F.) of 10th L.N. Lancs. to temporary medical charge.	E.S.
	4/8		Medical Board on O.R.'s now attached to 49 F.Amb. President Lt.Col. S.O.J. Pine, Honey, Captain D.S. Forsyth M.C. Members. No. 36270 Ot Marshall C.S. 49 Field Ambulance died of wounds at Lord Howe A.D.S.	E.S.
	5/8		Capt. A. O'Bruce R.A.M.C. returned from Gas Course at IX Corps Gas School. A.D.M.S., 37th Division Army returned from leave, Lt.Col. H.O. returned to Field Ambulance.	E.S.

Army Form C. 2118.

WAR DIARY
or
INTELLIGENCE SUMMARY. 49 Field Ambulance
(Erase heading not required.)

Place	Date	Hour	Summary of Events and Information	Remarks and references to Appendices
Kemmel	6/7/18		Lt. Col. W.T. Rae D.S.O. RAMC proceeded to England on leave, for period 4/7/18 to 6/7/18. Lieut Jenten M.O.R.C. U.S.A. proceeded to attend Army Musketry School (I.O.M.S. Instruction). Pay Parade at 2.0 pm. Sgt Roth O.J. RAMC 49th Field Ambulance awarded Meritorious Service Medal.	W.J.
	7/18		A.D.M.S. called in the morning, with D.A.D.M.S. 49th Division. Capt. A.P. Piggott RAMC returned from leave. Sg. Paxman who had been attached to 48th F.A. returned to HQ for duty.	W.J.
	8/5		Visited 112 Bgde H.Q. with reference to moving 49th F.A. transport. Capt. ex. Brunn RAMC visited D.H.Q. arrange about billets in new area.	W.J.

Army Form C. 2118.

WAR DIARY
or
INTELLIGENCE SUMMARY. 49 Field Ambce

(Erase heading not required.)

Place	Date	Hour	Summary of Events and Information	Remarks and references to Appendices
Kemmel	9/18		Field Ambulance transport moved off for new area in charge of Capt Crewe Payne. The transport was billetted at Strazeele for night of 9th to 10th. Heavy enemy action during day.	W.J.
EBBLINGHEM	10/18		49th Field Ambulance less Capt. A.P. Boyd Payne & 21 O.R. moved from Kemmel, entrained at Strazeele, & detrained at Ebblinghem. The 49th F.A. went into billets Ebbinghem area, Simon Ling & Cope Reserve.	W.J.
	11/18		Made arrangements at Ebbinghem for 49th F.A. to receive patients from 112th Brigade. Also arrangt with Col. Taylor RAMC, O.C. 13th Casd. to look after & retain as far as possible cases sent to 13th Casd. from 37th Division, the F.A. accommodation for retaining patients being inadequate. Capt Crewe Payne went to 9th Bde R.G.A. to try any duty Kentish 112 B.M.Y. reference Bgde medical arrangements	W.J.

WAR DIARY
or
INTELLIGENCE SUMMARY. 49th Field Ambulance

Army Form C. 2118.

(Erase heading not required.)

Place	Date	Hour	Summary of Events and Information	Remarks and references to Appendices
Effingham	12/7/18		Capt A.R. Piggot & 20. O.R. returned from Kennel other morning having handed over Main Dressing Station at Kennel to O.C. 13th Australian Field Ambulance. A.D.M.S called this afternoon. Field Ambulance commenced scheme of training.	W.S.
	13/7/18		Visited A.D.M.S. in afternoon reference Training & reduced arrangements called in O.C. 15 C.C.S. reference arrangements whereby 37th Sand patients not to 15 C.C.S should not be evacuated if possible.	W.S.
	14/7/18		G.O.C. 37th Division inspected hospital & for three Heavy wind during night 14, 15, & 16. part of "B" section letter blown in – no casualties.	W.S.
	15/7/18		Capt J.G.T. Thom M.C. R.A.M.C attached for temporary duty. Visited No 4 Coy & 37th Sanitary.	W.S.
	16/7/18		ADMS 37th Division called in the morning C.O.S. fell Parade.	W.S.

WAR DIARY

INTELLIGENCE SUMMARY.

Army Form C. 2118.

49th Field Ambulance

Place	Date	Hour	Summary of Events and Information	Remarks and references to Appendices
Effingham	M 1/18		Inspection Visits etc of 63rd M.G.C. Capt W.A. Semple M.C. R.A.M.C. (T.C.) Lieut J.T. Hill R.A.M.C. (T.C.) } reported for duty from England. Lieut N.C. Horn R.A.M.C. (T.C.) Capt. G.R. Menzies R.A.M.C. (T.F.) posted to permanent medical charge of 10th Batt: L.N. Lancs. Capt. L.S.J. Thomas M.C. R.A.M.C. (T.C.) posted temporal charge of 8.A. Lincolns - to report to O.C. 8th Lincolns on return from leave.	
	18/1/18		Capt V.G.L. Thomas M.C. R.A.M.C. (T.C.) proceeded to England on leave.	W.T.
	19/1/18		Lieut O.G. Hill R.A.M.C. (T.C.) proceeded to Division D.M.S. Service for temporary duty. The weather during the past week has been exceptionally cold & has interfered with the training.	W.T.
	20/1/18		Pay Parade in afternoon.	W.T.

Army Form C. 2118.

WAR DIARY
or
INTELLIGENCE SUMMARY. 49th Field Ambulance

(Erase heading not required.)

Instructions regarding War Diaries and Intelligence Summaries are contained in F.S. Regs., Part II. and the Staff Manual respectively. Title pages will be prepared in manuscript.

Place	Date	Hour	Summary of Events and Information	Remarks and references to Appendices
EBBLINGHEM	21/1/18		Visit by A.D.M.S. & D.A.D.M.O. Visited 112th M.G.C.	W.T.
	22/1/18		Gas demonstration by Divisional Gas N.C.O. Lecture to Officers by Comdg Officer	W.T.
	23/1/18		Presentation of Medal Ribands by 4th Army Commdr. at Aynes:— Recipients:— S.S. Coates, A.C. D.C.M. & bar to M.M. Sgt Preston, S. — M.M. Pte Whittaker, T. — M.M. Pte McKellen, R. — M.M. Sgt Park, P.J. — M.S.M. Field Ambulance Photo & Confirmations in afternoon. A.D.M.S. attended & distributed prizes.	W.T.
	26/1/8		Suspicion of serum of Pte H. Craig, R.A.M.C., received by G.O.C. 37th Division, noted edned case sent tangle forward for further consideration no 26 4/18	W.T.

Army Form C. 2118.

WAR DIARY
or
INTELLIGENCE SUMMARY. 49th Field Ambulance
(Erase heading not required.)

Instructions regarding War Diaries and Intelligence Summaries are contained in F. S. Regs., Part II. and the Staff Manual respectively. Title pages will be prepared in manuscript.

Place	Date	Hour	Summary of Events and Information	Remarks and references to Appendices
EBBLINGHEM	27/1/18		Inspection of Field Ambulance & Transport by G.O.C. 37th Division Lt. Hon. A.Q. and Sgt. Preston to IX Corps Gas School for course.	W.T.
	28/1/18		To see A.D.M.S. & A.P.M. re enemy.	W.T.
	29/1/18		Visit by Lt. Col Humphries, A/C, O.C. 37th Divisional Train	W.T.
	31/1/18		Visit & inspection of 112 M.S. Co's Hutts. Dinner A.D.M.S. in morning. During the present the Ambulance has been at EBBLINGHEM it has undergone training, special attention being been given to Gas drills	W.T.

31-1-18

T. Scrivenich
Capt. RAMC.
Comd. 9. 49th Field Ambulance.

Confidential

War Diary
of
49th Field Ambulance

From 1st February to 28th February 1918

[Volume 31]

Army Form C. 2118.

WAR DIARY
INTELLIGENCE SUMMARY. 49th Field Ambulance

(Erase heading not required.)

Place	Date	Hour	Summary of Events and Information	Remarks and references to Appendices
EBBLINGHEM	1/2/18		Capt Cook RAMC returned to Headquarters from temporary medical charge of No. 9 Bgde R.G.A.	W.T.
	2/2/18		Lieut Henn RAMC returned to unit from IX Corps Gas School. Visited 63rd Bgde H.Q.	W.T.
	3/2/18		Capt Temp. M.C. RAMC posted for temporary medical charge of 104 Bgde R.F.A. Pay Parade in afternoon	W.T.
	4/2/18		Capt Crux RAMC to 70th L.N. Lancs for temp? duty in relief of Capt Menzies RAMC(T) - sick	W.T.
	5/2/18		Ambulance turn out this morning to Ebbinghem point. O.C. XV C.C.S. called	W.T.
	6/2/18		Col Humphreys, O.C. 39th Fd Amb, allotted open mmmmy of evidence re 2no Roatay, Synch & Feather	W.T.

Army Form C. 2118.

WAR DIARY
INTELLIGENCE SUMMARY.
(Erase heading not required.)

49th Field Ambulance

Place	Date	Hour	Summary of Events and Information	Remarks and references to Appendices
ESSLINGHEM	7/2/18		Attended Conference of C.O.'s & Staff Officers, 3rd Division, with Chemical Advisor at School Room, Blaringhem. Lt. Col. W.P. Ros D.S.O. R.A.M.C. returned from leave.	W/-
"	8/2/18		Lt. Col. W.P. Ros D.S.O. returned command of the unit yesterday on return from leave to U.K.	W/R
"	9/2/18		C.O. & Capt Serves his Officers attended lecture by O/C for officers at Bn H.Q. 16 O.R. reported from cyclist Base Depot as reinforcement.	W/R
"	10/2/18		Cont[inued] hostilities at 10 h and M. Comm Bros, on Dr Fette, A.R., Rosling E.P., and Lynch with all R.S.C. H.T. Changes with "Meeuwen", knowing them who take Italian protein fort" after Scrap hub notes in proceeds. Admns returns callers.	W/R

Army Form C. 2118.

WAR DIARY
or
INTELLIGENCE SUMMARY. 49th Field Ambce
(Erase heading not required.)

Instructions regarding War Diaries and Intelligence Summaries are contained in F. S. Regs., Part II. and the Staff Manual respectively. Title pages will be prepared in manuscript.

Place	Date	Hour	Summary of Events and Information	Remarks and references to Appendices
EBBLINGHEM	11/3/18		Received orders from ADMS 20th Divn over from O.C. 61st F. Amb in the line in rel. to 15/6. & thankt necessary arrangement with him. Obtained from Temp. dr/s with 20th Div to the firing line with 50th F. Amb.	
"	12/3/18		I went to see O.C. 61st F. Amb. at REININGHEIST & arranged for taking over his positions there viz. at MENIN ROAD & the forward bearer relay posts North of MENIN ROAD.	W.O.R.
"	13		49 F. Amb HTransport moved at 9 a.m. under Major G.O.C. 63rd Brigade to REININGHEIST, staying the night of 63rd Brigade. I sent 2 Sgt + 12 Bearers + 3 N. Orderlies N. STRAZEELE. I reported MO.C. 61st F. Amb as an Advance party. Received Proceeding of at MENIN ROAD A.D.S. Received from Private J.C. Gr. Dr. Jetter, Raddop + hyneck sent from F. P. amb attached to 57 drup F. P. No I. Capt Puntschau reported for duty from 8th F. Amb.	W.O.R.

(AFonn) We. W2771/M2931. 750,000. 5/17. **Sch. 50** Forms/C2118/14
P. D. & L., London, E.C.

Army Form C. 2118.

WAR DIARY
or
INTELLIGENCE SUMMARY. 49th Field Ambulance
(Erase heading not required.)

Instructions regarding War Diaries and Intelligence Summaries are contained in F. S. Regs., Part II. and the Staff Manual respectively. Title pages will be prepared in manuscript.

Place	Date	Hour	Summary of Events and Information	Remarks and references to Appendices
RENINGHELST	1/4/18		Bivouacked personnel of Fd. Amb. moved by train from FROLINGHEM, who Command (P. Coptn?) which they detrained at DICKEBUSCH. Capt Sampbrick hence marched with to O.P. to MENIN ROAD & took over the forward A.D.S. Bearers and relay posts from officer of 61st Fd Ambulance & left an Advance party at the A.D.S. MENIN ROAD. The remainder under Capt Piggot moved to RENINGHELST & went into billets. Later 5 p.m. Capt Piggot proceeded to MENIN ROAD to take over the A.D.S. from officer of 31st Fd Ambulance. Lt Hill J.T. proceeded to FROLINGHEM by road with the M. Ambulance Cars & came here from FROLINGHEM by road with the M. Ambulance Cars & accordingly struck off Strength 1/4/18 two lorries conveying excess stores. duty to 50th Field Ambulance & accordingly struck off Strength 1/4/18 J.A.	

Army Form C. 2118.

WAR DIARY
or
INTELLIGENCE SUMMARY.

(Erase heading not required.)

4 G+y Field Ambce

Instructions regarding War Diaries and Intelligence Summaries are contained in F. S. Regs., Part II. and the Staff Manual respectively. Title pages will be prepared in manuscript.

Place	Date	Hour	Summary of Events and Information	Remarks and references to Appendices
RENINGHELST	15/7/18	10 am	I promulgated sentence of F.G.C.M. on Dr Rorking, Fitter and Lynch, all A.S.C. attached. Each was found guilty and sentenced to 56 days F.P. No 1. I completed relief of 61st Fd. Amb. at A.D.S. at MENIN ROAD. I went to visit A.D.S. at MENIN ROAD & it very quiet. Pvr Capt Brough t advance party unser Cm unk to O.C. 61 st Fd Amb. as M.D.S. RENINGHELST.	WM
	16/7/18		I took over M.D.S. & bivets & horse lines at RENINGHELST from O.C. 61st Fd. Amb. who became responsible for clearing the Brigade on the immediate left of the MENIN RD. At noon proceeded to XXIInd Corps Med. officers school BAILLEUL for a course lasting from 17/7/18 to 28/7/18	WM

Army Form C. 2118.

WAR DIARY
or
INTELLIGENCE SUMMARY. 49th Field Ambulance
(Erase heading not required.)

Instructions regarding War Diaries and Intelligence Summaries are contained in F. S. Regs., Part II. and the Staff Manual respectively. Title pages will be prepared in manuscript.

Place	Date	Hour	Summary of Events and Information	Remarks and references to Appendices
RENINGHELST	17/7/18		ADMS visited aid posts at RENINGHELST, & desires that it please be used a Sick Collecting Station, hour XXII Corps Scheme, & that Cars could be detained here for 48 hours. O.C. F.A. and conveul	
MENIN ROAD I.9.c.6.6.		5 p.m.	his H.Q.G. MENIN ROAD. I.9.c.6.6. Sheet 28. Wounded are evacuated by 14 M.A.C. Cars fr C.R.S. & by Train from Y PRES h 11 C.C.S. GODSVERVELDE. Other Cars are attached to Sick Collecting Station at RENINGHELST. Capt Brough & Capt Buchanan now duty at RENINGHELST. O.C. & Capt Pyjoh at H.Q. Capt Schmidt h H.Q. at A.D.S. CLAPHAM JUNCTION. J.13.d.9.8.	
MENIN RD I.9.c.6.6.	18/7/18		O.C. visited CLAPHAM JUNCTION. A.D.S. BEARER POSTS at HOOGE (RATER & JACKDAW TUNNELS (J.19.b.1.9), and 112th BRIGADE H.Q. JACKDAW TUNNELS W.D.R. (J.19.a.3.6). A.D.M.S. inspected M.D.S. here to day.	
"	19/7/18		O.C. visited CLAPHAM JUNCTION A.D.S. GLENCORSE TUNNELS (J.14.a+b) post & R.A.P. and Bearer post at BLACKWATCH CORNER J.15.b.1.9. Sheet 28.	

WAR DIARY

INTELLIGENCE SUMMARY. 49th Field Ambulance

Army Form C. 2118.

Place	Date	Hour	Summary of Events and Information	Remarks and references to Appendices
MENIN RD. I.9.c.6.6. Sheet 28	20/2/18		A.D.M.S. called 11 am & proceeded to inspect the forward A.D.S. & Rear of Relay Posts. Medical Boards assembled to examine Gnr Clifton, 113 Siege Bty R.G.A. & found him fit for service with his unit. Pres. Lt Col W.E. Thew D.S.O. Member Capt Riddoch. Name Capt Pigot. R.A.M.C. 1 man lectures at XXII Corps School for Medical officers on "Red Shock, Haematuria and Malingering". Capt W.A. Trump M.C. R.F. M.C. reported for duty from temp. duty with 124 Bgde R.F.A.	WM
"	21/2/18		Lieut Carl of Engineers, referred by me, awarded 2 days field 1 No 36272 Pte MILLS.J. Pres. Capt Trump M.C. Member Capt Pigot. Capt D. Brough M.C. proceeded to England on completion of his contract.	MR
	22/2/18		2 Sgts & 20 Bearers returned to this Unit by 2 ambulance launches from Wks, notified by A.D.M.S. that Capt R.A. CROUX R.A.M.C. is attached to Unit & to L.N. Lancs as from 15.2.18. Capt Sainsbury returned Capt Trump from the base.	MR

Army Form C. 2118.

WAR DIARY
or
INTELLIGENCE SUMMARY. 49th Field Ambulance

(Erase heading not required.)

Instructions regarding War Diaries and Intelligence Summaries are contained in F. S. Regs., Part II. and the Staff Manual respectively. Title pages will be prepared in manuscript.

Place	Date	Hour	Summary of Events and Information	Remarks and references to Appendices
MENIN ROAD	23/9/17		Capt Scrimich relieved in the line by Capt Dunlop M.C. 3rd Batt. Lt Mason reported as M.O.	
I.9.c.66 (M.D.S)			Reinforcements (B. category) arrived from attending course of XII Corps School for R.O.	WM
"	25/9/17		Capt Scrimich took over charge of Sick Collecting Stn, Kenningherst. Lt Mason reported for duty at M.D.S.	won
"	26/9/17		A.D.M.S. called and discussed plans for evacuation of hit & wounded in expected enemy attack on our front.	
"	27/9/17		A.D.M.S. orders & orders as to take precautions because his SB detected enemy attack tomorrow morning. I sent Capt Scrimich up to A.D.S. to take charge of moving bearers & others. Capt Dunlop M.C. to be located at GLENCORSE TUNNEL. Adv. orders R.A.P. of the One battalion in our front the Norwood Pioneers to INVERNESS COPSE. I reinforce all the forward bearer & bearer party with WALKING WOUNDED from plan trenches & bearers our route from line to	

WAR DIARY

INTELLIGENCE SUMMARY. 49th Field Ambulance

Army Form C. 2118.

Place	Date	Hour	Summary of Events and Information	Remarks and references to Appendices
Continued	27/1/15		BIRR CROSS ROADS (Walking Wounded Collecting Sta.) Received 1 Bearer Subdivision, 2 horse hs/ds Ambulance Wagons and 1 Motor Ambulance Wagon from O.C. 4th Field Ambulance. have brought up all our reserve bearers from RENINGHELST. Also 3 Motor Ambulances Wagons.	WDR
MENIN RD	28/2/15		Expected attack on our front did not come off. A/Snt. Celeer stone hire instructions to still take the Cantonary prisoners. Very few Casualties have come through this Ambulance since we took over here on Feb 15/16 a.m.	WDR

W. Francis Roy R
Lt Col 4 49th Fd. Ambulance
Commanding 49th Fd. Ambulance

Confidential

War Diary
of
149th Field Ambulance

from 1st March 1918 to 31st March 1918

COMMITTEE FOR THE
MEDICAL HISTORY OF THE WAR
Date 12 MAY 1918

WAR DIARY
INTELLIGENCE SUMMARY

49th Field Ambulance

Army Form C. 2118.

Place	Date	Hour	Summary of Events and Information	Remarks and references to Appendices
MENIN ROAD I.9.c.6.6. Sheet 28	March 1918 1		Received orders from A.D.M.S. to resume normal arrangements in this as "Precautionary Orders" orders had been cancelled. I returned horse Ambulance Wagon, 2 Horse Ambulances and 38 Bearers belonging to 45th Field Ambulance to their Unit. At about 5-30 p.m. the Elephant Shelter at Hooge Crater an emerging post was struck by heavy shell. 20 Bearers who were inside were unhurt, they came out & went into the tunnel & immediately afterwards another shell struck the Shelter + WAR broke in the Western half of it. There were one Casualty. 4.N.C.O.s reported for duty (Temp) from 48th Fd Amb in between Sanitary Officers & Inf Bde as I reported the bearers in the line to Coy. and Capt Trump M.C. + the a/c to bearers I took up. Capt. B. Sich Officer	
,,	2/3/8		Trump proceeded to RENINGHELST + took charge B. Sich Collecting St. Capt Schmid visiting tonight Curlis afternoon turn over to St Capt Schmid to take steps to have the Advance Shelter repaired. I reported the removal of wound + sickness M.	

Army Form C. 2118.

WAR DIARY
or
INTELLIGENCE SUMMARY.
(Erase heading not required.)

49TH FIELD AMBULANCE.

1918

Place	Date	Hour	Summary of Events and Information	Remarks and references to Appendices
MENIN Road I.9.c.6.6. Central Sheet 28	2 3/18		For R.B. Assistance is referring it. Appointments in accordance with ADMS instructions. Made arrangements for the Sanitary Sq: of dugouts & tunnels in the Divisional area left of MENIN Rd. to be inspected by the Officer i/c Forward Bearers, Dugouts near ZILLEBEKE Lake & near to be checked with collecting	W.D.L.
"	3 3/18		Visited RENINGHELST in afternoon & to Checker Hill Collecting Station & Transport Lines	W.D.L.
"	(4) 4 3/18		We continued to carry out improvements at the M.D.S. Which is constructed with Cellars & Elephant shelters. Reconstruction work Composes of Cellars & Elephant shelters proceedings. R.B. on demand shelter at HUGOS CRATER proceedings. Capt Buchanan proceeded to A.D.S. at CLAPHAM JUNCTION to relieve Capt Scanlurch in charge of forward Bearers.	W.D.L.
"	5 3/18			W.D.L.
"	6 3/18		ADMS called this morning. Capt. Scanlurch in relief in the line by Capt Buchanan proceeded Home on Leave & took Collecting Station RENINGHELST.	W.D.L.

WAR DIARY or INTELLIGENCE SUMMARY

Army Form C. 2118.

49TH FIELD AMBULANCE.

Place	Date	Hour	Summary of Events and Information	Remarks and references to Appendices
MENIN RD. I.9.c.6.6. Sheet 28. (M.D.S.)	7/3/18		Received orders from A.D.M.S. that "Precautionary measures" 10.15 p.m. I sent Capt TROUP. M.C. to GLENCORSE WOOD & the reserve Bearers to report to O.C. Front Bearers for reinforcement of Bearers to the Line. Orders 3 horse ambulance wagons to come to M.D.S. from KENINGHURST. One Bearer Subdivision under Sgt. Ronzi, with 2 Motor Amb Cars & 1 Horse Ambulance Wagon reported here from 45th Field Amb. & are in reserve.	W2R
"	8/3/18		No attack this morning. I visited Bearer post at HOOGE CRATER & saw that the repairs & drainage were being proceeded with. I visited through Cadi tunnels, mended Tray 10th R.F. & found that situation improved in sanitation was progressing, though Stanley was in station of A.D.M.S. I returned the 2 Motor Amb. Cars & Fd. Amb. sent to O.C. [?]. Capt B. GRAVES R.A.M.C. (T.C.) reported for duty from England. I received orders from A.D.M.S. that Capt TROUP M.C. would take first Reserve Change of 13. R.B. in relief of Capt Nicholson who wished in writing report to this unit for duty. I have written to Capt Lt Morgan to relieve him in the "Precautionary measures" Stay Plant. Troop Received orders	W2R

WAR DIARY
or
INTELLIGENCE SUMMARY.

Army Form C. 2118.

49TH FIELD AMBULANCE.

Place	Date	Hour	Summary of Events and Information	Remarks and references to Appendices
MENIN RD I.Q.c.6.6. Centre	7/3/15	6 pm	Enemy heavily shelling front and back all day. Carrying Casualties away at 6 pm. Advancing behind a Smoke Cloud attacked & occupied our front & support trenches. [struck through] About 7 pm Casualties began to arrive at M.D.S., and up to 11 p.m. 4 Offrs & 11 O.R. had passed through.	
M.D.S.	9/3/15		Evacuation of wounded continues from R.A.P. & INVERNESS COPSE to HOOGE (CRATER went on satisfactorily. Here too difficulty in getting cars down from the line owing to the enemy occupying the communication trench. At 11 am. O/c of former Bearers reported that Line had been cleared. No 6 Coy from 5 pm 8/3/15 to 12 noon 9/3/15. 7 Offs. 57 O.R. [illegible] evacuated. Further open Change [illegible]	

WAR DIARY
or
INTELLIGENCE SUMMARY.

Army Form C. 2118.

49TH FIELD AMBULANCE

Place	Date	Hour	Summary of Events and Information	Remarks and references to Appendices
MENIN RD T.9.c.6.6. M.D.S.	9/3		9 Sick Collecting Stn. RENINGHELST. Capt Tombs M.C. proceeded to take over duties & charge of 13 R.B. Enemy drives out enemy this morning by 13. R.B. Capt Jeffrys R.A.	WM
"	10/3/18		A.D.M.S. Called & went with him to form field ambce near junction from Hellfire Corner. We then inspected some battery positions. Stella is improving. Casualties passed through M.D.S. in Mr.9H + 10H. 13 Officers 93 O.R. Capt Gunn relieved Capt Buchanan in the line. Capt Buchanan proceeded to RENINGHELST. Lt Jos on leave to UK tomorrow. Front Quiet.	WM
"	11/3/18		Front quiet. Lt Heron returned to RHQ from GLENCORSE WOOD. Been Post. S Lines now relieved the Scouse at all the posts & week & moves at M.D.S. Capt Buchanan proceeded to England on leave. Wounded passing through post 12h - 12h 10 O.R.	WM

11TH L.O.H. B.O.R.

Army Form C. 2118.

WAR DIARY
or
INTELLIGENCE SUMMARY.
(Erase heading not required.)

49TH FIELD AMBULANCE.

Instructions regarding War Diaries and Intelligence Summaries are contained in F. S. Regs., Part II. and the Staff Manual respectively. Title pages will be prepared in manuscript.

Place	Date	Hour	Summary of Events and Information	Remarks and references to Appendices
MENIN RD M.D.S. I.9.c.6.6. (Sheet 28)	12/3/18		A.D.M.S. called in forenoon. I sent back Horse Ambulance Wagons to Reinforcements & to 48th Fd Amb. I visited Sick collecting Post at REININGHELST. Wounded passing through 11/12th thro' 6700 - 1 Off. 8 O.R.	WAR
"	13/3/18		I visited G.O.C. 111 Bgde in afternoon. Raining in afternoon. Supervision of former area - left hundred leaks being carried on with marked improvement in sanitary condition of Command & Regt. areas. My men twice to have been in this area have labour and enormous amount of valuable Government property. Wounded passing through 12/13th = 12 O.R.	WAR
"	14/3/18		M.O.S. in Motor Lorry o/s at 8:30 am. XXII Corps. Wounded passing through, nearly known from 13/14th 1 Off. 7 O.R.	WAR

Army Form C. 2118.

WAR DIARY
or
INTELLIGENCE SUMMARY.
(Erase heading not required.)

49TH FIELD AMBULANCE.

Instructions regarding War Diaries and Intelligence Summaries are contained in F.S. Regs, Part II. and the Staff Manual respectively. Title pages will be prepared in manuscript.

Place	Date	Hour	Summary of Events and Information	Remarks and references to Appendices
MENIN RD M.D.S. I C.9. c.6. (Sheet 28)	15/9/18		Wounded passing through from them 14/15th 26 O.R. (This is above 23 graved (shell) also belonging to AUSTRALIAN TUNNELLING Coy.	WD
"	16/9/18		At 7.10 a.m. a bomb dropped about 80 yards behind the M.D.S. doing no damage. It is stated by the guns in charge at the time that 2 British planes were passing over. No F.A. were observers. Pieces of bomb dug up & sent to 37 Stri G. Wounded passing through from them 15/16th. 1 Off. 7 O.R.	WD
"	17/9/18		A.D.M.S. called in forenoon. Daimler M.A. Car damaged by shell (radiator perforated). Capt Gram reported at 16.00 from the line & proceeded for duty to Remingshot. Pay Parade. I went to Reningshot & interred S.C.O.R. Wounded passing through from them 16/17th = 8. O.R.	WD
"	18/9/18		A.D.M.S. called in forenoon. A good deal of enemy shelling & aeroplane activity. Shelling gap & hospital yards. Station & Amm Q. Gas Fountain & few howitzer yards. Wounded from 17/18th - 19. O.R. at M.D.S. includes 12 O.R.	WD

Army Form C. 2118.

WAR DIARY
or
INTELLIGENCE SUMMARY.
(Erase heading not required.)

49TH FIELD AMBULANCE.

Instructions regarding War Diaries and Intelligence Summaries are contained in F.S. Regs., Part II. and the Staff Manual respectively. Title pages will be prepared in manuscript.

Place	Date	Hour	Summary of Events and Information	Remarks and references to Appendices
MENIN RD I.9.c.66 Shot 28 M.D.S.	19 3/18		Enemy shells (H.E. gas & shrapnel) continue to burst within a few hundred yards of M.D.S. Wounded passing through now known 18/19th 1 Off. 48 O.R.	War
"	20 3/18		Wounded passing through now known 19/20th 1 Off. 38 O.R. Enemy shelling continues heavy.	War
"	21 3/18		Sunbeam Ambulance Car No.10. damaged by enemy action. Wounded passing through now known 20/21st 13 O.R.	War
"	22 3/18		Returns & Sanitary N.Co. & 45th Fd. Amb. were attached for duty. Wounded passing through now known 21/22 1 Off. 40 O.R.	War
"	23 3/18		Wounded passing through now known 22/23 1 Off. 31 O.R.	War

Army Form C. 2118.

WAR DIARY
or
INTELLIGENCE SUMMARY

(Erase heading not required.)

49TH FIELD AMBULANCE.

Place	Date	Hour	Summary of Events and Information	Remarks and references to Appendices
MENIN RD (MDS) I.9.c.6.6. Sheet 28	24/7/18		A/D.M.S. called. Capt Graves relieved Lt Hearn – stationed the latter (pre-arranged) for duty to RENINGHELST. Wounded passing through from Brown to Brown 23/24 12 O.R. Received news from others to Brown from Bearer Post at BLACK WATCH CORNER to O.C. Unit W. Riding Fd. Amb. Arranged to take this tomorrow morning.	W/Man
"	25/7/18		A.D.M.S. D.A.D.M.S. Corps Called & brought a Surg-Gen. R.N. & Lt-Col. M.O.S. A.D.M.S. called. Received orders from A.D.M.S. re relieving Bearers & got 3rd and 4th R.A.P. South of Menin Road. J.20.t. 6.4. Have now Bearer post at BLACK WATCH CORNER to ½ W.Riding Fd Amb. Health of the personnel has been on the whole, throughout the journey slight except from heat rashes in the form of papular eruptions. A few cases of pharyngitis occur, apparently due to inhaling air which has been affected by gas shells.	*Sheet 25

Army Form C. 2118.

WAR DIARY
or
INTELLIGENCE SUMMARY.
(Erase heading not required.)

49TH FIELD AMBULANCE

Instructions regarding War Diaries and Intelligence Summaries are contained in F. S. Regs., Part II. and the Staff Manual respectively. Title pages will be prepared in manuscript.

Place	Date	Hour	Summary of Events and Information	Remarks and references to Appendices
MENIN RD I.9.c.6.6 Sheet 28	26/3/18		Received orders to the ready to be relieved and to move at very short notice.	WD
GODESVERDELDE	27/3/18		Received orders to relieve reserve bearers belonging to 48th Field Ambulance which I complied with. Handed over the M.D.S. A.D.S. & Bearer posts in the line to O.C. 1/2nd West Riding Field Ambulance & moved the Fd Ambulance to GODESVERDELDE & there in billets. Bearers & transport sections moved by truck train from the line to POPERINGHE & thence there. On arrival at GODESVERDELDE we received orders of G.O.C. 63rd Brigade & are awaiting orders &c in readiness known by train at short notice to an unknown destination.	WD
"	28/3/18		Received orders to move by train (entrained), with men of 111th Brigade tomorrow morning at 9.55 a.m. Pay Parade. Round called.	WD
BEAUVEMAISON	29/3/18		Transport moved at 4.30 a.m. & remainder of Fd Ambulance at 6.10 a.m. under orders of G.O.C. 111 Brigade and travelled to HOPOUTRE SIDING S.E. POPERINGHE. Entrained there. Detrained at BEAUVEMAISON & received verbal orders to remain here in billets for the night.	WD

WAR DIARY

Army Form C. 2118.

49TH FIELD AMBULANCE

Place	Date	Hour	Summary of Events and Information	Remarks and references to Appendices
GRINCOURT lès PAS	30/3/18		7th Ambulance marched by roops to PAS, & went with Chiels at GRINCOURT. Very wet day.	WR
"	31/3/18		Received orders from A.D.M.S. to take over from 6C. of West Riding Fd Amb. at LA COUCHE on 2nd April, and to form M.D.S. for the Division. I visited LA COUCHE & made arrangements for taking over. Personnel resting & cleaning up.	WR

W.Morris Lt.Col.
Commanding 49th Fd. Ambulance

31/3/18

WO 34

140/2902-

COMMITTEE FOR THE
MEDICAL HISTORY...
Date -6 JUN.1918

M

Confidential

War Diary
of
49th Field Ambulance

From 1st April to 30th April 1918

WAR DIARY
INTELLIGENCE SUMMARY

49th Field Ambulance

Army Form C. 2118

Place	Date	Hour	Summary of Events and Information	Remarks and references to Appendices
GRINCOURT LEZ PAS	1/4/18		Sgt Bryan + 38 Bearers sent to O.C. 48th Field Ambulance as temporary orderlies. Capt Pigott and advance party sent to LA CAUCHIE to report to O.C. West Riding Fd Ambulance preparatory to 178th Div arr.	W.R.
LA CAUCHIE	2/4/18		I moved Head Quarters of Fd Amb to LA CAUCHIE and took over M.D.S. from O.C. West Riding Fd Amb. (62nd Division) with 1 tent subdivision. Leaving Lieut A.M. Stuart & remainder of Ambulance behind here to take over premises of West Riding Fd Amb in GRINCOURT. Received orders to arrange to take over premises in SOUASTRE in 2nd visit and to establish a M.D.S. I went to SOUASTRE to inspect premises which consists of a large school occupied by A & Q 37 Div. Capt Pannefurth of 48th Fd Ambulance in temporary duty.	W.R.
"	3/4/18		Patrol of Fd Amb. remaining at GRINCOURT marched to SOUASTRE under command of Maj. Nicholas & took over No 78 Rideout and against Rue Main Dressing Sta and preparing an entrance thro' the M.D.S. at LA CAUCHIE on to divert at 9 am. Transfer from F.A. am 2/3rd & 2 A.M. 5.5. P.R. to Clos. Wounded passing through from F.A. am 1 am F.A. am.	W.R.

Army Form C. 2118.

WAR DIARY
or
INTELLIGENCE SUMMARY.
(Erase heading not required.)

Instructions regarding War Diaries and Intelligence Summaries are contained in F. S. Regs., Part II. and the Staff Manual respectively. Title pages will be prepared in manuscript.

Place	Date	Hour	Summary of Events and Information	Remarks and references to Appendices
SOUASTRE	4/4/18	9.am	Handed over Ambulance SIt'S at LACOUCHIE to an Officer of 4th Fd Amb. GUARDS Division, & moved M.D.S. back to SOUASTRE.	General
		9.30am	M.D.S. at SOUASTRE & Commenced to take in. I attended Conference at Adv.H.Q. Office. Colvin & received instructions re Forthcoming battle operations. J + Major Dickson visited AUTHIE + Prospected in available Sites for Aracin Dressing Station, a large area about 400 yds EAST of the Village, with a view to the possibility of a withdrawal from our present front. 1 Sgt + 37 Bearers sent to O.C. Scott Fd Ambulance in for temporary duty. Women leaving through M.D.S. 12 noon to 12 noon 3/4th 3 Off - 37 O.R.	
"	5/4/18		Attack by 63rd Brigade S. Down. Casualties commenced to come in from A.D.S.S at 7.30 p.m. Casualties 12 noon to 12 noon 4/5/4 6 Off. 51 O.R. S.C.Prisoner O.R. 4 Buses placed at our disposal for evacuation of walking wounded. No. 21 M.A.C. Clearing M.D.S. Evacuation very slow owing to trains + motor Ambulances being held up at C.C.S. 3 enemy Planes bombed SOUASTRE	
		2.40 pm	Several Casualties.	W.M.

Army Form C. 2118.

WAR DIARY
or
INTELLIGENCE SUMMARY.
(Erase heading not required.)

Instructions regarding War Diaries and Intelligence Summaries are contained in F.S. Regs., Part II. and the Staff Manual respectively. Title pages will be prepared in manuscript.

Place	Date	Hour	Summary of Events and Information	Remarks and references to Appendices
SOUASTRE	6/4/18	1:30 a.m.	Attained "S" Ammunition Lorries through "D" 37 Div which cleared all walking wounded awaiting evacuation. M.A.C. Cars being held up at C.C.S. delayed evacuation of Stretcher Cases, but we were all clear by 9 a.m.	M/R
		9 am	A.D.M.S. called at 10:30 a.m. Wounded passing through M.D.S. 12 noon to 12 noon 5/6/15 — 20 Officers + 562 O.R. (this includes 14 O.R. Germans). This has been a quiet day # evacuation has been fairly easy. 12 noon to 12 noon 5/6/15 — French Feet 157 + Passed (sheet) 1111 — 6/7 — 10 Officers 164 O.R. (includes 83 passed(s) 4 Officers 52 O.R.: (includes 31 T.Feet.)	M/R
"	7/4/18		Wounded passing through (12h to 12h.) Sick	"
"	8/4/18		Very wet for the past 3 days. Wounded passing through from 12 noon to 12 noon 7/8/18 4 Off. 65 o.r.: (includes 14 Gassed Shell). Sick 12 noon to 12 noon 7/8/18 121 O.R.: (includes 96 Trench feet.)	M/R
"	9/4/18		A.D.M.S. called in am — Capt. B. Graves posted for permanent duty to 474 Field Amb + 1 bunch off Staff. Wounded passing through 12 to 12 = 8/9/18 1 Off. 36 O.R. (6 gasses Shell) " " " " = 3 Off. 62 O.R. (40 Trench Foot.) Sick	M/R

Army Form C. 2118.

WAR DIARY
or
INTELLIGENCE SUMMARY.
(Erase heading not required.)

Instructions regarding War Diaries and Intelligence Summaries are contained in F. S. Regs., Part II. and the Staff Manual respectively. Title pages will be prepared in manuscript.

Place	Date	Hour	Summary of Events and Information	Remarks and references to Appendices
SOUASTRE	10/7/15		Capt R.C. Mick. C.A.M.C. reported for duty from No 5 Stationary Hospital.	
(M.D.S.)			Wounded passing through from 12 noon to 6 noon 9/10 2 Off. 31.O.R. (Officer (SA) 5. 2 Off. 90 O.R. (Punct. ppt 40. WM	
			Sick " " " " " " 2 Off. 90.O.R. (Punct ppt 40. WM	
"	11/7/15		Wounded passing through from noon to 6 in noon 10/11 1 Off. 38.O.R. (Hosp(SA)8	
			Sick " " " " " " 1 Off. 63 O.R. (Read ppt 20 ppt	
			A.D.M.S. called in afternoon	
"	12/7/15		Conference of Fd. Amb. C.O.s at A.D.M.S. Office re impending movements in the line. I went to AUTHIE to inspect probable sites for M.D.S. in the event of a retirement of the Division.	
			Wounded passing through in noon to 6 noon 11/12 37 O.R. (General-1 (SA)) WM	
			" " " " " " - 2 Off. 95 O.R. (T.Rep 31)	
			Sick	
"	13/7/15		Wounded in noon to 6 noon 12/13/15 2 off. 40 O.R. (General-1 (SA))	
			" " " " " " 2 Off. 63 O.R. (T.Rcpt 1)	
			Sick	
			Orders telephoned instructions at 10 p.m. to be prepared for numerous casualties WM. to-morrow morning.	

WAR DIARY or INTELLIGENCE SUMMARY

Army Form C. 2118.

Place	Date	Hour	Summary of Events and Information	Remarks and references to Appendices
SOUASTRE	14/8		Normal cancelled all day. Wounded passing through 12 months mean 13/14th 1 Off. 15 O.R. (Closed 2 days) 3 Off. 65 O.R. (Trench feet 4.) Sick	WAR
"	15/8		Receiving orders that over to O.C. from EAST LANCS Field Amb on 17th inst. & to move in to billets at HENU. Wounded passing through 15 to 12 (noon) 14/15/17 19 O.R. (General Shell 4.) Such " " " " 1 Off. 40 O.R. (Trench feet 1) N.Coms. Coller. 9 Supplier 2 horses ambulance wagons to Corps stragglers post 13th Brigade coming out of the line in being relieved.	WAR
"	16/8		Received orders from A.D.M.S. to take over The Mill at AUTHIE from & open up a CORPS REST STATION on being relieved at SOUASTRE. Section plus 1 Nurse Subaltern, under Major J Cambell with Corps Rest Station the Mill now form a relieving party of the 1/1 as	

WAR DIARY or INTELLIGENCE SUMMARY

Army Form C. 2118.

Place	Date	Hour	Summary of Events and Information	Remarks and references to Appendices
ConTd	16/9/16		EAST LANCS Fd Amb & to prepare the premises for the reception of 250 Cases of slight sickness & wounds. ATrs cases the "Dummy". An Officer and advanced party from 3rd E. Lancs Fd Amb taking over the M.D.S. Tomorrow. Wounded passing through 12 hrs 15 to noon 17/9/16 2 Off. 35 O.R. (Gassed (O.3)) — " — 15/9/16 3 Off. 46 O.R. (T. Fri. 2) Sick — " — —	
AUTHIE	17/9/16		Remainder of Fd Amb moved to AUTHIE – leaving however M.D.S. at SOUASTRE (BAYEN COURT Rd) to O.C. 3rd E. Lancs Fd Amb. Opened C.R. Station at AUTHIE 2pm. Visited by at 9 a.m. D.D.M.S. IV Corps Divisional Staff etc. in At 11.8 a.m later by D.A.D.M.S. IV Corps. knowing nothing of at 2 hours notice known at I have orders during night — at 2 hours later during day. In case of sudden move I come under orders of G.O.C. 125th Inf Bde attached whilst in reserve to N.Z. Divn & Eventual to be signed for his medical arrangements N.Z. Divn & Renewal his medical arrangements.	

Army Form C. 2118.

WAR DIARY
or
INTELLIGENCE SUMMARY.
(Erase heading not required.)

Place	Date	Hour	Summary of Events and Information	Remarks and references to Appendices
AUTHIE	18/4/18		Visited the A.D.S, & M.D.S. of the N.Z. Division at MAILLY MAILLY, BEAUSART & BERTRANCOURT, with the 2nd N.Z. Div. Attended Conference at A.D.M.S Office. Received orders to open up a M.D.S at THE MILL in the event of active operations in this front, & have 1 Lieut Subcommission tier sections to be found & establish A.D.S. of regiment, instead of the Subcommission party proceeding at once in the Albert band position.	MR
"	19/4/18		K.A.Ind Coleur. Major Nicholson & 4 Bearer S/Bs reconnoitred the line of anticipated evacuation from heavy attacked acts. Returned at dust. Watched in the front. Acting Colour Capt. Mick. C.A.M.C. proceeded to Canadian Base depot Whitecroft Yesterday. Brot. Nicholson	MR
"	20/4/18		G.O.C from Coller is married & looking round the Front Stations 1 & 4 Officers attended conference with A/DMSs & A.A.R.H.E at Divl HQ.	

WAR DIARY or INTELLIGENCE SUMMARY

Army Form C. 2118.

Place	Date	Hour	Summary of Events and Information	Remarks and references to Appendices
AUTHIE	21/4/18		A.D.M.S. & A.D.O.S. IV Corps called & gave me authority to draw 300 pullovers & 3 bales of pillows from IV Corps Salvage Dump, and to take away any useful furniture from IV Corps School at VACQUERIE. Capt Cullen.	War
	22/4/18		A.D.M.S. called. I received orders to take over A.D.S. BIENVILLERS from and to hand over C.R.S. at AUTHIE to O.C. 2/3rd West Riding Field Amb. on the 24th inst. I visited A.D.S. at BIENVILLERS, & hutment lines & Dressing Stn at HENU & MARIEUX with O.C. 2/3rd West Riding Fd Amb for the purpose.	War
	23/4/18		Major Nicholson proceeded with 2 N.C.O.s & 24 bearers on an advance party at 9.15 am. to report to O.C. 2/3rd W.R. Fd Amb. 63rd Brigade received to be re-inforcement to N.Z. Division at 5 pm. Capt Buchanan proceeded with 2 Reserve Autoplaninis (sic – those that went yesterday) to return to O.C. 2/3 W.Riding Fd Amb for transport to line. Capt Pigot + 1 Lieut/Administra proceeded forward to O.C. 2/3rd W.R. Fd Amb at BIENVILLERS. 2 officers & 16 O.R. from 2/3rd W.R. Fd Amb arrived at AUTHIE (C.R.S.) as an advance party.	War

WAR DIARY
or
INTELLIGENCE SUMMARY.
(Erase heading not required.)

Army Form C. 2118.

Place	Date	Hour	Summary of Events and Information	Remarks and references to Appendices
BIENVILLERS. E.2.d.5.8. (Sh57.D)	24/4/18		Handed over at C.R.S. AUTHIE to Major Sneddon R.A.M.C, & O.C. 2/3rd West Riding Field Ambulance. Remainder of Ambulance moved by Motor head to BIENVILLERS. The transport moved to HENU. Took over A.D.S. (E.2.d.5.8) from O.C. 2/3rd W. Riding Field Ambulance, and responsibility for clearing the Divisional front, at 12 noon. All the bearers of W.R.Fd.Amb. relieved by my bearers in the line by 8.30 pm/Relief. I have from 48th + 50th Fd Ambs 1 Bearer Subdivision + 3 horse motor Amb. Cars each. Between 6 & 7 pm 3 bursts of enemy shelling took place in the village, wounding 14 men. About 130 yards away from the A.D.S. 2 or 3 shells burst quite close to the A.D.S.	
" HENU "	25/4/18	6 p.m	A.D.M.S. visited A.D.S. today and others are to move away H.Q. & all personnel who are not required at A.D.S. to HENU. This order complies with at 5 p.m. We are taken over at HENU	

Army Form C. 2118.

WAR DIARY
or
INTELLIGENCE SUMMARY.
(Erase heading not required.)

Place	Date	Hour	Summary of Events and Information	Remarks and references to Appendices
HENU	26/4/18		Scheme of evacuation from the R.A.P.'s is divided into 2 branches R & L. On Right Scheme Cases are brought by hand carry & Wheeler Stretcher by relays of bearers to FONQUEVILLERS & thence by Motor Amb. Car to A.D.S. at BIENVILLERS. On Left Cases are conveyed by hand carry & Wheeler Stretcher by relays of bearers to MONCHY-AU-BOIS & thence by Motor Amb. Car to A.D.S. BIENVILLERS. From A.D.S. Cases are conveyed to M.D.S. SOUASTRE, by Divisional Motor Amb. Cars. I visited A.D.S. this afternoon. BIENVILLERS has been subjected to fairly heavy shelling at intervals through the night & day. There is practically unobstructed passage heavy shelling at A.D.S. There are a certain number of shell cellars in the village which most of the personnel can find cover.	

Army Form C. 2118.

WAR DIARY
or
INTELLIGENCE SUMMARY.
(Erase heading not required.)

Place	Date	Hour	Summary of Events and Information	Remarks and references to Appendices
HENU	27/4/18		Visited forward Aerial & Relay posts in Right Sector, with Major Nicholson. (O/C Forward Bearers) between 7 & 9 a.m. Passing through W.O.S. 6 p.m. to 9 p.m. 26/27th ELR 12 Sick. 3 wounded.	
"	28/4/18		Visited forward Bearer & Relay Posts — Left sector, with Major Nicholson between 7 to 10 a.m.; Also A.D.S. BIENVILLERS. Passing through A.D.S. 6-6.30 p.m. 27/28th. 15 Sick. 6 wounded.	MR
"	29/4/18		Passing through A.D.S. 6 p.m. to 6 p.m. (27/30 Oct) Sick 15 OR. Held 8.	
"	30/4/18		Visited A.D.S. BIENVILLERS. Passing through A.D.S. Sick 19. 15 O.R. Unit. 1 Off. S. O.R. Case of No.35571 Pte H CRAIG R.A.M.C. reviewed by Brid. Commander who has remitted the two sentences by Pte. Craig (R.S.T.) of 12mo I.H.L. in c/c of B Army Road home — the pieces	

30.IV.18

Confidential

War Diary
- of -
49th Field Ambulance

From 1st May to 31st May 1918

Volume 34

WO 35
140/2983

COMMITTEE FOR THE
MEDICAL HISTORY OF THE WAR
Date 9 JUL 1918

49TH
FIELD AMBULANCE

M

Army Form C. 2118.

WAR DIARY
or
INTELLIGENCE SUMMARY.
(Erase heading not required.)

49TH FIELD AMBULANCE

Place	Date	Hour	Summary of Events and Information	Remarks and references to Appendices
HENU	1/5/18		Visited A.D.S. Brévillers, and Fonquevillers. WD found sheltors etc for Creation of additional A.D.S. at latter place we were unable to erect in between for erection of Elephant dug out shelter. Churn passing through A.D.S. 6pm to 6pm 30/1st happen Sick 14. Wounded 10.	WD
"	2/5/18		Sick passing through A.D.S. 6pm to 6pm 1/2nd 17 O.R. Sick. 2 off. 10 O.R. Wounded. GREEN CARD awarded to No.36524 Pte J. Carless by G.O.C. Divn.	WD
"	3/5/18		Visited R.A.P.s in the line + all bearer + relay posts + A.D.S. with District from 9 am. Today all evacuation from the line (left + right sectors) are being cleared through Fonquevillers + to have pine up the route through Hunchy-au-Bois. Drew Material from C.R.E. for Erection of Elephant dug out at FONQUEVILLERS. Case passing through A.D.S. 6pm to 6pm 2/3rd Sick 1 off. 13 O.R. Wounded 21 O.R. (including 12 Gassed)	WD
"	4/5/18		Passing through A.D.S. Sick 15 O.R. Wounded 1 Off. 9 O.R. Capt. J.R.M. HEGGS. RAMC (T.F) admitted to hospital nosto from 9/05 Fr Amb.	WD

WAR DIARY
or
INTELLIGENCE SUMMARY.

Army Form C. 2118.

49TH FIELD AMBULANCE.

Place	Date	Hour	Summary of Events and Information	Remarks and references to Appendices
HENU	5/4/18		I visited A.D.S. at BIENVILLERS + CAR LOADING POST at FONQUEVILLERS, both in Efficient state, proceeding satisfactorily at latter place. Military Medal awarded to No 74657 Pte GUNTON, J. and No 92203 Pte FOWLER, S.T.R. for gallant conduct near COMMECOURT on 10th + 11th April 1918. Cars passing through A.D.S. 6pm to 6pm 4/5th Sick 2 off. 19.O.R. Wounded 6. O.R. (H.V.)	W
"	6/4/18		Enemy shelling vicinity of HENU in afternoon. Cars passing through A.D.S. 6pm to 6pm 5/6th Sick 10.O.R. Wounded 5.O.R.	W
"	7/4/18		I visited A.D.S. at BIENVILLERS, also FONQUEVILLERS. Capt O.E. WARD. R.A.M.C.(T.C.) returned to duty from Base. Sgt SIMMONS, L. awarded "TEMOIGNEGE DE SATISFACTION" by French Division with British Army for gallant conduct during Enemy bombardment of BAILLEUL in March 23/24 1918. Cars passing through A.D.S. 6pm to 6pm 6/7th Sick 20.O.R. Wounded 13. O.R.	W

Army Form C. 2118.

WAR DIARY
or
INTELLIGENCE SUMMARY.
(Erase heading not required.)

49TH FIELD AMBULANCE.

Place	Date	Hour	Summary of Events and Information	Remarks and references to Appendices
HENU.	8/8/18		Stand sent but one 10 a.m. to form in rear station as clearing Cavalry etc. "Main advance" by 111 Brigade on left flank. I visited BRONVILLERS. For evacuees & rumours. 111 Brigade attack 2 p.m. Cases passing through A.D.S. 6pm to 8pm 7/8th Sick 1 off 24 O.R. Wounded 22 O.R. (including 10 Grave) (R.A.M.C.) Casualties few. Main enterprise did not commence till 8 p.m. The majority being caused by enemy shelling after the objective had been gained.	
	9/8/18		I visited A.D.S. BRONVILLERS. Cases passing through A.D.S. 24h to 8pm 7/8th Sick 1 Off 28 O.R. Wd 8 off 79 O.R. Rations 4 O.R. 1 Off. Wd 8 Off 79 O.R. (1 Off. 1 O.R. died)	
	10/8/18		Military head ordered to 303412 gpl (6/8th) S. Parker R.A.M.C. &c. Conditions following demonstrate on 10am April rue COMMANDOURT. Cases passing through ADS 6pm-6pm 9/10th Sick O.R. 14 Wounds - 8 W.R. including S.G. 2 frozen ears (? due to drinking the hole water others cleaner than are uncommon).	

D.D. & L., London, E.C.
(A8004) Wt. W1771/M2 31 730,000 5/17 Sch. 53 Forms/C2118/14

WAR DIARY or INTELLIGENCE SUMMARY

Army Form C. 2118.

49TH FIELD AMBULANCE

Place	Date	Hour	Summary of Events and Information	Remarks and references to Appendices
HENU	1/15/17		MDnS called the morning & taken over home lines. Coys pass through A.D.S. from 6pm to 8pm. Relief 7 O.R.	
	12/1/17		Enemy bombarded FONQUEVILLERS lines with Gas shells for several hours last night. Coys passing through A.D.S. 6pm to 8pm. Relief 7 O.R. Between 10 O.R. Wrtk Sick 10 O.R. Wounded G.S. 1 Off. 10 O.R. Hostile Gunfire 4 & 6 Off. 7 & 5 O.R. Capt Rankanu, Capt Hays + 30 O.R. of this Unit Evacuated. General. Pleise. All appeared at same time the personnel turned by a Go. shell burst up that same time the personnel turned by a rickshaw, were always excellent & cleared large numbers of Severe cases, were very trying anxious times. This being Severe Gas Shell burst at the Car loading Post, FONQUEVILLERS rendered the place untenable so I was able to Move to places away from the vicinity. Coming through FONQUEVILLERS, to Front a Relay Post at E.22.b.6.7 to HANNES CAMP. Evacuation of Horse Lines.	(Sketch)
Sheet 57D				

Army Form C. 2118.

WAR DIARY
or
INTELLIGENCE SUMMARY.
(Erase heading not required.)

49TH FIELD AMBULANCE.

Place	Date	Hour	Summary of Events and Information	Remarks and references to Appendices
HENU.	13/5/18		Green Cross from FINCHVILLERS through PIERNEVILLERS (A.D.S.) to M.D.S. Bearers worked without a hitch. Capt Pigott R.A.M.C. + the A.D.S. personnel worked splendidly, as did Major Mitchelson, Capt Muldoon & the staff at FINCHVILLERS. The M.A.C. on arrival of 1st, 49 & 51st cars did splendidly from start to cleaning the cars. By Motor. R.A.M.C. personnel for Stretcher duty attd. to 10th R.F. Cross proceeding through A.D.S. 6pm 12th to 6pm 13th. 2 Offrs. 9 O.R. GASSED (Blue) 4 Offs. 127 O.R. FINCHVILLERS still full of gas. Arrangements for cleaning the air [illegible] put off for being taken. Meanwhile in-exertion is being [illegible] instructs through MANNEQUIN CAMP. 3 ...sent in the following recommendations: Capt A/Major C Mickleham jr M.C.; Sgt ROUSELL of 49th Field Amb for M.M.	M.C.
HENU.	14/5/18		Received to hand new A.D.S. + Bearer post to O.C. 2/5 W. Riding Fd Amb. Relief being achieved 18th May 1918. O.C. 2/5 W. R. Fd. Amb. called in to arrange hrs and make arrangements for the relief. I recommend 1 Clergy hon. nursing recommendation forwarded :- Capt Buchanan for M.C.	

Army Form C. 2118.

WAR DIARY
or
INTELLIGENCE SUMMARY.
(Erase heading not required.)

49TH FIELD AMBULANCE

Place	Date	Hour	Summary of Events and Information	Remarks and references to Appendices
	14/8/16 contd.		Pte DOWNEY. R.A.M.C + Pte TASSELL. A.S.C.(M.T) att. to M.A. awarded (Card?) D.S.M. M.M. Sgt Major RUSE & Pte M. KEELAN. M.M. All in connection with Gas Bombardment of FONQUEVILLERS on 19/6/16. except Sgt ROVERT, which took part in connection with attack by 13 R.B. on 8.7.16. One passing through A.D.S. Sick 10. O.R. wounded 3 O.R. Gas Shell 4 O.R. Evacuation still being carried on through HANNESCAMP. CAR LOADING POST at FONQUEVILLERS is now in use by As.	
HENU	15/8/16		Visits A.D.S. at BIENVILLERS & arranged for evacuation to come through FONQUEVILLERS again. Advance party of 2/1 West Riding Fd Ambulance reported at (BIENVILLERS) Receiving trans/ A.D.S. Lieut F.S.R. Warner 1/off 9 O.R. (general sd)	
		11.45pm	E.A. Moffatt 7 horses at HENV. One horse in our camp. I.H.D. horses kit. I tent to hospital. Several tents & a horse cart damaged. Many 7 the personnel were saved by the trout protecting bank round the tents	M.R.

WAR DIARY
or
INTELLIGENCE SUMMARY.

Army Form C. 2118.

49TH FIELD AMBULANCE

Place	Date	Hour	Summary of Events and Information	Remarks and references to Appendices
HENU	16/5/18		Further Collance Party from 2/7 West Riding F. Amb. reported at PRONVILLERS. 17 Reinforcements arrived from the Base. Cars busy through day. Sick 1 Off., 1 O.R. Wounded 8 O.R. (6pm to 6pm 15/16/17)	WM
	17/5/18		O.C. 2/7 West Riding F.A. took over the evacuation of sick & wounded of Divn at midnight. 49th Bearers have been proceeded Estables, under charge of Capt. Hart, to ST LEGER, leaving Smithick & 1 Lieut + 3rd Division & A Captain, Det ST LEGER. 1 Tent Subdivision & H.Q Bearer Divne bearer proceeded to ST LEGER. Divne (72 O.R.) Came under orders of G.O.C. 63rd Brigade. Ready to have at short notice, in reserve to New Zealand Div. Transport & remained at Henu, to keep C.O. & D.O.R. proceeded to wounded & known at 5 pm. I remain here till I know over the evacuation of St Regis at 5 pm. Cars busy through A.D.S. 6 pm to 8 pm 16/17/17. A line at 6 am 17th Cars busy through A.D.S. & A.D.S. BRONVILLERS known now to O.C. 2/7	WM
HENU 17/5/18			Evacuation of left Corps Sect & A.D.S. BRONVILLERS to West Riding Field Ambulance 6 am.	WM

WAR DIARY
or
INTELLIGENCE SUMMARY.
(Erase heading not required.)

Army Form C. 2118.

49TH FIELD AMBULANCE

Place	Date	Hour	Summary of Events and Information	Remarks and references to Appendices
AUTHIE ST. LEGER	18/5/18		Major Hitchen having handed over to the O.C. 2/1 West Riding Ft. Ambulance proceeded to Buire = ST LEGER with all personnel for Reserve. M.A. Corps + Nuclear Stretcher bearers belonging to [Khi.] L.d.H. + Stretcher Ambulance returning to their units. Sick of F.A. lent. Moved to AUTHIE ST LEGER 9.30 a.m.	nil
"	19/5/18		Capt R. E. F. Nash. R.A.M.C. (S.R.) reported for duty from No 7 Stationary Hosp. B.M.Q. Wonders M.B.R.C. U.S.A. reported for duty from 39th Division. Church Parade. M.S. Non Com't our R.C. Pay Parade. [illeg.] hospital clean + scrub hick recommended to Reserve afternoon	Scott [illeg.]
"	20/5/18		Personnel occupied today in cleaning up equipment, baggage &c.	
"	21/5/18		[illeg.] Reveer [illeg.] Amin'n 4.30 Pkgs kitchen, + Fans Div'n 4/9 hrs in Scrub hick, next to rate hoard + Whitewash the Property of the Country. We had this we have taught in the [illeg.] of history Operation [illeg.] recommended this to [illeg.] no what [illeg.] of [illeg.] are Whit to take place.	[illeg.]

Army Form C. 2118.

WAR DIARY or INTELLIGENCE SUMMARY.

(Erase heading not required.)

49TH FIELD AMBULANCE

Place	Date	Hour	Summary of Events and Information	Remarks and references to Appendices
AUTHIE ST LEGER	22/9/18		Received Divisional Order "Practise Battle Positions" at 7.30 p.m. Lt/n Nicholson took the Bearer Division to 63rd Brigade Rendezvous at Bois de WARNIMONT arriving there at 9.25 am. The remainder of the unit is charge of [?] stand-by ready tomorrow by 9.30 am. I and the Officer i/c the Unit's attached a lecture on Anti-gas protection to Corps Chemical Adviser at 6.15 pm. Unless orders of C.O.s to division. All ranks have been lifted responsible for 1 hour each day from 22/9/18 to 26/9/18 inclusive. 3 of these exercises are to be at night. Box respirators worn by all ranks - this month from 9.30 to 10.30 pm. tonight.	K.M.
"	23/9/18		Box respirators worn by all ranks from 9.30 am to 10.30 am.	
"	24/9/18		On 63rd Brigade relieving our N.Z. Brigade in the line, this unit seem to be attached to G.O.C. 63rd Bgn. Bearer Division + 1 Tent Sub-Division [?] to be disposed of by Sgt N.Z. Divn of reserve in the mine [?]. Box respirators worn by all ranks 9.30 pm to 10.30 pm.	K.M.

WAR DIARY or INTELLIGENCE SUMMARY

Army Form C. 2118.

[Stamp: 49TH FIELD AMBULANCE]

Place	Date	Hour	Summary of Events and Information	Remarks and references to Appendices
ST LEGER LES AUTHIE	25/5/18		Box respirators worn by all ranks 9.30 – 10.30 p.m. I visited O.C. M.D.S. N.Z. Div. at Pvs. I also visited A.D.M.S. N.Z. Div.	WM
"	26/5/18		A quiet day, new street car work have except necessary. Box respirators worn by all ranks from 9am to 10 am. Commenced training under Section Commanders.	WM
"	27/5/18		Continued training. Visited by G.O.C. Division in the field during training.	WM
"	28/5/18		Continued training. Visited by G.O.C. Division & the following: No 37128 Cpl / 9/04/Sgt. No 34417 Sgt Maj. F.H.RUSE.: No No 2/153494 Pte A.C.CARTY D.C.M. M.M.: R. M. KELLAN M.M. A.S.C. M.T. attached.	WM
"	29/5/18		GREEN CARDS issued to following. Training continued. Lecture on "Precautions against gas" by divisl Gas Officer. C.O. attended Conference at HAMEL.	WM
"	30/5/18		Diphtheria Epidemic filled from S. Box Mobriston: Training Continued. Lt Omsted M.O.R.C. U.S.A. reported for duty. From No 4 General Hospital Lt Col Heron hurried to R.F. Vice Capt Cranmer M.C. held.	WM

WAR DIARY
or
INTELLIGENCE SUMMARY.

Army Form C. 2118.

49TH FIELD AMBULANCE.

Place	Date	Hour	Summary of Events and Information	Remarks and references to Appendices
AUTHIE - ST - LEGER	31/3/18		Admd. & A.A. resug & tea & both unwel Enphtheire Training Continued.	M

[signature]
LT. COL. R.A.M.C.
COMDG 49th. FIELD AMBULANCE.
31.3.18

Confidential

War Diary
of
49th Field Ambulance
from 1st June 1918 to 30th June 1918

Volume 35

Army Form C. 2118.

WAR DIARY
or
INTELLIGENCE SUMMARY.

(Erase heading not required.)

49TH FIELD AMBULANCE.

Place	Date	Hour	Summary of Events and Information	Remarks and references to Appendices
AUTHIE ST LEGER	June 1918		Training continues. Athletic sports held in the afternoon. Classes for Toinal + Physical phases of the men are given. Officers attended a lecture by the Consulting Surgeon to the Army, on "The Principles of Surgical treatment in forward areas". The F.A. is still prepared to move at 1 hour notice.	
	2/6/18		Field Ambulance Transport Competition been today. The teams went out very fond of the judges difficult. Received instructions from W.E.Lancs F.A. in the Training Continues.	
	3/6/18		Training Continues. Visited O.C. W.E.Lancs F.D.Amb. Couin + had arrangements taken over from him on 7th with on arrival heard at hrs. Cavan. Found a line from A.D.M.S. Saying that we would be ready to move tomorrow 5th. 49 F.A. transferred to 111 Brigade for the purpose of new Area.	
	4/6/18			
	5/6/18		F.A. Transport moves bryn. Scam hate, Arrives with Transport at 111 Brigade to stay at CANAPLES, leaving AUTHIE 12.30 a.m. Billeting party left at 7.30 a.m. to meet billeting officer at AUCY. W.B. + Capt Piggott AMIENS.	

Army Form C. 2118.

49TH FIELD AMBULANCE

WAR DIARY or INTELLIGENCE SUMMARY.
(Erase heading not required.)

Instructions regarding War Diaries and Intelligence Summaries are contained in F. S. Regs., Part II. and the Staff Manual respectively. Title pages will be prepared in manuscript.

Place	Date	Hour	Summary of Events and Information	Remarks and references to Appendices
DREUIL LES AMIENS	6/8/18		Transport arrived here at 3.30 a.m. Remainder of F.A. moved by Lorries, under 111 Brigade orders, from ST LEGER-LES-AUTHIE to XXII CORPS + 4TH ARMY arrived here at 12 noon. The Division are now in G.H.Q. Reserve.	WD
"	7/8/18		C.O. & 2nd in Command attended Conference at A.D.M.S. 11 a.m.	WD
"	8/8/18		C.O. & 2nd in Command reconnoitred over the ground in which the Division are now to work.	WD
"	9/8/18		C.O. & Major Sims reconnoitred the ground South of AMIENS.	WD
PLACHY-BUYON	10/8/18		Field Ambulance in answer to PLACHY-BUYON, under orders of G.O.C. 111 Brigade. (Transport by route march, remainder personnel by lorry). Unit went into billets. At Oliveton M.R.C. U.S.A. evacuated sick.	

Army Form C. 2118.

49TH FIELD AMBULANCE

WAR DIARY
or
INTELLIGENCE SUMMARY.
(Erase heading not required.)

Instructions regarding War Diaries and Intelligence Summaries are contained in F. S. Regs., Part II. and the Staff Manual respectively. Title pages will be prepared in manuscript.

Place	Date	Hour	Summary of Events and Information	Remarks and references to Appendices
PLACHY-BUYON	11/8		C.O. & Major Scewihich reconnoitred road Mont West of JUMEL. & reconnoitred.	War
"	12/8		The Division is under orders to be ready to move at 1 hours notice. Major Kitchin with the ambulance transport between JUMEL & CATTENCHY. C.O. & Capt Puget visited French "TRIAGE" in the ESSARTAUX — JUMEL Road, and reconnoitred the line between JUMEL & CATTENCHY.	nr
"	13/8		Major Scewihich & Major Kitchen reconnoitred the line between JUMEL & CATTENCHY. The latter took the Bearer N.C.O.s & showed them the country.	nr
"	14/8		Major Kitchen & D.A.D.M.S reconnoitred the line — hour of BOVES.	nr

WAR DIARY or INTELLIGENCE SUMMARY

Army Form C. 2118.

49TH FIELD AMBULANCE

Place	Date	Hour	Summary of Events and Information	Remarks and references to Appendices
PLACHY-BUYON	15/8		C.O. with Capts. Pigott & Nutt, & some N.C.O.s reconnoitred the front S.E. of BOVES & prospected for Suitable positions for A.D.S. at Boves, in the event of enemy attack. Maj. Scrivener presence in Special Reserve for 14 days to U.K. C.O. attended Conference of M.O.s at 2-30pm.	WM
"	16/8		C.O. took Capts. Pigott & Nutt & prospected BOVES for Suitable positions for A.D.S. & spent some time in the BOVE-CAGNY ROAD, also prospected for Suitable Site for Surround M.D.S. There are very few places in FUSCHEN, but it is anticipated that if the enemy attacks that village will be heavily shelled. A place suitable for a further M.D.S. in the vicinity of PETIT-CAGNY has been selected. Ony persons W.M. 6 p.m.	
"	17/8		C.O. with Major Kitchen, Capt. Nutt & 1st N.C.O.s. reconnoitred the vicinity of Boves having in view the clearing of Casualties from the enemy attack.	WM

Army Form C. 2118.

WAR DIARY
or
INTELLIGENCE SUMMARY.
(Erase heading not required.)

49TH FIELD AMBULANCE

Instructions regarding War Diaries and Intelligence Summaries are contained in F. S. Regs., Part II. and the Staff Manual respectively. Title pages will be prepared in manuscript.

Place	Date	Hour	Summary of Events and Information	Remarks and references to Appendices
PLACHY	18/6/18		Major Michelson & Bearer N.C.Os recommended for Military Medals re the Noye bie H<u>t</u> Viers & Boves. Q.M. S.A.W. BURDEN awarded the M.S.M. London Gazette Supplement June 17.'18.f. H.T. not arrived.	MR
"	19/6/18		Received orders to prepare to move into 4th Corps. First Army on the 20/2/18.	MR
"	20/6/18		Given orders to be in reserve to XXXI Corps (French), all transport moved off by road to arrive to PAS area.	MR
"	21/6/18 22/6/18		Remainder of Ambulance moved by train to MONDICOURT & marched to LILLERS at THIEVRES. HOrs and Eng moved by road to THIEVRES. Div remain in GHQ Reserve, & act with either XVII or Corps or IV Corps.	MR

Army Form C. 2118.

49TH FIELD AMBULANCE

WAR DIARY
or
INTELLIGENCE SUMMARY.
(Erase heading not required.)

Place	Date	Hour	Summary of Events and Information	Remarks and references to Appendices
THEVRES	23/6/18		Lt. Col. W.J. Roe left to-day to take over Command of 37th C.C.S. Major Nicholson took over temporary Charge. Capt. Pigot proceeded with advance party to take over Main Dressing Station at	Cu.
THEVRES	24/6/18		SOUASTRE	Cu.
SOUASTRE	25/6/18		This Ambulance took over Divisional Main Dressing Station at SOUASTRE from 2/1st West Riding Field Ambulance 62nd Division. Dressing Station is established in Farm and Annexes on the SOUASTRE - ST AMAND Road D.22.a.2.5 Sheet 57D. Receiving Casualties from Advanced Dressing Station BIENVILLERS (50th Field Amb.) and evacuates to C.C.S. via M.A.C. Cars. Transport lines are at HENU D.13.a.4.4 and Sgt. Teakin proceeded for temporary duty Sheet 57 D. One Tented Subdivision c/o Sgt. Teakin proceeded for temporary duty with 50th Field Ambulance.	Cu.
SOUASTRE	26/6/18		Capt. GREEN M.O.R.C. U.S.A. reported for duty from 67th Field Ambulance.	Cu.
SOUASTRE	29/6/18		Conference held at A.D.M.S.' Office. Owing to the outbreak of an epidemic of Influenza in the division it is necessary to increase the accommodation for sick in the division. This Field Ambulance opens an Influenza hospital under its own Tentage at Transport lines HENU Sheet 57D D.13.a.4.4.; Capacity 72 Cases.	Cu.

WAR DIARY
or
INTELLIGENCE SUMMARY.

Army Form C. 2118.

49TH FIELD AMBULANCE

Place	Date	Hour	Summary of Events and Information	Remarks and references to Appendices
SOUASTRE	30/6/18		Lt. Col. R.E. Todd arrived yesterday evening to take over command of the unit. Lt. Col. R.E. Todd to-day inspected the Dressing Station and Transport Lines of the unit and visited the A.D.M.S.	A.

Cuth Wedington
Lt. Col. R.A.M.C.
COMDG 49th FIELD AMBULANCE

SECRET.

WAR DIARY

of

49th. FIELD AMBULANCE

From 1st. July to 31st. July 1918.

Appendices IV and V are filed with Plans under "Main Dressing Stations."

yet his memory survives.

mention in despatches an

rewarded by a posthumous

a brave man and value d

presented him or his me

  Finally, on the 2

of the 2nd.Highland Lig

total of medical office

Division was so large i

the advisability of per

into the trenches came

point of fact, issued o

Yet there are frequent

officer in the front li

in the height of an act

Army Form C. 2118.

WAR DIARY
or
INTELLIGENCE SUMMARY.

49th. FIELD AMBULANCE.

JULY 1918

(Erase heading not required.)

Instructions regarding War Diaries and Intelligence Summaries are contained in F.S. Regs., Part II. and the Staff Manual respectively. Title pages will be prepared in manuscript.

Place	Date	Hour	Summary of Events and Information	Remarks and references to Appendices
SOUASTRE.	July 1st.	a.m.	Fine. Hot. Routine office & inspection of quarters &c. Visited Salvage Dump, Souastre with a view to obtaining a boiler to attach to a Disinfesting Box Chamber & any other material likely to be of value for constructional work.	
		p/m.	To visit HEMU with reference to the accommodation there for INFLUENZA, & general clearing of area & cleansing of vehicles suggested yesterday. No of INFLUENZA admitted for the day shows a marked rise on yesterday. NEW ZEALAND DIVISION relieving 57th in the line tonight. Lt LISA, M.O., U.S.A. reported after/his course of instruction with 50th FIELD AMBULANCE.	
	2nd.	a.m.	Fine. Hot. Picking of Wards for stretchers & General cleaning proceeding apace. Visited new site for Elephant Shelter Dressing Station on SOUASTRE-ST. AMAND Road. Met R.E. Officer in charge of the work & spoke to him about several improvements that might be made in constructions. The question of water supply to the site must be gone into. The place was started by the 62nd. DIVISION & was not very satisfactorily planned. Major SCARISBRICK returned from leave late last night. He will be O.C. of the Detachment at HEMU. Major NICHOLSON to visit M.T. Coy to try & get a boiler for a Disinfesting Chamber with piping to lay on steam.	
		p.m.	Lt LISA called for & departed to join his Division which is now under training with our 66th. Divisional Nucleus. Officer R.E. called to go into question of canvas roofing for the wards' Waiting room shelter for M.I. Room and a lean-to corrugated iron shelter for the Sergeants' Mess Kitchen. He states that the broken bricks for a Car stand which it is proposed to build can be obtained, without authority, from either FONQUEVILLERS or HANNESCAMPS. Telegram received from Chief Constable of Oldham stating that Pte H. CRAIG's wife was seriously ill. application for Leave for him was made immediately. Letter regarding our requirements in Stoves, lamps &c. for the coming winter received from D..A..Q..M..G. Triplicate copies of War Diary D.D.M.S. VIIIth Corps despatched to Base for safe custody. A.D.M.S. telephoned that M.O i/c 1st ESSEX REGT. complained about non-receipt of drugs from this Unit. The complaint was groundless. 112th INF. BDE. relieves 111th INF. BDE. in the line tonight.	
	3rd.	a.m.	Cloudy dull day. Colder. Cleared towards afternoon. Sent in estimate for Heating & Lighting apparatus for the coming winter to A.D.M.S. Certain R.E. material Felting &c. drawn from the R.E. Dump. Went round Baths, SOUASTRE with Baths Officer. Found suitable chambers for disinfestation had been made but they did not know how to use them. Suggested he should let me know when the R.E. Officer constructing the new Baths would conduct experiments with me. The steam is to be supplied from a small protable Galloway Petrol Boiler which can raise 150 lbs. pressure. A.D.M.S & O.C. 48th FIELD AMBULANCE had called & been taken round by Major NICHOLSON. Spoke to TOWN MAJOR regarding complaints from certain farmers about the methods of transforming barns into wards. /p.m. Visited	

Army Form C. 2118.

WAR DIARY
or
INTELLIGENCE SUMMARY.

(Erase heading not required.)

49th. FIELD AMBULANCE.   JULY 1918.

Instructions regarding War Diaries and Intelligence Summaries are contained in F. S. Regs., Part II. and the Staff Manual respectively. Title pages will be prepared in manuscript.

Place	Date	Hour	Summary of Events and Information	Remarks and references to Appendices
SOUASTRE.	July 3rd.	p.m.	Visited 48th FIELD AMBULANCE, PAS, & Supply Refilling Point. Captn. E.L.F. NASH, R.A.M.C, from HENU to be M.O i/c 1st* ESSEX REGT. Captn. H. GREEN. M.O.R.C. U.S.A. evacuated (sick) & struck off strength. Pte PARKIN W, R.A.M.C. Groom to D.D.M.S. VIII Corps joined.	
	4th.	a.m.	Cloudy & cold early, cleared later. 2 or 3 cases badly wounded by shell fire admitted early. 1 case of SCABIES admitted from 13th RIFLE BDE. Visited Divl Baths to watch new Disinfestation Chambers & Galloway Boiler at work. These should prove satisfactory when the chambers have been lined with blanket material or felt. To visit detachment at HENU on inspection & to see about practices being held for "stand to" "turn-out" orders in case of hurried exits, also re promotion of Sgt TATAM, A.S.C,M.T. To A.D.M.S Office to discuss questions of accommodation at M.D.S.- treatment of GAS CASES and the formation of a GAS CENTRE, also INFLUENZA EPIDEMIC. Lieut W. I. SUMMERS, M.O.R.C,U.S.A. arrived and posted for duty with HENU detachment.	
		p/m.	Orders for medical care of 92nd BDE.R.G.A. issued to O.C. HENU & Captn PIGGOT. Batteries are too far spread out to allow of one Officer doing the work as well as his ambulance duties} Some 3 or 4 shells put into SOUASTRE area between 2-30 & 3 p.m. Orders regarding SPLINTS to be carried by Motor Ambce Cars & method of exchange with Units issued. Fifth man from the Unit admitted to hospital with INFLUENZA. Wrote private note to O.C. Detachment HENU re striking a daily balance between serious cases of INFLUENZA transferred to 48th FIELD AMB. discharged to duty, & vacant beds in hand daily. Today 32 cases were transferred to 48th FIELD AMB. &there are 34 beds vacant (HENU) At 12.30 past midnight a Projector attack was made on ABLAINZEVILLE, 850 drums of GAS being fired, the gas drifting south along the enemy's line. Artillery Smoke & THERMITE bombs were also used to mask the attack. Enemy transport was heard entering the village previous to the attack. 10 of our patrols out. 13 wounded cases passed through M.D.S. during the day. 12 of these had not had A.T.S. at the A.D.S. About 11.45 p.m. enemy shelled roads & approaches to SOUASTRE with heavy shrapnel, continuing at intervals till about 2.30 a.m. No casualties were caused apparently. Revd. THOMAS, C.F.(Nonconformist) took to bed suffering from Influenza. He is quartered in the same billet as the three Ambulance Officers.	
	5th.	a.m.	Cloudy & dull. Pte H. CRAIG, R.A.M.C. left on special leave.	/Weekly

2353 Wt.W3544/1454 700,000 5/15 D. D. & L. A.D.S.S./Forms/C. 2118.

Army Form C. 2118.

WAR DIARY
or
INTELLIGENCE SUMMARY.

(Erase heading not required.)

49th FIELD AMBULANCE.

JULY 1918.

Instructions regarding War Diaries and Intelligence Summaries are contained in F. S. Regs., Part II. and the Staff Manual respectively. Title pages will be prepared in manuscript.

Place	Date	Hour	Summary of Events and Information	Remarks and references to Appendices
SOUASTRE.	July 5th.	a.m.	Weekly Sanitary & Health Report for unit rendered. Description of improvised splint as devised by Lt Stanley R Maxeimer M.O.R.C./U.S.A. M.O i/c 8th LINCOLNS received. Economy Returns for the Division received. 49th F.Amb do well in the saving of rations. Met O.C. 154 Field Co, R.L. Major Horsfield, who stated that the new Elephant Shelter Dressing Station was nearly completed. He promised any help we required to convert the hut, obtained from Town Major this morning, into a Divl Gas Centre. O.C. 55th Sanitary Sec (Captn A Banks-Ruffle M.C.) called. Orders for damping of Incinerator during hours of darkness issued in view of danger from Enemy aircraft. Permission of G.O.C. 37 Divn for O.C. 49th F. Amb. to wear Lieut Col's badges of rank pending grant of acting rank, received. Authy 4/1854/1A 37 Div, A.D.M.S. 5/10/35 both dated 1/7/18. Arrangements made to inoculate 20 men of No 2 Coy Divl Train with T.A.B. tomorrow at HENU.	(By.)
		p.m.	Notification received from O.G. 28 Mobile Vet Sec re evacuation of Brown Gelding Charger-Fistula Withers. 6-30. L/Cpl BOND to be interviewed by G.O.C. 111th Inf Bde., reference his application for a commission. Telegram from England that Pte CRAIG's wife dead & Mother-in-law very ill. 11 Gassed cases from 4th MIDDLESEX & 8th SOMERSET L.I. passed through M.D.S. during the day with ? mixture of Di-phenyl-chlor-arsine & Di-chlor-ethyl-sulphide (Blue & Yellow-cross Shells) 7 of these gassed between 11 & 2 last night did not arrive at M.D.S. till after 6-30 p.m.	
	6th.	a.m.	Cloudy - fine morning. Dull & sultry afternoon. A/L/Cpl BOND's papers forwarded to A.D.M.S. after interview with G.O.C. 111 Bde who recommends Commission. 1 case GONORRHOEA sent to No 47 C.C.S. & O.C. asked to notify A.P.M. XXII Corps in accordance with request of A.P.M. 37 Divn. O.C. 50th F. Amb called reference relief of our Bearer Sub-division on the 8th, details for which were arranged. It was also decided that his Unit should give all XX A.T. Serum at the A.D.S. as far as possible & mark both wrists with a "T" in all cases after administration. A.D.M.S. called. Showed him wards in course of construction, also hut taken over for Gassed cases, which he approved of. Details of retirement of Medical Units in the event of the line falling back were gone into & main points fixed were :- /50th. F. Amb.	

Army Form C. 2118.

WAR DIARY
or
INTELLIGENCE SUMMARY.

49th FIELD AMBULANCE.   JULY 1918.

(Erase heading not required.)

Instructions regarding War Diaries and Intelligence Summaries are contained in F.S. Regs., Part II. and the Staff Manual respectively. Title pages will be prepared in manuscript.

Place	Date	Hour	Summary of Events and Information	Remarks and references to Appendices
SOUASTRE.	July 6th. (con)		50th Field Ambulance will take over M.D.S. SOUASTRE, which becomes A.D.S. & continues clearance of new line. 48th Field Ambulance will open as M.D.S. at PAS. 49th Field Ambulance Tent Sub-divisions rendezvous at HENU await orders at "Stand-to" to return either to PAS or further West & be held in reserve. Major Nicholson to HENU to go into stock of Stretchers & Blankets now held at SOUASTRE & HENU.	
		p.m.	O.C. to HENU on inspection &c. O i/c Supplies to be written to regarding provision of Fresh Milk & Tinned Fruit for INFLUENZA cases at HENU. Further application for special leave for Pte J. H. BROWN put in, telegraphic police confirmation of his father's illness having been obtained. Captn Mc GIURE, R.A.M.C. M.O i/c R.E. admitted with Shrapnel wound Rt Scapula Region. No of "SICK" dealt with by 49th F. Amb for week:- 155. of these, 37th Division :- 117. Small Clinical Chart devised, & duplicated for use with Field Medical Cards in the case of Sick.	Copy App.I.
	7th	a.m.	Warm. Fine. Interviewed No 38138 Dr Wilson J.T. R.F.A. asking for advance of pay. Fr 40 allowed. do No 174670 Dr Barker H.V. R.G.A. asking for special leave owing to Mother's illness Instructed him to get Police confirmation. Notification received that Lt Col F.A. BESLEY, M.C.N.A., U.S.A., appointed Consultant I' American Corps & facilities to be afforded to visit American patients in all Medical Units, also to confer with Consultants in the area. Written Orders issued for the relief in the line of "C" Sec Bearer -Subdivision by those of "B" Sec tomorrow. Visited 153 Co, R.E. & asked the adjutant to try & obtain whitewash for use in this Unit. Fr 6,000 drawn by Major Nicholson & paid into Imprest. Captn Piggot refunded Fr 240 lent from Canteen Funds for purpose of advancing pay to men going on leave &c.	
		p.m.	M.O. i/c 13th K.R.R.C. (Captn Rutherford, R.A.M.C) called to make arrangements for care of Influenza patients to be left in SOUASTRE when the Regiment goes into the line tonight. /It	

Army Form C. 2118.

WAR DIARY
or
INTELLIGENCE SUMMARY.

(Erase heading not required.)

49th. FIELD AMBULANCE.

JULY 1918.

Instructions regarding War Diaries and Intelligence Summaries are contained in F.S. Regs., Part II. and the Staff Manual respectively. Title pages will be prepared in manuscript.

Place	Date	Hour	Summary of Events and Information	Remarks and references to Appendices
SOUASTRE.	JULY 7th.		It was suggested that the M.O. of the Battn being relieved should take charge of them as the accumulation of work for officers of this Unit, which is under strength & in two detachments is becoming more than they can manage. Report called for by A.D.M.S. on the use of Bicarbonate of Soda as a prophylactic draught. L/Cpl J. F. Lintott & Pte G.S. Norman to Third Army Rest Camp.	App.II A.J.—
	8th.	a.m.	Cloudy & dull. 12 further Gassed cases from the same two Units as previously notified, passed through M.D.S. in last 24 hours. " Delayed action cases. Notice received that Indents for Medical Comforts on No 5 Supply Depot, PREVENT, were to be in by 12 noon on Mondays & Thursdays for our Medical Units. Notice regarding scheme for selling fresh Vegetables & Fruit at cost price in Divisional Canteens received. Assessment of requirements to be submitted by Units. O.C. 37th M.T.Co asked to hasten discharge of Sunbeam Ambulance Car which was sent to Workshop for overhaul. Run on cars at present is great in view of the Influenza epidemic & the fact that we are assisting 50th Field Ambce with 2 cars to clear the line. Unit's Gas N.C.O. took mouth piece & container of 2 S.B.Rs for repair to Gas School, also to fit C.O's mask with triplex Eye-pieces. Relief of "C" Sec bearers by "B" Sec started at noon today. O.C. & Major Nicholson to visit Lt.Col. Jackson,D.S.O. O.C. 13th F.R.R.C. ill with Influenza On to Divl Baths to see if the Disinfestation Chambers had yet been got going. Met A.D.M.S. at Baths.	
		p/m.	Notification received of opening of Corps Rest Station at MONT RENAULT BERNE, staffed from Division in Corps Reserve, with 1 clerk of each of the other Divisions. Cases for transfer will be collected at Field Ambce, MARIEUX WOOD, I.19.c.2.2. (Sh 57D) Accommodation at first 300. Allotment to Left (37th) Divn, 100 cases. D.R.O. 5607 (Horsemastership) received & to be brought to special notice of O i/c & Senior M.O. i/c Transport. O.C. to visit 41st 65th & 61st Labour Co Camps to arrange Medical supervision by an Officer of this Unit as a temporary measure. Captn PIGGOT detailed & written orders issued, copies being sent to all concerned. 92nd Bde, B.G.A. having now received a M.O. Reinforcement, our Officer is relieved of duty. Winter Hutting required sent in. O.C. Detachment, HENU, called on routine matters. /Telegram	App.III. A.J.— 

Army Form C. 2118.

WAR DIARY
or
INTELLIGENCE SUMMARY.

49th FIELD AMBULANCE. JULY 1918

(Erase heading not required.)

Instructions regarding War Diaries and Intelligence Summaries are contained in F. S. Regs., Part II. and the Staff Manual respectively. Title pages will be prepared in manuscript.

Place	Date	Hour	Summary of Events and Information	Remarks and references to Appendices
SQUASTRE	July 8th (Con)		Telegram notifying illness of Dr Wilkes' wife received & forwarded to A.D.M.S. He was last home on leave in Feby on the same plea.	(sgd)
	9th.	a.m.	Thunderstorm & some rain during night. Fine & cooler today. Dr Wilkes to get Police confirmation & Medical Certificate as to Wife's illness. Officers' Mess windows & Kitchen fly-proofed this day. "C" Sec Bearers engaged in arranging bivouacs &c. Party to get bath & change of clothing this evening. Several men required new clothing - S.D. Jackets & Trousers &c to replace kit torn by barbed wire. O.C. to HENU on inspection where A.D.M.S. went round Camp also. Later went to see Russian Pit Delousing Chamber in 50th Field Ambce Lines. I regard it as unsatisfactory & unscientific, requiring considerable effort to deal with very small amounts of clothing which have to be exposed to the heat for a considerable time.	
		p.m.	Precautionary orders on Yellow Cross Gas Shelling issued. C.R.S. PONT RENAULT FARM opens tomorrow 10th. List of clothing &c. required by "C" Sec obtained at Parade of kit. In accordance with "G" Orders Gas Masks will be worn for 1 hour daily as practice. Orders for one week issued. Advanced Depot Medical Stores unable to supply Quinine & other antipyretics usually used for treatment of Influenza. A.D.M.S. asked if anything can be done to expedite supplies. Sent a further copy of Hutting Return to A.D.M.S. in response to wire to expedite & replied that this Return had been rendered direct to "Q" there being no A.D.M.S. stamp on original memo. Clouded over & rained during the afternoon. About 6-45 p.m. one enemy Aircraft brought down apparently by Anti-aircraft fire.	
	10th.	a.m.	Cloudy, cooler. All ranks wore S.B.R. for one hour. A.F.M. sent in Ford Car for Dental treatment. Same car conveyed a Venereal case to 12 C.C.S. LONGPRE. Estimate of quantities of Fresh Vegetables & Fruit for the Unit received from Quartermaster's Dept. Local prices obtaining at present are far too high for the canteen funds available to allow of issue generally. Further details of probable cost will be obtained from O i/c Divl Canteens. Notification received that only 10 case for the Divn per day would be sent to C.R.S. till /allotment	(sgd)

Army Form C. 2118.

WAR DIARY
or
INTELLIGENCE SUMMARY. 49th FIELD AMBULANCE.

(Erase heading not required.)

Instructions regarding War Diaries and Intelligence Summaries are contained in F.S. Regs., Part II. and the Staff Manual respectively. Title pages will be prepared in manuscript.

Place	Date	Hour	Summary of Events and Information	Remarks and references to Appendices
SOUASTRE.	JULY 10th. (Con)		allotment is filled. We transfer through 48th Field Ambce which makes for simplicity of Returns &c. Further special Indent for Medical Stores sent in. Drugs are urgently required. Under 37 Div No Q.246 the monthly Tonnage Return will be rendered on a special pro-forma.	
		Noon	O.C. asked to meet A.D.M.S. & A.A.Q.M.G. (Lt. Col Reid, D.S.O) at the Divl Baths to discuss the question of Disinfestation. There is still too much attention paid to an individual man picking up stray verminous insects & too little to the General mass of infestation in the whole Division. The speed & frequency with which men can be put through are the main features to be considered. It is putting too great a strain on any Divl Baths to expect them to deal with the disinfestation of:— (a) Outer clothing. (b) Dirty underclothing going to Laundry. (c) Clean underclothing coming from Laundry. I am against disinfestation by Ironing.	

		p.m.	The following extracts from Divl Intelligence Summary for period 6 a.m. to 6 a.m. 8th/9th. are of interest:—
			"Under cover of heavy Trench Mortar bombardment, enemy made an unsuccessful attempt to raid our post at I.3.c.1.7".
			1 Officer & 10 O.R. Wounded passed through M.D.S. during that period.
			Under distribution of Enemy forces:—
			  Group Prince Rupprecht available 26 Divisions.
			  Group Crown Prince " 20 "
			  Groups other. " 6 "
			    Total Reserves available 52 Divisions.
			General Plan of Main Dressing Station, SOUASTRE, copies added.
			General Plan of alternative Protected Dressing Station on SOUASTRE-STAMAND Road, copies added. This Station was originally designed & started by 62nd Divn R.E. It consists of a series of English Elephant Shelters let into the side of the road & covered by sand-bags & earth for splinter protection only. From the air it would resemble gun-pits and if by chance a shell did drop into the excavation between two shelters, it would seriously damage any occupants of both who happened to be there. It is not Gas-proof & is difficult to render so. Water tank would have to be filled from Water carts by hand-pump.
				APP. IV.
				APP. V.
				(filed with Nara-W.D.)

		6 p.m.	Lieut & Qmr. PYLES (Harry Leyland) reported for duty with this Unit from 1/1 E. Lancs F. Amb. 42nd Divn under Authy D.G. No /92/9 d/-5.7.18.	

Army Form C. 2118.

WAR DIARY
or
INTELLIGENCE SUMMARY.
(Erase heading not required.)

49th FIELD AMBULANCE.

JULY 1918.

Place	Date	Hour	Summary of Events and Information	Remarks and references to Appendices
SOUASTRE.	July 11th	a.m.	Windy & cloudy. Further rain during night. Lt Manuel Garrido MORALES M.O.R.C.,U.S.A. evacuated from this Unit on 25/6/18 rejoined for duty late last night under D.M.S. 4th Army authority from EU. Wounded admitted during the night were 1 Officer & 17 O.R's 37 Divn & Corps Troops 10 O.R's, which includes 4 gassed cases Yellow Cross Shell. 1 man admitted dead with very severe injuries to abdomen & both thighs fractured. C.O. to HENU to inspect with special reference to Gas Mask practice & accommodation for Lt & Qmr Fyles. Visited new Divl Baths which are operating today for the first time, the delousing of outer garments being done by ironing. Went over structural alterations & additions to g hut, which we shall convert into a Divl Gas Centre, with an Officer from 154 Coy, R.E. Whitewashing Canvas roofing & rails for C.G.S. Evacuation ward at M.D.S. completed today. stretchers make a wonderful difference in the appearance of a Mud walled French Barn. Midden in front of Officers' Mess being cleared by the farmer today.	
		p.m.	One Ford Car to workshop today. Lt & Qmr Fyles to HENU to take over duty as Quartermaster from Q.M.S. Burden who has acted in that capacity since 26th Novr 1917. "A" 37 Divn asked if St ANAND Cemetery could now be used. Reply "yes" - authority 2nd Divn "Q" Burial arranged for tomorrow afternoon 3 p.m. 4 men of the Unit will dig the grave. C of E Padre called reference burial. Brief synopsis of results of American Research Commission on Trench Fever received. The disease is caused by a virus permeable to filters. Can be conveyed by the bite of a louse for 12 days. Virus present in urine & saliva of the cases. Full report to be published later. Rained heavily during afternoon & at night. Some hail. Signal for Cloud Gas attack will be ringing of SOUASTRE Church bell for 15 minutes.	
	12th.	a.m.	Cloudy. Heavy showers. A.P.M. 37 Divn & Capt Robertson, R.E. to Dental Surgeon. Pamphlet of instruction in the abolition of Flies received. The following appears to be a particularly useful formula for House & Yard use. Soak blotting-paper & spread in Formaldehyde ..... 2 tablespoonsful. a soup plate or saucer, keeping Sugar ..... 1 Dessert spoonful. moist. Filtered lime Water ½ pint. Water add to make up ½ pint.	

Army Form C. 2118.

WAR DIARY
or
INTELLIGENCE SUMMARY. 49th FIELD AMBULANCE. JULY 1918.
(Erase heading not required.)

Place	Date	Hour	Summary of Events and Information	Remarks and references to Appendices
SOUASTRE.	JULY 12th. (Con)		Instructions regarding latest date after manufacture that Sera & Vaccines may be used received. Personnel of T.M. Batteries & Intrenching Battns to have previous Unit shown on all Casualty reports & orders issued to that effect. Orders issued for Lt M. G. MORALES, M.O.R.C.,U.S.A. to proceed to PERU this afternoon for duty in relief of Lt SUMMERS,M.O.R.C.,U.S.A. who will report to SOUASTRE for duty & instruction. Papers regarding Lt & Qmr PYLES sent to Messrs HOLT & Co. Points requiring more attention in precautions against GAS recd from "G" thro' A.D.M.S. 37 Div. Started obtaining cart-loads of bricks from FONQUEVILLERS with which to floor Gas Centre & make a Gas stand.	
		p.m.	Sergt J. DONKIN reported for duty as a reinforcement from Divl Reception Camp, Orville. A design for Divl Xmas Card defining a heavy gun in action submitted by Pte SWIFT of this unit. also 2 designs by Pte HALFORD. C.E. Chaplain, Revd HARDY, V.C;D.S.O;M.C; called at M.D.S. SOUASTRE.	
	13th.	a.m.	Cloudy but fine. Designs for Xmas cards sent to "Q" 37 Divn. Aeroplane photographs of Hospital signs taken at 18,000 feet arrived showing good & bad examples. Passed on to 50th F. Amb. after noting that:- The minimum minimum dimensions considered effective are:-	

EXAMPLE

FILLIEVRES.

Best sign at PRENVIN. Cross 72 feet across with 24 feet breadth. Black cross best colour. Take care not to shadow by buildings or trees. Signs on sloping roofs show badly. Weekly Returns &c. to A.D.M.S. Report asked for from Lt MORALES as to circumstances under which he lost Frs 600 & certain Identity Cards between 3/6/18 & 4/6/18 while at ST.LEGER. He complains they were stolen. The matter had been previously enquired into by A.P.M. Divn & Corps but nothing could be ascertained. Owing to his broken English he had previously been arrested as a "German spy" A.D.M.S. & D.A.D.M.S. called on inspection.

Army Form C. 2118.

WAR DIARY
or
INTELLIGENCE SUMMARY.

49th. FIELD AMBULANCE.

(Erase heading not required.)

Instructions regarding War Diaries and Intelligence Summaries are contained in F.S. Regs., Part II. and the Staff Manual respectively. Title pages will be prepared in manuscript.

Place	Date	Hour	Summary of Events and Information	Remarks and references to Appendices
SOUASTRE.	JULY 13th. (Con)		As 63rd Bde are relieving 112th Bde in the line tonight went to see the Town Major to ascertain that the hut for Gassed cases, previously occupied by 112 Bde Signals would still be ours. He states 112 Bde want it. Asked him to arrange with H.Q. & let me know when A.A & Q.M.G. called. Latter called at Lunch time & said we could have the hut by right of possession.	
		p.m.	To see Staff Captn 112 Bde on the question & warn him of possible danger in using hut. Later in the evening Town Major called to say that he still proposed to put Signals in the hut, so I wrote him a letter again refusing to waive our right especially as other accommodation had been provided for the men. The body of No 47083 Pte T. OTHEN, R.A.M.C. killed by shell fire at 6-15 p.m. today was received from 50th F. Amb. He was on duty at "Z" Post. Orders received from A.D.M.S. to detail a M.O. for duty with 9th M. STAFFS Regt. in relief of Captn A.E. NORTON A.A.M.C. to 1st Australian General Hosp. Lt M. G. MORALES, M.O.R.C., U.S.A., detailed to take over on 15th inst & report compliance. 16 Wounded passed through during the day, of which 9 were of 1st Herts Regt. All evacuated to C.C.S.	
	14th.	a.m.	Cloudy. Tendency to showers. Church Parades held. Stocks of Standard Dressings applied for from D.G.V.O. Lieut Johnston, 154 Co, R.E. called regarding alterations to Gas Hut, & question of taking temperature of chambers at the Baths. The 5 Privates (reinforcements) who reported last night were interviewed this morning. Vaccine phials are required to be returned to the Base Depot Med. Stores. Orders issued to return carefully to Advanced Depots from this Unit. M.O. i/c 1st Essex (Captn NASH) called.	
		p.m.	Papers of Unit taken charge this afternoon. Administrative Instructions No 8 under No 271/32 regarding issue of Lime Juice in lieu of Fresh Vegetables received from A.D.M.S. No 6/35/73. O.C. to HENU on inspection with special reference to condition of horse lines in the present wet weather. They drain fairly well. Gave instructions that ashes from Cook-houses & Incinerator should be sprinkled daily on standings. Charger "Johnson" kicked on near fore shoulder now has well marked purulent discharge, & the leg generally is very oedematous. Gave instructions as to procuring Veterinary services at once, with a view to evacuation for operation. The animal is old & not of great value to the unit. One of the Operating Tents becoming unserviceable, replacement to be asked for. New billet for Officers & Sgts' Mess HENU inspected. It was taken over yesterday. O.C. reports	

Army Form C. 2118.

WAR DIARY
or
INTELLIGENCE SUMMARY.

49th. FIELD AMBULANCE.   JULY 1918.

(Erase heading not required.)

Instructions regarding War Diaries and Intelligence Summaries are contained in F.S. Regs., Part II. and the Staff Manual respectively. Title pages will be prepared in manuscript.

Place	Date	Hour	Summary of Events and Information	Remarks and references to Appendices
SOUASTRE	JULY 14th (Con)		that Patients relish tinned fruit now provided. Fresh Milk is not procurable. General condition of site & tent hospital accommodation good, despite the heavy rain. Telegram from Police, W.Hampstead re dangerous illness of the son of Pte Tyrrell, R.A.M.C. Application put in through A.D.M.S. for Pecial leave. Approval of L/Cpl Brown's special leave has come through. To sail on 18th. Sick admissions for the week .. 169 do. returned to duty .. ~~total~~ ~~169~~ .. 85 Battle Casualties dealt with .. ~~85~~ .. 102 of which 98 were from 37th Divn. TOTAL cases dea't with .. 482 of which 400 cases were from 37th Divn. Recovery of 3rd class Dripping from swill & Grease traps started in the unit. O.C. M.T. Column written to regarding a replacement for Pte Mc Kellan A.S.C. to be cadet for R.A.F.	
	15th.	a.m.	Rained heavily last night. Heavy cloud banks this a.m. Some sunshine. Pte SPENCER departed for Corps School for instruction in Brick-laying. Lt M.G. MORALES to 9th N. Staffs Regt fur duty. One Officer 1st Essex sent to 56 C.C.S. for dental treatment. Lt SUMMERS, M.O.R.C. sick in quarters with Influenza. A.D.M.S., D.A.D.M.S. & Area Sanitary Officer called, all bent upon inspection of the state of sanitation of SOUASTRE. The A.A.& Q.M.G. had apparently complained to Corps H.Q. that he was not satisfied with it. When pressed however specific complaint was not forthcoming. A.A.& Q.M.G. came about 11.30 a.m.& went all round unit with O.C. He agreed that at present there was not sufficient accommodation at the M.D.S. & that the present site was far from satisfactory. Alternative proposals for a new site were discussed. O.C. pressed for either the erection of further accommodation near new Elephant Shelter Station or complete removal back to HENU which latter it is thought would be the better proposal.	
		3 pm.	No 48073 Pte T. OTHEN, R.A.M.C. was buried with as full a parade as possible at StAMAND. O.C. attended parade. Note from Town Major re sanitation in SOUASTRE, he having received a complaint from Division. Two men of the last batch of reinforcements received have not had leave for some 2 years. An allotment for them will be applied for as soon as possible. Provision of appliances in case of Fire demands attention in the unit. Returns have to be sent in by the 22nd as to requirements in accordance with scale in G.R.O. 3269. /Rumours	

2353   Wt. W3544/1454   700,000   5/15   D. D. & L.   A.D.S.S./Forms/C. 2118.

Army Form C. 2118.

WAR DIARY
or
INTELLIGENCE SUMMARY.

49th FIELD AMBULANCE.

JULY 1918

(Erase heading not required.)

Instructions regarding War Diaries and Intelligence Summaries are contained in F. S. Regs., Part II. and the Staff Manual respectively. Title pages will be prepared in manuscript.

Place	Date	Hour	Summary of Events and Information	Remarks and references to Appendices
SOUASTRE	July 15th (Con)		Rumour of a commencement of a GERMAN offensive in the South received. 62nd Divn has moved in that direction.	(sgd)
	16th	a.m.	Thunderstorm with heavy rain at 5-30 a.m. Cleared later. In a raid last night on the front held by the New Zealand Divn it is stated that 70 prisoners were captured with only 6 casualties on our side. German offensive East & West of RHEIMS confirmed by Intelligence wire this morning. Some progress made by the enemy. Details lacking. Under authority A.D.M.S. instructions were issued to M.O's of 112 Bde that they should attend the sick at the Brigade Rest Station while they are in SOUASTRE. At present they all flock down to this Unit. Orders regarding Sanitation & Regularity in the Unit published in order to avoid any ground for complaint against 49th F. Amb. R.E. work on Gas Centre commenced this morning. New list of locations Corps Troops received. Spoke to D.A.D.M.S. IV Corps regarding our getting a supply of Syphon Soda from Corps Soda Water Factory. (Got information that there had been some trouble in the G.H.Q. South direction.) D.D.M.S. IV Corps had been sent to take over. With reference to returns required by "Q" they will be rendered as under:- Direct to "Q" 1. Surplus & deficiencies in transport. 6 p.m. Fridays. 2. Tentage return. 9 a.m. 12th of the month. 3. Personnel under canvas. (G.R.O.3148). 9 a.m. 11th do. Through A.D.M.S. Economy in man-power & expenditure) generally (G.R.O.2988)) ... 15th of every second month.	
		p.m.	Next of kin of Pte T. OTHEN written to giving details of death & expressing the sympathy of the Unit with the family. Leave applied for on behalf of :- (a) No 24766 Pte ROBERTS, W. R.A.M.C. Date of last leave Octr 1915. (b) No 77259 Pte NUTTALL, A.E. do do do Aug. 1916. O.C. to HKNU on inspection with special reference to provision of Fire appliances to conform with G.R.O. 3 Extincteurs will be indented for which, with present Fire buckets, will suffice for needs of Unit. /Training	(sgd)

Army Form C. 2118.

WAR DIARY
or
INTELLIGENCE SUMMARY.

49th FIELD AMBULANCE.   JULY 1918.

(Erase heading not required.)

Instructions regarding War Diaries and Intelligence Summaries are contained in F.S. Regs., Part II. and the Staff Manual respectively. Title pages will be prepared in manuscript.

Place	Date	Hour	Summary of Events and Information	Remarks and references to Appendices
SOUASTRE.	July 16th (Con)		Training of Cooks & Sanitary men gone into. "Charger" Johnson's leg better as the result of opening for drainage by Veterinary Officer. Authority for Lt. & Qmr H. L. FYLES to wear Territorial Efficiency Medal received & published in Orders. Later to 48th F. Amb. PAS to look at improvised baths & Disinfestation Chambers devised by Lt.Col. Clarke, D.S.O. Good but difficult to apply on an extended scale. L/Cpl Brown paid 180 francs advance of pay before leave. Last night of S.B.R. practice. Lieut SUMMER's surplus kit deposited at Divisional Dump & due receipts obtained & issued.	
	17th a.m.		Cloudy. Hot & humid but More breeze than yesterday. Enemy shelling of area recommenced. L/Cpl Brown departed for leave & Pte McKellan A.S.C. to join R.A.F. Special instructions regarding proceedure in the event of the occurrence of cases of ANTHRAX received under D.G.M.S. No D.G./11/1 d/-8.7.18-D.A.D.M.S.(San) 3rd Army No 159/6/Circ 149 d/-11.7.18 D.D.M.S. IV Corps No 3/MA/1 d/-16.7.18. A.D.M.S. No 6/31/30 d/-16.7.18. Full report by M.O. to A.D.M.S.(San) B.M.F. Copy through usual channels to D.A.D.H.S.(San) Army. Wire A.D.M.S. Sanitation. Repeating D.A.D.M.S.(San) 3rd Army. Medical, IV Corps. Medical, 37th Divn. Lt & Qmr Fyles to H.Q. to discuss various matters of routine with O.C. notably:- 1. Getting rid of further equipment, not really required by the Unit. 2. Obtaining Fresh Vegetables & Fruit to supplement rations against payment out of Canteen funds. 3. Provision of standard Notice boards to conform to Divl Orders. ? material to be used for. 4. Provision of Carpenters tools by purchase from Canteen fund. 5. Extra duty pay for Cooks. 6. Question of assessment of real saving in dripping - 1st & 3rd class, to be gone into. Orders issued for necessary entry to be made in History sheet of Box Respirators, i.e. Drill 7 hours from 10.7.18 to 16.7.18 inclusive. Notice received that Hydrogen Peroxide would not be issued except for special cases, other antiseptics to be used as substitute. Order to this effect issued.	

Army Form C. 2118.

WAR DIARY
or
INTELLIGENCE SUMMARY.

49th. FIELD AMBULANCE.   JULY 1918.

(Erase heading not required.)

Instructions regarding War Diaries and Intelligence Summaries are contained in F.S. Regs., Part II. and the Staff Manual respectively. Title pages will be prepared in manuscript.

Place	Date	Hour	Summary of Events and Information	Remarks and references to Appendices
SOUASTRE.	July 17th (Con)		Sergt Bristow brought from line for jobs requiring carpentry. Sergt Donkin sent in his place. Private note to O.C. 50th F.A. One case N.Y.D.Mumps from 8th Somerset L.I. reported - No 40769 Pte WHITMORE, A. Order regarding Box Respirator entries cancelled as with the new containers the number of hours occupied in drill is not of importance & need not be noted. Heavy thunderstorm about 8.30 p.m. News of latest offensive meagre. Pte RICKARDS (MT) reported in the place of Pte McKellan.	
	18th.	a.m.	Fine, cloudy, cooler. A.P.M. Captn Robertson, Lt Summers M.O.R.C. and Captn Cousins (A.S.C) from HENU sent for Dental treatment. Indent on B.R.C. Stores sent in. In accordance with instructions received from A.D.M.S. Major Nicholson was detailed to supervise the sanitation of the Transport lines of the 3 Infantry Brigades of the Division, with special instructions from O.C. 49th F.A. regarding points of interest with regard to Water Carts & Kitchens. Interviewed new Driver (M.T) reinforcement. A case of ? ENTERIC notified from C.R.S. a man of 124 Bde R.F.A. who passed through this unit on 24.6.18 diagnosed "I.C.T.Finger" & was sent to II N.Z.F.AMB (who were then running C.R.S.) on same day.	
		p.m.	New ovens & fire-range completed by Pte LAMPITT. Shed will be erected over it and used as a subsidiary kitchen. P.M.G. No 3 Mess, D.H.Q. asked leave to draw water from our Cart. Granted. Answered enquiry re PLUVINSIN waterproof material required in lieu of Ground sheets which will not be issued further to Medical Units. Asked for 136 sq.yards per section of a F.Amb. This will complete to same standard as laid down for Ground sheets i.e. 50, other than the 10 carried on each Medical Store Cart. Size of Ground sheet - 6'6" x 3'. One Officer of 13th Rifle Bde sent to 45 C.C.S. as a case of N.Y.D.N. Had shell concussion and has got no better. Heavy shower of rain during the afternoon. One of our posts was lost last night by a raid. Enemy apparently obtained 10 identifications One man managed to fight his way back after capture & passed through M.D.S. having been hit on the head by a stick grenade.	/19th.

Army Form C. 2118.

WAR DIARY
or
INTELLIGENCE SUMMARY.
(Erase heading not required.)

49th FIELD AMBULANCE.

JULY 1918

Instructions regarding War Diaries and Intelligence Summaries are contained in F.S. Regs., Part II. and the Staff Manual respectively. Title pages will be prepared in manuscript.

Place	Date	Hour	Summary of Events and Information	Remarks and references to Appendices
SOUASTRE.	JULY 19th.		Cloudy. Dull. Report that French had taken 8,000 prisoners and 100 guns received. Captn WALKER RAMC one of the Army Shock experts called regarding the question of administration of Gum Infusion in cases of Haemorrhage and Shock. Stayed to talk to ADMS who had stated on telephone that he proposed to visit the unit this morning. The matter of the General treatment of Shock was discussed with him. He left a stopper canula for infusion with the unit. ADMS and DADMS round the unit with O.C. as also alternative sites for the Field Ambce. Lt. W.K. MARTIN MORC, USA reported for duty and was posted to HENU as a temporary measure under instruction.	
		p.m.	Major Nicholson began his round of Sanitary inspections. Later reports indicate that the French have taken 13,000 prisoners and 200 guns. No 24766 Pte W. Roberts RAMC paid 150 Frs advance of pay before proceeding on leave to U.K. Paid Messrs Cox & Edwards Frs.11.60 (8/8d) out of Imprest A/c AUTHY D.A.D.O.S. 37 Divn L.P. 196 d/- 26.6.18. 3 or 4 shells into this area today.	
	20th.	a.m.	Fine. Warm. Two Enemy Aircraft over early. Spasmodic H.V. shelling of area continues. Owner of field objects to Car Standing we are making on the ground that it will spoil the field for ploughing. As the land has never been used for anything but pasture & not good at that, the N.C.O. Interpreter was told to let him lodge his claim & the Claims Commission can deal with him. Administrative Instructions No 10 Q343 "Improved method of fixing Eye Fringes for horses" received. The exact advantage is not immediately apparent. Pte Roberts left on leave to U.K. Reply received to M. letter asking that the system of Ambulance Car Inspection might be modified. In view of recent D.R.O. the correspondence can now cease. Regular inspections being provided for. Intelligence Summary 6 a.m. to 6 a.m. 18/19th. reports fairly heavy Yellow Cross Shelling of MESSRES & F.21. No increase of Gassed cases for that period passed through A.D.S. There was marked increase in the activity of the artillery last night in the sector of the line occupied by the N.Z. Divn.	
		p.m.	C.C. to HENU on inspection special reference t Transport, Clothing of Cooks, training of /Lieut.	

Army Form C. 2118.

WAR DIARY
or
INTELLIGENCE SUMMARY.
(Erase heading not required.)

49th FIELD AMBULANCE.

Instructions regarding War Diaries and Intelligence Summaries are contained in F.S. Regs., Part II. and the Staff Manual respectively. Title pages will be prepared in manuscript.

JULY 1918.

Place	Date	Hour	Summary of Events and Information	Remarks and references to Appendices
SOUASTRE	JULY 20th		MARTIN, &c. G.O.C. Divn had inspected Transport this morning and expressed satisfaction with the state of the animals lines and vehicles. Officers charger reinforcement arrived. A light built, useful, rather showy bay horse - mouth hard, but no vices. Action Good - despite evidence of having been down at some time. Clouded over during afternoon and rained heavily. Arranged with Lt Johnson R.E. & Lt Huyton (Divl Baths Officer) to test new Disinfestation chamber tomorrow morning at 11.30 a.m. Considerable increase in the number of Battle casualties passing through, especially GASSED cases from 10th ROYAL FUSILIERS. News of Franco-American & Franco-British offensives in the South is Good. Captn H. GREEN, MORC, USA, reported his arrival on return from ROUEN.	(Sgd)
	21st.	a.m.	Cloudy & windy. Some rain early. Number of Shell Gassed cases (Yellow Cross) which were dealt with from 6 a.m. to 6 a.m. 20th/21st were - 53 from 10th Royal Fusiliers. 2 " 9th North Staffs. In two instances the men were badly splashed from top to toe. In this Unit bathing and Soda Bicarb. treatment for Mustard Gas is no longer allowed. Routine is as follows:- (a) Completely strip patient. (b) Instil pure Vaseline or Paraffin into eyes. (c) Dry mop blisters or ulcerative skin surfaces - cleaning surrounding skin with gauze mops damped with Picric Acid Solution. (d) Paint over with Ambrine. This antiseptic waxy compound has to be applied warm to melt it & causes some inconvenience during application owing to its temperature, but the immediate relief is most marked as it soon cools down & forms a wax film over the raw cutaneous surfaces. (e) Dress in clean pyjamas. (f) Shock & Symptomatic treatment as required. Patients clothing is hung in the open air & taken away after 3 days by Divl Gas Officer. Pte Park having developed a further temperature Pte Bowker will be sent in his stead to III Army Rest Camp. Administrative Instruction No 11 Q.349 "Canteen Supplies" received. This and III Army Routine Order re Canteen Accounts to be brought specially to the notice of P.R.I.(Captn Piggot, RAMC) /Notice	(Sgd)

Army Form C. 2118.

WAR DIARY
or
INTELLIGENCE SUMMARY.
(Erase heading not required.)

49th FIELD AMBULANCE.

JULY 1918.

Instructions regarding War Diaries and Intelligence Summaries are contained in F.S. Regs., Part II. and the Staff Manual respectively. Title pages will be prepared in manuscript.

Place	Date	Hour	Summary of Events and Information	Remarks and references to Appendices
SOUASTRE	JULY 21st.		Notice re further Gas Shells used by the enemy & notes on masks - New Blue Cross now used. Orders for Captn. GREEN, M.O.R.C. to proceed to Casual Officers' Depot, A.E.F. received and transmitted to him. He reported departure forthwith. O.C. to new Baths to conduct test of new Disinfestation Chamber. A.D.M.S., who had called, watched the experiment. The chamber used, was too big for the steam generated but the point of displacement of the air by steam was completely proved by taking temperature at different levels.	
		p.m.	Intelligence Summary 19/20th records heavy Yellow Cross shelling F.20,21 & 22. Divl Zone Calls received. Divl Gas Officer called re casualties passed through during the past 24 hours. Weekly Statistics as under:-	

			37th Div. Other Fmns. TOTAL
			Sick admitted. 93 59 152
			   " evacuated. 31 37 68
			Wounded (includes 55 Gassed) 125 3 128
			48th F.Amb (direct admissions) 165 36 201
			    TOTALS through Unit 383 98 481	

			Lt & Qmstr Fyles came to H.Q. on various routine questions. He was given Frs 500 from Canteen Funds to supplement the Fresh Fruit & Vegetable Ration. Weather cleared p.m. with fine afternoon and night.	(sgd.)
	22nd.	a.m.	Fine - cloudy. Orders, warning all ranks to let their relatives know that Police confirmation & medical certificate are required to support applications for special leave on account of illness or death in families, published yesterday. Order regarding telegraphic recall from Leave published. Medical Officers attention directed to the order against giving recommendations for leave on Medical grounds to anyone. Pte Tyrell having received a letter from his wife regarding the condition of his son, his case was again submitted to Divl. H.Q. for further consideration. Arrangements for relief of "C" Sec Bearers in the line by "B" Sec on Wednesday next 24th inst drafted and sent to all concerned. 2 Cwt. of used Carbide for whitewashing received from C.R.E. Divn.	(sgd.) /Captn.

Army Form C. 2118.

WAR DIARY
or
INTELLIGENCE SUMMARY.
(Erase heading not required.)

49th FIELD AMBULANCE

Instructions regarding War Diaries and Intelligence Summaries are contained in F.S. Regs., Part II. and the Staff Manual respectively. Title pages will be prepared in manuscript.

JULY 1918.

Place	Date	Hour	Summary of Events and Information	Remarks and references to Appendices
SOUASTRE.	JULY 22nd.		Captn Ward R.A.M.C. attended as witness in a F.G.C.M. on a case of S-I Injury which occurred 10 days ago. There would appear to be no doubt of the guilt of the man. Wrote to A.D.M.S. asking for allotment of 1 place per course for the next 3 courses of training at the Army School of Cookery. At present there are no fully trained Cooks with the unit, and though they provide fair meals, the knowledge of those now acting as cooks with regard to Economical cookery, variation of Menu &c. is not as satisfactory as it might be. Went into question of change of clothing & the administration of A.T.S. to Gassed Cases with Officers. Changes & Serum are to be left at their discretion. Dripping Return for Economy Returns received from H.Q. This unit shows well in ration saving. the period was not entered. Administrative Instruction No 12, Q 287 d/-21.7.18 "Canadian Boiler" for horses food. Bottom and ends one sheet iron 6', wood sides nailed & plugged with tarred hemp- 2" x 11" wood. Heated over trench fire/. Cheap, light, simple, large capacity. Will boil 2 sacks of barley. Saw Town Major re complete evacuation of hut for Gassed cases, 112 Bde having gone into the line again. The outer sheds being now practically complete, work on the interior furnishings of the central hut can be started. Urgent Report called for by A.D.M.S. on Gassed cases for information of G.O.C. Division.	App. VI.
		P.M.	Sgt SIMMONS, R.A.M.C. (on duty at Baths) arrested by Police for selling Whiskey to Imperial Troops. Copies added.	
	July 23rd.	a.m.	Raining. Three Officers sent to C.C.S. for Dental treatment; Captn Robertson, R.E., Captn Kerr, R.E., & Revd. Kick, C.F. No 30188 Sgt SIMMONS R.A.M.C. was brought up on a charge of "When on Active Service conduct to the prejudice of good order & military discipline in "that he did:- 1. Procure Whisky. 2. Sell whisky to Colonial Troops on 19th July 1918. Section 40 Army Act. After taking evidence and the prisoner's plea of "Not Guilty" he was remanded for trial by Court Martial. A day for taking further evidence will be notified by A.P.M. 37 Divn. The case is likely to be a large one involving more than one department including A.S.C. E.F. Canteen &c. /Went	

Army Form C. 2118.

JULY 1918. 49th. FIELD AMBULANCE.

WAR DIARY
or
INTELLIGENCE SUMMARY.
(Erase heading not required.)

Instructions regarding War Diaries and Intelligence Summaries are contained in F.S. Regs., Part II. and the Staff Manual respectively. Title pages will be prepared in manuscript.

Place	Date	Hour	Summary of Events and Information	Remarks and references to Appendices
SOUASTRE	JULY 23rd.		Went into question of payment and advancement in Corps Pay of Specialists under letter No A.G. Base R.A.M.C. Sec No 18/91/18 which now required a full List of all Specialists serving with Units.	
		11 am.	The new D.D.M.S IVth Corps (Col Gibbard C.M.G. D.S.O) with Major R. Gale D.S.O. his D.A.D.M.S. and the A.D.M.S. 37 Divn inspected the unit and its adjuncts. Our last Projector attack at ABLAINZEVILLE resulted in 120 casualties. We have a considerable amount of useful information to the Intelligence Officer who interviewed him. The rations of the German Army do not appear to be satisfactory according to his story. The prisoner however did not appear to be underfed or unhealthy. He was in fact a good specimen of a man, said to be an Alsatian. Made application to A.D.M.S. to expedite the despatch of a Tailor for the unit from the base. We have been without one since 12th April and application was made on 20th June for another to replace the former who was wounded and died at C.C.S. Notice received from a.H.Q. D.M.S. through usual channels regarding Maximax Geneva Conventional markings on ground. Cross 24 feet. Spray ground first with Cresol to prevent weeds growing. White Ground 72 feet. A.O. 211 of 1918 abolishing left-hand salute for all ranks received with A.O's 192 to 219. Rained very heavily all the afternoon. Cleared during the night. Civilian Case N.Y.D. Diphtheria reported from Billet 113 SOUASTRE which is 112 Bde H.Qrs. Precautions taken.	(sd):/
	July 24th. am.		Weather unsettled. O i/c R.A.M.C. Sec G.H.Q. asked if Q.M.Sergts, R.A.M.C. could be classed as F.O's Class II under terms of A.O. 194. That classification would give them an increase of 6d per day Field Allowance. Major RUSSELL of 13th Rifle Brigade very kindly undertook to interview Sgt Simmons and advise him as to the conduct or his defence at F.G.C.M. Copies of III Army Pamphlet on "The treatment of Wounded men in R.A.P's & Field Ambces" received and distributed to the Officers of the Unit. A special point was made that the two Officers M.O.R.C. U.S.A. now undergoing instruction with 49th F. Amb. should each have a copy The pamphlet is a useful addition to Medical literature on treatment in forward areas & the illustrations of methods of applying special splints, rechauffement, blanket-folding &c. are simple and clear. /Letter	(sd):/

Army Form C. 2118.

WAR DIARY
or
INTELLIGENCE SUMMARY.
(Erase heading not required.)

49th FIELD AMBULANCE.   JULY 1918.

Place	Date	Hour	Summary of Events and Information	Remarks and references to Appendices
SOUASTRE	JULY 24th.		Letter asking for sketches of things and places of interest from Units for the Imperial War Museum received from D.H.Q. O.C. 50th F. Amb. called regarding relief of Bearers today, also to discuss the condition of patients being sent down the line from A.D.S. on arrival at M.D.S. One or two minor defects were pointed out which could be remedied. Area Sanitary Officer called regarding question of Civilian case? Diphtheria reported yesterday. Went with him to examine it and found that an abscess on the right side of the Fances had burst during the night and membranes had all practically disappeared though leaving inflamed traces of their presence on soft and hard Palates. Result of Bacteriological examination of the swab will be awaited before taking stringent measures about disinfection and action decided on reported to A.D.M.S.	
		pm.	O.C. to HHNU on inspection with special reference to condition of tents, dug-outs & Horse-standings after the heavy rain of yesterday. They were satisfactory. Operating Tent in exchange for one unserviceable has arrived. Salvage of Nails for past 2 weeks satisfactory 3 lbs and ½ lb. having been collected. Complaint of a sack of Oats heavily contaminated with stones and grit is to be enquired into by O i/c Supplies & Veterinary Officer. In a raid by the 4th Middlesex Regt last night 6 prisoners were taken. Returns show a rise of wounded to 25 today as a consequence, 7 of whom were returned to duty after getting A.T.S. Summary of Evidence in the case of Sergt Simmons taken by Major C. Nicholson, R.A.M.C. Weather cleared in late afternoon & evening. Artillery during the night strikingly quiet.	
	25th.	am.	Weather unsettled and showery. Special leave Warrants for Cpl Magill and Pte Tyrrell both of whose previous applications had been refused, were received this morning for sailings tomorrow. They were despatched as quickly as possible to Orville by Car, being given Fr 100 and Fr 50 respectively as advances of pay. Name of Corpl WOODWATCH R.A.M.C. submitted as candidate for Gas Course tom report to IVth Corps School ARGOULES on 29th July. Administrative Instruction No 17 No 347/1Q "Improved Hay-sieve" received. This is designed to collect seeds, flowers & short hay & so prevent waste. It is eminently portable. A.D.M.S. orders that when a Bearer Sub-division of a Field Ambce is attached to another in the line, full complement of 3 wheeled stretcher carriers will be taken with them. One extra. was sent forthwith to 50th F. Amb from whom we already hold a receipt for two.	

Army Form C. 2118.

WAR DIARY
or
INTELLIGENCE SUMMARY.

(Erase heading not required.)

49th. FIELD AMBULANCE.   JULY 1918.

Instructions regarding War Diaries and Intelligence Summaries are contained in F.S. Regs., Part II. and the Staff Manual respectively. Title pages will be prepared in manuscript.

Place	Date	Hour	Summary of Events and Information	Remarks and references to Appendices
SOUASTRE	July 25th	pm.	Nominal Roll of Specialists R.A.M.C. N.C.O's & Men submitted through A.D.M.S. in accordance with instructions from the Base (R.A.M.C. Sec. G.H.Q) i.e. Dispensers 3 Dental Mechanics 1 Linguists (French) 3 (two 2nd class Interpreters & 1 Conversational) Chiropodists 1 Bootmakers 1 Clerks & Shorthand) 2 Typists. Writers) Having examined the Summary of Evidence as taken down by Major Nicholson yesterday in the case of Sergt Simmons, a confidential letter was sent with documents to A.D.M.S. asking that Regulations should be quoted which prohibited a N.C.O. from procuring Whisky or selling it, even at a profit, to a comrade. In the absence of such, it was asked if it would be in order to submit a formal application for P.G.C.M. on a point of law as to whether it was prejudicial to good order and military discipline (A.A. Sec 40) for one N.C.O. of good-conduct to sell intoxicants to another N.C.O, a Corporal of Police, in such limited quantities. Pte CRAIG, R.A.M.C. who was granted special leave and was due to return to France on 20th was reported as an Absentee, not having yet returned. On his last leave he overstayed and was duly punished. Bacteriological examination of Swab from Civilian case of Diphtheria reported as negative. A.D.M.S. and French Mission to be informed by wire that hospital accommodation at HESDIN is not now required. A.D.M.S. telephoned O.C. to discuss case of Sgt Simmons.	(sig.)
	July 26th	am.	Weather dull and showery. L/Cpl BOND to DOULLENS for Interviewing Officer R.A.F. reference commission. Pte MARTIN seen by O.C. regarding the desirability of getting him a Commission in R.A.F. He will be recommended. Instructions, Pamphlets & Circulars which arrived day before yesterday from Base Staty Depot were checked against the list we asked for. The new Protected Shelter Dressing Station was rendered damp, uncomfortable and muddy by the recent wet weather. It will not be satisfactory in the winter. O.C. & Major Nicholson /explored	(sig.)

Army Form C. 2118.

WAR DIARY
or
INTELLIGENCE SUMMARY.
(Erase heading not required.)

49th FIELD AMBULANCE.

Instructions regarding War Diaries and Intelligence Summaries are contained in F. S. Regs., Part II. and the Staff Manual respectively. Title pages will be prepared in manuscript.

Place	Date	Hour	Summary of Events and Information	Remarks and references to Appendices
SOUASTRE.	JULY 26th.		explored the excavations into the chalk which have been dug some 150 to 200 feet below the ground surface. They are entered by a steep stepped approach and could scarcely be used as a Dressing Station unless better approach and suitable arrangements for lighting were made. Otherwise would be absolutely safe and commodious. Later to see Baths, sanitation.	
		p.m.	14 cases from 10th Royal Fusiliers with delayed symptoms of "Mustard" Yellow Cross Shell poisoning were sent in. They had been treated by their R.M.O. for six days. Every case presented blistering of the scrotum and Perineal region and two men at least had temperatures and lung symptoms. The blisters had been treated with Soda Bicarb. powder without much result, but they seemed to agree that the solution for their eyes eased the pain a little. Five men were markedly hoarse including the two with lung symptoms. No men presented signs of face blistering. Two men had well marked erythema of the whole genital region and one or two, blistering of the elbows and knees. Two N.Y.D. Mental cases from 65th Labour Coy sent to 45 C.C.S. the N.Y.D.N. Centre, the special instructions in D.G/1108/2 d.22.3.16 being complied with. M.O. i/c 9th N. Staffs (Lt Morales) called regarding his instructions to test the wells in the FONQUEVILLERS area. Rained heavily during the night.	
	27th.	am.	Dull - Showery. Ground very wet. Captn Robertson, R.E. sent for dental treatment. Application of Pte Martin for R.A.F. forwarded and recommended with reasons. Report on "GLAXO" as a substitute for milk sent to A.D.M.S. This was not favourable. Instructions received that all indents on D.G.V.O. must be submitted through proper channels. Report to A.D.M.S. with copy to Divl Gas Officer by request, on Combination Suiting impregnated with Linseed Oil as protection against "Mustard Gas" sent in. There has been no opportunity of really testing its resistance to penetration but one or two points were called attention to which appeared to detract from their utility. D.M.S. III Army No 2690/9 re standard of oxygen to be maintained per Division received under A.D.M.S. No 6/17/37 d.26.7.18. 240 Cub feet per Divn in 20 & 40 C.F. Cylinders. 120 Cub ft at A.D.S. i.e. 120 Cub feet at M.D.S. Report to be rendered by July 30th that Ambulances are in possession according to scale. All Cylinders to be treated as Area Stores.	

Army Form C. 2118.

WAR DIARY
or
INTELLIGENCE SUMMARY.

(Erase heading not required.)

49th FIELD AMBULANCE.

JULY 1918.

Instructions regarding War Diaries and Intelligence Summaries are contained in F.S. Regs., Part II. and the Staff Manual respectively. Title pages will be prepared in manuscript.

Place	Date	Hour	Summary of Events and Information	Remarks and references to Appendices
SOUASTRE.	JULY 27th (Con)	11am.	Medical Board in accordance with orders from A.D.M.S. under terms of G.R.O. 4480 held on C.Q.M.S. W.G. DYSON, 65th Labour Coy, a Candidate for a Commission in the Labour Corps. He was categorized BII in view of Eye-sight & history of Corneal Ulcer. In view of a previous entry on 10.7.18 the following extract from Intelligence Summary d/- 27.7.18 is of considerable interest. Prince Rupprecht's Group of Armies - 80 Divisions, of which 28 are in reserve. On the Aisne-Marne front - 27 Divisions including 15 from reserve are reported engaged. In all 36 Divisions in reserve on Western Theatre are available for operations. Weekly Returns of Dripping saved shows a considerable improvement in this Unit. Rations saved compare more than favourably with any other Unit in the Division.	(sgd)
		pm.	O.C. to HENU on inspection. Several of the dugouts have suffered badly from the present rain and the store tent floor badly wetted. O.C. & Q.Mr both out. Questioned Lt Martin on instructional progress. Information from O i/c R.A.M.C. Section A.G's Office Base No 612/1915 d.26.7.18 that Q.M.Sgts R.A.M.C. are now classed as W.O's Class II under terms of A.O. 194 of 1918. Very heavy rain during afternoon. LT & QMr visited H.Qrs SOUASTRE. A.D.M.S. telephoned to say that there was only vacancy for a Refresher Course at the School of Cookery at present. Weekly Returns all rendered up to date.	
	28th.	am.	Dull, unsettled, showers. Cpl. WOODHATCH R.A.M.C. sent to ARGOULES for course at Gas School. Paid Fr 30 before departure. In response to Memo from D.M.S. III Army, reported through A.D.M.S. that there was no delay so far as this Unit is concerned in sending venereal cases to centres where treatment could be instituted as soon as possible. Ruling re Q.M.Sgt. R.A.M.C. being W.O. Cl.II published in today's Orders. Separate Indents for Medical Stores will be submitted in the case of:- (a) Prisoners of War Cos: (b) Prisoners of War Cages: (c) Prisoners of War Camps in future & stating whether (a)(b) or (c) D.M.S. III Army No 3049/229 d.26/7/18. Corps Intelligence Summary reports that 34 Enemy Divisions are available in reserve. Since July 15th 66, of which 44 were put in from reserve, have taken part in the Southern Battle. Checked balance of cash, Imprest A/c remaining in Cash Box. Correct.	(sgd)

Army Form C. 2118.

WAR DIARY
or
INTELLIGENCE SUMMARY.

49th. FIELD AMBULANCE.

(Erase heading not required.)

Instructions regarding War Diaries and Intelligence Summaries are contained in F.S. Regs., Part II. and the Staff Manual respectively. Title pages will be prepared in manuscript.

Place	Date	Hour	Summary of Events and Information	Remarks and references to Appendices
SOUASTRE	July 28th. (Con)		O.C. to draw Fr.4,600 from Field Cashier for purposes of payment of Unit. After this was carried out Fr.125.30 remained as cash balance. Later to HENU on inspection with special reference to new constructional work, the ruination of mens clothing at the Divisional Baths and improper exchange of clothing stated to be unserviceable. Gave orders that no more clothing was to be sent to Divisional Baths for disinfection. A local chamber is to be provided Lt SUMMERS received a good deal of instructions during the round. Inspected a very ingenious Clockwork Fly-trap. Went into question of marking and separation of horse's nosebags and eye-fringes.	
		pm.	Band of 8th Somerset Light Infantry played at HENU Camp for the benefit of patients and personnel there. Several of the Officers walked over to tea there from SOUASTRE. A farmer's complaint about our putting down tins to make a car stand received through the Town Major. Under orders of A.D.M.S. remaining Ford Car detailed for duty with 50th Field Ambce. Summary of cases dealt with during the past week:-	
			SICK admissions ... : 37th Divn. 58. Other Fmns. 11. TOTAL 69.	
			do evacuations ... : do. 37. do. 11. do. 48.	
			WOUNDED admissions .. : do. 86. do. 3. do. 89.	
			To 48th F.A. for direct) admission.) do. 147. do. 30. do.177.	
			TOTALS.passing) through) do. 291. do. 44. do. 335.	Ct
	29th.	am.	Weather dull and unsettled looking, but no rain. O.C. in quarters sick. Major Nicholson acting. Instructions regarding disposal of clothing and accoutrements of American personnel admitted to British Medical Units received. D.M.S. III Army 3090/S. A.D.M.S 6/17/49d d.28.7.12. Names of men for next period at III Army Rest Camp sent in. Pte Halford & Dr West. To go on 4th August from WARLINCOURT to ST VALERY.	
		pm	Names of Sergt Bristow & Pte Bell (M.T) submitted to fill 2 vacancies of allotment or leave in France. Copies of Pamphlets "Special Sanitary Rules on the occurrence of Infectious Diseases" and "Notes for Regimental Medical Officers" issued by D.M.S. III Army received & distributed to officers. On the departure of an Officer these are to be returned.	RN

Army Form C. 2118.

WAR DIARY
or
INTELLIGENCE SUMMARY.

49th. FIELD AMBULANCE.

JULY 1918.

(Erase heading not required.)

Instructions regarding War Diaries and Intelligence Summaries are contained in F.S. Regs., Part II. and the Staff Manual respectively. Title pages will be prepared in manuscript.

Place	Date	Hour	Summary of Events and Information	Remarks and references to Appendices
SOUASTRE.	July 30th.	am.	Fine. Warmer again. Orders issued for Lt. J. W. SUMMERS, M.O.R.C., U.S.A. to proceed today for temporary duty with 8th Somerset L.I. vice Lt. S.R. MAXEINER, M.O.R.C., U.S.A. to 32 C.C.S. as Radiologist. D.G. No 128/1 d.25.7.18 & A.D.M.S. 6/7/40 d.29.7.18. No 40817 Pte MOORE departed for course of Cooking in accordance with orders in D.R.C.3640 and urgent notice from A.D.M.S. who had previously said we could only have a "refresher course" The area in the immediate vicinity of the Dressing Station being heavily shelled from about 9.45 am. Advisability of moving forthwith considered. Sick Parade and Ambulance Cars despatched out of harms way. 2 or 3 killed & 6 wounded as a result of the shelling, mostly A.S.C. M.T. (SuppPark) Issued detail of Medical Board for 1st August to be held on Pte Elkington, 41st Labour Coy. In response to enquiry from Army & Corps, reported that in my opinion payment of patients on discharge from Medical Units would considerably increase clerical and other labour and that the necessity for the procedure when discharging from Medical Units in Divisional areas is not apparent. Reported, in response to enquiry by A.D.M.S. re vacancy for a Sergt Dispenser, that one of the vacancies in this Unit is held by a Corporal, but that I am not anxious for an exchange unless he deems it advisable. Sent Messrs BOOSEY & Co, 295 Regent Street, London, W.1. a cheque for £31-6-1 in payment of account for Side Drums, Fifes & Music procured (Canteen Fund A/c) R.A.M.C. Order No 97 received from A.D.M.S. regarding Medical arrangements for the Raid by 1st Battn ESSEX Regt. to be held tonight. Should it be necessary to postpone the raid, the code work "Cucumber" will be sent. Claims for Allowances for Officers & W.O's for the past month despatched to Command Paymaster Base. Instructions regarding Burials A.G.3212 (O) received.	
		pm. 6.15 p.m.	A.D.M.S. visited M.D.S. to enquire as to damage &c. done by this morning's shelling.	
	31st.	a.m.	Weather fine, inclined to Greyness. Visibility poor. The raid by ESSEX Regt. last night was a failure so far as can be at present ascertained. Out of 60 taking part, 21 casualties had passed through M.D.S. by 8.30 this morning, most of them being stretcher cases. Report asked for regarding Omnopon and Scopolomine for anaesthesia in operative work as compared with Morphine or other anaesthetics. D.G./75/50. D.M.S. III Army No 3712. Completed documents of Pte Mc Kellar, again sent to O i/c A.S.C. Sec. answering certain questions by him.	

Army Form C. 2118.

WAR DIARY
or
INTELLIGENCE SUMMARY.

49th FIELD AMBULANCE.

JULY 1918.

(Erase heading not required.)

Instructions regarding War Diaries and Intelligence Summaries are contained in F.S. Regs., Part II. and the Staff Manual respectively. Title pages will be prepared in manuscript.

Place	Date	Hour	Summary of Events and Information	Remarks and references to Appendices
SOUASTRE.	JULY 31st.		New forms giving full particulars of Officers R.A.M.C. completed and sent in for this Unit to A.D.M.S.	
			Notice received that Clinical Meetings will be held on the first Sunday in each month at Nos. 29, 56 & 3 Casualty Clearing Stations in that order. To commence on 4th Augt.	
			Went thoroughly into question of scheme for hurried removal of M.D.S. to a new site in case of necessity. The protected Shelters on the St AMAND Road are now whitewashed, cleaned and ready for occupation.	
			Good progress has been made with the Divisional Gas Centre being made by the Unit. Reception & evacuation sheds have been put up, the interior whitewashed and the floor which has been levelled and is being covered with brick rubble will be ready for cementing within the next two or three days.	
			A shelter for the Medical Inspection Room is now complete, the floor having been bricked and seats provided.	
			A new subsidiary Kitchen with Oven, shelter & cemented floor is completed.	
			At HENU, Fly-proofed portable meat-safe in a proper cutting up room, also a shed for food distribution to patients and personnel have been erected. A brick Oven has also been provided there.	
			Other minor improvements have been installed, including a Dining room in the Barn billet at SOUASTRE.	
			Sick & Evacuation Wards are complete.	
			Dripping-saving has been actively taken up and more than double is now being sent down to the Base. Administrative Instruction No 18.Q/147/120 which was received this morning deals with the question on lines already laid down in this unit.	
			Completed Pay Books and Claims for N.C.O's & Men entitled to Additional & Extra-duty pay, Barber's Account Frs.25 paid and receipt obtained.	
	pm.		Board on Pte ELKINGTON, 41st Labour Coy cancelled as he has been admitted to Hospital. O.C. on inspection to HENU. Pte FAULKNER R.A.M.C. renewed Engagement for further period of service to 21 years.	
			Accounts of the expenditure of the 500 Frs from Canteen Funds to supplement Vegetable Ration by local purchase submitted for approval by Lt Pyles.	
			The Battle Order for the greater part of the month in this sector of the line is of interest to record:-	
			IV Corps. III Army. (A) In the line	

Army Form C. 2118.

WAR DIARY
or
INTELLIGENCE SUMMARY. 49th FIELD AMBULANCE
(Erase heading not required.)

JULY 1918.

Instructions regarding War Diaries and Intelligence Summaries are contained in F. S. Regs., Part II. and the Staff Manual respectively. Title pages will be prepared in manuscript.

Place	Date	Hour	Summary of Events and Information	Remarks and references to Appendices

SOUASTRE.	JULY 31st. (Con)		(a) In the line:
			    Left. 37th Division.
			    Centre. New Zealand Division.
			    Right. 42nd Division.
			(b) Reserve:
			    57th Division.
			    62nd Division, now left for South.
			    ? 18th American Division.
			On the left of IV Corps is VI Corps.
			On the right of IV Corps is III Corps (IVth Army).
			The Division on our left is the 2nd.
			When this Division is likely to be relieved in the line is at present most uncertain. It has not had an ultra-trying time in any way during the past month.
			With the advent of rain the Influenza Epidemic is fast disappearing, and Battle casualties have not been heavy on any one day, in the Division. The total for the month to noon today being - 448, of which 432 are 37th Division.
			Our view as to the ridiculous nature of the claim made by the owner of the field where we are making a Car Stand is upheld by the 37 Div¹ Claims Officer (Claims Officer 37 Div¹ No 2625 d. 31.7.18).	

[signature]

LT. COL. R.A.M.C.
COMDG 49th. FIELD AMBULANCE.

Month								Treatment
Date								
Temp								
Pulse								
Resp								
Bowels								

49TH FIELD AMBULANCE.

II.

            Objective.   4th Objectiv

         ANT COPSE - Enemy's
         ANT TRENCH   trench from
         L.25.c.93   L.26.c.3½.5
         .74   L.26.c.4.7½
         nce to   thence N.W.
         er of   to L.25.a.74
         ard   Infantry
         .a.26.   arrive 5.30.
         antry
         ve 1.50.

         _____

         carry triangular

         tween the shoulders.

         latoon, will be carried

         one half - yellow one
                        half.

         above - yellow below.

REPORTS on the use of BICARBONATE of SODA to counteract the effects of MUSTARD GAS.

I have no experience of the use of this chemical as a prophylactic after exposure to low concentrations of the Gas either as a gargle or for use in the eyes.

In Cases that have been exposed to a high concentration I have found that:-

(I) it has no effect in relieving pain when the conjunctivae are already involved; &

(II) it has no effect in arresting the conjunctivitis even if applied immediately after symptoms are first observed.

(sgd) CLARK NICHOLSON,
Major R.A.M.C.
49th Field Ambce.

4-7-18.

I. EYES. There is considerable doubt as to whether the treatment by bathing is of any value. Some patients say that the pain is relieved, whilst others complain that it is increased. For prolonged treatment in slight cases, no useful effect has been observed.

II. WASHING BODY. No evidence to show that this is of any value.

III. GARGLING & WASHING NOSE. No evidence as to value.

4-7-18-

(sgd) A. P. PIGGOT.
Captn. R.A.M.C.
49th Field Ambulance.

In my experience based on some hundreds of cases passing through the BIENVILLERS A.D.S. the immediate benefit derived from bathing with Sod. Bic. Sol. was very doubtful. In fact I am inclined to consider wetting the skin with water may be harmful.

Liquid Paraffin or Paraffin Wax No 7 is, in my opinion, well worth trying.

(sgd) O. E. WARD.
Captn. R.A.M.C.
49th Field Ambce.

4-7-18-

A.D.M.S
37th Divn.

With reference to your letter No 5/24/148 d/- 3/7/18, Report on "Soda Bicarbonate as a prophylactic treatment to counteract the effects of Mustard Gas" I submit the attached Reports of three Officers of this Unit who have had experience in dealing with a number of cases affected by Dichlorethyl sulphide at FONQUEVILLERS, & the place.

It will seem that their experience at present does not warrant the expression of an opinion on the use of the medicament as a prophylactic, and so far as I am aware, there is no definite reason, from a chemical standpoint, why it should act as such.

From personal experience of the effects of "Mustard Gas" in Flanders, even in very low concentrations, I should hesitate to rely on any special means of protection for eyes and air passages, other than the small Box Respirator, unless it was of proven value. The sense of false security induced by its use might lead to serious results.

As a means of treatment after the onset of the effects of the gas, I am in agreement with the opinion expressed in the reports, that Soda Bicarbonate is of very doubtful value.

In dealing with clothing contaminated with Dichlorethyl-Sulphide by means of steam - which hydrolyses the compound into ?Thiodiglycol & Hydrochloric Acid, it is possible that a preliminary soaking of the fabric in a solution of Soda Bicarbonate might act as a deterrent to the action of the H.Cl. liberated, in destroying the cloth.

Lt.Col. R.A.M.C.
Comdg. 49th Field Ambce.,

49TH FIELD AMBULANCE.
No.............
Date...7/7/1918.

"Q"
37th Divn.

With reference to 37 Div No Q 230 dated 7/7/18, herewith table showing requirements for this Unit for the forthcoming winter.

                    (sgd) R.L.TODD.
                    Lt.Col. R.A.M.C.
8/7/18.   Comdg. 49th Field Ambce.

49th FIELD AMBULANCE.

ACCOMMODATION RETURN.

Class of Accommodatn.	Numbers to be accommodated.			Remarks.
	Officers	O.R'S	Patients.	
Sleeping.	9 M.O's. 1 C.F.	232	150	Usual assessment of Nos to be accommodated (2 Hospital Nissens or Adrian Huts as hands)
Officers' Messes.				1 Hut for 10 Officers. 1 Hut for Sergts' Mess.
Dining Rooms.				1 Patients) Hospital Nissens 1 (Personnel) or Adrian Huts.
Recreation Rooms.				Recreation Room & Canteen combined, either Adrian or Hospital Nissen.

8.7.18.

SECRET.

A.D.M.S.
37th Division.

App. VI

With reference to your letter No 6/24/4 of today's date asking for particulars of Gassed (Shell) Cases admitted during period from 6 a.m. 20.7.18 to 6 a.m. 22.7.18 for the information of G.O.C. 37th Division, I beg to report as follows:-

1. NUMBER of CASES by UNITS.

	Officers.	O.R.	TOTAL.
10th Royal Fusiliers.	3	52	55
4th Middlesex Regt.	-	1	1
37th M.G.Battn.	-	5	5
TOTALS.	3	58	61

2. TYPE of GAS.

All the cases exhibited symptoms pointing to poisoning by Dichlorethylsulphide (Yellow Cross Shell). There was nothing to indicate, from a Medical point of view, that sternutators such as Diphenylchlorarsine or Phosgene had been employed by the enemy. Officers and men were unanimously of the opinion that it was "Mustard" that had caused their symptoms.

3. SEVERITY.

    10th Royal Fusiliers. - 26 moderate.   29 severe.
    4th Middlesex. - 1 slight.
    37th M.G. Battn. - 5 moderate.

The severe cases exhibited marked eye symptoms. Rhinitis and
    , some cases, Larygeal involvment, & blistering of the skin.
Moderate cases. Eye symptoms - slight Rhinitis & slight
    erythematous patches.

Slight cases. Some degree of conjunctivitis and slight
    hoarseness of voice.

It must be noted that this classification is made solely from the symptoms observed at this Main Dressing Station, and that cases, there classified as moderate, might later exhibit pulmonary and other changes of a severe character.

4. SPECIAL POINTS or ATYPICAL SYMPTOMS.
    None were noted.

5. PARTICULARS GATHERED FROM CASES THEMSELVES.

There is nothing of special interest to note. All cases had relied solely on their Small Box Respirators for protection, and these once adjusted appear to have been worn for considerable periods of time.

It would appear that the bombardment broke out very suddenly and was fairly concentrated, and certainly in the severe cases the men seemed to have been caught before adjustment of Respirators was possible, and several exhibited marked and extensive blistering of the body and limbs.

Severe cases were mainly received in the first batches of men admitted, and slight cases later. It is suggested that this indicates that the latter cases were possibly ones of "delayed action" of the poison in question. There is nothing to indicate that they were caused by reinhabitation of gassed areas before the effects of the compound had passed off.

No evidence could be adduced by Medical Officers of any lack of discipline or want of knowledge of necessary precautions on the part of the casualties or those who commanded them at the time.

Sd.
Lt.Col. R.A.M.C.
Comdg. 49th Field Ambulance.

22.7.18.

Confidential

War Diary
— of —
49th Field Ambulance

From 1st to 31st August 1918

49TH FIELD AMBULANCE

No. 49. F.A. Aug. 1918.

Plans of Field Kitchen have been detached & filed under "Plans Maps & Charts" – "Sanitation" Plans

Sketch showing Petrol Tin Shower has been detached & filed under & "Plans Maps & Charts – "Sanitation Plans.

Army Form C. 2118.

WAR DIARY
or
INTELLIGENCE SUMMARY.   49th FIELD AMBULANCE.
(Erase heading not required.)

AUGUST 1918.

Instructions regarding War Diaries and Intelligence Summaries are contained in F.S. Regs., Part II. and the Staff Manual respectively. Title pages will be prepared in manuscript.

Place	Date	Hour	Summary of Events and Information	Remarks and references to Appendices
SOUASTRE.	AUGT. 1st.	a.m.	Fine. Warmer. Signed up Pay Books (A.B.64) for all personnel entitled to the 4th Chevron on 30-7-18. Completed Summary of Imprest Account for despatch to Paymaster. Obtained Report from Major NICHOLSON regarding special points of interest arrived at by him during his Sanitary Inspection of the Rear H.Q. and Transport Lines of the Division. Interviewed A.P.M. regarding the state of his digestion and sent him to Captn PIGGOT for treatment. Visited H.Q. 63rd Brigade with Major Nicholson to make the acquaintance of the Brigadier and Staff (Bdr Genl CHALLONER,C.M.G.,D.S.O) A Corporal M.C.O. from the Tent Sub-division Went into question of Equipment with Cr'r. of each Section will be appointed as N.C.O i/c Equipment of the Section to which he belongs. It is discovered that none of the panniers are provided with locks and their contents require carefully going into. A.A. & Q.M.G. called. Discussed a large number of interesting points affecting the internal economy of the Division:- e.g. Bathing, Laundry and Disinfestation. Refuse and Dead Horse Salvage. Canteen Share System. Venereal Prophylaxis &c.	
		pm.	Paid Pte NUTTALL, R.A.M.C. proceeding on leave tomorrow advance of pay (Fr.100) P.R.I (Captn Piggot) balanced and checked Canteen Funds and Lt QrMr's Account for Supplementary Rations &c. Received notice A.D.M.S. 5/12/30 d.1-8-18 No 285 that No 16670 Sgt POLLARD Master Cook 37th Division will visit all Units to advise on cooking arrangements of those whose standard is not sufficiently high to be satisfactory. Reported names of N.C.O's and Men suitable for duty at Advanced Operating Centre. Reported on reason for not sending Ambulance Cars to Workshop up to date. Issued Orders that in future Cars should not be sent in regularly no matter what number were already there for overhaul or repairs. Corrected and despatched War Diary for July to A.D.M.S. 37th Divn. New Senior Chaplain 37th Divn. The Revd (Major) MARSHALL, called.	
		6 pm.	One Enemy Aircraft passed over M.D.S. flying at a great height.	
		7-30.	Two cases of N.Y.D. DIPHTHERIA from New Zealand Entrenching Batn passed on to 21 C.C.S. Four MARKED D. Contacts of a case of Tonsilitis from 13th Rifle Brigade given prophylactic doses	

Army Form C. 2118.

WAR DIARY
or
INTELLIGENCE SUMMARY.

49th FIELD AMBULANCE.   AUGUST 1918.

(Erase heading not required.)

Instructions regarding War Diaries and Intelligence Summaries are contained in F. S. Regs., Part II. and the Staff Manual respectively. Title pages will be prepared in manuscript.

Place	Date	Hour	Summary of Events and Information	Remarks and references to Appendices
SOUASTRE.	AUG. 1st.		of Anti-Diph.Serum and sent to Transport lines and to attend for Medical Inspection with DO/78/33. Raining. Cooler.	
	2nd.	am.	Nil Return of French Sick and Wounded admitted to Unit sent through A.D.M.S. in accordance Notice received that No 93628 A/Cpl WHITTAKER H will shortly be posted to this Unit. There are 94 Category "A" Corporals R.A.M.C. at the Base available for posting who have all to be absorbed before further recommendations for promotion to A/Corporal can be considered. (R.A.M.C.Sec.No 65/942/18 & A.D.M.S. No.6/4/31) Lieut Mills Education Officer 37th Division called with reference to formation of classes in subjects likely to be of value to the Men. After some discussion sent him to talk the matter over with Major Nicholson, who will, after having been given a Full Nominal Roll of the Unit shewing Trades in civil life, go into the question of what subjects are most likely to be of interest and profit. Notification of Field Ambce Commanders' Conference at 11 am. tomorrow received from ADMS. A.F.B.136. Re-engagement papers of Pte FAULKNER forwarded to A.D.M.S. for approval. Engineers started cementing floor of Gas Hut. Went into question of provision of proper drainage being provided on the floor to enable the hut to be thoroughly swilled out when necessary.	
		pm.	O.C. to DOULLENS taking down an Officer of the 13th RIFLE BDE for Dental Treatment, on to HEM to collect some B.R.C.Stores and later to MARIEUX (IV Corps H.Q) to draw Frs.6,000 from Field Cashier.	
	3rd.	am.	Dull, showery and unsettled. Cleared towards evening. Correspondence dealt with. O.C. attended Conference at A.D.M.S. Office. The following points were discussed. 1. Use of Ambulance Cars. Horse Transport to be used for Sick as far as possible. O.C. 48th Field Ambce can draw on 49th & 50th as he requires. 2. Reception of Inspecting Officers. Complaints have been received that they are not properly treated when visiting Medical Units. 3. Lorry for Medical Stores. 3 cwt. Lorry will draw for the three Field Ambulances and distribute them. 4. Training of M.O's attached. Sanitation to be made an important point of, and 11am Military Diaries to be kept by Regimental M.O's.	

Army Form C. 2118.

WAR DIARY
or
INTELLIGENCE SUMMARY.

49th FIELD AMBULANCE.   AUGUST 1918.

(Erase heading not required.)

Instructions regarding War Diaries and Intelligence Summaries are contained in F. S. Regs., Part II. and the Staff Manual respectively. Title pages will be prepared in manuscript.

Place	Date	Hour	Summary of Events and Information	Remarks and references to Appendices
SCUASTRE.	Aug. 3rd. (Con)		5. Anti-Typhoid Inoculation Returns. Numbers for Ambulances are not satisfactory.	
			6. Bacteriological Swabs. Field Ambulances to keep stock of and distribute as required.	
			7. Infectious and Dysentery. Send in as N.Y.D. Action with regard to contacts depending on the case. All cases of N.Y.D. DYSENTERY and DIARRHOEA to be sent in first instance to 48th Field Ambulance.	
			8. Supernumerary Acting Corporals. Posted to Units supernumerarily xx to Establishment, will xxx draw pay as Corporals and will be absorbed at first opportunity.	
			9. Advanced Operating Centre. The need for this was not apparent. Considered that all the orderlies recommended would require more training. Copies added.	App. I.
			Correspondence relating thereto.	
			10. Venereal Disease. Prophylactic Measures discussed. A N.C.O. from 48th Field Amb. will lecture men going on leave from Divisional Reception Camp.	
			11. Action in case of Retirement. Altered.	
			50th. Clear line and spads Tent Sub-Division to HENU. Reinforced by Bearers of 49th Field Ambce.	
			49th. Becomes A.D.S. SCUASTRE, with 1 Tent Sub-division. Remainder to HENU.	
			48th. Opens M.D.S. at PAS.	
	pm.		Went Round Unit.	
			Major Scarisbrick reported privately that two sets of Harness had been stolen from Transport lines. Later reported as replaced and called himself to give account of loss. Lt. & QrMr Fyles called. Various instructions regarding his department given.	
			Communique gives news of readiness of enemy to retire on River ANCRE &c. Cellars in ALBERT &c. &c. mined to hinder occupation of territory. Look out to be kept on this front for any such attitude on part of the enemy.	
	4th.	am.	Unsettled. Cloudy.	
			Thefts from New Zealand and O.C. Servant's bivouac reported. Inquired into the matter and reported it to A.P.M. 37th Divn. An expert thief must have done it. Suspicion cast on Pte Whittle servant to Revd Thomas. No real ground for this.	
			O.C. and Major Nicholson rode to HENU Camp. The latter to collect information with regard to Education Scheme, the former on inspection and with special reference to harness lost, kitchen regime and instruction of Lieut MARTIN. A.D.M.S. called at the Camp xx at the	

Army Form C. 2118.

WAR DIARY
or
INTELLIGENCE SUMMARY. 49th FIELD AMBULANCE.

AUGUST 1918.

(Erase heading not required.)

Instructions regarding War Diaries and Intelligence Summaries are contained in F.S. Regs., Part II. and the Staff Manual respectively. Title pages will be prepared in manuscript.

Place	Date	Hour	Summary of Events and Information	Remarks and references to Appendices
SOUASTRE.	AUG. 4th. (Con)		conclusion of the round. O.C. visited Dressing Station St AMAND on journey back to SOUASTRE. A heavy-draught horse had fallen between two of the sections and done some slight damage which will be repaired forthwith.	
		pm.	Orders issued for Sgt TATAM A.S.C.(H.T) to proceed tomorrow to Base Depot H.T & S. Authy.A.S.C.Section.No P.33/14418 d/-1/8/18. 37th Divl Train. No 1251 d/-3/8/18. Information received D.G.96/13 D.A.S.No 3726 that a certain number of men had transferred from Non-Combatant Corps to R.A.M.C. and will be posted for duty as Stretcher-Bearers to Field Ambulances. Orders regarding DIARRHOEA and DYSENTERY issued. Captns PIGGOT and WARD, M.O. i/c 1st HERTS and Major SCARISBRICK to attend Clinical Meeting at 29 C.C.S. this afternoon. O.C. & Major Nicholson take charge of M.D.S. On the return from the clinical meeting it was ascertained that the following points, which have been strongly urged during discussions in this unit, were borne out by C.C.S. experience. 1. The danger of treating "Influenza" in forward areas. Recurrent cases are common and generally result in Bronco-Pneumonia in which the mortality has been high. 2. The usefulness of the little charts sent to C.C.S. recording clinical details sent in of all cases sent down as "sick".	
		8.45 pm.	A Captn F. F. Moratt of the 4th Middlesex Regt was sent to M.D.S. suffering from Pyrexia - Temperature 104º. A letter accompanied him asking that he might if possible be treated at Rear Battalion H.Q. This was not allowed, it being considered contrary to the interests of both the patient and this unit. Requests of this nature appear to be common in this Division. They evince a great and natural keenness on the part of Commanding officers to retain good men whom they know, and if complied with would no doubt tend to lower the figures for evacuation in the Division. But it appears questionable if this constant straining against evacuation is in the end a sound measure for husbanding Man-Power in the Armies as a whole. It is a pity that reinforcements sent from Base cannot more frequently be sent back to Divisions from which they were evacuated when an inter-regimental exchange might be effected. Weather cleared towards evening.	

WAR DIARY
INTELLIGENCE SUMMARY

Army Form C. 2118.

AUGUST 1918. 49th FIELD AMBULANCE.

Place	Date	Hour	Summary of Events and Information	Remarks and references to Appendices
SOUASTRE.	Aug. 4th. (Con.)		Weekly Summary of Sick and Wounded are as under:-	

```
                        57th     Other           57th   Other
                        Divn.    Frmns.   TOTAL. Divn.  Frmns.  Total
   SICK admitted. ..     75       17       92 ..Evacuated 54    15    69
   WOUNDED admitted.     66        6       72
   To 48th F.Amb.direct.121       33      154
      Total. ..          262      56      318
```

| | 5th. | am. | Dull, unsettled, damp. | |

Notice of Meeting on Surgical Shock to be held at Officers Hospital GEZAINCOURT at 2.30 pm. 9th inst. received.

Economy Returns received. There is considerable improvement in Dripping saved throughout the Division.

Wrote to A.D.M.S. asking that arrangements might be made to have notification of C.C.S. to which patients are evacuated sent by post. The present method of stamping the duplicate roll and returning by M.A.C. Drivers is still uncertain, and in view of constant enquiries as to whereabouts of patients and the necessity of satisfactorily completing our records, some certain method is desirable.

Lists of men requiring Inoculation i.e. who have not been done within the last 12 months being made out.

An interesting memo on Poisoning by Chloracetin Compounds (D.G.53/21) drawn up by Major Genl. W. P. Herringham, Consulting Physician, received.

| | | pm. | Rained heavily during afternoon. | |

Sent Pr 120 to O.C. HSMU for payment of Pte Halford and Cpr West proceeding to III Army Rest Camp tomorrow.

Paid L/Cpl BOND Frs 100 before going home tomorrow.

D.A.D.M.S. 42nd Divn (Major Dalziell, J.C. R.A.M.C.) called.

Major Scarisbrick submitted a paper for typing entitled "Influenza & Chest Diseases" with a view to publication.

A wet night.

| | 6th. | am. | Cloudy, unsettled. Some showers. | |

L/Cpl BOND proceeded to England as Cadet for R.A.F. (Pilot) Authy R.A.F.929/368 (A) d.27-7-18. A.C. to G.148/519(O) d.12/7/18. 57 Divn No A/39/406 d.4-8-18.

Army Form C. 2118.

WAR DIARY
or
INTELLIGENCE SUMMARY.
(Erase heading not required.)

49th FIELD AMBULANCE.   AUGUST 1918

Instructions regarding War Diaries and Intelligence Summaries are contained in F.S. Regs., Part II. and the Staff Manual respectively. Title pages will be prepared in manuscript.

Place	Date	Hour	Summary of Events and Information	Remarks and references to Appendices
SQUASTRE.	Aug. 6th. (Con)		Replied to D.G.157/4 d.2/8/18 (ADMS 5/8/18 - Postal Restrictions-R.A.M.C. which is being made the subject of a War Office enquiry. 1. None other than prescribed by Censorship Regulations. 2. I wish all correspondence could be restricted 2 letters a week. Replied DG/197/2 d.2/8/18 (ADMS 6/11/16) regarding disposal of Field Medical Cards of Men sent to duty or died. Replied to 37 Div G.9865 Educational Training Scheme, submitting the name of Major Nicholson R.A.M.C. as representative of this Unit. Provided with a complete list of O.R. personnel, their ages, civil occupations &c. & their wishes as regards subjects for study he has already elaborated a workable scheme in so far as 49th Field Ambce is concerned. It is apparently desired that representatives should meet and discuss scheme for the Division. O.C.'s asked to give the matter their sympathetic attention. Administrative Instructions No 20 embodying all important routine orders of daily import received. These will be read to the Unit or 6 a.m. parade and to all ranks on first joining as reinforcements. New list Station Code Calls for Division received and acknowledged last evening. Come into operation on night 7/8 August. Administration Instructions No 21 (2168/365) - Improvised Curry-Comb made out of corrugated iron received.	
		pm.	G.R.O. 4680 allows for 6 Anti-gas rattles per Field Ambce being held as equipment. Certified true extract of Birth Certificate of daughter of Sgt Daveney sent to O i/c RAMC Section. Two cases Diarrhoea - Ptes Alexander and Blackford - sent sick to 48th Field Ambce. This occurrence of diarrhoea, after the notification of 2 cases of Dysentery requires further investigating and thorough disinfection of quarters. Both men were Bearers up the line during the last shift. Neither have been employed on any duty in connection with food or drink. Sent typed paper to Major Scarisbrick for correction, stops &c. before sending it forward for publication. Later notified that Dr Newcombe A.S.C. from HDQU was admitted to 48th Field Ambce suffering from Diarrhoea. Pte W.Roberts returned from Leave. L/Cpl Bowker returned from III Army Rest Camp. Pte Halford and Cpl West proceeded to III Army Rest Camp.	

Army Form C. 2118.

WAR DIARY
or
INTELLIGENCE SUMMARY.
(Erase heading not required.)

49th FIELD AMBULANCE.

AUGUST 1918.

Instructions regarding War Diaries and Intelligence Summaries are contained in F. S. Regs., Part II. and the Staff Manual respectively. Title pages will be prepared in manuscript.

Place	Date	Hour	Summary of Events and Information	Remarks and references to Appendices
SOUASTRE.	Aug 7th.	am.	Finer. Cloudy. Enemy shelled BIENVILLERS during the night and 11 casualties passed through, of which one (a New Zealander) was received practically dead - a fractured Femur. He had become delirious on the way down and had fought hard with the car orderly. He had managed to turn completely round despite the Thomas' Splint in which he was fixed. One shell had wounded 7 of the New Zealand Entrenching Battn in one billet. Answered/ question regarding Pte T. Cubbons & others of the 10th Royal Fusiliers now queried by "A" Branch Army as "Self-Inflicted". In future Boards on Officers will be furnished on A.F. A.45 unless we are otherwise instructed (Authy DMS III Army No 3051/51 d.3/8/18.) ADMS telephoned that O.C. was to take up quarters at Divisional H.Q., while acting as ADMS 37th Divn. Also discussed experiments with regard to Disinfestation Chamber at Bethe. The following Lance Corporals are appointed as under:- No 27172 A/L/Cpl H. PARSONS, M.M. to be Acting Paid L/Cpl Vice No 36780 A/L/Cpl R.M. BOND, M.M. to R.A.F. 5/8/18. No 37739 A/L/Cpl W.L.GILLMAN, to be Acting Unpaid Local Corporal whilst employed as N.C.O. i/c Equipment of "A" Section. No 89483 A/L/Cpl M.J. NEVILLE, do. do. "B" Section. No 34167 A/L/Cpl W.J.LINTOTT, M.M. do. do. "C" Section. The last 3 named Will be attached to the Quartermasters Department for instruction in their duties. The Local Rank is not to be shown on any official documents. Wrote to H.Q. for authority to make the promotions in accordance with K.R. 394. A.F.M. sent for Dental treatment. Another New Zealander dead sent down from 50th Field Ambce (C.S.W. Spine - penetrating)	
		pm.	C.O. and Major Nicholson visited Rear H.Q. of 13th Rifle Brigade and inspected the excellent Kitchen and Catering arrangements now installed. Lt. & Qmr Clements is the responsible agent under the advice of Major Nicholson. It is a pity more Units cannot be induced to copy their example. The oven to bake for a whole Battalion is a good modification of the usual pattern and only requires 400 bricks and 4 sheets of corrugated iron to construct. A.D.M.S. telephoned that Sgt Simmons was to be relieved at the Divl Baths and replaced by another W.G.O. R.A.M.C. from this Unit. Corpl Cale, M.M. was detailed, His orders expressly stating that he was there to detect Skin Disease and Foot Ailments and not as General Manager. C.O. also instructed to get into touch with A.D.M.S. New Zealand Division, while he is Acting A.D.M.S./ with reference to the necessity for an A.D.S. at HENU in case we should fall	

Army Form C. 2118.

WAR DIARY
or
INTELLIGENCE SUMMARY.

49th FIELD AMBULANCE.

AUGUST 1918.

(Erase heading not required.)

Instructions regarding War Diaries and Intelligence Summaries are contained in F.S. Regs., Part II. and the Staff Manual respectively. Title pages will be prepared in manuscript.

Place	Date	Hour	Summary of Events and Information	Remarks and references to Appendices
SOUASTRE	Aug. 7th. (Con)		back to the Purple line. Major Scarisbrick's paper sent with forwarding letter to A.D.M.S. for publication in R.A.M.C. Journal. L/Cpl Brown reported for duty from leave having been granted an extension of 5 days. No 46303 Pte Tucker C, R.A.M.C. reported for duty as reinforcement. "Tailor" was employed at Vipples the Tailor in Exeter in civil life. Notification received that on 12th inst 2 Officers & 27 O.R. of 60th American American Divn Sanitary train will be attached to the unit for one week. Arrival to be reported to A.D.M.S. Weather cleared in afternoon. Warmer.	
	8th.	am.	Fine but cloudy. Warmer. Following men departed On leave having been given advances of pay last night as against their names. Pte Edgar, RAMC 73 Fr. " Standen, do 100 Fr. " Woolhouse, do 30 Fr. Dr Rosling, ASC 100 Fr. Replied to D.M.S. question as to why Ptes WOOD & RICHARDS 65th Labour Coy diagnosed "N.Y.D. Mental" on 26/7/18 were sent to 45 C.C.S. the M.Y.D. Centre. Alteration in leave train service notified from D.H... MONDICOURT will now be the most convenient station for this unit – not OMIELL as heretofore. Orders issued for relief of C Section bearers by those of B tomorrow. The men will march to take up their posts, as G.O.C. Divn objects to their transport by Horsed ambulance, and in fact no great hardship is involved. Pte Jennings who has been employed as Butcher in a General Hospital in to replace Pte Ferguson at present on that duty with this unit from tomorrow's date.	
		pm.	Correspondence regarding charge against Sgt Simmons R.A.M.C. with ruling by D.A.G. 3rd Army received. He will be tried under sec 40 Army Act - Conduct to the prejudice of good order and military discipline in that he did:- 1. Sell one bottle of whiskey to Cpl Parker MMP on 19-7-18. 2. Sell two bottles of whiskey to the said Corpl Barker on 22-7-18. Pte Appleby will be tried under the same section for aiding and abetting. They may be tried together unless they object. Orders quoted which have been contravened by the alleged offence are as follows:- G.R.O. 1252 & 1567; 3rd Army R.O. 1043 as amended by 1223 & No 760.	

Army Form C. 2118.

WAR DIARY
or
INTELLIGENCE SUMMARY.
(Erase heading not required.)

49th FIELD AMBULANCE.

Instructions regarding War Diaries and Intelligence Summaries are contained in F.S. Regs., Part II. and the Staff Manual respectively. Title pages will be prepared in manuscript.

AUGUST 1918.

Place	Date	Hour	Summary of Events and Information	Remarks and references to Appendices
SOUASTRE	Aug 8th (Con)		Report by Major Nicholson R.A.M.C. in accordance with G.R.O. 4664 on the necessity for standard fittings for the carriage of extra water on water carts & G.S. Wagons sent to ADMS. ADMS notified under his No 5/1/36 that the Acting Local Unpaid Promotions to Corporal of N.C.O's i/c Section equipment did not appear necessary. Saw two typical cases from 1st Herts Regt of poisoning with Chlor-Arsine compounds by drinking from unknown comrades water-bottle. Both sent down as Self-Inflicted though it is doubtful if the two men in question were wilfully guilty. Water Discipline on working parties does not appear to be good. Neither of the men had been able to fill their own bottles before starting out, so they said. Full notes by Captn Piggot accompanied them. O.C. to Divisional H.Q. to take over duties as Acting A.D.M.S. Major Nicholson assumes command of the Unit in his absence.	
	9th.	5.30 pm.	Weather dull and warm. Memo from O.C. 5 C.C.S. ref Pte Thomas who wishes to exchange. Agreed. Lt Johnson R.E. called ref. trial of disinfestation Chamber at Baths. A/ADMS called ref. cases of Mental disease sent to 45 C.C.S. Arranged to try disinfestation Chamber at 11-30 tomorrow. Notification received that No 40481 Pte Blackford was evacuated N.Y.D.Dysentery. News of Offensive on AMIENS front received.	
	10th.		Very bright and warm. 112th Brigade relieved 111th Bde in the line last night. 13th R.Fusiliers had 4 killed & 6 wounded by 2 shells during relief. There is only 1 car for duty with Unit. A/A.D.M.S. visited the Unit and went on to the Baths.	
	11th.	pm.	Very bright and warm. 7 Gassed cases admitted during the night from 8th Somersets. Gas porbably Blue Cross all of moderate severity. Went to HENU. Visited A.D.M.S. Drew cash for Unit's pay Fr.2,000. Visited Camp and Hospital and inspected new Spray bath installed there. Captn Piggot paid the Personnel here. Sgt Bristow R.A.M.C. & Pte Bell, A.S.C. R.H. went on leave to PARIS. 8th Lincolns had 2 killed & 8 wounded by a shell falling in a Pay Parade.	

Army Form C. 2118.

WAR DIARY
or
INTELLIGENCE SUMMARY. 49th FIELD AMBULANCE.

AUGUST. 1918.

(Erase heading not required.)

Instructions regarding War Diaries and Intelligence Summaries are contained in F. S. Regs., Part II. and the Staff Manual respectively. Title pages will be prepared in manuscript.

Place	Date	Hour	Summary of Events and Information	Remarks and references to Appendices
SQUASTRE	Aug. 11th. (Con)		Casualties through during the week:-	
			37 Div. Other Fmns. Total.	
			Sick admissions ... 55 15 70.	
			Wounded admissions.. 56 12 68.	
			To 48th Field Ambce. 106 25 131.	
			TOTALS.. 217 52 269.	Evacuations 39 of 37 Div & 11 O. Fmns. Cn
	12.	pm.	Dull and warm. Reported adversely on suggestion that a man's medical classification should be entered on Field Medical Card. Note Verbale by Enemy Medical Officer regarding his treatment during the Battle of ARRAS 23-4-17. He states that he was not permitted to dress his own wounded. Major Nicholson and Captn Piccot knew nothing of this matter. Reported to that effect. Sgt Simmons tried by F.G.C.M. Visit from A/A.D.M.S. 25 stretchers and 50 Blankets returned by 48th Field Ambce (loaned on 28-5-18)	Cn
	13.	pm.	Very bright and warm. 12 wounded from an unsuccessful raid by 8th Somerset L.I. All bomb wounds and slight except one penetrating wound of chest. Captn Salley & Captn Scott FORG and 28 O.R. arrived to be attached for instruction. They belong to 320 Field Hospital Sanitary Train 80th Div. A.E.F.	Cn
	14.	pm.	Bright and warm. American personnel attached distributed to various departments. Captn Salley attended Orderly Room and accompanied O.C. on his inspection. Major Nicholson & Captn Salley and Captn Scott called on A.D.M.S. and discussed instruction and thereafter inspected Transport camp MENU. Major Nicholson & Captn Piccot explain system of evacuation of wounded during active operations and quiet periods.	Cn
	15.		Bright and warm. Enemy reported retiring from the front of Divisions on each flank. PUNISIEUX occupied. Water system of SQUASTRE inspected and demonstrated to Captns Sall & Scott. Ford Motor Ambulance for duty with A.D.M.S.	Cn

Army Form C. 2118.

WAR DIARY
or
INTELLIGENCE SUMMARY.

49th FIELD AMBULANCE.

AUGUST 1918

(Erase heading not required.)

Instructions regarding War Diaries and Intelligence Summaries are contained in F. S. Regs., Part II. and the Staff Manual respectively. Title pages will be prepared in manuscript.

Place	Date	Hour	Summary of Events and Information	Remarks and references to Appendices
SOUASTRE	Aug. 15 (Con) 16th.		Discussion with Captns Salter and Scott on treatment of wounded in Field Ambce. Sentence on Sgt SIMMONS promulgated "Reduced to the ranks"	
			Bright and warm. Enemy reported holding positions as before in front of BUCQUOY. Outbreak of Diarrhoea in the Unit traced to tainted meat. Captn Piggot asked for report. Pte SIMMONS transferred to 46th Field Ambce on orders from A.D.M.S. News of offensive on Italian front, received.	Cx
	17th		Duller but still warm. Fighting patrols of 13th R. Fusiliers in conjunction with A. troops moved forward and occupied new ground last night - opposition b.g. fire only about 6 casualties. 1st Essex continue the movement today. Much artillery and some Tanks moving up through SOUASTRE Pte CRAIG who was declared an absentee by Court of Inquiry reported to have embarked for France. Visited Transport Camp at HENU with Captns Salter and Scott and went on to visit 48th Field Ambce at PAS. 49th F.Amb played No 2 Coy Train at Cricket.	Cx
	18th.	4.m.	Dull and warm Visited baths and rear Battalion H'qrs with Captn Salley Visited A.D.S. BIENVILLERS and FONQUEVILLERS and RAP RETTEMOY Farm with Captns Sally and Scott. Ten Casualties from explosion of a dump of our own Gas Shell admitted Weekly Summary of cases through M.D.S.	Cx

	37 Div	Other armies	Total
Sick Admissions	43	23	66
Wounded -do-	72	6	78
To 43 F. Ambce	132	19	151
Totals	247	48	295

WAR DIARY
INTELLIGENCE SUMMARY.

49th Field Ambulance

August 1918

Place	Date	Hour	Summary of Events and Information	Remarks and references to Appendices
SOUASTRE	19th	4 pm	Bright and warm. A.D.M.S. called with reference to active operations in the future. Visited transport camp HENU and saw Lt & Qmr FYLES with reference to supply of food in case of heavy casualties, inspected Camp and saw Major SCARISBRICK with regard to establishing Walking Wounded Station at Reserve M.D.S. 63rd (R.N.) Division are moving into SOUASTRE and to "red line". O.C. 50 F.Amb. called - also O.C. 149 F.Amb. - personnel of latter accommodated in Gas Shelter for the night. American personnel left expressing satisfaction with their treatment while with this unit. 63rd Inf. Bde relieves 112th Inf. Bde in the line tonight.	
	20th		Dull but warm - A little rain fell during the night but not more than lays the dust. Went over Reserve M.D.S. with Major Scarisbrick and Lt & Qmr Fyles with a view to its equipment as a Walking Wounded Station this afternoon.	
		4 pm	Conference of O's C Field Ambs at Office of ADMS this afternoon and final arrangements for active operations completed. Summary of arrangements affecting the Unit:- 1. Personnel (a) One Tent Sub Division and HQr Section at M.D.S. SOUASTRE. D.22.a.2.5. (Sheet 57D)	

WAR DIARY
INTELLIGENCE SUMMARY. 149th Field Ambulance

Army Form C. 2118.

August 1918

Place	Date	Hour	Summary of Events and Information	Remarks and references to Appendices
SOUASTRE	20th (Cont'd)		**Officers** - Capt. Piggott, Capt. Ward and Capt. Shaw (M.O i/c 3/Div R.E) (a) One Tent sub division at Walking Wounded M.D.S. D.15.d.9.6 - **Officers** - Major Scambrick, Lieut Martin. (b) Two-bearer sub divisions attached to 50th Field Ambulance (2) Motor Transport All Cars pooled for work back to M.D.S. One Ford with A.D.M.S. Its other Ford working from Nac Z to FONQUEVILLERS. One Motor Cyclist with 50th Field Ambulance. (3) Transport lines remain at HENU with one section packed.	
		4 p.m.	A.D.M.S. called and inspected Walking Wounded station.	Cn
	21st	6 a.m.	Zero hour was 4:55 a.m. At that hour a heavy wet mist covered everything and the sound of the opening Barrage was not well heard. Both branches of M.D.S. ready to receive Wounded.	
		9 a.m.	A.D.M.S. 5th Div called and asked help in evacuation of walking wounded from his Division at FONQUEVILLERS. Arranged that he should send across clothes and chicken to Walking Wounded M.D.S.	
		10 a.m.	Wounded began to arrive at both branches at 8 a.m. and increasing numbers kept coming in. Orders received from A.D.M.S. to move transport camp to Walking Wounded M.D.S. Pilch Canvas and be ready to accommodate sick Sit stretches given orders accordingly and available men and transport sent to help.	
		12 m	D.D.M.S. IV Corps arrived at noon and inspected both branches of the Station. M.C.	

Army Form C. 2118.

WAR DIARY
or
INTELLIGENCE SUMMARY.
(Erase heading not required.)

49th Field Ambulance

August 1918

Place	Date	Hour	Summary of Events and Information	Remarks and references to Appendices
SOUASTRE	21st (Cont'd)		suggested that too many cases were lying out in the sun. Went out to M.D.S. N.Z. Divn with D.D.M.S. arranged to avoid all stretcher cases there until Divn M.D.S. was clear. Arranged for supply of A.T.S. which is low. Evacuation of stretcher cases satisfactory but walking wounded accumulating. D.G.M.S. with A.D.C. called after inspecting Walking Wounded Station and inspected this Station. He suggested that some shade should be provided for men lying in who then awaiting dressing.	
		5 p.m.	Most of stretcher cases dressed and O.C. N.Z. Divn M.D.S. informed - Large numbers of Walking wounded awaiting evacuation. A.D.M.S. 37 Divn and D.D.M.S. IV Corps called. Figures of Daily State at 12 noon were as under:-	

	Sick		Wounded		Total	
	Offrs	O.R.	Offrs	O.R.	Offrs	O.R.
37 Divon	1	29	2	24	3	53
Other Formations	2	42	-	50	2	92
Prisoners of War	-	-	-	1	-	1
Totals	3	71	2	75	5	146

		9 p.m.	Six lorries from the 2nd Divn M.T. Coy arrived and the situation at Walking Wounded Station practically clear.	
		11 p.m.	Cases still coming in slowly but evacuation satisfactory. Both Stations practically clear.	
	22nd	9 a.m.	Exceedingly warm. In view of the small number of cases coming in, decided to stop admission at Walking Wounded Post and treat all wounded at SOUASTRE.	

Army Form C. 2118.

WAR DIARY
or
INTELLIGENCE SUMMARY.
(Erase heading not required.)

149th Field Ambulance

1918 August

Place	Date	Hour	Summary of Events and Information	Remarks and references to Appendices
SOUASTRE	2nd (cont.)		Casualties in the Unit yesterday – 2 killed (Ptes Ong and Johnston) – two Wounded (Ptes Perkins and Travis) and two Gassed – Three Cases (Ptes Park and Whigham Third Army Consulting Surgeon called. He suggested forceps for taking axolis and dressings from Marriers and said that cases were arriving at B.C.S in good condition.	
		2 pm	Figures for Daily State at 12 noon were:-	

	Sick		Wounded		Total	
	Offrs	O.R.	Offrs	O.R.	Offrs	O.R.
37 Divn	–	14	7	164	7	178
Other Divns	1	51	13	428	14	479
Prisoners of War	–	–	–	38	–	38
Totals	1	65	20	630	21	695

| | | 3 pm | D.M.S. Third Army with D.D.M.S. IV Corps called and inspected M.D.S, Walking Wounded Station and car Park and expressed satisfaction. | |
| | | 10 pm | Conference at A.D.M.S. Office. 111th and 112th Brigades attack tomorrow morning – 50th Field Ambce clear Vie line as before – 148th Field Ambce Walking Wounded M.D.S. at BIENVILLERS – 149th Field Ambce M.D.S. Stretcher Cases, SOUASTRE and all clearing – Arranged to cover receiving yard with wagon covers and to draw supplies of medical stores and medical comforts | |

Army Form C. 2118.

WAR DIARY
or
INTELLIGENCE SUMMARY.
(Erase heading not required.)

40th Field Ambulance

1918 August

Place	Date	Hour	Summary of Events and Information	Remarks and references to Appendices
SOUASTRE	23rd	4 P.m.	Bright and warm. New hour at 11 a.m. and fresh cases received at 2 p.m. and coming in since then in very large numbers. At 3 p.m. D.G.M.S. inspected the Station with D.D.M.S. IV Corps. He expressed displeasure at the state of the Cookhouse but was satisfied with the manner in which the wounded were handled. Daily State 12 noon figures:-	

	Sick		Wounded		Total	
	Off	O.R.	Off	O.R.	Off	O.R.
3rd Division	1	30	1	88	2	118
Other Formations	1	43	3	31	4	85 (?)
Prisoners of War	-	-	-	4	-	4
Totals	2	73	4	123	6	207

		3 p.m.	Evacuation is exceedingly slow and the receiving yard has been kept full since 6 p.m. and wounded awaiting dressing are lying in the Officers Mess Yard and Cookhouse yard without cover. Captain James of R.t M.F.C. has seen the conditions and has promised army lorries that can be spared. The evening is still and suggests main lorries.	
	24th	4 a.m.	A.D.M.S. called and arranged to refill medical supplies and comforts for further operations. No change in medical arrangements. There are over 100 cases awaiting evacuation and as many admissions as about 40 cases still unattended.	

Army Form C. 2118.

WAR DIARY
or
INTELLIGENCE SUMMARY.
(Erase heading not required.)

149th Field Ambulance

1918 August

Place	Date	Hour	Summary of Events and Information	Remarks and references to Appendices
SOUASTRE	R.H./8 (Cont)	6am	21 M.A.C. provided 14 cars at 4.30 am and the situation is with more or acute less severe cases have been accommodated in the Hut. 30 cases will undergoing.	
		10am	Evacuations proceeding more satisfactory – 20 British and 30 Enemy cases left. No cases to dress – The day is dull and cold after the shell of night. Divisional Troops have been requisitioned as internal bearers to relieve men of the Ambulance tired out.	
			Daily State (12 noon) Figures:–	

	Sick		Wounded		Total	
	Offrs	O.R.	Offrs	O.R.	Offrs	O.R.
37 Division	–	19	27	711	27	730
Other Formations	1	43	8	242	3	315
Prisoners of War	–	–	3	72	3	72
Totals	1	62	38	1,055	38	1,117

			Enemy Aeroplane dropped some bombs on 63rd C.C.S. on Transport lines at SOUASTRE, killing 1 man and 18 horses and wounding 1 man.	
			Fine – very hot and dusty	
			Col. Hopkins A.D.M.S. returned from leave last evening and took over from A/A.D.M.S. Spent the day going round Medical situations of Units – visiting 50th Fd Amb. ESSARTS near BUCQUOY – Forward A.D.S. Forest Lodge – just E of LOG EAST WOOD and Car loading Point E of ACHIET-LE-GRAND, with a forward post at BIHUCOURT – Selected site of A.D.S. Post E of ACHIET-LE-GRAND, with a forward post at BIHUCOURT – a reinforced concrete structure, a strong site capable of in former German Dressing Station – standing a direct but worth any shell – Visited Brigade	Ci
	25/8			

Army Form C. 2118.

WAR DIARY
or
INTELLIGENCE SUMMARY.
(Erase heading not required.)

HQ & Field Ambulance
19/8 August

Place	Date	Hour	Summary of Events and Information	Remarks and references to Appendices
SOUASTRE	25 (contd)	a.m.	H.Q. 63rd and 111th Bdes - Former Brigade holding BAPAUME - SAPIGNIES Road; FAVREUIL and BEUGNÂTRE to be taken this evening beginning 6.30 p.m. G.O.C Division and Staff going round. Figures for Daily State (12 noon):-	

	Sick		Wounded		Total	
	Off	OR	Off	OR	Off	OR
3/1 R Division	-	10	6	193	7	203
Other Formations	1	33	8	69	9	102
Prisoners of War	-	-	1	22	1	22
Totals	2	43	15	284	17	327

	Totals for week ending				
	S		W	to 43 R.A.	Totals
	Off	OR	Off	OR	Off	OR
	129	1239	41	—	37=852	1409
	229	390	15	—	—	1134
	—	142	—	—	—	142
	358	3,270	56	—	—	2685

p.m. Returned with A.D.M.S. to Lunch at SOUASTRE
Following arrangements now decided on:-
50th F. Amb. - Clear the line and find A.D.S.
48th " " - to be M.D.S. for Walking and Lying Wounded - near BUQUOY
14/3 " " - to push forward and prepare a M.D.S. somewhere W of LOGEAST WOOD over which to be released by O.C. Orders issued accordingly.
Unit to move at daybreak.
Sick and Wounded evacuated to C.C.S. in lorries obtained from various sources.
Enough left out to deal with any urgent cases that might arise in during the night -
Preparations for move completed by 10.30 p.m.-

Army Form C. 2118.

WAR DIARY
or
INTELLIGENCE SUMMARY.
(Erase heading not required.)

49th Field Ambulance

August 1918

Place	Date	Hour	Summary of Events and Information	Remarks and references to Appendices
Near LOGEAST WOOD F.30.a.6.d (Sheet 51P)	26th	a.m.	Weather unsettled - Heavy showers - Colder	
		5.30	Unit marched out under command of Major Nicholson	
		9 a.m	O.C. and Capt. Piggot in Ford Car to select site and leave guide at ABLAINZEVELLE corner. He joined Unit. Site selected at F.30.a.5.0 just west of LOGEAST WOOD - near Corps Ammunition Dump and the light railway supplying it. Unit marched in at 10 a.m. - setting in after arrangements for plan of camp had been detailed. Bearers of this Unit assisting in batches from 50th Field Ambulance. Received report that one Ford Car of this Unit was rendered useless and the driver Pte BOUSFIELD killed by shell fire last night. Divisions as to be in rest for a few days with Brigade areas as under:-
63rd - ACHIET-LE-PETIT
111th }
112th } - LOGEAST WOOD	
		2 p.m	D.A.D.M.S called.	
		3 p.m	A.A & Q.M.G called. Stated that G.O.C. was pleased with all administrative arrangements. By darkness the Unit has settled down fairly comfortably and useful structural work like metalled Car road entrance with bridges for the ditch, latrines, kitchens &c got well under way. The whole camp area has also been fenced with barbed wire.	
	27th		Dull and cooler - looks like rain	
			Office routine - Men of unit all busily engaged in structural work - A.D.M.S & D.A.D.M.S called to discuss points of routine - Medical arrangements received - 49th will collect sick of 63rd & 111th Bdes and send to 48th F.Amb. 50th F.A. will do 112 Bde.	

D. D. & L., London, E.C.
(10340) W₁ W5900/P713 750,000 3/18 H 1688 Forms/C2118/16

Army Form C. 2118.

WAR DIARY
or
INTELLIGENCE SUMMARY.
(Erase heading not required.)

HQ 1/1 Field Ambce

1918 AUGUST

Instructions regarding War Diaries and Intelligence
Summaries are contained in F.S. Regs., Part II
and the Staff Manual respectively. Title pages
will be prepared in manuscript.

Place	Date	Hour	Summary of Events and Information	Remarks and references to Appendices
F.30.a.5.0 (nr LOGEAST WOOD) (Card) Sheet 57"	27th		The Division after two or three days rest will go into the attack again in which case 48th Field Ambce will be M.D.S. lying cases. 49th " " " - " - M.D.S. Walking cases 50th " " - " - continue clearing the line. As advance continues, 49th will become M.D.S. walking and 48th close and again advance ahead, so overlapping. Congratulatory letter from Corps Commander to the Division. News sheet states that just over 3,000 prisoners, including 33 Officers have passed through the Divisional Cage since the 22nd.	A.Y.
	28th	a.m.	Weather dull and unsettled. - Cold with heavy showers. "Preparation of M.D.S. proceeding apace - Dispensary, Reception shed, Baths, improvements to Kitchen and trench boarding of Camp all being gradually completed. Three horsed Ambulances from 48th Field Ambce reported for duty. Mark I Horsed Ambce wagon sent to I.O.M. for condemnation returned without anything visible in the nature of repairs having been done to it. A.D.M.S & D.A.R.R.G. called. The former seemed pleased with what he saw of the Camp work. - 2nd Lieut Newson, 13 Bde sent to 48th for transmission to N.Y.D.N Centre suffering from ? hysteria - Epilepsy ? Projectilphobia. O.C. and Lt Styles to SOUASTRE and HENU to bring back stores and to salvage of Corrugated iron and other material. - Called at A.D.M.S Office FONQUEVILLERS on return journey and completed his office Diary for last two days the A/A.D.M.S was in charge. Arranged with D.A.D.O.S to send Lorry to bring back remainder of stores still left at SOUASTRE	A.Y.

Army Form C. 2118.

WAR DIARY
or
INTELLIGENCE SUMMARY.
(Erase heading not required.)

49th Field Ambulance

1918 AUGUST

Place	Date	Hour	Summary of Events and Information	Remarks and references to Appendices
F.30.a.5.0. (Sh.57.D)	28th (Contd)	5 pm	Got back to Camp. Paid men as under proceeding on leave tomorrow. Pte Backhouse RAMC 150 fr; Pte Curry RAMC 100 fr; Pte Richards 200 fr; Pte Robson RAMC 200; Pte Richards 200 fr (MT). Parties for leave now proceed to Refilling Point by 11 a.m and are transported in returning lorries to Railhead AUTHIEULE. 100 clean changes received from "Q". News of our offensive continues good. It is reported that enemy resistance is stiffening as we approach the Hindenburg Line.	Ayi
	29th a.m		Colder. Fine but heavy clouds about. Two heavy showers afternoon. Notice received that 56th San. Sec. leaving IV Corps area. 62nd San. Sec. takes over left forward area and 14th the Right forward area. Capt. W. P. Piggot RAMC and 4 O.R. left on leave to U.K. Wired A.D.M.S. "Immediate Awards" – Nil. Presumed that 50th Field Ambce will deal with personnel of 49% attached to them during operations. Replied to an Officer of 63rd Div. (Lt. H.E. Pearson RNVR) who stated he had lost his boots in this Unit – They cannot be traced. Field Cashier at Divl H.Q. (Brickworks near ACHIET-LE-GRAND) 10am – 12-30. DADVS and O.C. Mobile Veterinary Section went round horse lines and seemed pleased with the animals. D.A.D.M.S. called and was shown round camp. O.C. went to D.H.Q with him and heard from D.A.Q.M.G. that we should probably be moved as Corps Commander considered we were too close to the Ammunition Dump. D.A.D.M.S and O.C. prospected for new site East of LOGEAST WOOD. but not very satisfactory.	Ayi

Army Form C. 2118.

WAR DIARY
INTELLIGENCE SUMMARY.
(Erase heading not required.)

49th Field Ambulance

1918 AUGUST

Place	Date	Hour	Summary of Events and Information	Remarks and references to Appendices
F.30.a.5.0. (Sheet 57D) (LOGEAST WOOD)	29th (Contd)		On return to Camp found that AA+QMG had been round and said he would try to get the Dump moved rather than ourselves.	
		2pm	Lorry load of Stores, Stretchers and Blankets etc. arrived from SOUASTRE. Lt Qmr Styles went in an Ambulance Car to St AMAND Dressing Stn to bring back Canteen stuff and oil for the cars.	
		6pm	C.O. and Major Nicholson rode to look out for alternative sites for M.D.S. selected one in G.C.3. Behind ACHIET-LE-GRAND. On the D.H.Q. and saw A.A+QMG who advised standing fast as the advance having gone forward some 3 or 4 miles, site of M.D.S. behind ACHIET line would be too far back. Division will probably not go into the line again for about two days. QC to see OC 50th Ft. Amb. regarding immediate awards for men of 49's Stretcher Bearers, also receipts for Stretchers & Blankets sent up during present operations.	
		9pm	Sent in Situation Report and replied to ADMS wire regarding equipment surplus to Mobilization tables held at this unit as follows:- (1) Stretchers = 189 ; (2) Blankets = 600: (3) Thomas Splints (a) Arm 26 (b) Knee 34 News from ARRAS front very good - Our troops have crossed HINDENBERG LINE at one point. Weather Finer - Cloudy.	R.N.
	30th	a.m	At intervals of 10 minutes to 15 minutes from about 11.30 p.m last night to 4.30 a.m. the LOGEAST WOOD B.W.T. LATRINE area shelled by the enemy with H.V. Gun. They appeared to be searching for Ammunition Dumps in and round the wood. - 13th KRRC had 4 men severely wounded	

Army Form C. 2118.

WAR DIARY
or
INTELLIGENCE SUMMARY.
(Erase heading not required.)

49th Field Ambulance

1918 AUGUST

Place	Date	Hour	Summary of Events and Information	Remarks and references to Appendices
F.30.a.5.0 (Sheet 51D)	30th (Contd)		and two horses killed. Men dressed by Orderly Officer and sent to 143rd Field Amb.	
		10.30 a.m.	A.D.M.S. called and went to see M.O. i/c 13 K.R.R.C. Monthly Returns dealt with. Further instructions regarding use of Sera & Vaccines received from D.G. Office through usual channels. Instructions received that dose of Tetanus Antitoxin should be 1500 units in all cases - D.G. 72/14 dt. 24/5/18. This was embodied in orders.	
		11.45 a.m.	G.O.C. Division with his A.D.C. called regarding our proximity to Ammunition Refilling Point for Heavy Artillery. He seemed good tempered and amused with tips & pleased with efforts in the Camps.	
		3 p.m.	A.D.M.S. Conference of all Medical Officers of the Division who could be spared from duty at site of 48th Ft. Amb. F.36.c.7.7. A general survey of the Medical Services during recent operations was gone into. The need for extra accommodation for Wounded in Field Ambces working under their own strength was emphasized especially where clearance of M.D.S. area was slow owing to long Car runs to Cas Clearing Stns. or other cases. A.D.M.S. stated that these Tarpaulins for Ambulance had been recommended, of which shelters could be made. The figures given for wounded dealt with by our Divl Medical Units from 21st to 27th Aug. are interesting	

	Offrs	O.R.
37 Division	58	1,378
Other Divisions	19	479
Corps Troops		
Total	77	1,857

Detts with by our Medical units
other formations
1st & 37th Division

Army Form C. 2118.

WAR DIARY
or
INTELLIGENCE SUMMARY.
(Erase heading not required.)

49th Field Ambulance

1918 August

Instructions regarding War Diaries and Intelligence Summaries are contained in F.S. Regs., Part II. and the Staff Manual respectively. Title pages will be prepared in manuscript.

Place	Date	Hour	Summary of Events and Information	Remarks and references to Appendices
F.30.a.5.0 (sheet 51.D)	30th (Cont)		No Regimental Medical Officer had any suggestions to make for improvements, or complaints. All commented on the satisfactory and rapid clearance of Regt. Aid Posts. News from the various fronts continues good. On this front FREMICOURT was taken this morning, the 5th Division and New Zealanders pushing rapidly forward. Replacement of Ford Ambulance Car destroyed by shell fire received with admin reinforcement in place of Pte BOUSFIELD killed. Baths have been completed today in the Camp and all bearers bathed and clean clothing given. New stock of Field Medical Cards received from the Base - We now have about 2,000.	A.B.
	31st		Small - windy - cold. Rain early morning - showers during the day - Enemy aircraft over last night. Monthly and weekly returns dealt with. A.D.M.S. asked if Lieut SUMMERS, MOrc might now be struck off our strength, to allow us to demand two M.O.'s reinforcements. This is still shown as on temporary charge of 8th Somerset Light Infy. Bde Refilling Point for 111 Bde changes to G.4.a.5.4 near railway north of ROMET LE GRAND. One man of the Unit sent to 48th F.Amb suffering from intractable Diarrhoea, there have been three other cases of the complaint during the week all of which have yielded to simple treatment with Ol:Ric: & Bismuth Salicylate. Protective trenching of Horse lines started. The standings will be bricked. Wooden Officers' Mess with Kitchen was taken into use last night.	

D.D. & L, London, E.C.
(10340) Wt W5300/P713 750,000 5/18 H 4688 Forms/C2118/16

Army Form C. 2118.

WAR DIARY
or
INTELLIGENCE SUMMARY.
(Erase heading not required.)

1918
August

49th Field Ambulance

Place	Date	Hour	Summary of Events and Information	Remarks and references to Appendices
F.30.a.50. (Sheet 57D)	31st (Contd)		Orders given to replenish stock of reserve water. After bathing parade yesterday it has run low. Clao wrote a private note to Capt. Willis in O/C Office asking if one of the Water Tank lorries in his charge could refill our tanks. Canteen funds checked by the Acting P.R.I. (Lt. Secombrick) in the absence of Capt. Pigg. A deposit of £n 500 cash opened with Divl Canteen in accordance with instructions received yesterday, viz. a basis of 2/3 a man of Unit. It is hoped that some cigarettes will be procurable shortly. At present they cannot be obtained at all and the men have had to subsist on their tobacco ration which is by no means sufficient.	
		1.45 p.m.	D.M.S. III Army (Sgr Gnl Murray I.M.S.) called regarding safety of GREVILLERS and other places he was apparently going to prospect for C.C.S. sites in. The road diverted to D.H.Q. to A.D.M.S. Office	
		2.15 p.m.	D.A.D.M.S. called, en route to take up quarters near ACHIET-LE-GRAND with T.A.B. so that Advanced H.Q. whither ADMS Office moves today.	
			During the month 63 Offrs & O.R. have been inoculated with T.A.B. so that Inoculation Return now shows:-	

Under 12 months   Over 12 months   Over 24 months
91.66%   8.34%   Nil

The confrere will with April 1918:-

Under 12 months   Over 12 months   Over 24 months
61.39   26.06   12.55

Army Form C. 2118.

WAR DIARY
or
INTELLIGENCE SUMMARY.

(Erase heading not required.)

1918
49th Field Ambulance
Original

Place	Date	Hour	Summary of Events and Information	Remarks and references to Appendices
F.30.a.5.0 (St.51D)	31st (Cont.)		Plans of Kitchen appliances in use with 49th Field Amb added in Appendices. Motor Cyclist D.R. attached for duty with 50th F. Amb. returned to Unit in response to our request. Note from A.D.M.S. that the undermentioned number of casualties of formations other than 37 Divn have been dealt with by 37 Divn Medical Units during period 21/25 Aug (incl) :— Offrs O.Rs Others 39 1056 37 Divn 58 1348 Total 97 2404 Total Batt. str. of 37th Div'l Med. Units. 49 R.F.A. need. Information received that Ammunition Refilling Point will be moved. A brief summary of operations in which the 37th Divn have taken a conspicuous part is as follows:— 21.8.18. Took high ground East of BUCQUOY and ABLAINZEVELLE consolidating it for defence in depth while 5th & 63rd Divisions passed through on R & L respectively. 23.8.18. Passed through 63rd Divn who had been held up – Bleared LOGEAST WOOD – took ACHIET-LE-GRAND – GOMMIECOURT line – into BIHUCOURT 24.8.18. – Took BIEFVILLERS – SAPIGNIES line 25.8.18. Took SAPIGNIES – BAPAUME road and attacked FAVREUIL. New Zealand Divn operating on our right in the BAPAUME sector. Night 25/26. Division relieved in the line by 5th Division. The IV Corps when we passed through the 63rd & 5th Divns on 23rd Aug, now	Appx

(A7092). Wt. W12839/M1293. 75'000. 4/17. D.D. & L., Ltd. Forms/C.2118/14.

WAR DIARY
or
INTELLIGENCE SUMMARY.

Army Form C. 2118.

40th Field Ambulance

1918 August

Place	Date	Hour	Summary of Events and Information	Remarks and references to Appendices

F.30.a.5.0 (Sheet 57D)	31st (Cont'd)		Held by Divisions as under from North to South :-
			
			 3rd ⊡ ACHIET-LE-GRAND
			      63rd
			      5th
			      N.Z.
			      42nd
			
			          ⊡ BAPAUME
			
			 The two attempts to ride the 1st Cavalry Divn during the attacks were of no avail.
			
			 Notification from A.D.M.S. (No. 6/4/354/. 34715) that Lt. Col. J. Summers, M.O.R.C., U.S.A. is posted to permanent Medical charge of 8th Somerset Light Infantry.
			
			 Summary of Cases dealt with during August 1918
			
			                  3rd Divn Other formations Totals
			 Sick Admissions 276 291 567
			 Wounded admissions 1,474 991 2,465
			 To 48th F.Amb. for direct admission 392 77 469
			       Totals 2,142 1,359 3,501	

COPY.
A.D.M.S.
37th Divn.

      In the event of an Advanced Operating Centre being opened in this area, please inform me the number of Nursing Orderlies in the Field Ambulances on your Division who have had sufficient training and experience to justify their being entrusted with the nursing of abdominal and other cases which would be dealt with at such a Centre.

                         (sgd) R. GALE, Major.
H.Q. IV Corps.   for Colonel, A.M.S.
  30-7-18.   D.D.M.S. IV Corps.

O.C. 48th Field Ambulance.   6/29/G/67.
O.C. 49th Field Ambulance.
O.C. 50th Field Ambulance.

      Reference above, please inform me if you have any men so qualified.

                     (sgd) E. M. MORPHEW.
                            Colonel A.M.S.
                      A.D.M.S. 37th Division.

A.D.M.S.
 37th Division.

      With reference to your No 6/29/G/67 d. 30-7-18 (Nursing Orderlies qualified for duty at an Advanced Operating Centre) - the u/mentioned N.C.O's and Men of this Unit would be quite suitable.

No 36921 Sgt CHILTON, B.A.   No 36939 L/C HEAP H.
   34906 Cpl ADAMS   F.   37172 " PARSONS H.
   34935 L/C BURTON   A.   105751 Pte HOPKINS A.J.
   40482 " BOWKER   R.   48625 " JONES H.C.D.
      36259 Pte LEEMING L.

                     (sgd) R. E. TODD, Lt. Col. R.A.M.C.
                     COMDG 49th. FIELD AMBULANCE.

A.D.M.S.
   37 Division.

       The notification of the C.C.S. to which cases are evacuated is still very irregular in arrival.

       Can it be arranged please that the duplicate Nominal Roll sent down with patients may be sent back to Field Ambulance by post?

       The present method of stamping it and sending it back by the Driver of the M.A.C. Car which conveys the patients is not satisfactory.

       Enquiries from all sources are constantly being made of the whereabouts of patients evacuated to C.C.S. and the certain receipt of the notification is necessary in order to enable our records to be satisfactorily completed.

5. 8. 18.

Lt. Col. R.A.M.C.
Comdg 49 Field Ambulance.

Confidential

War Diary

of

49th Field Ambulance

From 1st September to 30th September 1918

WAR DIARY
or
INTELLIGENCE SUMMARY

Army Form C. 2118.

(Erase heading not required.)

Title pages September 1918

49th Field Ambulance

Place	Date	Hour	Summary of Events and Information	Remarks and references to Appendices
F.30.a.5.0 Sheet 57D (LA FOREST WOOD)	1st	a.m.	Fair. Windy - Cool. A.D.M.S. called and went round Ammunition Dump which is steadily filling instead of emptying as we had hoped. O.C. rode with him across country to D.H.Q. We are to hold ourselves in readiness to move to a new site if necessary. Visited 63rd Bde H.Q with a view to obtaining a lease exchange if possible so that SB styles could proceed - No use - Received Order No 105 which states 49th F.A. to be M.D.S. on present site 48th F.A. to close and park near 49th for further instructions - Perish on books to be transferred to 49th. To commence noon 2nd Sept.	
		p.m.	This Order was cancelled by wire T 98 at about 6.15 p.m and 49th ordered to pack and hold ready to move at from 6 a.m. Packing & dismantling of ambulance put up completed by 8.30 p.m. dumps of all material being arranged. Rear Marquees Operating Tent left up equipped in case of accidents - Monthly statement of Ops Impt sent to Base Cashier - balance checked = £2,669.90. O.C. 48 F. Amb. called about Teachne. War Diary for August corrected & sent to ADMS Weekly figures :-	

Sick admissions — 37 Div: 21, Other Forms: 18, Total: 39
Wounded — 97, 8, 105
To 48 F.A. for clinical adm. — 53, 4, 51
Total — 171, 30, 201

[signature]

Army Form C. 2118.

WAR DIARY
or
INTELLIGENCE SUMMARY.

(Erase heading not required.)

1918 September   **49th Field Ambce**

Instructions regarding War Diaries and Intelligence Summaries are contained in F.S. Regs., Part II. and the Staff Manual respectively. Title pages will be prepared in manuscript.

Place	Date	Hour	Summary of Events and Information	Remarks and references to Appendices
F.30.a.5.0 Sheet 57D (LOG EAST WOOD)	1st (cont)		L/Sgt Dyson paid Fr. 40 before proceeding to Catering Course. Barker paid 24 x 40 Obi. (for August) Dull - windy - heavy showers. Unit standing by ready to move.	
	2nd	a.m 10.30	No orders having been received O.C. went to D.H.Q. saw D.A.D.M.S. who said A.D.M.S. would like a reconnaissance of sites for a M.D.S. carried out. Went back to Unit & picked up Lt Styles and set out. Visited ACHIET-LE-PETIT, MIRAUMONT - R/5th IRISH RIFLES (MDS 42 Dn) then on to GREVILLERS where we met and spoke to G.O.C 42nd Divn (Mjr Gnl SULLY FLOOD) G.O.C. & Staff Captain R.A. of IV Corps. Good ride beyond GREVILLERS where we went to a C.C.S. decided on - Visited N.Z. Divn H.Q. saw Col McGAVIN the A.D.M.S. and we went back to site which we decided would be curve of approach road. his M.D.S. be the other opposite side of the road. At present 6 met Bondgeons are spreadeagled among the huts - These will mean forward today, the time having now advanced. At noon it was roughly BEUGNY - DELSAUX FARM - West of HAPLINCOURT. - between VILLERS-AU-FLOS & BARASTRE - E of TRANSLOY. Divisions in line from N to S of IV Corps front = 5th - N.Z - 42nd. Heard that G.O.C. 9 SDI and a Brigadier of 63rd Divn had been killed and a Brigadier of 42nd Divn. Returned through BIHUCOURT to D.H.Q. vf of ACHIET-LE-GRAND and reported to A.D.M.S. No news of a move for us yet. Returned to Unit at 3.15 p.m. Office - Paid Gles Parkinson and Rees Fr 100 each before proceeding to III Army Rest Camp at 6.15 p.m. today.	

Army Form C. 2118.

WAR DIARY
or
INTELLIGENCE SUMMARY.
(Erase heading not required.)

49th Field Ambulance

1918 Sept.

Instructions regarding War Diaries and Intelligence Summaries are contained in F. S. Regs., Part II. and the Staff Manual respectively. Title pages will be prepared in manuscript.

Place	Date	Hour	Summary of Events and Information	Remarks and references to Appendices
F.30.a.5.0 (Sh.57D) LOG EAST WOOD	2nd (Cont)		Copies of Army Orders 220-256 (August) received. Transfusion Sets now available for supply to Medical Units from No.1 Base Depot Medl. Stores, BOULOGNE. One set for each F. Amb & C.C.S. through usual channel (D.G. 15/35 d/d 29/7/18. This will be indented for on next indent from A.D.M. Stores.	
	3rd	Wet a.m.	Cleared later. A.D.M.S. called. The enemy have decamped and troops have lost touch with them. General forward move to be made. General idea at present is that 37 Div takes over from 5th Div on rough line in front of BERUMETZ.	
		a.m	48th F.Amb open M.D.S at G.9.b (Sh.57c) near ACHIET-LE-GRAND. 49th F.Amb to form M.D.S near FAVREUIL. 50th F.Amb to clear line with A.D.S. BEUGNATRE. Advanced D.H.Q moves to FAVREUIL.	
FAVREUIL H.16.c.2.7 (Sheet 57c)			Unit moved en masse at 2.30 p.m. O.C. & Capt. Ward forward to select site. We managed to secure temporary site in grounds of a completely ruined Chateau with a few riddled Nissen Bow tents irregularly arranged in the Park at H.16.C.2.7 - Unit marched in about 5 p.m. Fixed up Dressing Room with two Operating tents. Personnel accommodated on dugouts and shelters in the wood. Also Transport lines. Ready to receive at 9.30 p.m. Area fairly heavily bombed by E.A. up to about midnight - Difficult to shade lights and carry on in ruined huts under such conditions. At midnight area shelled by H.V. heavy gun till about 4.30 a.m. 5 wounded admitted during the night as result of bombing.	

WAR DIARY or INTELLIGENCE SUMMARY

Army Form C. 2118.

1918 September — HQ ½ Field Ambce

Place	Date	Hour	Summary of Events and Information	Remarks
FAVREUIL	3rd (Contd)		At 5:30 OC visited H.Q. 50th F. Amb. now at I.13.b (54c) and learnt that ADS will be at LEBUCQUIERE - Two Bearer Sub-Divisions and two large Cars to report to A.D.S. to clear line.	
	4th	a.m.	Fine - Bearers and Cars went off at dawn. Clouded over p.m. Some showers. OC & Major Nicholson to take over site of 5th Divl MDS at H.17.c.1.7. 'C' See to move at once and establish Dressing Station. 'B' See carry on at present site until 'C' See ready to receive. OC 21 MAC called & arranged about Cars for evacuation. D.D.M.S. called. 'C' See moved off at 9-45 a.m. with Major Nicholson & Capt. Marrot.	
H.17.C.1.7 (Sh 54c)			At noon Major Nicholson reported himself as ready to receive. The 3 large cars with the Unit getting odd stores to new site - Transport lines will remain in situ for the present as horse standings are good and transport vehicles are parked under trees which screen them from observation. 'B' See packed and moved off to new site.	
		3:10	OC & remaining men having cleared site, moved to new location at H.17.C.1.7.	
		4 p.m.	Found 16 Stretcher & 12 sitting cases awaiting evacuation - Sent urgent letter to M.A.C. asking for Cars by Major Despatch rider. Paid following men proceeding on leave tonight £1.50 each - 36390 Pte A.26 Bowens } RAMC T/025843 Sgt Usher a } 48625 " H.C. Jones } " T4/038202 Sgt Clulee R } ASC (HT) 3. ½ . " A.M. Aitcheson } T4/033125 " Sutherland D } 17962 Pte Wilson W, Bmen attached	

WAR DIARY or INTELLIGENCE SUMMARY

Army Form C. 2118.

49th Field Ambulance

1918 September

Place	Date	Hour	Summary of Events and Information	Remarks and references to Appendices
H-17. C-1-1 Sheet 57C	4th (Contd)		Lt Col Styles also proceeded on leave — Asked him to see into questions concerning purchase of (a) Cooks white clothing (b) Cigarettes while in Lancashire (c) Carpenters' tools	

		6pm	Wounded who reads = 6am to 6pm
			       Off OR
			 37 Bn 3 94 Evacuated 4 Offrs 75 OR
			 5 " 1 4 Rem 9: Lying 16
			 C.T. — 1 Sitting 10
			 P of W — 2
			           4 101
			
			 At 5.50 pm total numbers really awaiting were Lying 22
			                                                                 Sitting 12
			                                                                 Sick 8
			
			 At 6pm a passing empty lorry of 2nd N.Z. A.F.A. cleared some 18 W.W. to CCS in camps
			 At 6.10 O.C. 2 MAC called & we had 34 stretcher cases awaiting evacuation	

		6.15	D.A.D.M.S. called and promised he would try & arrange a lorry to bring up remaining stores from LOG EAST WOOD tomorrow morning.	
		6.20	1 MAC Cars cleared 28 cases leaving only 8 awaiting evacuation.	
		6.30	Situation Report sent to A.D.M.S. Mentioned therein that the 2 M.C.O.s 74 men at PUISEUX W.W. Clearing Station have to collect their rations from this Unit still — Asked	

Army Form C. 2118.

WAR DIARY
or
INTELLIGENCE SUMMARY.

49th Field Ambce

1918 Sept.

(Erase heading not required.)

Place	Date	Hour	Summary of Events and Information	Remarks and references to Appendices
H-17.c.1-7 (sh. 57c)	4th (cont'd) (2)		What T.S.O. Railhead might arrange to ration them. The area immediately around the Camp was fairly heavily shelled by heavy H.V. Guns. News from the Northern fronts is good. On this front - fair - 37th Divn are across the Canal and into HAVRINCOURT - 2nd Divn & N.Z. Divn on flanks rather held up. Enemy offering considerable resistance on the Canal line. Special Order regarding saluting & Distinguishing Flagged Cars published. At 4.10 pm today the Unit had dealt with 6 Offrs & 135 Other Ranks, including 2 German P of W, Wounded, & about 20 sick and no direct admissions to 48 F.A. After 8.30 pm cases came in very slowly till about 3 a.m. 5/9/18. Revd Marshall & Revd Thomas helped considerably in the "Restaurant Depot" keeping wounded supplied with hot drinks & cigarettes to	

		6 am	time - colder. Wounded evac:-
			      Offr OR
			 37 Divn 3 96
			 63 " 1 43
			 5th " 1 4
			 C.T. - 2
			    Total 4 51
			 Total last period 4 101
			 Grand total 8 152
				} Gas (Shell) Cases Nil
				 N.Y.D.N.; N.Y.D.Gassed, S.I. totalled 15
				 Evacuated since 6 pm last night 4 Offs 41 OR
				 Remaining Nil

	5th			

Place	Date	Hour	Summary of Events and Information	Remarks and references to Appendices
H.17.c.1.7 (Sh 57a)	5th (Contd)		Refilling point for Divnl Troops changed from BIEFVILLERS to near BEUGNATRE H.13.c.7.7. Of individual units in the Divn the 1st Berks had 13 sick and 62 Wounded sent to CCS 13th Royal Fusiliers had 60 Wounded.	
		10.30 a.m	ADMS called with OC 42 F.A. and gave news that one of our Brigades is to take over a two Batn front on our right from the N.Z. Divn, also that our Tent Sub- Divn of 142 F.A. are in position near FREMICOURT and will act as a Walking Wounded Dressing Station. This is more convenient as being on a main lorry route. It appears likely that we shall have two days comparative rest.	
		11 a.m	OC to see OC MT Column at ABLAINZEVELLE and arranged (a) For lorry to convey residuum of stores from LOGEAST WOOD to present site. (b) To try & get rid of the new Ford Car driver No M/338212 Pte C.P.Ball who is in every way unsatisfactory as a car driver. Called at old site on return journey & gave instructions about stores to be sent & ordered return of 2/Cpl Lintott & 5 OR. Left there as guard.	
		2 p.m	S.C.F Rev C/F Rev Major Kempster called about Y.M.C.A. Booths in connection with R.D.S. & M.D.S. Y.M.C.A. have opened a large Marquee Canteen opposite our present site. Did away with a large number of insanitary structures used by the enemy in this Camp area & effected a considerable improvement in the general cleanliness of Camp. With two Bearer Sub Divisions away and remaining staff divided into day and night shifts it is difficult to get a reasonably large fatigue party to work on improvements	
		2.15	Enemy plane brought down 2 of our Balloons in flames on our front	

Army Form C. 2118.

WAR DIARY
or
INTELLIGENCE SUMMARY.

(Erase heading not required.)

49th Field Ambulance

1918 September

Place	Date	Hour	Summary of Events and Information	Remarks and references to Appendices
H.Q. C.I.9. (Sheet 57c)	5th (Cont)		While O.C. was out this morning the D.D.M.S. called. Stated he was getting the Walking Wounded Railhead removed to BIHUCOURT. It would benefit more to the point if a definite lorry service could be arranged to clear M.D.S. during specially active periods of operations.	
		6 pm	Wounded were as follows:-	

			Offrs O.R.
			 37 Divn — 7
			 2nd " — 1
			 Pol M — 2
			      Total — 10
			   Growing total 8 162	

			Wrote to O.C. M.T. Coy regarding Pte Wall & re reinforcement in place of Pte McKellow who departed for England on 17/7/18 to join R.A.F.	
			A.A.Q.M.G. called and went round camp.	
			News from North excellent - LENS has fallen and 1st Army has taken 10,000 prisoners	
	6th	am	Fine - hot day.	
			E.A. active on reconnaissance duty.	
			63rd Bde relieved N.Z. Bde in the line last night.	
			111th Bde in reserve in BEUGNATRE area & this Unit to collect their sick.	

			Wounded were 6 pm to 6 am Offrs O.R.
			            37 Divn 1 15
			            5 " — 2
			            N.Z. — 3
			            P.W. 1 22
			    Remaining (sitting) cases - 3
			   Growing Total 9/9 184 O.R.	

Army Form C. 2118.

WAR DIARY
or
INTELLIGENCE SUMMARY.
(Erase heading not required.)

49th Field Ambulance

1918 September

Place	Date	Hour	Summary of Events and Information	Remarks and references to Appendices
H.17.C.1.7 (Sheet 57c)	6th (Cont)		Officer who passed through about midnight stated that the car he came down in took as long time to arrive as the driver lost his way. This aid is rather awkwardly placed off the beaten track. Letter re arrangements for visit of 111 Bde sent to H.Q. Bde and all M.Os of Bde. Administrative Instructions No A.Q.203 37 Div received. Dressing Baths will be at VELU Supplies at H.17.C.7.7 for 111 Bde. Water " " Salvage sent to Supply Refilling Points FAVREUIL H.16.a.2.3 Dirt Garden " FAVREUIL H.15.d.7.8 Evacuation of Civilians in Captured Localities - to DOULLENS by empty supply trains. A.D.M.S, O.C. 43 F.A. & O.C. 21 M.A.C called. Letter regarding delay in sending Diacetmorph Nivals received. Dental cases 13 for the Divn allotted at 29 C.C.S. Report re supply of water sent down by O.C. 50 F.Amb from forward area. By Major Scarisbrick shews - no trace of Metallic poisons or Cyanide - Requires 2 scoops Chloride lime per Water Cart. A.R.O. regarding explosives published. The Post & Bates of the Unit notified by 48 F.A. on evacuated to C.C.S. Kitchen has been greatly improved today - Extra Latrine accommodation has been provided and a Mortuary & Salvage Dump put into one of the derived huts. The fly nuisance is considerable despite the amount of cleaning effected - Fly traps, papers & formalin are installed in the Camp - Baths & Ablution bench put up in one of the huts near the Patches and will be installed next.	MA

Army Form C. 2118.

WAR DIARY
or
INTELLIGENCE SUMMARY.
(Erase heading not required.)

149th Field Ambce

1918 September

Place	Date	Hour	Summary of Events and Information	Remarks and references to Appendices
H.19.c.1.7 (Sheet 57ᴬ)	6th (Contd) 2		C.C. R.C. Capt Brookfield came into residence with the Ambulance today. 6 pm Wounded nine	
			37 from	
			T. of M.	
			off O.R.
			— 9
			— 1
			— 10 mobiles & Sawed cases (Green & Skull)	
			Evening total 9 / 194	
			Plans of Ambulance at M.D.S. LOGEAST WOOD added (Drawn by Sgt Chilton). The Unit had reason to be pleased with the action of the Service Dress Clothing left at old site under lock & key & marked up previous day. Salvage all articles were made of material rescued from the ruined camps nearby are Sgt Emett when he went down this morning — Loss notes reported to A.D.M.S. in the Evening Disturbance Report.	AF I
	7th.	a.m	Cloudy — more windy — E.A. active during early part of last night — No bombs especially near to this site — Shelling of back areas continues. Administrative Instructions A.Q. 243 received (Col. 67/2) Civil Boundaries, Water supplies + are all now clearly defined. The Divis is through HAVRINCOURT WOOD but held up on the left flank near HERMIES Wounded Mine 6 am =	
			37 from off O.R.
			C.T. 1 3
			2 —
			3 3
			12 / 197 Evening total	

Army Form C. 2118.

WAR DIARY
or
INTELLIGENCE SUMMARY.
(Erase heading not required.)

49th Field Ambulance

1918 September

Instructions regarding War Diaries and Intelligence Summaries are contained in F. S. Regs., Part II. and the Staff Manual respectively. Title pages will be prepared in manuscript.

Place	Date	Hour	Summary of Events and Information	Remarks and references to Appendices
H.17.c.1.7. (S.570)	1st (Sunday)		Weekly Returns to dealt with Pte Spencer – Perionsillar abscess sent to 4 F.A. with a private note to O.C. Letaford. P? Para Typhoid.	
		11 am	A.D.M.S called and went round Camp. Arranged that I might now get rid of the large excess of Stretchers, Blankets, Splints is now held by the Unit. Stretchers and Blankets to M.A.C. Dump – Letter to "Q" to arrange for destruction of unexploded shells and bombs which the salvage people refuse to take over. Various C. & B. balances notified by Regl Paymaster received and entered on AB 64 of men concerned –	
		1 pm	Attention again drawn to lack of proper Traffic Control & Road discipline on some Units (DRO 3746) Order brought to notice of all personnel HQ & M.T. Order against givens unauthorized lifts to troops. Officers & O.R. published in Unit Orders. Notification of appointment Acting Lieut. Col. R.E. Todd, as O.C. 49 Field Ambce from 8th July 1918 received on extract from List of Appointments to N°202 of 25/8/18 3/ Div A 9 6/14 28 A - 6 9/13 – ADMS 5/10/ 35 off. 9 9/12 received. 100 Blankets sent to O.C. 50 7 Amb at his request O.C. 48 7 Amb asked if certain excess Medical comforts which were now held by this Unit would be of use to him –	
		3.30 pm	The pilot and observer of an A.W. Reconnaissance plane which had to make a forced landing near here, this morning owing to Engine failure, given lunch	

(A7092) Wt. W12839/M1393. 75,000. 1/17. D.D. & L., Ltd. Forms/C.2118/14.

Army Form C. 2118.

WAR DIARY
or
INTELLIGENCE SUMMARY

(Erase heading not required.)

149th Field Ambulance

1918 September

Instructions regarding War Diaries and Intelligence Summaries are contained in F.S. Regs., Part II. and the Staff Manual respectively. Title pages will be prepared in manuscript.

Place	Date	Hour	Summary of Events and Information	Remarks and references to Appendices
H.17.c.1.4 (Sh. 57 c)	4th (Con't)		Officer R.A.M.C. also asks for Certificate of qualification for the post of Dispenser in case of S/S Bland 3 Jenks. R.A.M.C. of this Unit. Certificates will be obtained by them & forwarded later. Condemned a sample of 70lbs of meat forwarded for inspection from H.Q. 111 Bde. Wounded Men:-	
		5pm	34 Division — 9½ — S.R. — 11	
			12th — — 1 — 1	
			Corp. Troops — — 1	
			— 13	
			Running Total 12 210	
		6pm	Remaining 2 sitting — these will probably be sent back to their unit. Very slightly wounded. When they recover their rifles & equipment will be noted here.	(A)/S
	5th	a.m.	Cloudy — cold — very windy. Gotha reported over about 3 a.m. dropped bombs also to present are - Report on loss of S.D. Clothing submitted to A.D.M.S. The loss was noticed on 31st Ult. Situation Report. Submitted name of Staff Sergt. T.D. Warwick for course of Gunnery. No names for the Bricklaying Course. Stock of Medical comforts sent to Offr 48th. F.Amb. Last evening, he having notified they would be very acceptable for D.R.S. cases.	
	8th		N° 40819 Pte E Woods R.A.M.C. reported as having paraded satisfactorily as a cook. Further Administrative Instructions A.Q. 255 giving short reports on adequacy of Water supplies received. Order issued re non-billetting of men in houses or marked ROUGE = (Seabies) Divisional Location Est received	W.S

Army Form C. 2118.

WAR DIARY
or
INTELLIGENCE SUMMARY.
(Erase heading not required.)

Instructions regarding War Diaries and Intelligence Summaries are contained in F. S. Regs., Part II. and the Staff Manual respectively. Title pages will be prepared in manuscript.

104 Field Ambulance

September 1918

Place	Date	Hour	Summary of Events and Information	Remarks and references to Appendices
H.14 c.14 (Sheet 57°)	8th (Cont)		Own Wounded Men:— Off OR 37 Division — 1 10 Running total 13 220 — Remaining 1 officer & 12 men	
		11am	O.C. visited Transport lines. These were not satisfactory. Wagons not fraked properly. Tailboard of one of the limbers broken. — Wagon covers blown off wagons — Senior N.C.O. still showing — The one bright spot was the fact that stabling had been cleaned out and was almost ready for use by the horses. Went on to Div. H.Q. and drew £6,000 for Imprest A/c. — Visted G.S.O.1, L.O. R.T.O. and got a view of the situation. The enemy apparently pivoting on HAVRINCOURT, which remains in command of a valley approach, and falling back on the Hindenberg Line, the Canal du NORD north of HAVRINCOURT has banks 99 feet deep and affords a difficult passage for troops in that sector. Met Lt.Col. SAUNDERS, C.M.G. D.S.O. Legion of Honour O/C 1st Essex Regt. who was just leaving the Division to assume command of a Brigade. Visited A.D.M.S. Office	
		12.20 pm	Returned to Unit. — Start raining which will lay the dust it is hoped— Notification received that Rations for personnel now at Walking Wounded Railhead would be drawn under Corps Arrangements. This in response to our request. Change of underclothing were sent to the Superintendent Company hand out by Major Ashburn	
		5.15 pm	Now raining very heavily. News from the South Good — COUCY — CHAULNY and HAM are to reported as taken	B Noakes

Army Form C. 2118.

WAR DIARY
or
INTELLIGENCE SUMMARY.
(Erase heading not required.)

49th Field Ambulance

1918. September

Instructions regarding War Diaries and Intelligence Summaries are contained in F. S. Regs., Part II. and the Staff Manual respectively. Title pages will be prepared in manuscript.

Place	Date	Hour	Summary of Events and Information	Remarks and references to Appendices
H.if. C.i.Y (sheet 54C) (Cont.)	8th		Weekly Summary of Cases:-	
			37 Div Attd.Arms P.O.W. Total	
			Sick Admissions 23 13 - 36	
			Wounded do. 198 23 6 233	
			To 143 FA died 100 21 - 121	
			Totals 321 64 6 390	
		6 p.m.	Wounded Wave:- Off OR	
			37 Div Nil 10 Evacuated 150R	
			Evening total 13 220 Remaining Nil	
			Paid out yesterday Fr. 3,550.	
			Balance Fr. 2,519.90	
	9th	a.m.	Cloudy, very windy - Rained heavily early a.m. -	
			Signed Acquittance Rolls for transmission to Cashier, Base -	
			Important correspondence received as under:-	
			(a) D.G. 32/10 dt. 5/9/18. 94 Lences within ½" of each correction cannot be furnished to American troops, indents should be submitted to A.D.M.S. PARIS area.	
			(b) D.G. 75/3 dt. 14/9/18. Specimens derived of ISOETHYLHYDROCUPREINE captured from German Medical Units. It has a high value as a disinfectant. Reported through usual channels that no samples had been captured by this Unit.	
			(c) 37 Div. G. 511 dt. 5/9/18. Samples of batches of prisoners to be sent without delay to Div. Cage. Not all to be retained for work as bearers in Medical Units.	
			(d) D.G. Sth/1254 dt. 3.9.18. All acting unpaid N.C.Os. + N.C.Os. in excess of ranks authorised forthwith. Acting unpaid appointments will in future be regulated from G.H.Q. - Compliance reported.	

WAR DIARY
or
INTELLIGENCE SUMMARY

Army Form C. 2118.

1918 September

HQ of Field Ambulance

Place	Date	Hour	Summary of Events and Information	Remarks and references to Appendices
H.17.c.1.4. (Sheet 57C)	9th (Contd)		to A.D.M.S. and application made for appointment as Officiating S.C.F. for the following men stating reasons for asking :- Pte Brown J.H. Receiving Room Clerk etc. Pte Bowker } Ho Operating Theatre & Dressing Room " Heap } " Crawford } " Leslie } Ho Stretcher Squads " Baker } " Gillman Ho Refreshment Room & Ho Deskin Equipment " Neville Ho Unit's Band & Ho Deskin Equipment Divl Order No 3748 regarding practice of lightly wounded men discarding Arms and Equipment before reaching a Dressing Station. A.D.M.S. to arrange for names of offenders to be reported for disciplinary action. Both Road and Albuhera Benches now maintest & Camp generally greatly improved.	
		11.30 am	A.D.M.S. called. This unit to move and open M.D.S. at LEBUCQUIÈRE. A.D.S. moves to RUYAUCOURT. 62nd Divn to take HAVRINCOURT - 37 Divn to take FRESCAULT & onwards toward HINDENBURG LINE. Attack to begin ? 11th inst.	
			Lt 190 sent to O.C. N.M Railhead for Map of our personnel there. Impress balance £2.32.4.70. Wrote A.D.M.S. asking that something might be done regarding delay in forwarding of tracks of men of unit who pass through Divl Reception Camp. The instances in which it occurs are numerous & frequent.	
		p.m.	O.C. B/114 D. & Nicholson to LEBUCQUIÈRE to arrange how to fit site of present A.D.S. as a M.D.S. for Walking and Lying Wounded. The site is cramped -	AMS

WAR DIARY
or
INTELLIGENCE SUMMARY.

Army Form C. 2118.

49th Field Ambulance

1918 September

Place	Date	Hour	Summary of Events and Information	Remarks and references to Appendices

H.17.c.1.4.
(Sheet 57°)
(Contd)
	9th
	2
			dirty - and accommodation poor - Also visited BEUGNY to try and arrange Transport lines. Finally decided to leave them where they are till Water situation is more settled. Ptes Boff & Savage returned from Army Rest Camp. Pte Johnson W. from 43 S. Amb. - Ptes Lail & Kempson returned from leave. Pte Kempson reported 5 days late at Victoria Station. Asked ADMS if this case could be dealt with by me as Comdg Officer - We already have one F.G. C.M. pending. Wounded 6.h. on 8/9/18 to 6.h.m. 9/9/18 :-
			
			            O/R O/R
			34 Divn 1 34 ×
			63 " - 3
			C.T. - 2
			                  1 45
			Growing Total 14 265
			
			× Includes 29 gassed Yellow Cross
			              1 OR - - Blue Cross
			
			Settled details of move tomorrow with O.C Sections of 81/pr Res.
			B. Sec moves 10 am H.Q. & details by exp as soon as able is cleared
			    opens 3.30 p.m. leaving a holding party of 1 N.C.O. & 2 O.R. as
			C " moves 4 pm guard to stores to -
			    opens 6 pm
			
			Reported action on Situation Report pending definite orders from ADMS
			Special Order regarding NYDN & NYD Gassed cases published to prevent any confusion which is said to exist in some Field Ambces. (D.G. letter No 8053/1209 of 5/9/18)
			Orders received regarding relief of Brigades in line as under tonight—
			63 rd relieves 112 R. without withdrawing to BEUGNY less 1 Bat.n in support of 63 rd - 111 Bde takes	

WAR DIARY
or
INTELLIGENCE SUMMARY

Army Form C. 2118.

1918 September   HQ X Field Ambulance

Place	Date	Hour	Summary of Events and Information	Remarks and references to Appendices
H.17.c.1.7 (Sh.57c)		a.m.	over main line of resistance P.29 – J.33 central –	
			Raining - Very windy	
			Orders for move received from ADMS early, as follows :-	
			50% to open ADS at RUYAULCOURT	
		10 am	1/9 X { One Tent Sub Divn to take over present site LEBUCQUIÈRE I.30.a.6.6 from 50% & form MDS as from noon 11th Sept	
			{ Two Tent Sub Divns and present MDS close at FAVREUIL & form LEQUVIÈRE GRAND and DRS	
			48% { Two Tent Sub Divns remain at ACHIET LE GRAND as DRS	
			{ One Tent Sub Divn man FREMICOURT remain closed and be prepared to move at short notice	
			Acted on follows :- "B" Secs and all personnel that could be spared moved to new site at 10 am with sufficient necessary transport details – "D" Sec. of men going on leave tomorrow + holding party of 3 remain at present site as also Officer.	
			OC to see ADMS re getting 6 Bandsmen to act as Bearers for today at MDS - also other details.	
			Went on to LEBUCQUIÈRE to arrange details of taking over with OC 50% F.Amb. When open "B" Sec will act for a short time as ADS. to allow 50 F.A. to leave the site of their stuff & personnel.	
			Back to lunch -	
			Removal of YMCA Marquee arranged – This will be useful for Walking Wounded reception at the new site - Note from ADMS stating that half a Bearer Office Sub Divn could not be spared from the line for duty with the Unit as asked for in last nights Situation Report	[initials]

Army Form C. 2118.

WAR DIARY
or
INTELLIGENCE SUMMARY.
(Erase heading not required.)

49th Field Ambulance   September 1918

Place	Date	Hour	Summary of Events and Information	Remarks and references to Appendices
H.17.c.1/9. (Sh. 57c)	10th (cont)	2.45 pm	6 Bandsmen reported for duty as Bearers. The remainder of the Band will form up at LEBASQUIÈRE at a date to be arranged later.	
		3 pm	Went to LESBOEUFS - B Sec. rapidly installing and now functioning as A.D.S. till 50% are installed at RUYAUCOURT. Arranged for Transport horses in the village near M.D.S. The water situation for horses is rather precarious but it will settle and it is far better that the Unit should be complete with transport. It is hoped that enemy will not continue bombing the area as heavily as he has done recently.	
		5 pm	Returned to Unit. Paid out men who proceed on leave tomorrow morning:- Sgt J.J. Lord fr.100 : Pte Buskin fr.150 : Pte Bay fr.150 : Pte Linton fr.75 : " Thomson fr.150 :- Total fr.650 = Pte Walton R.S.C. also goes on leave - he was paid on Sunday. Refused application of No 1 Coy 37 Bn Tanks to medically categorize a man of their unit - Stated that authority should be obtained from H.Q. Tank Cs. as we have no authority to do so. Warned 6pm 9/9/18 to 6pm 10/9/18	

```
              Off    O.R
       3/     1     48 *   + Includes 25 Bearers (Yellow Cross)
       62     -      2
    Corps Troops  1      1
                 ___    ___
                  1     51
                 16     36
```

Ground total 16 36

Orders issued for complete move of Unit tomorrow. Situation Personnel will reinstall unit

WAR DIARY or INTELLIGENCE SUMMARY.

Army Form C. 2118.

49th Field Ambulance

1918 September

Place	Date	Hour	Summary of Events and Information	Remarks and references to Appendices
LEBUCQUIERE 11th (I.30.a.6.6) Sh.57c		a.m.	Stormy - cold. Considerable bombing of area last night - Section at LEBUCQUIERE sent down some 20 cases of bomb wounds to during the night. Bore front instructions regarding move.	
		10.30	Conference of F.Amb. Commanders at A.D.M.S. Office. Details of the attack were gone into and medical arrangements in connection therewith. This Unit has to deal with Walking & Lying Wounded and open a Gas Centre as well - 50th F.Amb run clearance of him 2.A.D.S. at RUYAULCOURT (F.16.a.2.6) - 148th F.Amb D.R.S. at ACHIET LE GRAND whither slightly wounded, Injured Cases and Sick will be transferred - 62nd Div on the left attack HAVRINCOURT 37th Div. Centre } TRESCAULT Spur and area beyond to Hindenburg Line - N.Z. Div. Right }	
			Remainder of Unit and Transport & Band details attached left H.16.d.9.6 at 11.55am & arrived at LEBUCQUIERE (I.30.a.6.6) at 1.25 p.m. -O.C. joined at 1.30 p.m. having visited 56 C.C.S. GREVILLERS en route from Conference. Camp rapidly being improved and cleanliness now being established. It was infested with flies and rats and had large quantities of refuse lying about.	
		3.30 p.m.	D.D.M.S. IV Corps with A.D.M.S. 37 Div. § O.C. 31 M.A.C. called and went round proposed arrangements. 37 Divisional Orders out § 242 for attack tomorrow received and acknowledged.	
		5.45	Horsed Ambces (2 each from 153rd & 114th F.Ambs - 5th Div) reported for duty with 2 days rations. Notification received that Major Wilton Mondol, M.C. U.S.A. attached Senior Dive Consultant in General Medicine to IV Corps A.E.F. facilities to be afforded to meet American patients. Copy of 37 Div § Wire 609 M. 10th states that N.Z. Div report enemy putting over volleys of behind 200 & 300 projectiles about any of orange covering an area of	

Army Form C. 2118.

WAR DIARY
or
INTELLIGENCE SUMMARY.
(Erase heading not required.)

49th Field Ambulance

September 1918

Place	Date	Hour	Summary of Events and Information	Remarks and references to Appendices
LEBUCQUIERE	11th (Contd)		Last 3 ones which burst on contact giving off gas - When gas clears ground & grass are burnt. The Wire Beats on the necessity for Gas accommodation. 200 further blankets sent to OC 50th F. Amb which makes 300 transferred in last 3 days. Some 200 sets of gas-col clothing received from 50th F Amb this afternoon - Wounded. 6pm 10th to 6 pm 11th.	

			                       ORs offs
			37 D. Auto 35 (includes 32 Yellow Cross & 9 Blue Cross - Gassed (shell)
			62 " 3
			N.Z. " 1
			C.T. 4
			                  43
			Growing total 16 350	

			Weather cleared & wind dropped towards evening - Fairly heavy long range shelling of area round this side - Place is stocked with horses. Transport lines to left no casualties in large numbers at present -	
		9 pm	Zero hour notified at 5:25 a.m.	N.S.
	12th		A miserably wet windy day - Some 33 cases through it up to 6 am this morning. Barrage started at Zero hour. - First cases commenced arriving at M.D.S. about 7:15 am	
		10 am	Cases coming down steadily & evacuation keeping pace with entry - Bus & lorry reported for duty for Walking Wounded. 8 MAC Cars - sent note to OC 21 MAC to forward 100 more blankets	
		10:45	ADMS, DADMS & Lt Col Clarke called - were shewn round - seemed pleased OC 21 MAC called	

Army Form C. 2118.

WAR DIARY
or
INTELLIGENCE SUMMARY.

(Erase heading not required.)

 1918 September   49th Field Ambulance

Place	Date	Hour	Summary of Events and Information	Remarks and references to Appendices
LESCOUVIERES	12th (Cont)	11.30 a.m.	D.D.M.S. & DADG IV Corps called - They also seemed satisfied. Road for cars built of old bricks proceeding well - The heavy rain during morning rather flooded canvas erections but these were dealt with by drainage. G.S. Wagons sent to our old site to collect the heap of head bands we had salved. Evacuation is keeping pace with entry quite satisfactorily. Up to noon today figures for wounded dealt with & evacuated were:—	

			            Offr OR
			3rd Divn 2 34
			62 " " 4 65
			3 " " 1 4
			Corps Troops - 6
			P of W - 9
			              7 118	

			Weather cleared a little towards noon but still looks stormy. By 1.30 p.m. dressings were sufficiently slack to allow of staff taking lunch in relays.	
		1 p.m.	200 Blankets received from M.A.C. News seems to be good - All the Corps objectives are reported by the wounded as having been taken - With the exception of Machine Gunners the enemy are stated not to be fighting hard but either surrendering or retreating hurriedly. Our barrage is reported as excellent - Very few casualties claimed to have been the result of our gunnery.	
		3 p.m.	Capt Drew took M.O.s RE attached for duty today. I went forward to A.D.S. at Ecoust S Mein where Cases were being easily dealt with and there was	A.S.A.

Army Form C. 2118.

WAR DIARY
or
INTELLIGENCE SUMMARY.
(Erase heading not required.)

49th Field Ambulance

1918 September

Place	Date	Hour	Summary of Events and Information	Remarks and references to Appendices
LEBUCQUERE	Sept 12 (Contd)		no news of any large numbers likely to be coming down from the line. OC 50th FA did not think we could help him in any way. A few extra splints & a further stock of dressings had been sent from M.D.S. just before I started.	
		5.10 pm	D.D.M.S. called again & went round. His visit was mainly concerned with the possible visit of the D.M.S. (General Murray Irwin). Wire from the Div'n & surrounding Units dealt with at 6.30 this afternoon by Orderly Officer. Letter received from the mother of Pte Bonfield ASC who was killed by shell fire at ACHIET-LE-GRAND, asking for particulars of his death and burial	
		6.15 pm	A.D.M.S. called again. He states that some of the Units estimate their casualties at up to 100, which is strange in view of the fact that only 80 have passed through our hands for the Division. He states that the N.Z. Division are being withdrawn from the line and relieved by the 5th Div'n. Wounded 6 pm 11th to 6 pm 12th —	

	Offrs	OR
37th Division	3	7 (includes 2 O.R. Gassed (Blue X Shell))
62nd "	6	94
2nd "	–	4
3rd "	1	4
5th "	–	1
Corps Troops	1	10
Prisoners of War	1	33
	12	223
Grand Total	28	582

Army Form C. 2118.

WAR DIARY
or
INTELLIGENCE SUMMARY.
(Erase heading not required.)

49th Field Ambulance

1918 September

Instructions regarding War Diaries and Intelligence Summaries are contained in F. S. Regs., Part II. and the Staff Manual respectively. Title pages will be prepared in manuscript.

Place	Date	Hour	Summary of Events and Information	Remarks and references to Appendices
LEGUCQUIERE	Sept 12 (Contd)		A.D.M.S. 62 Divn called at Office to enquire number of casualties from his Divn which had passed through our hands – He could not wait to see me – Refilling points moved to I 28 a 3 b from today. Letter D.M.S. 61 Div/33 regarding attachment of M.A.C. Cars to M.D.S. received Capt. Fletcher M.O. of D.A.C. came over this afternoon to help & relieve Capt. Ward who was sent to bed as he had been up most of the day – Cloudy & stormy. Rained heavily during the night. Done 12 stretcher cases & 26 sitting cases were dealt with during the night.	(ks)
	13th	a.m.	"C" Communique received states that at 4.30 pm yesterday "37 Divn are on offensive on whole front – BILHEM & TRESCAULT villages & – total prisoners captured by 37 Divn = 250. 13 KR R.C. captured DERBY TRENCH after hand fighting – This Balln captured about 140 unwounded 2 Field Guns, 18 Machine Guns and 2 Trench Mortars. A rough idea of the proportion of various cases as the result of yesterdays fighting may be gained from the following figures – Stretcher cases 100 } serious and Sitting cases 144 } moderately serious Walking cases 56 } lighter D.A.D.O.S. moved to 1660 yesterday – Respirator Exchange held 21.C.5.7.4 following items of correspondence received – (a) D.D.M.S. II Corps 2/786/4. If S. Clyn claimants of exchange to 42 Staty Hosp. Replied "No" (2) D.G. 100/34 dt 7%/18 M.Os required for RAF (1) Wing M.O. under 40 active, be prepared to fly, & take an active part in the life of the Wing (2) Not M.Os. "B" Officers eligible – but prepared to fly when required to do so	NT

Army Form C. 2118.

WAR DIARY
or
INTELLIGENCE SUMMARY.
(Erase heading not required.)

49th Field Ambulance

1918 September

Instructions regarding War Diaries and Intelligence Summaries are contained in F.S. Regs., Part II. and the Staff Manual respectively. Title pages will be prepared in manuscript.

Place	Date	Hour	Summary of Events and Information	Remarks and references to Appendices
LEBUCQUER	13th (Cont)		(c) D.G. 75/81 calling attention to serious shortage of Quinine Salts	
			i Stocks to be carefully watched	
			ii Undue accumulations to be reported	
			iii Indents carefully limited to actual requirements	
			(d) III Army Dental Centre from LIGNY sur CANCHE opens FREVENT close to No 15 R.D.M. Stores on 17-9-18	
			(e) Forms of Renewal of Contract for Capt. WARD, R.A.M.C.	
			Camp being got into order – trench boarded, Road Completed, Refuse burned, extra Equipment and Baths being installed. Transport lines improved	
	11.45 am		O.C. 21 M.A.C called to talk over question of evacuation	
	12.25 pm		O.C. 62 San. Sec. (Capt. Braydon) called & asked if 2 Sergts & 6 OR. could be billetted & rationed by us – Arrangements were made to do so.	
			Receipt for 200 blankets received from O.C. 50 F. Amb.	
			City Wire D.D.M.S. M/3286 all cases lying & Walking from IV Corps to 56 CCS GREVILLERS file further orders	
			Notification received that Pte GALISS V.C. would be sent to this Unit. Our reasons were evidently in the interests of the Service.	
			An interesting case of vascular pigmentation of the arm affecting ? Mme J. Medicus Calcareous Nerve distribution was seen among the sick this morning – It would appear from the history to be the possible result of a bayonet wound of the forefinger left hand received about a year ago. Boy aged 20 of 13 KRRC –	
			Board in Command 8 Som. L.I. came to ask permission to use Y.M.C.A. Marquee for a Concert tonight – This was granted	
	1 pm		Went round Camp & inspected various improvements – It is a beastly site & almost impossible to render really sanitary without immense labour – Code Codes originally issued for use from 20/23 Aug. will be taken into use midnight 13/14 Sep.	

(A7092). Wt W12859/M1293. 75,000. 1/17. D.D. & L., Ltd. Forms/C.2118/14.

Army Form C. 2118.

WAR DIARY
or
INTELLIGENCE SUMMARY.

(Erase heading not required.)

49 Cy Field Amb ce

1918 September

Place	Date	Hour	Summary of Events and Information	Remarks and references to Appendices
LESQUIELRE	13th (Cont'd)		others to be destroyed & certificate rendered -	
			Reinforcement T/039729 Pr E. Webb A.S.C. reported from 3rd Corps Train -	
			News of a Franco-American offensive on the ST MIHIEL salient	
			Enemy planes active over this area - One seen to be brought down	
			Wounded 6 pm 12th to 6 pm 13th :-	
				O/R	O.R.	
			37 Div	1	56*	*Includes 2 Yellow X and 1 Blue X Gassed (Shell)
			62 "	1	22	
			63 "	-	1	
			Corps Troops	-	6*	*Includes 8 Yellow X and 1 Blue X Gassed (Shell)
			P of W	-	15	
				2	100	
			Growing total	30	682	
						W.I.
			Ptes Spencer & Lotchford rejoined from Hospital.	
	14th	am	Cloudy - windy -	
			11 Stretcher cases & 10 sitting passed through during the night, includes the orderly of G.O.C. 8th Div badly wounded by shell fire & not expected to live -	
			A.D.M.S. notified special Medical Arrangements for Active Operations most revert to normal -	
			Lieut Martin detailed to look after A.A. searchlight section at H.18. Cent. on Tent Sub-division of 48 F. Amb. FREMICOURT are going to assist 56 C.C.S.	
			O.O. 3 Army in command 8th Somerset L.I. called to thank us for loan of Marquee for Concert & brought news that St MIHIEL salient had been obliterated by Franco-American offensive & 29,000 prisoners taken -	

Army Form C. 2118.

WAR DIARY
or
INTELLIGENCE SUMMARY.
(Erase heading not required.)

1918 September   49th Field Ambulance

Place	Date	Hour	Summary of Events and Information	Remarks and references to Appendices
LEBUCQUIERE	14th (Contd)		O.C. 21 M.A.C. called & notified that cases for Special Centre would be collected at N.Z. D.R.S. on BAPAUME Road so as to avoid wastage of cars on the long run to FILLIEVRES. Weekly Returns dealt with. Number of German P of W. wounded who have passed through this Unit from 21/8/18 to 11/9/13 = 4 Offrs 192 O.R. of which total, notified to A.D.M.S. for information of Q Branch. Administrative Instructions A.Q.340 received (a) Div. Recep. Camp moves to FAVREUIL today (b) Order regarding prevention of Trench foot published. Tram to 4/Iam Camphor Soap and Powder which will be made up by 148 F. Amb. (c) Spray Baths ready at VELU Station. Letter of sympathy sent to Mrs Bonfield in response to her enquiries. A.D.M.S. asks for name of an Officer who is desirous of can be recommended for duties as D.A.D.M.S. of a Division. Wire confirming Southern successes received O.C. to see A.D.M.S. at D.H.Q about various matters — 48th sent Trench foot medicaments to this Amb.e. It was sent back again in accordance with Instructions noted above.	

Wounded 6 pm to 6 pm

	Offr	O.R.
37 Divn	1	60 → 3 Yellow X; 2 Green X & 1 Blue X Gassed (Shell)
5 Divn	–	1
C.T.	–	2 – lost Yellow X Gassed (Shell)
F.W.	–	1
Total	1	64
Grand Total		31	946

Army Form C. 2113.

WAR DIARY
or
INTELLIGENCE SUMMARY.
(Erase heading not required.)

49th Field Ambulance

1918 September

Place	Date	Hour	Summary of Events and Information	Remarks and references to Appendices
LEBUCQUIERE	14th (contd)		It being stormy - Enemy Aircraft were not active, but there was some H.V. shelling of the area	
	15th		Cloudy - less windy - Cleared afternoon - fine evening - 19 Lying cases & 14 sitting cases passed through during the night - Admin. Instructions A.D. 314 received, giving allotment of Baths at VELU Station - We shall not use it having now installed our own in the Gas Hut. Q. asked for changes of clothing & where dirty clothing is to be sent. Shelling all round over this morning - One of our Observation Balloons brought down in flames - Observer got clear in parachute - The name of Lt. Col. RAMS submitted for leave to PARIS in response to ADMS 7/33 df 14/9/18 Indent for 200 Pyjamas Suits & 3 Drums Distemper sent to A.D.M.S. for countersignature - State of Cars is low:- On road 1 Ford 1 Sunbeam A.D.M.S. 1 Sunbeam 50th F.A. 1 -do- Workshot 2 -do- 1 Ford Dicta transport to 48 F.A. being fairly heavy, half of M.T.C. may be needed - O.C. M.T.Coy asked to expedite discharge of Cars from Workshot. Pant Thomas left on leave to U.K. Wrote A.D.M.S. regarding a certain confidential letter received from O.C 37 Div Train not now in having now installed our own on 10th for Consumption on the 12th/ Wrote "Q" re shortage in French Oats Horse Ration issued One bag was 10lbs short - Wrote ADMS answering D.G. 100/34 stating that no Officer under my command was desirous of service with R.A.F. Also reported no Officer desirous of serving as DADMS of a Division - The Medical Board appointed for 11 am to examine The Lingham 13 R Fus in response to a letter to the Prime Minister from his wife, was dissolved as the man	ASR

Army Form C. 2118.

WAR DIARY
or
INTELLIGENCE SUMMARY.

(Erase heading not required.)

49th Field Ambulance

1918 September

Instructions regarding War Diaries and Intelligence Summaries are contained in F.S. Regs., Part II. and the Staff Manual respectively. Title pages will be prepared in manuscript.

Place	Date	Hour	Summary of Events and Information	Remarks and references to Appendices
LEBUCQUIERE	15th (Cont'd)		failed to appear. Papers returned to A.D.M.S. reporting non appearance. DADOS called and was asked about Tarpaulins - Difficulty in getting Ordnance Stores from the Base due to lack of railway transport. H.Q. 50 F.A. move from BERTINCOURT to RUYALCOURT today - Shelled out of their location. A.C.I. 940 of 1918 received re Articles for use in Army Hospitals which can be obtained from D.G.V.O. Following items received in correspondence - (a) W.O. Letter 129/Medical/3434 (A.D.M.S.) d/- 5/9/18. Tetanus anti toxin to be indented for as "phials 1500 units" or "phials 500 units" and for high potency serum "phials 8,000 units". Particulars required for French Soldiers on (B) D.G. 787/69 d/- 11/9/18 - Instructions regarding Particulars required for French Soldiers in British Medical Units who apply for leave. (c) D.G. 197/5 d/- 10/9/18 - Disposal of Field Medical Cards i. They will accompany from one Unit to another on transfer. ii Cards of patients discharged to duty or dying kept 3 months then sent to D.A.G. 3rd Echn. for transmission to Medical Records Committee. iii Under no circumstances will they be destroyed. (d) D.M.S. 3rd Army A.W. 138 d/- 12/9/18 - Statement of Soldiers on A.F.G. W. 3428 to be obtained wherever possible - Whenever impossible note to be made. Published in Units Orders. Received War Estab. for F.S. Amb. No. 1580 - Part VII A d/- 17/8/13 - supersedes W.E. No. 632.	
		7pm	Capt. A.P. Biggs R.A.M.C. returned from leave. Tarpaulin Shelter lent by 47 F. Amb. returned to them today - Another tarpaulin has been received as an issue. Form Observation Balloons have been brought down in flames within sight of this location.	E.A.

Army Form C. 2118.

WAR DIARY
or
INTELLIGENCE SUMMARY.
(Erase heading not required.)

49th Field Ambce
1918 Septr

Place	Date.	Hour	Summary of Events and Information	Remarks and references to Appendices
LEBUCQUIERE	15th (contd)		Reported to "Q" that shortage of Oats had been made up by receipt of 80lbs extra today. We also received 40lbs of salt which the horses & mules were badly in need of. Pvts. Geo. Letchford & Spencer Fr. 30 each - they were about sick last pay day. Dropping money Fr. 3.50 received & delivered to Canteen Funds. Wrote ADMS asking that arrangements might be made by which Chaplains attached during special phases of active operations should return to their normal Units when their services are no longer required. Weekly summary to noon today.	

Wounded
	37 Div	O.R.	P.M.	Total
Wounded	362	122	46	530
Sick	34	18	-	52
To 48 F.A.	136	67	-	203
Totals	532	207	46	785

Wounded 6 p.m - 6 p.m.
	Offrs	O.R.
37 Div	-	45 includes 15 Yellow x S' Green x Grand (shell)
62 "	-	3
C.T.	-	5 (2 Blue x Grand - shell)
P. of W.	-	3
	1	56
Growing total	-	
	34	802

In future N.Y.D.N & S.I.W. Cases from 14 Corps will be collected at New Zealand D.R.S. at H.28.d.3.4. (Sheet 57c) for transportation to the Special centre, No 6 Stationary Hospital.

Army Form C. 2118.

WAR DIARY
or
INTELLIGENCE SUMMARY.

(Erase heading not required.)

49th Field Ambulance

1918 September

Place	Date	Hour	Summary of Events and Information	Remarks and references to Appendices
LESUCQUIERE	16th		Clear & fine – Warmer. The whole area was kept much alive during the night by bombing & shelling – Two Bombing Planes were brought down, one quite close to this site, by one of our aircraft – S/S fall was received with great excitement & cheering by all who witnessed it – 20 Stretcher cases + 19 Sitting cases were evacuated from 7pm to 7am. One man in addition to other injuries had been considerably burned by the plane falling on him. Orders received to detail an Officer to take temp. Medical charge of 134 Rifle Bde for 30 days during absence on leave of Capt. A.W. Raymond RAMC. Lt Martin MORC USA was detailed & left during the morning for J. 27. d. 4. 3. H.Q. of Battn. Ordnance Stores to be drawn from dump opposite church at LESUCQUIERE. Warrants received for 5 O.R. to embark on 20th for leave to UK. "ADMS & DADMS called regarding casualties & other matters. Workshop Officer 24 MAC called re Car operation. 1 MAC Car has been despatched to DOULLENS, GEZAINCOURT and HEM to get Medical, Red Cross & other Stores – Admin. Instructions No 30 (Method of constructing & maintaining Chalk floors to Horse standings received – Very good, but whence the Labour to do it?!! O.M.S Burdens leave to PARIS with Warrant received approved – To start 25th inst. Grades of eligibility for different Orders of British Empire according to Rank received Officer (OBE), Lt Cols & Majors, Member (MBE), Capts, Lieuts & 2nd Lieuts. Notice received that clean clothing to be drawn from Baths daily to be returned to DADOS. OC Mobile Vety Sec had lunch in the Mess then inspected & passed the Horse standings from A.D. Vety DRO. OC to 63 Bde H.Q. LESUCQUIERE. Bde moving into the line tonight in relief of 111 Bde – Later washed all normal precautions of village lootings for another site for MDS at D.R.S. but	M.1.

Army Form C. 2118.

WAR DIARY
or
INTELLIGENCE SUMMARY.

(Erase heading not required.)

HQ 4th Field Ambulance

1918 September

Place	Date	Hour	Summary of Events and Information	Remarks and references to Appendices

LEBUCQUIERE	16th (cont'd)		could find none. Visited D.A.D.O.S. and enquired about various details regarding clothing & things mislaid. Pte Gates RAMC from No 3 F.Amb. who applied to come to this Unit, reported today. 4 OR (3 RAMC & 1 RSC (MT)) reported on return from leave – Return in entails sent to ADMS with Evening Situation Report. Wounded 6pm to 6pm :-
			
			            Off OR
			 37th Divn – 19
			 3rd – – 4
			 62nd – – 11
			 63rd – – 3
			 Cav Corps 3 13 – Includes 1 American returned to duty
			       Total 3 50
				RoR/

	17th	a.m	Fine – Heavy rain during the night but fine to midnight. Quiet night only 1 lying & 4 sitting cases having passed through. Stretcher case was an Officer of 13 KRRC with avulsion of lower jaw almost complete + of front of Left shoulder region – It was the result of H.V. Shell falling into a Niseen hut in VELU WOOD which 2 Officers, both of whom had just come down from the line, occupied. The other Officer occupying the hut was blown to pieces – Interviewed Pte Gates RAMC. Wrote ADMS asking if he still wished old ask at FAVREUIL held. It is reported that a Major had been there & ordered the NCO ic of the holding party to vacate the site – Submitted Indent for wood & coal to make supports for new tarpaulin shelter. O.C. 3 MAC called re Cars.	MN/

Army Form C. 2118.

WAR DIARY
or
INTELLIGENCE SUMMARY
(Erase heading not required.)

49th Field Ambulance

Title pages September 1918

Place	Date	Hour	Summary of Events and Information	Remarks and references to Appendices
LEBUCQUIERE	14th (contd)		ADMS & DADMS called. The Divn is going out of the line & this Unit is to move a DRS. Preparation to be made for Col Pilcher - Consulting Surgeon III Army to lecture tomorrow 2 p.m here. Approval given for issue of one Blanket per man. - QMG (QB) 24-14-9-13) CTD 1582. ADMS reply that old suits required by Corps for RAF & to be given up - GS Wagon sent forthwith to remove stores & turbinary party to rejoin unit. S.C.F. Now Cof E notified through ADMS that Revd Brookfield had been ordered to rejoin his unit (35 Somerset L.J.) from which he had been absent since 10th inst. Letter regarding application for transfer of S.S.M. Arthur, ASC received from 9 Stop Train & notice given to submit his application at an early date. Application for work in either State Medicine or Bacteriology R.A.M.C (T.F.) forwarded and recommended. Note received from D.D.M.S regarding lecture by Col Pilcher + a little later in telephone message forwarded from D.H.Q from him to say the lecture was postponed. Sent private letter to acknowledge. Application from S.S.M Arthur ASC forwarded & recommended for transfer. Recommendations for Honours & Awards for the month Feb. to Sept forwarded to A.D.M.S. Paid out the following O.R. preparatory to their proceeding on leave tomorrow morning. Sgt Downey M.J. Fr 200 Pte Ball T Fr 150 Pte Newman W Fr 150 Pte Ditch M.J " 50 " Radford W " 150 Reply received from Divn 'A' that Pte Hempson who reported late from leave was to be dealt with by O.C	

Army Form C. 2118.

WAR DIARY
or
INTELLIGENCE SUMMARY.
(Erase heading not required.)

49th Field Ambulance

Instructions regarding War Diaries and Intelligence Summaries are contained in F.S. Regs., Part II. and the Staff Manual respectively. Title pages will be prepared in manuscript.

September 1918

Place	Date	Hour	Summary of Events and Information	Remarks and references to Appendices

LE BUCQUIERE	17th (Cont)		Wounded 6pm to 6pm Off O/R
			 37 Divn 1 11
			 C.T. -- 1
			 P of W -- 1
			                   ─── ───
			                   1 13 Incl. 4 Yellow X	

		10.5 a.m.	Received Orders from ADMS that 112 Bde would attack on a small scale early tomorrow morning & we should be prepared for reception of increase of wounded. Replied that preparations would be made that our remaining Ambulances 1 Sunbeam & 1 Ford & 2 Ford Ambces would if necessary be placed at disposal of O/C 50.F.Amb	Evening total 37 Divn) 1 Off 30 OR from 16/9/15)
		11.30	Enemy plane brought down in flames quite close & mile beyond of our aircraft	
	18th		Grey cloudy. Rained heavily during the night 12 Stretchers to sitting cases passed through during the night - 7 Bombardments from 152 Field Coy. caught on parade near Gouzeaucourt Wood. One of Bertz Bath reported that 112 attack had started but it was found to be dos out. Pte Tempson R.A.M.C. brought up for overstaying Leave 5 days. Awarded 14 days FP.N2 & Forfeits 5 days pay under R.Warrant.	
		9.30 am	"B" Tent Sub Divn under Major Nicholson Scanbridge departed to form 49 F.A. & field form a D.R.S. on our old site at LOGEAST WOOD in accordance with orders received from ADMS last night to conform with 37 Div Instruction No 32 of 16/9/18. Also received last night as follows. 1. 2 or 3 or 4 days DHQ probably move to old site. Briskworthe ACHIET le GRAND 2 Div Reception Camp & Schools to arrive relieved by DAAG on 18th. 3. 48 F.Amb to arrive relieved by ADMS on 18th. Division	

Army Form C. 2118.

WAR DIARY
or
INTELLIGENCE SUMMARY.
(Erase heading not required.)

HQ 4 Field Ambce

Place	Date	Hour	Summary of Events and Information	Remarks and references to Appendices
LEBUCQUIERE	18.9		Division being relieved by 42 Divsn - When N.Z. Divs. goes into line again in about 14 days - HQ to FAVREUIL & Divs Reception Camp to Brickworks ACHIET. O.C. 31 MAC called re efficiency of Cars. Admin. Instruction No 31. Russian Baths:— Pit chamber 8 ft long 6 ft wide 4 ft high - Roof 2ft x 9ft. - Roof with beams and corrugated iron & spread earth over - Stoves, oil drums feet through chimney. Clothes turned inside out - Requires 25/30 minutes - D.D.M.S. IV Corps. 3 MA/misc. Lying & sitting cases to 34 & 56 CCS GREVILLERS Walking Wounded & } to Corp. M.Y. Station BIHUCOURT & whence to 149 CCS COUINCAMPS Lighter Sick Serious sick by Car to CCS COUINCAMPS 13 Mobile Lab: closed at GEZAINCOURT & fms BEAULENCOURT 29/9/18 Cyclist from M.A.C. attached under orders D.D.M.S. reported (Pte Clarke) One Char-a-Banc reported total to stand by for conveyance to BIHUCOURT (No 23154)	
		1pm	D.D.M.S. called & had lunch - Did not make any special comments	
		5.30	Fairly quiet afternoon - cases dribble slowly in - Brigade attack stated to have been moderately successful. 13th R.Fus on Right had a difficult time. Casualties up to present have been remarkably few - There is a wild rumour afloat that CAMBRAI has been taken from the North by our attack. In all directions. The present quietness of this front ? Enemy shelling does not bear this out.	

N.R.T.

Army Form C. 2118.

WAR DIARY
or
INTELLIGENCE SUMMARY.
(Erase heading not required.)

449th Field Ambce

Instructions regarding War Diaries and Intelligence Summaries are contained in F. S. Regs., Part II. and the Staff Manual respectively. Title pages will be prepared in manuscript.

Place	Date	Hour	Summary of Events and Information	Remarks and references to Appendices
LEBUCQUIERE	18.9 (Cont)		Capt. Drew M.O. 7th R.E. conveyed to 34 C.C.S. for temporary duty (F.D.M.S. 5/24/1423/t 16 9/18) On 37th L.T. Coy sent in very full report on the Betherdown Case, he says which he states will have to be evacuated (Sunbeam No 19114). Lothar will be discharged at end of work. Ptes Parkinson and Rice reported for duty on return from Army Rest Camp. The effects of 2/Lt. Hopwood, 152 7th Coy R.E. killed last night by the bomb which fell over the Coy, were sent to respective authorities & a pair of French Books forwarded by post to Officer's Cox & Co Agency. Wounded 6pm to 6pm	
			Offrs 9R 37 Division 5 47 includes 10 Offrs + 3 OR Yellow X 3rd 1 2 C.T. 1 1 Evening Total 37 Div 6 Offrs 80 OR 5 50 since 15 9/18 Some 14 cases, sick, requiring transfer to 48 F.Amb returned for the night in order to help D.R.S. which is on the move. One is a case of ? Malingering ? M.D.N. on Pte SAUNDERS of 1st Essex Regt, complaining of pains in back & loss of power in the legs. He has no appreciable signs of disease. D.T.I.C.s received :-	
			No 3771 Protection of animals against bombing, shelling - Question of available labour to raise revetments 5ft high round standings is difficulty for Units constantly moving to new sites No 3772 Diarrhoea - The precepts laid down are excellent & all well known - With regard to latrines it is stated that pails & oil drums will be used to	A.M.

Army Form C. 2118.

WAR DIARY
or
INTELLIGENCE SUMMARY.
(Erase heading not required.)

149th Field Ambulance

1918 Sept.

Place	Date	Hour	Summary of Events and Information	Remarks and references to Appendices
LEBUCQUERE	18th (Cont)		contents emptied down into specially dug pits. Pails not being available & use of All Arms forbidden by GRO in addition burn-incinerary the amount of fuel & wood labour involved by constantly digging pits considerably detracts from the force of the order.	
		7.30 pm	Casualties from enemy bombardment during afternoon began to flow in more rapidly. A fairly clear night, enemy aircraft actively astir.	
	19th	a.m.	Very noisy - heavy clouds & showers. Cleared later but cloudy. A total of 39 stretcher & 69 walking cases were dealt with between 1 am & 7 am. The steady stream of casualties did not slow up until about 2.30 am. The Regiments of this B'gde which suffered most heavily were those of 112 B'gde - 13 R Fus.; 1st Wilts; 1st Essex. Owing to fear of counter-attack all 3 were in fighting position 112th in the line, 63rd in support, 111th in reserve, behind 63rd. From reports by wounded officers & men it is gathered that the enemy tried to assault HAVRINCOURT on both sides, but failed & in consequence the 3rd Div. had to bear the brunt of the attack & suffered heavily. The bombardment of Bus. duf h'rt durin HAVRINCOURT Wood to its west & north has been most intense & with great ring & character of heavy & rapidly, but the enemy infantry are not fighting with grit & were kept farther back, no doubt. The Divisions of IV Corps taking part in yesterdays operations of attack & defence are → East } 3rd } 37th } 5th	

WAR DIARY
or
INTELLIGENCE SUMMARY.
(Erase heading not required.)

Army Form C. 2118.

49th Field Ambulance

1918 Sept

Place	Date	Hour	Summary of Events and Information	Remarks and references to Appendices
LEBUCQUIÈRE	19th (Cont'd)		The C.O. & Southwards were also notified in offensive of wations on a large scale, the results of which are not at present known.	
		11:45 am	A collection of some 25 beds were dispatched to 43rd F. Amb. by means of Charabanc. Orders for disposal of evacuations were received in order from ADMS 6/20/C/74. Sick to C.C.S. Colincamps in M.A.C. Cars & available cars via W.W. 54 BIHUCOURT. Lying & severe sitting to C.C.S. GREVILLERS. Walkers to W.M. Stn. M.I.D. N. & S.I.W. will be shown as admitted to receiving Ambulance N.Z. DRS only to be used as a tendency room. A case anonymously like ANTHRAX (a Gunner) with pustule on the chest reported sick this morning. On closer examination he proved not to be — ADMS called reference reliefs of our units by those of 42nd Div — 49 F. Amb will proceed first to IRLES BARQUE and later take over DRS LOGEAST WOOD from 42 F.D. Office received that 111th Bde withdrawn again to LEBUCQUIERE area again tonight. Intelligence Summary gives prisoners captured by 37 Div as follows :—	
			Aug 21st–26th	G.E 1955
			" 27 — " 31st	47 272
			Sept 1st — 19th	1 — 5 221
			Adm died at F.Hr. of 37 Div	
			Captured N. of FOIREUIL in combined operations on 25 Aug ('evacuated) through VI Corps. Lahnan	300 & 400
			Grand Total Captured by 37 Div	52 2,850

195

Army Form C. 2118.

WAR DIARY
or
INTELLIGENCE SUMMARY.

(Erase heading not required.)

49th Field Ambulance

Place	Date	Hour	Summary of Events and Information	Remarks and references to Appendices
LEBUCQUIERE	19th (Cont)	17.45	O.C. 1/1st E. Lancs F.Amb. and one of his Officers called to look round site preparatory to taking over from us.	
		6pm	Reported on Capt. Mackintosh - alternative uses of, in accordance with E.R.O. 1973 suggesting: 1/ Enamel sheets 2/ Covering Wounded on stretchers, in addition to blankets.	
			Wounded 6pm to 6pm	
			Offr OR	
			37 Div 3 97 29ff2 19 OR Gassed-Shell	
			3rd " 2 22 2 OR -do-	
			62nd " 1 13 3 GR -do-	
			63rd " 3 1	
			N.Z. - 2	
			C.T. 3 13	
			Y.M.C.A. Worker 1 (Burnt-Shell)	
			P. of W. - 5	
			11 152	
			1 Y.M.C.A. Worker	
			Evening total 37 Div 9 144	

WAR DIARY or INTELLIGENCE SUMMARY

Army Form C. 2118.

September 1918

Place	Date	Hour	Summary of Events and Information	Remarks and references to Appendices
LEBUCQUIERE	30th	am	L/Cpl R.E. TODD proceeded on 14 days leave to U.K. Temporary command assumed by Major Clark Nicholson. Arranged with 111th Bde to send 2 horsed Ambulances to follow troops on the move and wrote to 112th Bde asking for instructions with regard to taking their troops and to take over Camp at LA BARQUE.	(1)
		1 pm	Capt Riggs with 5 OR proceeded as advance party to take over accommodation for Officers and one tent sub division of 1/1 East Lancs Fd Ambce arrived at 7 pm with a group personnel party to take over. Dressing Room handed over on night duty.	(2)
	31st		Bright but showers. Night very quiet. Bearers returned from 50th Inf Bde. Last night and are being bathed this morning. RAD Boxe and surplus Stretchers, Blankets & other stores handed over to 1/1 East Lancs Fd Ambce.	(3)
LA BARQUE		5 pm	As the Ambulance was preparing to leave LEBUCQUIERE at 1 pm a H.V. Shell (probably 4.2" calibre) fell in the camp among the men's Barracks. Nobody was wounded but two minutes later another fell behind the horse lines and personnel was ordered to leave the Camp and the horses were got under cover. Shelling continued for half an hour all in close proximity to the Camp. Transport moved off at intervals and collected on the road at FREMICOURT. All was clear of the Camp by 2 pm and the Ambulance moved off from the rendezvous on the FREMICOURT Road at 2.15 pm marching here via FREMICOURT and BARQUE without incident. Personnel are accommodated in dugouts and the Units tents. One tent used as Medical Inspection Room. No accommodation for patients.	(4)

WAR DIARY
or
INTELLIGENCE SUMMARY.

Army Form C. 2118.

49th Field Ambulance

September 1918

Place	Date	Hour	Summary of Events and Information	Remarks and references to Appendices
LA BARQUE	21st (contd)		No reply was received from 112th Bde about horses Ambulances but two were detailed to find 13th Royal Fusiliers and 1st Essex – The front was uneventful – The latter not – 112th Bde asked for march tone and route of 1/1 Herts tomorrow.	(1)
	22		Dull morning. Reply from 112th Bde received during the night re/abovesaid 48th Fd Amb. - Wagon detailed to follow 1/1 Herts. – Visited 48th Fd Amb with a view to taking over D.R.S. D.P.M.S. F.D.M.S. and A.P.M.Q. also visiting Camp – Discussed possible sites and ADMS suggested improvements on present site. A.D.M.S. also discussed Operation Order not yet received by us, detailing action in case of enemy attack.	
		6 pm	Heavy rain during afternoon – Operation Order from ADMS received 4 pm – 49th F. Amb until relieved by 48th F.A. to go forward & establish M.D.S. in neighbourhood of VILLERS AU FLOS - Lt Col Blake. Cmds 48 Fd Amb. having reconnoitred this area called and reported that the only possible route of evacuation is by the road BUS, BAPAUME, HAPLINCOURT, BANCOURT and M.D.S. must be on this route – Details of relief of 48th F. Amb arranged.	(2)
	23rd		Fair & cold. 48th F. Amb took over site at LA BARQUE and 49th F. Amb moved out at 12 noon arriving at the new site at 2pm. D.R.S. is accommodated in 6 Marquees, 2 Officers' Tents and 6 Bell Tents – Dining Room in Bivouac giving only 4 feet head room –
LOGEAST WOOD F.30.c.9.9 (Sh 57 b)			Ablution Bench & Latrines are in the Camp & Bath horse on the other side of the road	

Army Form C. 2118.

WAR DIARY
or
INTELLIGENCE SUMMARY.
(Erase heading not required.)

November 1918   49th Field Ambulance

Place	Date	Hour	Summary of Events and Information	Remarks and references to Appendices
Lo EAST WOOD	22nd (cont)		Camp inspected and a general plan drawn up. Urgent work to be undertaken at once. The clearing of the ground fronting the road and the erection of a Cookhouse of hurdles. Personnel are accommodated in Bivouacs – Cooking being done in the Cookhouse evolved by this Unit on 27/5/18. Horse lines are arranged in shelter of the Wood N.E. of the Camp.	(a)
	24th		Fair + cold. Work on the Camp begun + progressing favourably. Spray Baths removed from ABLAINZEVELLE for re-erection in the Camp. ADMS called + suggested that the Rest Camp might be moved shortly – Care plans for detainer (57th Div) for trial. Report on recent operations called for and rendered. (Copy attached)	(a) Appdx II (a)
	25th		Wet morning – fair in the afternoon. Work progressing in the Camp. Many of the damaged Nissen Huts fronting the road have been removed + the pits filled in. The Patients Cookhouse is completed + also a Dispensary – Work has been begun on an Orderly Room + a Pack Store. Orders received from 37 Bri D "to replace Spray Baths in ABLAINZEVELLE	(a)
	26th		Fair + cold. Much work done in the Camp – Erection of a Bath house on this side of the road begun – Trench boards laid through the Camp – Re-erection of Baths at ABLAINZEVELLE proceeding – Trial stove for tent erected – Operation Orders IX Corps received	(a)

Army Form C. 2118.

WAR DIARY
or
INTELLIGENCE SUMMARY.
(Erase heading not required.)

49th Field Ambulance

September 1918

Instructions regarding War Diaries and Intelligence Summaries are contained in F.S. Regs., Part II. and the Staff Manual respectively. Title pages will be prepared in manuscript.

Place	Date	Hour	Summary of Events and Information	Remarks and references to Appendices
LOGEAST WOOD	27th		Fair & cold. Work proceeding in Camp. Orderly Room & Bath Store completed, also re erection of Baths at ABLAINZEVELLE. Bath Room almost finished & the work of digging out Friends Dining Hall to give head room commenced. Lethian Barrel for delousing on plans by Col Hunter RAMC published in "Lancet" constructed for trial. Work on permanent horse standings progressing well. News of Operations on ARGONNE front received. News of operations on this front doubtful.	
	28th		Fair and cold. Visited A.D.M.S. discussed possible move also operations. Drew 3,000 francs to pay men going on leave to. Work on the Camp proceeding, bath house almost completed. Lethian Barrel in use but too small to be effective as it takes only 2 blankets. (Plan of Camp at LOGEAST WOOD)	
	29th		Cold & showery. Lt. Summers, M.O.R.C. USA, M.O. & Serv L.I. admitted late last night & evacuated to C.C.S. Probably suffering from Trench Fever. Our instructions from ADMS Capt Piggot detailed to act for him & proceeded on this duty. A.D.M.S. called. D.R.S. to move tomorrow to site occupied by D.H.Q. G.9.6.(54c)	

Army Form C. 2118.

WAR DIARY
or
INTELLIGENCE SUMMARY.
(Erase heading not required.)

49th Field Ambce

1918 September

Place	Date	Hour	Summary of Events and Information	Remarks and references to Appendices
LOGEAST WOOD	29th (cont)		War news from all fronts is very good - A.D.M.S. extremely pleased with work put in on the Camp. Visited new Site (J.9.c.2) with Lieut Ingles and decided plan for the Camp. Holding party proceeded at 4 p.m. Lieut Warwick left on Catering Course - 7 O.R. went on leave	Cn
	30th		Bath and dull. Ambulance moved to new site, taking over camp vacated by Div. H.Q. "A large" quantity of excess stores necessitated frequent journeys by G.S. Wagons. Operation Order No 113 from A.D.M.S. Divn. Bearer Sub Divisions left to report to O.C. 50th Field Ambce at 3 p.m. and 2 large Cars left for 48th Field Ambce. Operation Order No 114 from A.D.M.S. - 49th Field Ambce to move D.T.S. to site vacated by 48th Fd Amb. near BANCOURT on 2/10 - Went over to new site with O.W.O. & Sgt Major. Accommodation consists of "Nissen Huts" in a very bad state of repair. Refilling missed owing to rain dump moving	Cn

Aust Nicholson.
Major R.A.M.C.
Comdg 49th Field Ambce

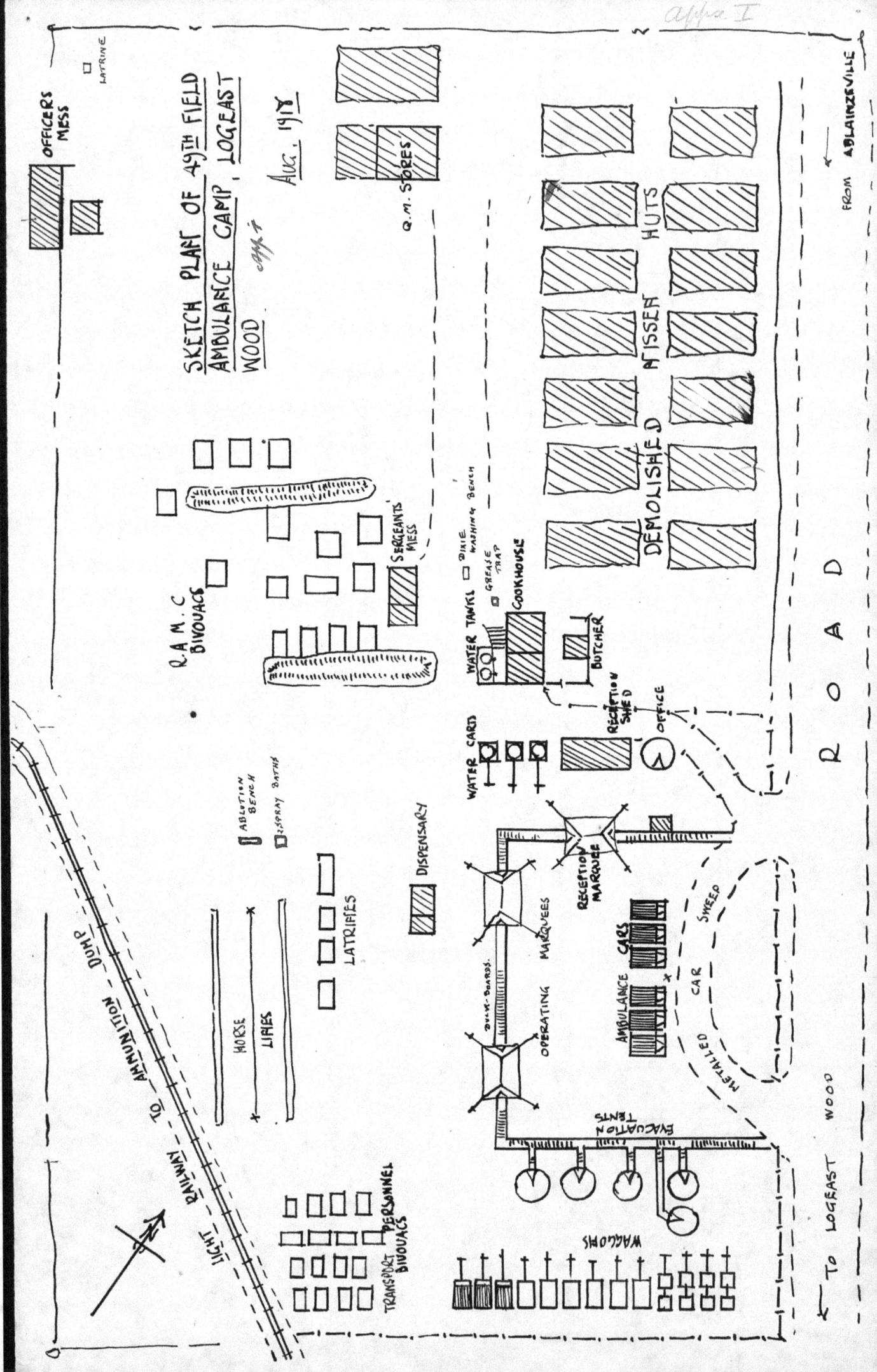

Appx II

Report on recent Operations

This Field Ambulance took over Divisional Main Dressing Station at SOUASTRE (D.22.a.4.6 - Sheet 57D) when 37th Divn relieved 62nd Division in the line on 25 June 1918.

The Dressing Station consisted of two tiled rooms which were used as Receiving Room and Dressing Room and a few barns which were used to accommodate cases awaiting evacuation and as Offices and Stores.

There was also a series of Elephant Shelters on the SOUASTRE - ST AMAND Road (D.15.d.7.9 - Sheet 57D) begun by the 62nd Divn and completed by this Division, which were designed as an alternative Main Dressing Station in the event of SOUASTRE being heavily shelled.

Later a hut was floored with concrete and additional shelter erected near the Main Dressing Station for dealing with Gas casualties.

For operations of 21st and 22nd August the buildings in SOUASTRE were used as a Main Dressing Station for Stretcher cases and the Shelter on the ST AMAND Road as a Main Dressing Station for Walking Wounded.

Casualties were dealt with expeditiously at both places and evacuation was never delayed to any alarming extent, although at one time nearly 200 Walking Wounded were awaiting evacuation.

Casualties dealt with from 6 am 21st August to 6 am 22nd August were :-
  Wounded   650
  Sick   66

For operations of 23rd August, 48th Field Ambulance dealt with Walking Wounded and this Unit continued to deal with Stretcher cases in SOUASTRE, the Shelters on the ST AMAND road were not used. Additional cover was provided by roofing in a yard with Wagon covers, but in spite of that accommodation proved inadequate and as casualties were very heavy, many of them lay in the open for the greater part of the night. The night was warm and the supply of blankets adequate, or this would have been extremely serious.

Total cases dealt with 6am 23rd Aug to 6am 24th August were:-

        Wounded 1,093
        Sick   62

On 25th August this Unit ceased to function a Main Dressing Station and on 26th August moved to LOGEAST WOOD (F.30.a.5.0 - Sheet 57c) where it prepared to open a Main Dressing Station under its own canvas.

On 3rd Sept. it moved to FAVREUIL (H.17.c.1.7 - Sheet 57c) and acted as Divisional Main Dressing Station from 4th to 10th September. Dressing and Waiting Rooms were in Nissen Huts a good deal damaged by shell fire. Casualties were not very heavy on any day and were dealt with and evacuated expeditiously.

On 11th Sept. this Unit moved to LEBUCQUIERE (I.30.a.6.6 - Sheet 57c) and continued to act as Divisional Main Dressing Station till the 21st, when relieved by 42nd Divn. Accommodation here was in 5 Nissen huts much damaged by shell fire, but they proved adequate to deal with casualties, and evacuation was extremely good.

Medical.

It is always difficult to secure suitable accommodation for a Main Dressing Station. It is not always realised what a large amount of actual floor space 100 men on stretchers require, and 100 stretcher cases is the minimum number that a Main Dressing Station must be prepared to deal with at one time. In addition it is of extreme importance in the treatment of wounded to provide a certain amount of security from shell fire and bombing. Sites close to railways, road junctions or other points liable to be shelled should be avoided if possible. The fact that the Dressing Rooms and other parts of a Main Dressing Station must be kept lighted even in the presence of enemy aeroplanes should give them a claim on material necessary to render them light proof.

Liaison between 149th Field Ambulance and 21st Motor Ambulance Convoy who were responsible for evacuation was very good throughout and the only time that there was any difficulty in evacuation was on 23rd August when casualties very heavy and Casualty Clearing Stations still at GEZAINCOURT.

Sick of detachments reporting at Main Dressing Stations during active operations were very troublesome, but these were dealt with by being told to report later in the day.

Advanced Depot of Medical Stores did not move forward throughout operations and it was found to involve loss of time and transport to have to send a Motor Ambulance Car to GEZAINCOURT or FREVENT for urgent supplies.

Administration of Localities

There seemed to be no system in the allocation of Camp sites and much trouble was caused by this Unit and Corps Ammunition choosing adjacent sites.

Animals

Water difficulties became acute in LEBUCQUIERE at one time, but the condition of the animals is very good. They have not done much work.

Baggage

Surplus Stretchers Blankets and Medical Stores which are necessary for a Main Dressing Station were a constant source of trouble during the forward movement and required a holding party on the old site and journeys for two or three days following the move; extra transport would be invaluable.

Baths

It has always been found possible to arrange baths in the Unit for personnel and to draw the underclothing required.

Burial of dead

It is not always possible for a Field Ambulance to find a party to dig graves for wounded who die in the Unit, but no provision seems to be made for this. Convalescent sick were used on one occasion for this duty.

Canteen Supplies

The supply of Cigarettes and Tobacco was never sufficient during the period. Other requirements were met and the system of supply was satisfactory.

Economy

The system of feeding wounded is that the Field Ambulance draws components of the ration as Medical Comforts from Railhead. As the rations for these wounded are already in the forward area, it is suggested that some arrangement might be made by which they could be transferred to Field Ambulances, thus saving double issue.

Prisoners of War

Doubt sometimes arises in Field Ambulances as to whether a Prisoner of War has passed through a Cage and has already been recorded. Some form of tally for attachment to the prisoner at the Cage before transfer to Field Ambulance would save confusion and difficulties in clerking. The services of an Interpreter at Main Dressing Station would be invaluable.

Provost Duties

Much unnecessary annoyance would be saved the wounded and confusion would be less at Main Dressing Stations if Police personnel could be detailed to deal with the morbidly curious crowd which invariably collects round the Dressing Station to stare at the wounded and get in the way of everybody who has work to do.

Salvage

A large quantity of salvage, rifles, clothing and equipment is collected at Main Dressing Stations from wounded. Field Ambulance personnel is not available to guard this and it is invariably picked over and thrown about by troops in the neighbourhood who are not employed. Could Salvage personnel be detailed to take charge of this?

Water

Could priority be given to Water Carts of Field Ambulances at refilling points; the supply of water at Main Dressing Stations is obviously of extreme importance and although there was always sufficient during recent operations, there were times when the situation was not comfortable.

(sgd) Clark Nicholson
R.A.M.
COMDG 49th. FIELD AMBULANCE

Army Form C. 2118.

WAR DIARY
or
INTELLIGENCE SUMMARY.

(Erase heading not required.)

Instructions regarding War Diaries and Intelligence Summaries are contained in F. S. Regs., Part II. and the Staff Manual respectively. Title pages will be prepared in manuscript.

Place	Date	Hour	Summary of Events and Information	Remarks and references to Appendices

Confidential

War Diary

of

49th Field Ambulance

From 1st October 1918 to 31st October 1918

Army Form C. 2118.

WAR DIARY
or
INTELLIGENCE SUMMARY.
(Erase heading not required.)

49th Field Ambulance

1918 October

Place	Date	Hour	Summary of Events and Information	Remarks and references to Appendices
ACHIET LE GRAND (G.9.b.5.9.)	1st		Visited new site and decided on plan for Rest Station. Hospital accommodation is in eleven Nissen huts in a reasonably good state of repair on the North side of the BANCOURT - HAPLINCOURT Road. Stores, Officers' and Sergeants' Messes are on the South side of the BANCOURT road in Nissen huts not in a good state of repair - 3 Motor lorries are to be provided from Division to assist in the move.	(1)
I.31.d. (near BANCOURT)	2nd		Fair. The Ambulance moved off at 9 a.m. and marched by ACHIET LE GRAND & BAPAUME to the new site. Patients unable to march were carried in Horsed and Motor Ambulances. Those able to march had their kits carried. Work was immediately commenced on the new site. Two Marquees were pitched together as a Dining Room for patients. A.S.M.S. forwarded a blanket indent signed by C.R.E. to draw R.E. Stores to complete work in the Camp. All surplus stores were carried by lorry and extra journeys by lorries brought a large quantity of miscellaneous building material which will be useful. D.D.M.S. IV Corps with O.C. 5b C.C.S. called. No remarks.	(2)
	3rd	a.m.	Fair & warmer. No material for construction was available at HUN DUMP and indent has again been forwarded to C.R.E. for material. Construction of patients' Cookhouse is proceeding but all Carpenters in the Unit are either on leave or on detached duty & work is slow. All patients in Rest Station will in future have a piece of bandage 2"x1" attached on the left sleeve to make identification easy. Rations for patients put in action.	(3)

WAR DIARY
or
INTELLIGENCE SUMMARY.

Army Form C. 2118.

HQ 1st Field Ambulance

1918 October

Place	Date	Hour	Summary of Events and Information	Remarks and references to Appendices
I.31.d (near BANCOURT)	3rd (Cont)	4 p.m.	R.D.M.S. called – discussed Capt Ward's renewal of Contract – contribution to R.A.M.C. Benevolent Fund – treatment and diagnosis of Diarrhea and Dysentery. He inspected Camp and was satisfied with amount of work done. Major Scarsbrick drew to 3,000 Imprest. Capt Ward renewed his Contract.	(1)
	4th		Fair and warm. Inspected patients in Camp at 9 am – on the whole well turned out – Inspected the Camp – construction of latrines + urinals is very slow – Lack of Carpenters is much felt. Patients Cookhouse nearly finished – 50 extra stretchers drawn from Corps Dump all without handles – All patients to be given a Shelter + Pillowcase. Issue of Dinner to patients inspected – food good + arrangement of Dining Room excellent.	(1)
	5th		Cold. Inspected patients at 9 am. Discipline good except among Turkish patients. Patients who are fit are doing work helping to clean up the camp. A squadron of RAF is preparing to occupy the ground to the north of the camp – Work on Camp very slow.	(1)
	6th		Cold & showery. Operation Order relating to the advance of the Division received from A.D.M.S. This front is not concerned. Enemy appears to be retiring on the whole front. 1 OR (RAMC) proceeding on leave tomorrow were paraded this evening. Bases for CCS are cleared at 1 p.m. to 3rd N.Z. Field Amb whence they are conveyed by car to Divisional Reception Camp.	(1)

WAR DIARY
or
INTELLIGENCE SUMMARY.
(Erase heading not required.)

Army Form C. 2118.

49th Field Ambulance

October 19/8

Place	Date	Hour	Summary of Events and Information	Remarks and references to Appendices
1-31-c (Sh 51c)	4th		Cold and showery. In accordance with a verbal message called on D.D.M.S. and went with him to inspect new site for M.D.M.S. at METZ en COUTURE. This is in the site occupied till yesterday by 50th Field Ambulance and consists of 8 Nissen huts on a small work and dugout and other shelters. There are 4 other Nissen huts at some distance which may be available - likely to be completed in 9/2.	(a)
		4 pm	Returned to new site with Major Davidson & S/M Sears - overtown shapes who will execute accommodation R.E. by him - Revised on plans.	
		4 pm	Order received from A.D.M.S. that move is to be completed by 3rd and lorries may be available - Operation Orders for above tomorrow.	
METZ EN COUTURE	5th		Wet morning - fair later.	
		8 am	Visited 21 M.A.C. & asked help in moving patients - arranged for 6 cars.	
		9 am	Capt. Ward moved off with horsed transport & walking patients.	
		10 am	Major Davidson moved off with remainder of patients in M.A.C. cars. Took 2 M.O. reinforcements. Visited new site - went on to D.H.Q. & to M.D.S. GOUZEAUCOURT where A.D.M.S. was met.	
		pm	Two lorries reported at old site at 13.00 and made long journeys back. Equipment has been moved. Windy, slightly showery and evening facing accommodation finishes. Field Ambulance columns then afternoon and evening that were finished to modest accommodation limit. See still tents and an operating - Operation Order for further advance received - 149 Inf. Brig. to	(a)

Army Form C. 2118.

WAR DIARY
or
INTELLIGENCE SUMMARY.
(Erase heading not required.)

47th Field Ambulance

Instructions regarding War Diaries and Intelligence Summaries are contained in F.S. Regs., Part II. and the Staff Manual respectively. Title pages will be prepared in manuscript.

1918 October

Place	Date	Hour	Summary of Events and Information	Remarks and references to Appendices
METZ EN COUTURE	8th (Cont'd)		Taken over Walking Wounded Entraining Station at GOUZEAUCOURT from 50th Fd Amb.	(1)
	9th	a.m.	Fair and mild. 1 officer Marquee and 3 EPIP opened to take over WW Entraining Station. Two Marquees fitted for Dressings and Bath house opened for patients. Visited GOUZEAUCOURT.	
		noon	Capt HAWES RAMC T.F. reported from D.R.C. made a short call on ADMS with him; he is to be taken on strength of this Unit. Little news from Battle front but progress is good. D.R.S. cannot expect to remain long and the present rate of progress likely to be put on 7 days to be evacuated. Cases not [illegible]	(1)
	10th		Cool and mild. Report on proposed change to A.S. Wagons sent to Divn. Sh. Wheelers sent to No 33 M.V.S. for Clipping. Cases in hospital during the night 202. Wire received from ADMS at 2.30 am. Ambce to be prepared to move to HAUCOURT tomorrow arriving at VAUCELLES. Patients to be sent to 50th Fd Ambce by lorry. Arranged to dispose of surplus stores. Called on D.M.TO with a view to their taking over surplus whelflers and blankets.	(1)
		11.00	Move is cancelled. 37 Div is still in the line. Advance continues.	(1)
	11th		Cool and dull. Wagons are being loaded with Mob. Equipment. 114 Patients are left site of action. RC for Heavy Drum and most of whom saw march.	(2)

Army Form C. 2118.

WAR DIARY or INTELLIGENCE SUMMARY.
(Erase heading not required.)

49th Field Ambulance

1918 October

Place	Date	Hour	Summary of Events and Information	Remarks and references to Appendices
METZ en Couture	12th	a.m.	Wet and windy. O.C. to A.D.M.S. Office to arrange various details in connection with (a) Obtaining supplies as we arrived ahead of all other details 16 miles behind D.H.Q. They will be sent by lorry daily and we submit indents to this Divisional Train. (b) Movements of Unit — Will not move for 2 days or so as lorries for patients conveyance cannot be obtained. Will then move to LIGNY. No further patients will be admitted. (c) Discharges to duty & transfers of Sick — also several other matters of minor importance. 37 Bde will be relieved on the line tonight by 5th Division.	
		p.m.	Orders received to detail M.O. for temporary charge 37 M.G. Bn. RDAS 5/14/9/58. Capt. Howes detailed to proceed. Reported at 10.30 p.m. D.G. Instructions received to return all A.T. & M. Lorries to Base. The horses and stretchers. 2/Lt. Norwood & 1 O.R. at Corps. W.M.G. Entraining stations who are going on leave to be relieved here & return to Unit. Notice received that orders for transference of St Nazaire to American Base Force are now cancelled. Number of Corporals taken by 37 Bde. 8/13 to 11/14 = 36 Officers and 834 Other Ranks. reported in Intelligence Summary.	
	13th	a.m.	Still and anything — Cold. Major Nicholson and droitings to D.R.C. en route to VILLERS au FLOS met Major Day the O.C. who stated that Reception Camp moved on its way to HAVRINCOURT stopping at GOUZEAUCOURT, on the journey return.	

Army Form C. 2118.

WAR DIARY
or
INTELLIGENCE SUMMARY.
(Erase heading not required.)

HQ 49th Field Ambulance

1918 October

Place	Date	Hour	Summary of Events and Information	Remarks and references to Appendices
METZ en COUTURE	13th (contd)		Sat. rep. at hospital and inspected all patients — reference patients & Pulmonary results obtained.—	
			Discharge to Div. Rest Camp — 29	
			Casualty Clearing Station — 11	
			Transfer to 51 D.R.S. — 2	
			R.T.U. Ytres to appear their Corps — 7	
			Duty with 49th Field Ambulance — 1	
			Kept in Hospital — 53	
			Total 103	
			Orders received for move to HAVRINCOURT on 15th. Patients in hospital will be transferred to D.R.S. LIGNY tomorrow by pooled Cars of the 3 Field Ambces. 29 dismounted accompanied by 1 horsed Ambulance will proceed by march route to HAVRINCOURT, preceding remainder of D.T.C. personnel at G.19.2 ERUCOURT WOOD at 8 a.m. Pass out personnel for Army Rest Camp and Leave the cinemas not against their names:—	
			Leave from 15.10.29 Oct:—	
			R.A.M.C. { S/Sgt Warnock T.B. 250 fr, Pte Adkins H 200, " Lightfoot H 200, " Logan J 200, " Stanridge C 100 }	
			Rest Camp (15th) R.A.M.C. { Pte Ferguson W 50, " Fitzsimons J 50 }	
			A.S.C. MT — Dr. Newcombe G 200 fr	
			A.S.C. MT { Pte Richards W 200, " Wilson H 200, Driver Lovatt J.C. 200 }	
			A.S.C. (HT) 2/Cpl Willis A 60 fr	
			Total Fr 1910-00	

Army Form C. 2118.

WAR DIARY
or
INTELLIGENCE SUMMARY.
(Erase heading not required.)

49th Field Ambulance

1918 October

Place	Date	Hour	Summary of Events and Information	Remarks and references to Appendices
METZ en COUTURE	13th (Cont)		Pte Tedford RAMC awarded 14 days F.P. No 2 and forfeits 4 days pay for overstaying his leave. Brigade Refilling Points situated near LIGNY from 13th onwards. Notification received that registration has been effected by Records of A/Cpl Bland as Pharmacist. Dispensers & Sgts as Dispensers. "Transfusion Leave" will not count as ordinary leave, does not affect transfer on ordinary leave Rota. Following entry will be made in A.B. 64 of men granted such leave "Special Leave. Authy. M.D Letter 111/Infantry/8274 (A.G.4.a) dt 29/9/18." Similar entry will be made on the medical certificate in the case of officers. Report on efficacy of Serum Transfusions and Blood Transfusion received.	At.
	14th	a.m	Snow fall during the night which was clear and moonlit. One Acute Abdomen sent direct to C.C.S. 53 patients transferred by Car to D.R.S at LIGNY. 350 Blankets, 105 Stretchers and 2 Marquees completely later by 21 M.A.C. Marquees to be collected later by 21 M.A.C 2 discharges sent with lorry which will convey them to D.R.C. HAUCOURT after unloading. Scabies patients and 50 Blankets of Scabies patients sent separately by car after disinfection. BRC Stores with kit separately by Car to LIGNY.	
		p.m	Lieut Ingles to VAUCELLES Chateau where a place for midday meal tomorrow was arranged. Site practically clear of surplus stores today. Arrangements for move tomorrow settled	At.

Army Form C. 2118.

WAR DIARY
or
INTELLIGENCE SUMMARY.
(Erase heading not required.)

10/13
Ahler
H.W. Field Ambulance

Instructions regarding War Diaries and Intelligence Summaries are contained in F.S. Regs., Part II. and the Staff Manual respectively. Title pages will be prepared in manuscript.

Place	Date	Hour	Summary of Events and Information	Remarks and references to Appendices
HAVCOURT	15th		Still self raining.	
		9 am	Main column of Unit left METZ en route for HAVCOURT – to halt for hot haversack ration at VAUCELLES Chateau whither a Watercart had been despatched starting at 4.30 a.m. Rations for the day had not arrived when the Unit whilst the same anxiety 10.15 and were sent on by Ambulance Car. Animals feeds were the main anxiety as they had started with a very meagre morning meal.	
		12.30	Arrived VAUCELLES Chateau	
		13.30	Left VAUCELLES Chateau	
		16.00	Arrived HAVCOURT – met by A.D.M.S. Taking the truck route was in error as I judged as I passed during route for the animals owing to softness of the ground. Unit collected 340 lbs salvage rubber en route. Orders received to move to CAUDRY tomorrow.	A.J.
			Raining slightly but steadily all day.	
CAUDRY	16th		Unit left HAVCOURT	
		9.30	Arrived CAUDRY – Ambulance H.Q. Rue Benoit Malon (Kriegskarte N° 10) Truffé Ø (T.18.c.99). Transport lines Rue André (T.18.d.3.7)	
		11.15	A.C. noted D.D.M.S. IV Corps and 50½ Field Ambce, D.R.S. at LIGNY en route. Transport animals temporarily accommodated at site of 48 F.Amb but stables having been found they will be moved tomorrow so that the solving of what would make an excellent hospital ward will be avoided. Bearers of the Unit repaired from 45th F.Amb. today. 90 lbs of Rubber was collected on the march today.	A.J.

Army Form C. 2118.

WAR DIARY
or
INTELLIGENCE SUMMARY.
(Erase heading not required.)

40th Field Ambulance

1918 October

Place	Date	Hour	Summary of Events and Information	Remarks and references to Appendices
CAUDRY	16/10 (Contd)		D.D.M.S. Corps A.D.M.S. Third Army and others called to view the site this afternoon. Supply trains are still running very satisfactorily, as the congestion at GOUZEAUCOURT is considerable. Party of I.W.G.C. and 8 O.R. at Walking Wounded Station GOUZEAUCOURT rejoin the Unit. rationed by R.S.D. there from tomorrow.	
	17/10	a.m.	Dull – drizzling – cold. General washing up of kits and cleaning and disinfestation now duties actively proceeding. The complete equipment of the whole Unit is being unpacked, will be overhauled and a further endeavour made to get rid of such articles as are never used. By sorting and repacking the panniers it is thought that two might be released in which Tailors and Shoemakers' materials and tools could be kept. Major Whitelaw to draw ₤1,000 Imprest and see D.A.D.S. Trans. regarding definite allotment of seats to Divisional trains daily. H. & Q.M. to Divisions to see about clean changes of clothing & Service Dress Clothing required for Unit. Bathing and Delousing van be done on this site. Stables more cleaned, disinfected and occupied. Cab obtained from Field Officers' Mess and quarters charged from 37th to N°5 Rue André.	
		p.m.	Football Match between 46 & 49 F. Ambs. resulted in a draw of 1 goal all.	
		12.00	Our Cadets' concert given in the evening at which 6 of the "Harm On's" kindly and very ably assisted.	

Army Form C. 2118.

WAR DIARY
or
INTELLIGENCE SUMMARY.
(Erase heading not required.)

40 L Field Ambulance

1918 October

Instructions regarding War Diaries and Intelligence Summaries are contained in F.S. Regs., Part II. and the Staff Manual respectively. Title pages will be prepared in manuscript.

Place	Date	Hour	Summary of Events and Information	Remarks and references to Appendices
CAUDRY	17th (contd)		Leader of Divisional Y.M.C.A. called to arrange Lectures for 47 & 49 F Ambs on Saturday & Monday next.	
		20.00	During night slight traces of gas ? Shell Gas in the atmosphere. All ranks warned to have Respirators handy.	
	18th		Lgt R.Cmd Lgt Challen & one O.R. returned from leave. Many early French later.	AG
		a.m.	Asked for 5000 wards from D.G.V.O. in reference to DMS III Army 2939/16 dt 14/3.	
			Made inspection of all quarters, billets, stables. Box Respirators not taken sufficient care of Unit Inspection R.A.M.C. regarding unit in units Quarters.	
		14.00	Visit Inspection R.A.M.C. regarding unit in units Quarters.	
		15.00	Leader of Divisional Y.M.C.A. called about Lecture tomorrow at 3/pm forestry St Aubin. Paid Unit with assistance of Major Whitham the Orderly Officer. Total fund nil in our Dining Hall. Informed A.D.M.S. that we have no Enem Engineer Jerkins in charge query from D.G. no 75/5 of 14 1/1/8.	
			Informed A.D.M.S. that 86 pheds of 1500 Civels ATS held – Ref D.M.S. 3065/19.	
	19.1 <s/>8 :		Called on OC 48 F.Ambl to talk over various questions. Interviewed 5 Candidates for Commissions recommended by Brigadier 63rd Inf Bde Town of CAUDRY shelled by enemy H.V Gun at intervals all day GRO 522 B/Ind more than one copy of War Diary being made.	RW

D.D. &L., London, E.C.
(A10260) Wt. W.5900/P713 750,000 2/18 Sch. 82 Forms/C2118/16

Army Form C. 2118.

WAR DIARY
or
INTELLIGENCE SUMMARY.
(Erase heading not required.)

49th Field Ambulance

1918 October

Place	Date	Hour	Summary of Events and Information	Remarks and references to Appendices
CAUDRY	19th		Dull - cold - heavy mist early. Whist Drive for men of Unit in evening. Pres Chapman and Rees proceeded on leave to U.K.	Ref.
	20th	12.40	Party at Walking Wounded Entraining Station reported Unit. G.O.C. 37 Divn accompanied by A.D.M.S. A.A.&Q.M.G. & A.D.C. inspected the Unit. Lieut W.M. Martin M.R.C. U.S.A. returned from temporary duty with 13th Rifle Brigade	
	21st		Visited 5th Divn H.Q. to ascertain situation and general locations of Medical Arrangements. F.G.B.M. on Rte CRAIG & held at Divl Reception Camp. HAUCOURT. Major Nicholson proceeded. Visited VIESLY and BRIASTRE to select A.D.S. site - decided on Chateau BRIASTRE. A.D.M.S. called regarding moves.	Ref.
VIESLY	22nd		Moved to VIESLY, the Chateau at BRIASTRE not being yet vacated. Visited Corps H.Q. and D.H.Q. Lieut Clarke, O.C. 143 F.Amb called. Bearers distributed to 111th Inf Bde Major Nicholson (Off. Bearers) went forward to take up position at Car Loading Post at BRIASTRE.	Ref.
BRIASTRE	23rd	3.30	"B" Section Tent Sub Divn moved off to form A.D.S. at BRIASTRE Chateau, "C" Section carrying on A.D.S. at VIESLY until "B" Section are ready.	
		6.30	Bearers distributed to 112 Inf. Bde at BRIASTRE Field Amb. HQ moved to BRIASTRE, Transport and Q.M. Stores remaining at VIESLY. Discharge of 42 days F.P. No 2 awarded to Pte W. CRAIG, RAMC promulgated. Casualties 6 p.m. 22nd to 6 p.m. 23rd = 36 Stretcher Cases & 73 Sitting Cases also 10 Prisoners of War	Ref.

Army Form C. 2118.

WAR DIARY
or
INTELLIGENCE SUMMARY.
(Erase heading not required.)

49th Field Ambulance

1918 October

Place	Date	Hour	Summary of Events and Information	Remarks and references to Appendices
BEAURAIN	24th		Major Nicholson established Car Loading Post at W. 24.c.6.0.3 with his HQ at NEUVILLE. Casualties 6 pm 23rd to 6 pm 24th = 93 Stretcher Cases, 54 sitting cases also 2 civilians and 11 Prisoners of War. Sick = 24. Cpl Magill to act as holding party at BRIASTRE Bholam.	Ref. Ref.
SALESCHES	25th	22.00	A.D.S. opened up at L'ECOLE and MAIRIE, SALESCHES. H.Q. + Transport remaining at BEAURAIN. Casualties 6 pm 24th to 6 pm 25th = 22 Stretcher Cases 41 Sitting Cases - also 1 civilian. Sick = 40. and 3 Prisoners of War.	Ref.
	26th		H.Qrs moved to SALESCHES - Transport + Q.M. Stores remain at BEAURAIN. Car Loading Post established at T.33.c.4.2 (BEAUDIGNIES). 13 of 45th F. Amb Gassed (Shell), Pte Pritchards Bearer of 48th F Amb Wounded (Shell). Pte Matthews ASC (M.T.) att 48th F. Amb Wounded (Shell). ASC (MT) att. 49 F.A. 22 Sick - Casualties 6pm 25th to 6pm 26th = 21 Stretcher Cases and 4 Sitting -	
	27th		SALESCHES shelled by H.V. Gun during last night. Casualties 6pm 26th to 6pm 27th = 25 Lying 31 sitting and 22 Sick.	Ref.
	28th		D.A.D. M.S. called. Visited 63rd Inf Bde HQ - Forward posts etc. Enemy shelled SALESCHES at 22 hours. Casualties 6pm 27th to 6pm 28th = 8 Lying, 28 sitting (includes 9 Gassed Cases) - 23 Sick.	Ref.

Army Form C. 2118.

WAR DIARY
or
INTELLIGENCE SUMMARY.
(Erase heading not required.)

49th Field Ambulance

1918 October

Place	Date	Hour	Summary of Events and Information	Remarks and references to Appendices
SALESCHES	29th		A.D.M.S. called. Lgt Blanchard A.S.C. (H.T.) att 49 F. Amb. Wounded by shell. Casualties 6 p.m. 28th to 6 p.m. 29th = 27 Lying 13 Sitting (includes 5 Gassed - shell) and 14 sick.	Ref.
	30th		Cellars at A.D.S. are being made Gas proof by 154 Field Coy. Beaurain was shelled and bombed last night. 6 bomb wounded and 3 shell wounded cases attended to by "C" Section there. Major Nicholson to GHISSIGNIES to evacuate 12 Civilians - these were brought down & sent on from ADS to BEAURAIN by lorry. Casualties 6 p.m. 29th to 6 p.m. 30th = 13 Lying 26 Sitting (includes 3 Gassed - shell) Wounded last night - 2 shell WO and 1 Gassed shell. 43 Sick. - 3 bearers of 50th F.Amb Wounded by same shell that wounded the 2 bearers at Ford Ambulance Car No 13 damaged by same Car Loading Post.	Ref.
	31st		Casualties 6 p.m. 30th to 6 p.m. 31st 7 Stretcher Cases 19 Sitting Cases and 42 Sick	Ref.

N Gott /Major
W A Lee Him.

2/11/18.

Confidential

War Diary
from
1st November to 30th November 1918

49th Field Ambulance

(352¼). Wt.10383—4032. 500,000. 10/15. McA & W Ltd   Forms A 36 / 19

FIELD

(To be compiled by the Commander of a Medical Unit and to be forwar

Hospital Return for the week ended_____ 19

This return is a nominal roll of all patients admitted to or discharged from hospital during the p
and a line ruled after the name of the last officer. A table will be added at the foot of the form, or be
the week for which the return is rendered. A separate return is not required for each unit.

N.B.—Reports of deaths of officers and men in hospital will, as they occur, be sent to the Adjutant-General's Office a
also be reported by telegraph to the Adjutant-General at General Headquarters. (*See* Field Service Regulations, Part II.)

Serial No. (Field Service Admission and Discharge Book)	Corps*		Regtl. No.	Rank	Name	Date of Admission	Nature
	Corps	Unit					

Hospital Return for the week ended_____

* Except Cavalry and Infantry, the unit of the Corps must be entered.

SERVICE.   Army Form A. 36.

(led weekly on Sunday to the Adjutant-General's Office at the Base.)

Hospital and Place_____

*revious week, and is to include civilians and prisoners of War. Officers' names will be entered first
ttached, showing, by ranks, the total number of patients in each unit, rationed on the Saturday in*

the Base as well as to their Commanding Officer, whether he is at the station or elsewhere. All officers' deaths should

disease or wound	Date of			Discharges	Transfers
	Death	Discharge	Transfer	Remarks as to †	Whither transferred and remarks

(led weekly on Sunday to the Adjutant-General's Office at the Base.)

† Specify whether discharged to join his unit or how otherwise disposed of.

Serial No. (Field Service Admission and Discharge Book)	Corps*		Regtl. No.	Rank	Name	Date of Admission	Na
	Corps	Unit					

D. A. G., Adjutant-General's Office at the Base.

Forwarded. The names of all officers and men (1) who have been admitted on account of

Place _____

Date _____

* Except Cavalry and Infantry, the unit of the Corps

WAR DIARY or INTELLIGENCE SUMMARY

Army Form C. 2118.

49th Field Ambulance

1918 November

Place	Date	Hour	Summary of Events and Information	Remarks and references to Appendices
SALESCHES	1st		Fine – cold	
		11.00	Medical Boards held on 2/Lieuts O'Sullivan and Newman.	
		am	Capt Beavis & C.O. visited forward posts, inspected possible ADS site at GHISSIGNIES and revised main road from GHISSIGNIES on return on foot – GHISSIGNIES end of the road though quiet while we passed showed signs of recent heavy shelling. Divisional front slightly increased to right by taking over about 500 yds from 24th Divn. Official confirmation of Armistice concluded with Turkey and Russia received today. DADMS called during the afternoon. Civilians evacuated from NEUVILLE to CAUDRY. Casualties 11 Lying 8 Sitting (4 Gassed) and 38 sick. (6 pm 3rd 16 Lying 20 Sitting)	
	2nd		Dull – cold – showers. Reported to "D" quantity of hay in Barn of Billet 108 – 6 G.S. Wagon loads. Went round all billets to – solo has been greatly improved. Dry proof latrines being installed. A good canvas Mortuary & good Bathhouse accommodation.	
		11.30	A.D.M.S. called – advised him round and took him up to Car Loading Post, BEAUDIGNIES, the GHISSIGNIES and giving up this site to 5th Divn for a M.D.S. I proposed putting A.D.S. in GHISSIGNIES and	
		p.m.	D.D.M.S. called to M.D.S. for 5th Divn accompanied by O.C. 53 F.Amb. Ford Car broke from BEAUDIGNIES into GHISSIGNIES reported road by Sgt Parker, who was bearer went up this morning to repair shell holes and clear the trunks which had fallen across the road.	
		16.00	O/P DMS 5th Divn called – looked round reference taking over as M.D.S. shewed him Farm Barrier and the event on it – prospect elsewhere.	

WAR DIARY
or INTELLIGENCE SUMMARY

(Erase heading not required.)

Army Form C. 2118.

HQ 149 Field Ambulance

November 1918

Place	Date	Hour	Summary of Events and Information	Remarks and references to Appendices
SALESCHES	2nd (cont)	17.15	March to 114th Inf Bde HQ to get details of objectives to ADMS Div Hours -	
		21.15	Conference of Officers — plans for medical arrangements for attack on morning of 4th at 5.30 hours discussed and settled. 114 Bde Orders and VI Corps Medical Arrangements received	
	3rd		March by 2nd Lincolns tonight. Casualties from 1st to 6 pm 2nd = 10 dying, 10 lying of Sitting, and 55 walk.	
			Dull - rain increasing & very dark. Result of last night's raid - Killed a large number of the enemy - Lincolns had 15 wounded and 15 missing -	
		a.m.	ADMS Orders Medical Arrangements for forthcoming attack received - Cap Beavers with two 5th Durh Med Officers to prospect CHISSIGNIES for an ADS.	
		10.00	Capt Thomas MC RAMC departed on leave.	
		11.00	Self to BEAURAIN - drew Imprest Cash Fr 5,000 from Field Cashier at NEUVILLE. Gave instructions at BEAURAIN regarding move of C Sec. Tent Sub Div @ 6am tomorrow	
		13.45	Set out with O.C. Beavers for ADMS Conference, where final details for arrangements were settled.	
		17.45	MDS (A & D Divit) opened at Carrier SOLESMES as from noon today & more following. Capt Beavers endeavoured to get to CHISSIGNIES last night & his black, very wet and road in bad state of confusion owing to heavy shelling which caught transports moving up. Will go tomorrow at 04.00 hours instead. Casualties 6 pm 2nd to 6 pm 3rd = 13 lying, 14 sitting and 46 walk. (13 Evacuated)	

Army Form C. 2118.

WAR DIARY
or
INTELLIGENCE SUMMARY.
(Erase heading not required.)

Army Form C. 2118. 49th Field Ambulance

Instructions regarding War Diaries and Intelligence Summaries are contained in F. S. Regs. Part II. and the Staff Manual respectively. Title pages will be prepared in manuscript.

November 1918

Place	Date	Hour	Summary of Events and Information	Remarks and references to Appendices
SALESCHES	4/11		A fine day -	
			There were some 70 total casualties from 6pm last night to 5am this morning, 30 of which were from a burn caused by shells fired from a which a shell fell.	
		04.00	Op Bearers established in GHISSIGNIES.	
		05.30	Barrage opened	
			Normal route of evacuation via BEAUDIGNIES.	
		07.30	Wounded arriving foot, especially walkers. Shared Ambulance Relays established at 06.30 hours on main GHISSIGNIES Road and LOUVIGNIES - GAY FARM - SALESCHES Road.	
		08.05	Op Bearers reported Ford Cars could get no further than ST ROCHE from BEAUDIGNIES - Shellholes accumulating there and at GHISSIGNIES. Direct route to GHISSIGNIES impossible owing to shelling. Horse was put on to clear.	
		08.40	Car Loading Post switched to GHISSIGNIES by direct route but continued clearing BEAUDIGNIES until all cases cleared and Relay Posts withdrawn.	
		09.00	Capt HALL, M.O. i/c M.G. Bn. reported for duty to assist	
		10.30	An American Officer (Lieut HSILLY) from a Heavy Batty. close by came to MDS and official assistance which was accepted gratefully - Field Amb. are kept far too short of M.O.s for active operations.	
		13.00	Op Bearers reported no being in LOUVIGNIES S.Y. d.2.8 and Car Loading Pst at GAY FARMS. Next up there - Road to LOUVIGNIES from GAY FARMS not possible for large Cars but being mended. A.D.S. Party by march route to LOUVIGNIES from A.D.S.	
		15.30	Returned to SALESCHES and ast C.the A.D.S. could be moved to SALESCHES while I went forward and D.A.D.M.S. off to see if M.D.S. could be moved to SALESCHES and fixed up site of A.D.S.	

Army Form C. 2118.

WAR DIARY
or
INTELLIGENCE SUMMARY.
(Erase heading not required.)

49th Field Ambce

1918 November

Place	Date	Hour	Summary of Events and Information	Remarks and references to Appendices
SALESCHES	4th (contd)	14.45	Cp Bearers reported by a note which I got on return that he wanted to move Car Loading Post to PONT AVRCHES. An return found M.D.S. could not be moved as cases had collected them & evacuation to CCS was slow. As LOUVIGNIES becomes subsidiary A.D.S. and they dress what they can and forward what they cannot home.	
		18.45	Our one nurse lent to 143 & D Amb. returned to us under verbal instructions of ADMS & 143 Amb. expressed his appreciation of the willing service they had given to MDS.	
		19.30	Capt HAMES went to help at A.D.S. LOUVIGNIES. Evacuation from A.D.S. during early part of the day was slow and cases collected badly - but with the aid of extra lorries and five cars from 5th Divn clearance was effected - A.D.S. at LOUVIGNIES had a fairly quiet time and managed to clear all casualties from 5 pm and forward them to SALESCHES. Front reported very quiet by Cp Bearers at 13.30 wks as no touch with enemy and RAPs 112th Bde in JOLIMETZ area - Total Car Loading Post in JOLIMETZ releaving by Northern Road to LOUVIGNIES.	
		21.10	9. left SALESCHES for LOUVIGNIES to see how they were going on. Found all quiet and Cp Bearers and Officers going to bed on my arrival. Returned at midnight bringing two last stretcher cases (Wounded enemy). Found D.A.D.M.S. wanting with news that 14th Field Amb. (5th Div) had been turned out of FERME BERNIER and they were held up for a MDS and their attachments for 05.30 tomorrow. Offered to become MDS for West Divn until they could get installed in LOUVIGNIES. Written Orders were drafted to that effect. Whole Unit very tired after a strenuous day.	

Army Form C. 2118.

WAR DIARY
or
INTELLIGENCE SUMMARY.
(Erase heading not required.)

49th Field Ambulance

November 1918

Place	Date	Hour	Summary of Events and Information	Remarks and references to Appendices
SALESCHES	4th (Cont'd) (?)		Details of casualties 6pm 3rd to 6pm 4th :-	
			Injury Sickness Totals	
			Wounded	
			37 Divn --- 101 184 (12 Gassed) 285	
			5 " --- 3 11 14	
			17 " --- 23 90 113	
			42 " --- - 3 3	
			62 " --- - 3 3	
			N.Z. --- 3 5 8	
			Guards --- 1 - 1	
			Corps Troops 20 19 (1 Gassed) 39	
			Total British 151 315 466	
			P. of War 10 47 57	
			Total Wounded 161 362 523	There are numbers of War Cases of whom we have particulars and who were dressed. At let out least 150 for cases of which we have no particulars and who did not need re-dressing and we get a total of some 650 of which about 120 were whether cases. There have been a strikingly large number of Wounded P.of W. today
			Sick 37 Divn 1 10 11	
			42 " - 1 1	
			1 11 12	
	5th		A miserably wet day and roads bad	
		01.15	S.O.Lt. RUSE reported A.D.S. SALESCHES as at last cleared of all cases	
		06.30	49th Field Amb. SALESCHES becomes M.D.S. for 5th Divn if needed and for any casualties from our detachment at A.D.S. LOUVIGNIES	
		09.30	Went to LOUVIGNIES which had a quiet night visiting D.H.Q NEUVILLE Fork. and met G.O.C. The few remaining casualties (about a dozen) from our Division easily cleared-	

Army Form C. 2118.

WAR DIARY
or
INTELLIGENCE SUMMARY.
(Erase heading not required.)

49th Field Ambulance

1918 November

Place	Date	Hour	Summary of Events and Information	Remarks and references to Appendices
SPLESCHES	5th (Cont)		Our line reported as the eastern side of the FOREST de MORMAL and the enemy retiring fast. Went to 5th Div. M.D.S. who LOUVIGNIES and found 14th Field Ambulance installed in a factory and nearly ready for receive. A.D.S. 13th F.Amb. was found beyond JOLIMETZ also reported ready, so no need for us to function for them. Arranged handing over excess blankets and stretchers at LOUVIGNIES to them. Met A.D.M.S. and got instructions after giving him the situation. Returned to SPLESCHES with two enemy stretcher cases on board. Arranged details for final clearance of A.D.S. and M.D.S.	
		10.30	Capt. James A.S.C. 2/M.T.C. called and took over further stock of excess blankets and stretchers for 5th Div. from us which were loaded on to M9 class G. lorry. Reg. Bearers reported H.Q. SPLESCHES	
		11.00	A.D.S. LOUVIGNIES closed, packed and reported H.Q. by march route. Officers, including O/C Bearers reported by car for lunch. By 12.0 whole place cleared and things settling down.	
		15.30	Attached Cars and Horsed Ambulances 45% & 50% F.Amb. sent to respective Units. Bearers returned. All further instructions from A.D.M.S. Large quantity of salvage - clothing and boots sent to BEAURAIN to be forwarded to Refilling Point. Went to H.Q. Units and attached Bearers settling in.	
		16.06	Sent in Information Report to A.D.M.S. detailing clearance and handing over to ...	

Army Form C. 2118.

WAR DIARY
or
INTELLIGENCE SUMMARY.

(Erase heading not required.)

2/1th Field Ambulance

1918
November

Place	Date	Hour	Summary of Events and Information	Remarks and references to Appendices
SALESCHES	5th (con'd)		A.D.M.S. Order received to transfer BEAVRAIN to 48th F. Amb. Orders received for move of O.M.T. Dept and Transport to SALESCHES tomorrow. Casualties 6pm 4th to 6pm 5th — 18 Lying, 24 Sitting (British) and 21 sick. 30 " — 5 " (Germans)	
	6th	am	A wet miserable day. 48th F. Amb. took over BEAVRAIN site. Bearers attached to 111th Bde. collected by Gen Fackers & after marching to load Stores at Beavrain joined H.Q. by march route.	
		1pm	Transport and Stores to move completed by 3pm	
		11.30	Visited A.D.M.S. and discussed various matters. Ins Qur. Doyles to see C.R.E. re obtaining oil linen for covering stretchers, metal tubing to experiment with water heating device for warming Operating Table suggested by Major Nicholson; also metal plating for larger A.D.S. signs. Present A.D.S. put in charge of Major Nicholson.	
			Collection of sick from Brigades a and their despatch to D.R.S. put in charge of Major Nicholson.	
			Wet and cold	
	7th	10.00	Issue of clothing to men nobody as requiring rest at CAUDRY being dealt with. Men whose boots require repair or replacement also paraded for same.	

Army Form C. 2118.

WAR DIARY
or
INTELLIGENCE SUMMARY.

(Erase heading not required.)

Army Form C. 2118.

409th Field Ambulance

1918 November

Place	Date	Hour	Summary of Events and Information	Remarks and references to Appendices
SALESCHES	1st (cont)		Lieut James Philip Walker Carson reported as missing – All MOs of Battery written to asking if any staff or their possession – All MOs of Battery received from OC 48 DIVH.	
			Details of Casualties from 12.00 3rd Nov to 12.00 5th/12 received from OC 48 DIVH as follows:-	
				Officers	OR	Total	
			3rd Divn	13	323	336	
			5th "	2	21	23	Army 1 Off. and 25 OR
			17th "	13	137	150	of these ORs were picked
			38th "	—	3	3	up at several points & squads
			42nd "	—	4	4	Divisions
			62nd "	—	25	25	
			Guards	—	12	12	
			Cavalry	—	2	2	
			N.Z.	—	18	18	
			Cav Corps	—	15	15	
			Army	2	22	24	
				1	—	—	
				31	575	606	
			Prisoners of War	—	152	152	
					Grand Total	758	
			Order received of moves tomorrow:-	
			42 FA to BRIASTRE (4 tables over DRS on LB.	
			49 FA to remain in SALESCHES	
			50 FA to ---------- BEAURAIN on 3h.	
			52 FA to LOUVIGNIES on 9h.	
			Render returns to be returned when information above available	

WAR DIARY or INTELLIGENCE SUMMARY

Army Form C. 2118.

Instructions regarding War Diaries and Intelligence Summaries are contained in F. S. Regs., Part II. and the Staff Manual respectively. Title pages will be prepared in manuscript.

1/9 Field Ambulance
1918 November

(Erase heading not required.)

Place	Date	Hour	Summary of Events and Information	Remarks and references to Appendices
SALESCHES	8th		Vet. & Col.	
			Four men of Unit admitted to Hospital today. 2 Influenza, 1 Diarrhoea, 1 Shrapnel.	
			Fit Infections as under today.	
			"C" Sec. 11.00 "B" do 14.00 "A" do to follow "B"	
		11.30	A.D.M.S. called. Went with him to select site for D.R.S. at JOLIMETZ	
		14.30	Conference of Medical Officers at A.D.M.S. Office. Points discussed were:-	
			(a) Venereal Prophylaxis	
			(b) Evacuation of Wounded during recent Operations. This was pronounced good. The fact was brought out that only 1 Off. + 25 OR of this Div. reached Medical Units of other Divisions whereas we treated some 13 Offrs + 233 OR of other Divisions engaged.	
			(c) Influenza	
			(d) Trench foot	
			(e) Arrangements for Medal Ribbon Presentation Parade tomorrow	
	9th		Fine clear day.	
			Capt. A.F. PIGGOT posted to permanent Medical Charge of 2 Son. L.D. (C "/B")	
			R.G.oll.S. called and gave instructions for Holding party of 45 F.A. to be sent to JOLIMETZ	
			No take over made of D.R.S. Party despatched with letter of authority	
			Medal Ribbon Presentation Parade postponed till 15 hours tomorrow.	
		12.4.5	Sent to Deputy Park Lodgeshall for credit of Captain Finch. 49 R.A.M.C.	
			Sent in recommendations for honours and awards "immediate" for recent operations.	

Army Form C. 2118.

WAR DIARY
or
INTELLIGENCE SUMMARY.

(Erase heading not required.)

149th Field Ambulance

1918 November

Place	Date	Hour	Summary of Events and Information	Remarks and references to Appendices
SOLESMES	9th (Cont)		Great improvement has been made in the general cleanliness of surroundings. Manure and carting away. Heaps of manure and refuse with which the farmyards occupied were filled. The stoning of horses lines much to be desired. Studied WEB Stow table with a view to seeing what we could dispense with in addition to reductions allowed by G.R.O. 5175. By a readjustment and refacking of the Panniers a good deal of space might be made by getting rid of useless material and stowing with Extra Dressings, Medical Comforts, Red Cross material, Splints &c, which are of real use. Not more during recent Operations than any of the transport, except ADS timber and material and Horsed Ambulances been of any value to us. Spoke to ADMS about the question yesterday. Fine – Clean.	
	10th	am	Orders received for Ambulances to move as under:– 149th unit 63rd Bde to CAUDRY 50th " 112th " BETHENCOURT 48th remain at BRIASTRE A.D.M.S. called re move tomorrow and recommendations submitted yesterday. Drew 3h 3 pro Imprest from Field Cashier. Visited BEAUDIGNIES and GUISSIGNIES roads looking for lost Stretcher Wheels without success.	149th Field Ambulance to CAUDRY area

WAR DIARY or INTELLIGENCE SUMMARY

Army Form C. 2118.

49th Field Ambulance

1918 November

Place	Date	Hour	Summary of Events and Information	Remarks and references to Appendices
SALESCHES	10th (cont)		Unit paid out - fr. 5,895. ADMS call with I/C Steele, OC 56 F.O.S., who is learning ADMS work. Major Nicholson and self to DHQ to receive any further instructions had been received. 63rd Bde Orders received – no arrangements made to transport Cpl. Bunten or Jenkins – no lorries available. Finest details and issued Orders for march tomorrow – Blankets will be conveyed by Car after site collection. Unit Parades 8 am to be in place in column at 8.36. Est. 4 wheeled Maltese Carriage from 50th Field Ambce through kindness of OC and Major Sergt. RAMC. News of Kaiser's abdication and Revolution in Germany received today. Paid on Leave party total fr. 1250 – Balance fr. 235.	
		21.15	Intimation that Unit proceed by march route to CAUDRY arriving about 2.30 pm. unit 63rd Bde W.F. 3.6.64 received (a) next from 63 Bde – 111 Bde – 9050. Division – no return. (b) Special arr. (Mental Ophthalmic etc)	
CAUDRY	11th		from 112 Bde BÉTHENCOURT area. 50th FA " " " " 4th FA " " " PONT SUR SAMBRE area. Div RE & N Staff on PONT SUR SAMBRE area. News of signing of Armistice received today.	

Army Form C. 2118.

WAR DIARY
or
INTELLIGENCE SUMMARY.
(Erase heading not required.)

49th Field Ambce

Month: November 1918

Place	Date	Hour	Summary of Events and Information	Remarks and references to Appendices
CAUDRY	12th		Fine – cold.	
		am	Cleaning up + generally settling down.	
			Called at A.D.M.S. Office – Tonight time named to see Units quarters to see over ordnance for D.R.S. offsite us, to be taken over by 143 F.A.	
		pm	Pmt Depot Kearns & Pt. Pulling on leave to Paris and Boulogne respectively. Report that 3/k Dixon is among those chosen for occupation of GERMANY.	
	13th		Fine – cold.	
			Orders regarding pathroal Medal Presentation Parade received.	
		11.00	Patronal Feast of Cavalry service in Church by Archbishop of Cambrai – a vast party from this Unit attended	
			Horses inspected by Veterinary Officer No 2 Coy Train to find any unfit for long marches – Reported 1 H.D. deficient – more condemned unfit. This was no reserve to replace same from A.D.M.S. T.G.	
			Units equipment unpacked for overhaul.	
			Arrangements for Concert tonight – Baths to completed.	
			Wrote O/C D.A.O Trains regarding deficiencies in M.T. Personnel.	
		14.30	Parade for presentation of Medal Ribbons by O/C Commander. Whole detachment paraded under command of Major Nicholson.	
			Actg A.D.M.S. by midst. Unit. Major Nicholson detailed for leave to U.K. Capt Ward will act as S.C. O/C pending return of Capt Thomas during Major Nicholson absence	

WAR DIARY
INTELLIGENCE SUMMARY

Army Form C. 2118.

Hd Qrs 2nd Field Ambce
November 1918

Place	Date	Hour	Summary of Events and Information	Remarks and references to Appendices
CAUDRY	14		Fine - showers. Lectures attended by Motor Convoy personnel - health & feet. Unit in excellent condition and ready for advance. Meeting with the Baswellier on transport and DTO not transport for advn alone. Blankets to ghaving nurse to Comny.	
		am	DADMS to lunch. Order received for Unit to return to D.Q.M.S. 6. 15th and to prepare to act tonight (Auth: TMS III Army wire 9/632/CM/) Athend & stelle (numbers disabled whole these a.c. 50 N.G. Nursing Sister W.R)	
			Whole Unit fitted up (less 1st & 2nd Sechs Convoy)	
	15	14:00	Capt Hawes to see site of Divis. Trainy Corps. Fine day. Oc to G.H.Q. in accordance with Orders.	
		11:00	Unit inspected by ADMS. Major Nicholson i/c of Parade.	
	16		OC returned from G.H.Q. Major Nicholson RAMC proceeded on leave to U.K.	W
	17		Fine but cold. Capt O.B Ward RAMC proceeded on leave to U.K. (19/11/18 to 3/12/18)	
	18		To see ADMS in morning	
	19	am	Capt. Hawes RAMC proceeded on leave to U.K. (20/11/18 to 4/12/18)	
	20	am	C.O. proceeded on Special leave to U.K. (22/11/18 to 6/12/18) handing over command of Field Ambce to Major M Scarisbrick RAMC	

Army Form C. 2118.

WAR DIARY
or
INTELLIGENCE SUMMARY. 49th Field Ambulance
(Erase heading not required.)

Instructions regarding War Diaries and Intelligence Summaries are contained in F.S. Regs., Part II. and the Staff Manual respectively. Title pages will be prepared in manuscript.

1918 November

Place	Date	Hour	Summary of Events and Information	Remarks and references to Appendices
Cambrai	20th		Capt R. Graves M.O. RAMC "A" Coy R. Fus. reported for temporary duty.	wt
	21st		Parade and Inspection by A.D.M.S. Practice Church Parade etc.	wt
	22nd	11.00	Inspection of Division by G.O.C. and March Past.	wt
	23rd		Capt Thomas M.C. returned from leave	wt
	24th		Cold and wintry. – Capt Graves returned to duty with R. Fusiliers	wt
	25th	a.m.	O.C. 6 Meeting of Educational Committee – Scheme or Education to meet of Unit.	wt
	26th	p.m.	Par Parade	
	27th		Fine but cold – Divisional Educational Officer called re Educational Scheme	wt
	28th	a.m.	Wet + cold	wt
	29th	p.m.	Visited 63rd Inf Bde HQ. A.D.M.S. called	wt
	30th	p.m.	A.D.M.S. called – 5 Reinforcements received from Base – Pass Pte. Burstow 20th to handed him Movement Order to proceed to Transportation Troops Base Sept Cm19's tomorrow morning – Authy DAG/AX 53 of dt. 29/11/3 Orders for move tomorrow received – Weekly Returns completed – Cash Bks completed – Cash cheques & A/cs despatched to Base (Balance £ 192-0-0)	wt

W Mansfield
Major RAMC
Comds 49th Field Ambulance

WA 42
MT/3681

Dec. 1918   Confidential

War Diary
— of —
49th Field Ambulance

From 1st December to 31st December 1918

COMMITTEE FOR THE
MEDICAL HISTORY OF THE WAR
6 MAR 1919
Date

49TH
FIELD AMBULANCE.
No.
Date

M

Army Form C. 2118.

WAR DIARY
or
INTELLIGENCE SUMMARY.   HQ 5 Field Ambulance
(Erase heading not required.)

December 1918

Instructions regarding War Diaries and Intelligence Summaries are contained in F. S. Regs., Part II. and the Staff Manual respectively. Title pages will be prepared in manuscript.

Place	Date	Hour	Summary of Events and Information	Remarks and references to Appendices
CAUDRY	1/12/18	—	3 ORs received on leave to U.K. Pour 2MS Brooks 100 france who proceeded on Special Leave - Pte Wilson (T.B. Machine) returned from C.C.S.	W.T.
HAUSSY	2/12/18		Unit moved from CAUDRY to HAUSSY. Chateau. Ambce moved from HAUSSY for VILLERS-POL	W.T. W.T.
VILLERS-POL	3/12/18		Highways, taking possession of the Girls School Pavilion in rue of town N. of Square. Pour Wp WHITAKER 50/00 who proceeded on Special leave to U.K. Major Nicholson Rambl returned from leave took over command at Unit and Major thereafter Rambl	W.T.
VILLERS-POL	4/12/18		Recd R.E. Tents 20 to and hauses W.C. Kitchen/Order Messroom to transform then Tents. Srivoughet Cellars - OrRty. DAD9/AXG2 2/13/18. U. O.C. collected Bootlaces of the 6 commanders at B.H.Q on New Area into take the strength of Unit.	W
VILLERS-POL	5/12/18		Relud by Major Nicholson in afternoon on arrangement	W.
VILLERS-POL	6/12/18		Relud by Major Nicholson all leavey or Evacuation who had been off Army - Capt Wood Norman from leave to U.K.	W.

Army Form C. 2118.

WAR DIARY
or
INTELLIGENCE SUMMARY.
(Erase heading not required.)

Acaula 49 Div. Sigs Cooks
1918

Instructions regarding War Diaries and Intelligence Summaries are contained in F.S. Regs., Part II. and the Staff Manual respectively. Title pages will be prepared in manuscript.

Place	Date	Hour	Summary of Events and Information	Remarks and references to Appendices
VILLERS-POL	7/7/18		Wk.	
VILLERS-POL	8/7/18		Church Parade in morning	
VILLERS-POL	9/7/18		Road Parades afternoon No RE Demonstration S.B. system employed No 3 Section B26 (Sgt)	
VILLERS-POL	10/7/18		Visit of Divisional General to System. Band from 09.15-10.00	
VILLERS-POL	11/7/18		Wired setting up during Brigadier Closing 09.15-10.00 French- 10.00-12.45 Musketry 16.00-14.45 Lectures and Bombing 17.15-18.00 Wiring and Shooting	
VILLERS-POL	12/7/18		Captain RW Mann Observed their home to O/C Reserve Canadian Chaos in road	
VILLERS-POL	13/7/18		Row McMahon and RE Safew and henew W. L.o. Warren O.C. Mental Conference of Adiud Afor 14.30 hrs - B Section Classes as usual	
VILLERS-POL	14/7/18		Ambulance moved from VILLERS-POL to ST WAAST- main (28/1.0.4)	

Army Form C. 2118.

WAR DIARY
or
INTELLIGENCE SUMMARY.

149 Field Ambulance

December 1918

(Erase heading not required.)

Instructions regarding War Diaries and Intelligence Summaries are contained in F. S. Regs., Part II. and the Staff Manual respectively. Title pages will be prepared in manuscript.

Place	Date	Hour	Summary of Events and Information	Remarks and references to Appendices
HOUDAIN	Dec 1st/14th		L.A. duties R.Amb. [unclear] and command of half unit	(X)
ST WAAST			Capt (A/Lt Col) R.F. Jones Tem to Emg Comm of Area W. of 13 R.E. rel'd at 6 p.m. (Auth: D.G.M.S. N.D.G. 113/326 Apl 24. N. 1/10) 1 O.R. struck off unit from Cpl Baines R.A.M.C.	
SOUS-LE-BOIS	15th		Ambulance moved from ST WAAST to SOUS-LE-BOIS. Capt Ward O.C. R.A.M.C. to 13 K.R.R.C. for temporary duty.	
ROUVEROY	17th		Ambulance moved from SOUS-LE-BOIS to ROUVEROY	
BINCHE	18th		Ambulance moved from ROUVEROY to BINCHE	
COURCELLES	19th		Ambulance moved from BINCHE to COURCELLES Capt (A/Major) Clark Nicholson R.A.M.C. awarded M.C. (2nd Army No HR/3997 14/12/18)	
LIBERCHIES	20th		Ambulance moved from COURCELLES to LIBERCHIES	
	22nd		2 N.C.Os. + 3 O.Rs from Field Ambs., IV Corps, Rft. Bookroom to 3 O.R. to England for demobilization (-Boatmen)	
	23rd		Pay Parade — 3 O.R. (1 Pivotal + 2 Coalminers to U.K. for demobilization	
	25th		2 O.R. (Long Service men) to U.K. for demobilization	
	26th		1 O.R. (Coalminer) to U.K. for demobilization	
	30th		2 O.R. (1 Pivotal + 1 Coalminer) to U.K. for demobilization	

C.W. Drew
LT. COL. R.A.M.C.
COMDG 149th FIELD AMBULANCE

37 DIV 98/43

140/3490

Confidential   Box 2326

War Diary

of

49th Field Ambulance

From 1st Jan 1919 to 31 Jan. 1919

Army Form C. 2118.

WAR DIARY
or
INTELLIGENCE SUMMARY.
(Erase heading not required.)

H.Q. 4th Field Ambulance

1919 January

Instructions regarding War Diaries and Intelligence Summaries are contained in F. S. Regs., Part II. and the Staff Manual respectively. Title pages will be prepared in manuscript.

Place	Date	Hour	Summary of Events and Information	Remarks and references to Appendices
LIBERCHIES BELGIUM	1st		Holiday – Monthly Returns and Cash A/c for Dec. completed and rendered	C.
	2nd		Educational Classes re-commenced – O.B. inspected billets &c	C.
	3rd		Major W. Scarsbrook RAMC returned from leave to U.K.	C.
	5th		Church Parades in morning. Capt J.H.S. Barnes RAMC returned from leave in U.K. Capt O.E. Ward RAMC returned from temporary medical charge of 13/K.R.R.C. Capt Figgis RAMC and Capt Custer RAMC called to see O.C.	C.
	6th		Divisional General inspected Hospital, Transport &c	
			Capt J.H.S Barnes RAMC to 123 Bde. R.F.A. for temporary medical duty vice Capt Martin M.R.C. called on O.C. Lecture to all ranks on "Demobilization" by Major Nicholson M.C. RAMC	C.
	8th		Capt O.E Ward RAMC to 34 D.A.C. for temporary duty as M.O i/c Capt J.H.S Barnes RAMC (now temporarily M.O i/c 123 Bde R.F.A.) posted to permanent Medical charge of 34 D.A.C.	
	9th		D.P.M.S. 37 Divn called in afternoon. Lecture to all ranks on "Parliament" by Major Scarsbrook RAMC Received D.R.O notifying award of Bar to M.C. to Major Albert Nicholson M.C. RAMC	C.

(37 D R/C 4820 d/- 10.1.19)

Army Form C. 2118.

WAR DIARY
or
INTELLIGENCE SUMMARY.
(Erase heading not required.)

H.Q. 7 Field Ambulance

1919 January (cont)

Place	Date	Hour	Summary of Events and Information	Remarks and references to Appendices
LIBERCHIES	12th		Capt. A.P. Piggott RAMC (M.O i/c 2 Somersets) (temporarily) for 293 Fd. Amb. F.9 & M.O i/c of 1/4th Running RAMC proceeding on leave – Lt Martin (M.O i/c 2 Somersets) to act as M.O i/c 2 Somersets in addition to his present duty during Capt Piggott's absence	A.
	13th		D.D.M.S. IV Corps called & inspected Hospital to –	A.
	18th		A.D.M.S. 37 Divn called and inspected Hospital to – 4 O.R. (RAMC) to U.K. for demobilization	A.
	20th		To see A.D.M.S. in morning – Major Nicholson inspected medical arrangements at 4th Division – Report satisfactory social Conference which was not quite satisfactory	A.
	21st		Attended Conference of O.C. 7th Field Ambulance at A.D.M.S. Office with Major Clark Nicholson, M.C. R.A.M.C., of Demobility xxxx and A.V.T. from 16.15 hrs. R.A.M.C. tracked Bournemouth (22.1.19 to 5.2.19)	A.
			1 O.R. (RAMC) to U.K. for demobilization Lecture to all ranks on "Waterloo" by Revd. H.G. Thomas, C.F.	A.
			11 O.R. to U.K. for demobilization	
	22nd 23rd 25th			
	26th		2 O.R. to U.K. for demobilization Revd. H.G. Thomas, C.F. proceeded to U.K. for demobilization To see A.D.M.S. in morning	A.
	27th		Revd. G.R.D. 6077 (Rankin) to full Parade of Ambulance in morning Lecture to all ranks "What caused the War" by Pte J. Dillon ("Bren Canls")	A.

Army Form C. 2118.

WAR DIARY
or
INTELLIGENCE SUMMARY.
(Erase heading not required.)

HQ H. Field Ambulance

1914 January

Place	Date	Hour	Summary of Events and Information	Remarks and references to Appendices
LIBERCHIES	28th	a.m.	C.O. went to D.M.S. South Army with Major C Nicholson MO RMC Capt Slaughter to 298 Field Amb for temporary duty in relief of Capt AS Riggs to M.K. on Leave. Handed in surplus Medical equipment to No 12 F.D.M. Stores CHARIEROI	Cu
	29th		Lieut G.M. Shaw RAMC to DHQ to act as A.D.M.S. during the absence on leave of Col. E.M. Morphew SM & DSO AMS ADMS 39 Div. (24/1/19 – 31/1/19) Capt OE Ward RAMC returned to Unit from 39 F.D.C. having been relieved by Capt J.J.S. Davies RAMC who took over permanent medical charge of the Column.	Cu

Auk Nicholson
Major RAMC
Comd'g HQ Field Ambce

Army Form C. 2118.

WAR DIARY
or
INTELLIGENCE SUMMARY.
(Erase heading not required.)

Instructions regarding War Diaries and Intelligence Summaries are contained in F. S. Regs., Part II. and the Staff Manual respectively. Title pages will be prepared in manuscript.

Place	Date	Hour	Summary of Events and Information	Remarks and references to Appendices

D. D. & L. London, E.C.
(A10460) W. W5300/P713 750,000 2/16 Sch. 82 Forms/C2118/16

Confidential

War Diary
of
49th Field Ambulance
From 1st February to 28th February 1919

Army Form C. 2118.

WAR DIARY
or
INTELLIGENCE SUMMARY.

(Erase heading not required.)

Instructions regarding War Diaries and Intelligence Summaries are contained in F. S. Regs., Part II. and the Staff Manual respectively. Title pages will be prepared in manuscript.

Place	Date	Hour	Summary of Events and Information	Remarks and references to Appendices

D. D. & L., London, E.C.
(A10266) Wt.W1300/P713 750,000 3/16 Sch. 52 Forms/C2118/16

Army Form C. 2118.

WAR DIARY
or
INTELLIGENCE SUMMARY. 4 O/R Field Amb clears
(Erase heading not required.)

Instructions regarding War Diaries and Intelligence Summaries are contained in F. S. Regs., Part II. and the Staff Manual respectively. Title pages will be prepared in manuscript.

1919 February

Place	Date	Hour	Summary of Events and Information	Remarks and references to Appendices
LIBERCHIES (Belgium)	1st		Monthly returns re completed & forwarded	Ch
	2nd		2 OR left for Concentration Camp for demobilization	Ch
	3rd		3 OR — do —	Ch
	5th		Group H.D Brood Mares despatched to the Base	Ch
	6th		3 OR left for Concentration Camp for demobilization	Ch
	8th		Medal Riband Presentation Parade at Gozalies by G.O.C. 37 Div. Major Black Nicholson attended for M.C. + Bar – Pte R.E Rasper for M.M.	Ch
	9th		Major Nicholson MC attended 50th Field Ambce as President of Board of Enquiry assembled to enquire into loss of certain Rums & ropes belonging to 50th F Ambce	Ch
		pm	3 OR to Concentration Camp for demobilization	Ch
		pm	Lt + Qmr H.E Staples returned from leave	Ch
	10th	am	Capt J.G. L Thomas MC to 143 Trails Ambce for temporary duty	Ch
		pm	Capt Slaughter returned from temporary duty with 298 Bde R.F.A	Ch
	12th		3 OR to Concentration Camp for demobilization	
			L/Cor CM Snow RAMC returned from D.H.Q. & resumed command of Field Ambce	Ch
	14th	am	Capt O.G Piggott RAMC returned from leave	Ch

Army Form C. 2118.

WAR DIARY
or
INTELLIGENCE SUMMARY.
(Erase heading not required.)

49th Field Ambulance

Instructions regarding War Diaries and Intelligence Summaries are contained in F. S. Regs., Part II. and the Staff Manual respectively. Title pages will be prepared in manuscript.

1919 February

Place	Date	Hour	Summary of Events and Information	Remarks and references to Appendices
LIBERCHIES BELGIUM	15th		Major Scanlebrick, Capt A.P. Piggot and Capt O.E. Ward proceeded to England for demobilisation – Yellapi Scanlebrick relinquished acting rank of Major on ceasing to command a Section –	Ap.
			Lt. H.O. Stone RAMC reported from 4th Middlesex and proceeded to take medical charge of 86 Bde, RFA	Ap.
	17th		Lt Col. C.M. Drew proceeded on leave to Scotland (17/2/19 to 5/3/19) Capt. E.A. Slaughter proceeded to take command of No.21 M.F.A Convoy	Ap.
	18th		Despatched 8 animals to the Base 3 O.R. to Concentration Camp for demobilisation	Ap.
	20th		2 O.R. (B men) to do	Ap.
	21st		3 O.R. (RAMC) to do	Ap.
	24th		2 O.R. (u.s.) to do	
		a.m.	A.D.M.S called & mobilised Hospital and statists. I went to H.Q. to see D.D.M.S. A Both S. & to meeting re "Golden November"	Ap.
			12 horses (Y class) despatched to the Base today.	Ap.
	25th		Court of Enquiry assembled to enquire into the loss of 2 officers saddles from the Harness Room on night 22/23 inst.	Ap.

Army Form C. 2118.

WAR DIARY
or
INTELLIGENCE SUMMARY.

49 & Field Amb.ce

(Erase heading not required.)

Instructions regarding War Diaries and Intelligence Summaries are contained in F. S. Regs., Part II. and the Staff Manual respectively. Title pages will be prepared in manuscript.

Place	Date	Hour	Summary of Events and Information	Remarks and references to Appendices
LIBERCHIES	20		Went to D.A.Q to see A.P.M.	
	28		Attended before a Board at N.8.C.C.S. NAMUR to give evidence on Equipment and organization of a Field Ambulance	

Auth Anderson
major
COMDG 49th FIELD AMBULANCE

Army Form C. 2118.

WAR DIARY
or
INTELLIGENCE SUMMARY.

(Erase heading not required.)

Place	Date	Hour	Summary of Events and Information	Remarks and references to Appendices

Instructions regarding War Diaries and Intelligence Summaries are contained in F. S. Regs., Part II. and the Staff Manual respectively. Title pages will be prepared in manuscript.

War Diary
of
49th Field Ambulance
From 1st March to 31st March 1919

Army Form C. 2118.

WAR DIARY
or
INTELLIGENCE SUMMARY.

(Erase heading not required.)

Place	Date	Hour	Summary of Events and Information	Remarks and references to Appendices

Instructions regarding War Diaries and Intelligence Summaries are contained in F. S. Regs., Part II. and the Staff Manual respectively. Title pages will be prepared in manuscript.

D.D. & L., London, E.C.
(A10260) W! W3900/P713 750,000 2/16 Sch. 88 Forms/C2118/16

Army Form C. 2118.

WAR DIARY or INTELLIGENCE SUMMARY.

(Erase heading not required.)

49th Field Ambulance

1919. March

Place	Date	Hour	Summary of Events and Information	Remarks and references to Appendices
LIBERCHIES (BELGIUM)	1st		Monthly Returns & Cash O/p completed & forwarded	
	2nd		3 O.R. to Concentration Camp for demobilisation	
	3rd		Pay Parade – Lecture to men on formation & of Cadre Establishment – Powers to	
	5th		To see A.D.M.S. & O.C. 37 Div. Train in early morning. 3 O.R proceeded to Concentration Camp for demobilisation. Lt Col C.M. Doxon returned from leave and resumed command of Unit. Marked A.D.M.S. in evening	
	7th		Received instructions from 63rd Inf Bde as to move of Bde to JUMET area early next week.	
	8th		C.O. & Lt. Dr Styles to see O.C. 48th Field Ambulance with reference to the billeting of this Unit at JUMET - later Lt Styles & Sgt Blood proceeded to localities to look for billets. 3 O.R. proceeded to U.K. for demobilisation Capt J.E.J. Thomas M.C. proceeded on leave U.K. (12.3.19 to 26.3.19) C.O. went to see MDMS	
	10th		Billeting & holding party of Lt & Dr Styles proceeded to JUMET Conference as to future War Establishment held at ADM's Office - attended by Major E. Nicholson M.C. Lt & Dr Styles & S Mjr Arthur (RAMC)	

Army Form C. 2118.

WAR DIARY
or
INTELLIGENCE SUMMARY.
(Erase heading not required.)

HQ 1/1 Field Ambulance

1919 March

Instructions regarding War Diaries and Intelligence Summaries are contained in F. S. Regs., Part II. and the Staff Manual respectively. Title pages will be prepared in manuscript.

Place	Date	Hour	Summary of Events and Information	Remarks and references to Appendices
LIBERCHIES (BELGIUM)	11th		6 "Class Z" Mules despatched to R.T.O. MARCHIENNE au PONT. 2 Riders (Class "Z") and 2 L.D. (Class Z) horses sent to O.C. 22 Mobile Vet Sec for inclusion in sale of "Z" animals at GOSSELIES tomorrow. The Unit has now only 1 Rider, 1 L.D, 3 H.D + 5 Mules in charge. 3 R.A.M.C and 1 R.D.S.C (HT) proceeded to Concentration Camp for demobilization. Transferred surplus Medical Comforts and Red Cross Stores to O.C. 48 Field Ambulance, all patients having been cleared from this Field Ambulance today. Approx 500 Animals from	
LODELINSART (CHARLEROI)	13th		Field Ambulance moved to LODELINSART (3 Rue Fr FERRER) - Receiving 48 & 5 Oth Field Ambulance to assist in moving vehicles. We have no Room only, all patients being sent on to 48th Field Ambulance for admission - (16 3/14 to 30 3/14)	
	14th		Major Clark Nicholson MC proceeded to U.K. on leave. 3 O.R. to Corps Concentration Camp for demobilization. 1 O.R. to U.K. on leave.	
	16th		Equipment sent to Infantry Barracks, CHARLEROI for storage viz - 4 O.R. leave to U.K	
	17th		To Corps HQ WAVRE to draw W 3,000 on Imprest - 3 O.R. to Concentration Camp for demobilization	
	18th		Pay Parade - I attended Conference at 37 @ 26.18 in morning	
	20th		3 O.R. to Corps Concentration Camp for demobilization	
	21st		1 O.R. to Corps Concentration Camp for demobilization	
	22nd		No A.D.M.S in morning	

Army Form C. 2118.

WAR DIARY
or
INTELLIGENCE SUMMARY.
(Erase heading not required.)

49th Field Ambulance

Place	Date	Hour	Summary of Events and Information	Remarks and references to Appendices
LODELINSART	24th		3 H.D. horses transferred to 34 Bn Machine Gun Corps.	
	26th		I went to Charleroi and checked Field Ambulance Equipment to 6 OR proceeded to Corps Concentration Camp for demobilization.	
	27th		to 34 D.H.Q in morning.	
	30th		1 Rider despatched to MARCHIENNE AU PONT for entraining for OUTREAUX Major Clark Nicholson MC returned from leave.	
	31st	10.00	I inspected RAMC and RASC personnel Pay Parade 1 L.D. Horse despatched to 28 Mobile Veterinary Section.	

McDrew Lt Col.
I/c 1 49th Ambce
Comdg 49 Fd Ambce
1/4/19

Army Form C. 2118.

WAR DIARY
or
INTELLIGENCE SUMMARY.

(Erase heading not required.)

Instructions regarding War Diaries and Intelligence Summaries are contained in F. S. Regs., Part II. and the Staff Manual respectively. Title pages will be prepared in manuscript.

Place	Date	Hour	Summary of Events and Information	Remarks and references to Appendices

D. D. & L., London, E.C.
(A10260) W¹ W4300/P713 250,000 2/15 Sch. 92 Forms/C2118/16

Confidential

War Diary
of —
49th Field Ambulance
from 1st April to 25 April 1919

MC 46
Reg 3550

April 1919

Army Form C. 2118.

WAR DIARY
or
INTELLIGENCE SUMMARY.

(Erase heading not required.)

Instructions regarding War Diaries and Intelligence Summaries are contained in F. S. Regs., Part II. and the Staff Manual respectively. Title pages will be prepared in manuscript.

Place	Date	Hour	Summary of Events and Information	Remarks and references to Appendices.

Army Form C. 2118.

WAR DIARY
or
INTELLIGENCE SUMMARY.
(Erase heading not required.)

49 Field Ambulance

April 1919

Place	Date	Hour	Summary of Events and Information	Remarks and references to Appendices
LODELINSART BELGIUM	1st		Monthly returns completed and despatched	
	2nd		1 OR despatched to Corps Concentration Camp for demobilization	
	3rd		Notification received from A.D.M.S. that Capt J.G.J. Thomas M.C. had been granted extension of leave to 5/4/19	
	5th		5 OR RASC (H.T.) to No 8 Army Aux. Horse Coy for duty	
	6th		Lt Col C.M. Drew to UK on short leave (7/4/19 – 13/4/19) Major Clark Nicholson M.C. assumed command of Unit.	
	12th		3 Mules despatched to IV Corps Heavy Artillery	
	13th		5 OR (RASC - H.T.) reported from No 3 Coy Train for duty.	
	14th		Lt Col C.M. Drew returned from leave – Pay Parade & Inspection	
	15th		Imprest O/c checked by Field Cashier, CHARLEROI, agreed and O/c closed.	
	16th		3 OR RAMC (Untransferable) transferred to 48 CCS, NAMUR, for duty. 2 Mules (Untransferable) transferred to No 11 Remount Squadron – the Ambulance has now no animals on charge –	
	17th		Maj. Nicholson handed over command of unit to Major C. Nicholson M.C. RAMC	

C.M. Drew Lt Col
Comdg 49 Fd Ambce

Army Form C. 2118.

WAR DIARY or INTELLIGENCE SUMMARY.

49th Field Ambulance

(Erase heading not required.)

1919 April

Place	Date	Hour	Summary of Events and Information	Remarks and references to Appendices
LODELINSART BELGIUM	17 (cont)		Lt Col G.W. DREW, RAMC proceeded to 55 C.C.S. CHARLEROI for duty. S.S.Mr Arthur and 3 OR RASC (H.T) transferred to No 8 Lry Army Amm. Base @ NAMUR for duty. Sgt Challen and 9 OR RASC (MT) transferred to 34 Ski M.T.Coy DAMPREMY for duty. Field Ambulance entrained at CHARLEROI and proceeded at 19.00 hours	G. G.
ANTWERP	18	a.m	Detrained at ANTWERP - Transport parked on Quay - Personnel proceeded to Embarkation Camp - Drew Fr 2,300 from Base Cashier and paid personnel.	G.
	20th	a.m	Transport loaded on S.S. "PRETORIAN" - Personnel embarked at 15:30 hours - i/c Major Clark Nicholson M.C. Lt + Qmr H.E. Inglis. 5 S.Sgts 2 Cpls 31 men RAMC - 3 Sgts and 12 men RASC (H.T) - Transport:- 6 G.S Wagons 2 Horsed Ambce Wagons - 2 Water Carts - 3 Limbers + 1 Maltese Cart.	G.
	21st	p.m	S.S. "PRETORIAN" proceeded to FLUSHING and anchored for the night	G.
TILBURY	22nd	a.m	do proceeded to TILBURY and anchored outside the Docks	G.
		a.m	do docked - personnel disembarked - Transport entrained & loaded on to train -	G.
	23rd	p.m	Personnel entrained & proceeded to CATTERICK (YORKS)	G.
CATTERICK YORKS	23rd		Ambulance detrained at CATTERICK and proceeded to Dispersal Camp - Transport unloaded from train and parked in the Camp	G.
	25th		Field Ambulance equipment etc. checked and handed over to Ordnance Officer & Clearance Certificate obtained.	G.

Clark Nicholson Major RAMC
Comds 49 Field Ambulance Centre

Army Form C. 2118.

WAR DIARY
or
INTELLIGENCE SUMMARY.

(Erase heading not required.)

Instructions regarding War Diaries and Intelligence Summaries are contained in F. S. Regs., Part II. and the Staff Manual respectively. Title pages will be prepared in manuscript.

Place	Date	Hour	Summary of Events and Information	Remarks and references to Appendices.

www.ingramcontent.com/pod-product-compliance
Lightning Source LLC
Chambersburg PA
CBHW080823010526
44111CB00015B/2596